New Directions in Instructional Pragmatics Research

Linguistic Insights

Studies in Language and Communication

Edited by Maurizio Gotti,
Emeritus Professor,
University of Bergamo (Italy).

Volume 315

PETER LANG

Lausanne - Berlin - Bruxelles - Chennai - New York - Oxford

Irene Guzmán-Alcón / Richard Nightingale (eds.)

New Directions in Instructional Pragmatics Research

PETER LANG
Lausanne - Berlin - Bruxelles - Chennai - New York - Oxford

Bibliographic information published by the Deutsche Nationalbibliothek
The Deutsche Nationalbibliothek lists this publication in the Deutsche Nationalbibliografie; detailed bibliographic data is available on the Internet at http://dnb.d-nb.de.

Library of Congress Cataloging-in-Publication

.

Names: Guzmán- Alcón, Irene, editor. | Nightingale, Richard (Professor of linguistics), editor.
Title: New directions in instructional pragmatics research / Irene Guzmán- Alcón & Richard Nightingale, eds.
Description: Bern ; New York : Peter Lang, [2025] | Series: Linguistic insight, 1424-8689 ; vol. no 315 | Includes bibliographical references. Identifiers: LCCN 2025000222 (print) | LCCN 2025000223 (ebook) | ISBN 9783034350990 (hardcover) | ISBN 9783034356848 (ebook) | ISBN 9783034356855 (epub)
Subjects: LCSH: Pragmatics—Study and teaching—Research. | Linguistics—Study and teaching—Research.
Classification: LCC P99.4.P72 N485 2022 (print) | LCC P99.4.P72 (ebook) | DDC 401/.45071—dc23/eng/20250520
LC record available at https://lccn.loc.gov/2025000222
LC ebook record available at https://lccn.loc.gov/2025000223

Financed by the Spanish Ministry of Science and Innovation (code: PID2020-117959GB-I00/ AEI /10.13039/501100011033).

MINISTERIO
DE CIENCIA, INNOVACIÓN
Y UNIVERSIDADES

AGENCIA
ESTATAL DE
INVESTIGACIÓN

ISSN 1424-8689
E-ISBN 978-3-0343-5684-8 (E-PDF)
DOI 10.3726/b22674
ISBN 978-3-0343-5099-0 (Print)
E-ISBN 978-3-0343-5685-5 (E-PUB)

Published by Peter Lang Group AG, Lausanne, Switzerland

info@peterlang.com - www.peterlang.com

Table of Contents

Section II Pragmatics at Tertiary Level

Section III Cyber Pragmatics

Section IV Multilingual Pragmatics

Acknowledgements

First and foremost, we would like to thank all members of the LAELA (Lingüística Aplicada a l'Ensenyament de la Llengua Anglesa) research group at Universitat Jaume I for their involvement in this project. We are also grateful to the reviewers of preliminary versions of some chapters for their comments and thoughtful suggestions. Special thanks to Dr. Eva Alcón Soler to whom we dedicate this book.

We also like to acknowledge that this book has been conducted within the framework of the research project PID2020-117959GB-I00 funded by MCIN/AEI/10.13039/501100011033. Additional funding has been granted by Projectes d'Innovació Educativa de la Unitat de Suport Educatiu from Universitat Jaume I (51020/24).

Dedication

It is with great pleasure that we have edited this book, New Directions in Instructional Pragmatics Research, in honour of Dr. Eva Alcón Soler. Eva's contributions to applied linguistics, particularly in the fields of second and third language acquisition, pragmatics, and multilingual education, have been both pioneering and transformative. Her work has shaped the landscape of language teaching and learning, not only in Spain but also internationally. All contributors to this book have known Eva Alcón for a long time. It was Eva who introduced pragmatics to most of us. Her passion for pragmatics and for teaching and learning pragmatics has inspired us and set us on our respective paths, and it continues to guide us each day.

Eva Alcón Soler is currently the Rector of the Universitat Jaume I in Castelló and serves as a Full Professor of English Philology. Since June 2023, she has held the position of President of the Conference of Spanish Rectors (CRUE). Her academic journey began with a degree in English Philology from the University of Valencia, where she also obtained her Ph.D. Since 1993, she has occupied various managerial positions at the Universitat Jaume I: Director of the English Philology degree (1999–2001); Vice-rector of academic and student orientation (2001–2006); and Vice-rector of international relations (2006–2010). Eva has been a key figure at Universitat Jaume I, contributing to its growth as a centre of excellence in research and education.

Eva has authored and co-authored more than 80 scholarly publications, including impactful works such as Pragmatics in Instructed Language Learning (*System*, 2005) and *Investigating Pragmatics in Foreign Language Learning, Teaching and Testing* (Multilingual Matters, 2008). Her studies have provided invaluable insights on the impact of instruction on pragmatic learning. In addition, work such as Development of Discourse-pragmatic Markers in a Multilingual Classroom: A Mixed-method Research Approach (*System*, 2018), Pragmatic Gains In The Study Abroad Context: Learners' Experiences And Recognition of Pragmatic Routines (*Journal of Pragmatics*, 2019), and Investigating Pragmatic Development In Study Abroad Contexts (John Benjamins, 2023) have provided invaluable insight into how learners acquire pragmatic skills, whether through study abroad programs or within multilingual classrooms. These contributions have advanced our understanding of pragmatic routines, discourse markers, and the influence of instruction on pragmatic learning.

Eva Alcón Soler's scholarly influence extends beyond her publications. She founded the Lingüística Aplicada a l'Ensenyament de la Llengua Anglesa (LAELA) research group in 1999, which she led until 2018. Under her guidance, LAELA became a prominent research group, exploring the interface between language instruction and pragmatic development. The members of LAELA, alongside other close academic colleagues of Eva, have contributed to this volume, reflecting the collaborative spirit that she has always fostered. Many of the chapters in this book are the result of academic partnerships with those who have shared Eva's vision of pragmatics and multilingual education.

Her contributions to the field of pragmatics and language education have been recognized at numerous international and national conferences. Eva has been an active participant and keynote speaker in prestigious forums, such as Pragmatics and Language Learning (PLL), Georgetown University Round Table (GURT) or Asociación Española de Estudios Anglo-Norteamericanos (AEDEAN) where she presented on topics like intercultural awareness in study abroad contexts and the integration of pragmatic instruction in foreign and multilingual contexts. Her work on pragmatic development during study abroad, such as her study on Spanish teenagers' request strategies published in the *Annual Review of Applied Linguistics* (2017), has provided a deeper understanding of how extended exposure to target languages shapes learners' pragmatic competence.

Eva's expertise has also been shared in Asociación Española de Lingüística Aplicada (AESLA), at the Association of Applied Linguistics (AILA) or the American Association of Applied Linguistics (AAAL), where she has consistently presented innovative research on the pragmatic dimensions of language learning. Her presentations reflect her ability to blend theory and practice, offering insights that resonate with both researchers and language educators. In addition, she not only is a member of the Consultation Board of the International Association for Teaching Pragmatics (ITAP) but she has also been an advisor for the following journals: *Language Learning, A Journal of Research in Language Studies, Studies in Second Language Acquisition, Intercultural Pragmatics, Language and Intercultural Communication, Language and Awareness, Issues in Applied Linguistics, and International Journal of Multilingualism.*

Her international reputation as a scholar is further reflected in her extensive experience as a visiting professor at institutions such as Birkbeck University (London), Macquarie University (Australia), the University of California (Los Angeles) and Trinity College (Dublin). These experiences have enriched her research with diverse perspectives, allowing her to engage with scholars and educators around the world. Eva's collaborative spirit has also been evident in her co-authored studies on pragmatics and multilingualism such as: Intercultural Language Use and Language Learning (Springer, 2007), Teachability of Request Act Peripheral Modifications Devices In Third Language Learning Content (John Benjamins, 2012), and Discourse And Language Learning Across L2 Instructional Settings (Brill, 2012).

Beyond her scholarly achievements, Eva Alcón Soler is known for her dedication to public service and her belief in the transformative power of education. Her role as a regional representative in les Corts Valencianes and her leadership in higher education reflect her unwavering commitment to social progress. She has consistently advocated for policies that promote equality, inclusivity, and academic excellence, making a lasting impact on the education system. As the president of the Conference of Spanish Rectors (CRUE), she has worked tirelessly to advance the position of Spanish universities in the global academic community, fostering greater collaboration and innovation.

This volume is a tribute to Eva Alcón Soler. It gathers contributions that reflect her wide-ranging impact on the field of language acquisition, with a special focus on the instructional dimensions of pragmatics and multilingualism. We hope this volume honours Eva's lifelong dedication to advancing the study of language acquisition and provides inspiration for future scholarship in this ever-evolving field. This book not only serves as a recognition of Eva's contributions to applied linguistics but also inspires future research in the field. Her passion for exploring the complexities of language acquisition and her commitment to fostering an inclusive, research-driven approach to language education have set a standard for excellence that will continue to guide the next generation of scholars.

LAELA Research Group

References

Alcón-Soler, Eva & Martínez-Flor, Alicia. 2005. Pragmatics in instructed language learning. *System,* 33/3, 381–546.

Alcón-Soler, Eva & Martínez-Flor, Alicia (eds). 2008. *Investigating pragmatics in foreign language learning, teaching and testing.* Bristol, Blue Ridge Summit: Multilingual Matters.

Alcón-Soler, Eva & Safont, Pilar (eds). 2007. *Intercultural language use and language learning*. Dordrecht: Springer.

Alcón-Soler, Eva & Safont, Pilar (eds). 2012. *Discourse and language learning across L2 instructional settings*. Leiden: Brill.

Alcón-Soler, Eva. 2017. Pragmatic development during study abroad: An analysis of Spanish teenagers' request strategies in English emails. *Annual Review of Applied Linguistics*, 37, 77–92. <https://doi.org/10.1017/S0267190517000125>

Benjamins, John. 2012. Teachability of request act peripheral modification devices in third language learning content. In Maria Economidou-Kogetsidis & Helen Woodfield (eds) *Interlanguage request modification*. Amsterdam: John Benjamins, 275–314.

Martín-Laguna, Sofía & Alcón-Soler, Eva. 2018. Development of discourse-pragmatic markers in a multilingual classroom: A mixed method research approach. *System*, 75, 68–79.

Nightingale, Richard & Alcón-Soler, Eva. 2023. Investigating pragmatic development in study abroad contexts. In Carmen Pérez-Vidal & Cristina Sanz (eds) *Methods in study abroad research: Past, present, and future.* Amsterdam: John Benjamins, 265–289.

Sánchez-Hernández, Ariadna & Alcón-Soler, Eva. 2019. Pragmatic gains in the study abroad context: Learners' experiences and recognition of pragmatic routines. *Journal of Pragmatics*, 146, 54–71. <https://doi.org/10.1016/j.pragma.2019.01.017>.

Irene Guzmán-Alcón and Richard Nightingale

New Directions in Instructional Pragmatics Research: An Introduction

As a discipline, pragmatics is concerned with the ways in which language is appropriately used within specific social and situational contexts, examining how speakers tailor their communicative choices based on situational demands and social norms (Taguchi, 2015, 2019; Alcón-Soler & Safont, 2018; Edmondson et al., 2023; Martí & Guzmán-Alcón, 2024). This foundational focus has shaped L2 pragmatics research, which, for decades, has aimed to cultivate learners' pragmatic skills primarily through traditional instructional settings such as classrooms and immersion experiences abroad. Within these contexts, the challenge has been to develop learners' pragmatic awareness and competence through both formal instruction and real-world applications, ensuring that they are equipped to manage culturally and contextually appropriate language use (Alcón-Soler & Martínez-Flor, 2008; Gesuato & Cheng 2015).

Building on these foundational efforts, L2/Interlanguage Pragmatics has emerged as a key area, addressing the complex journey that non-native speakers face as they develop pragmatic competence within their unique interlanguage. In L2/Interlanguage Pragmatics, learners blend the norms and conventions of both their native and target languages, creating an "interlanguage" space where pragmatic competence is actively negotiated and refined. This area of research investigates how L2 learners build both pragmalinguistic and sociopragmatic knowledge, often through the support of explicit instructional methods, feedback, and modelling within the classroom (Kasper & Rose, 2002; Taguchi, 2019).

Special attention has been given to instructional pragmatics, which has evolved to address the need for structured and explicit teaching of pragmatic skills, complementing L2/Interlanguage Pragmatics by embedding pragmatic instruction within curricula. Rather than relying solely on incidental learning, instructional pragmatics focuses on systematically developing learners' ability to manage communicative tasks (such as making requests, offering advice, or handling disagreements within the classroom). This area of research has gained prominence as it enables learners to practice real-world scenarios, preparing them for intercultural exchanges, by fostering awareness and adaptability (Bardovi-Harlig, 2018; Alcón-Soler, 2018; Ishihara & Cohen, 2021).

While the research mentioned above has centred on second language learners (Taguchi, 2012), foreign language learners (Alcón-Soler & Martínez-Flor, 2008), and learners during a study abroad period (Barron, 2019, 2020; Alcón-Soler, 2017; Alcón-Soler & Sánchez-Hernández, 2019; Sánchez-Hernández & Alcón-Soler, 2019; also see Nightingale & Alcón-Soler, 2023, for a recent methodological overview), the advent of globalization and the pervasive influence of technology has dramatically expanded the scope of pragmatics research. For example, increasing intercultural interactions challenge learners to navigate cross-cultural contexts where implicit norms and values may diverge from familiar frameworks, intensifying the need for flexible, interculturally sensitive pragmatic skills (Alcón-Soler, 2015a; Taguchi, 2014, 2019, 2022). Additionally, digital communication gives rise to new pragmatic concerns, as virtual environments offer unique speech communities, unbound from spatiotemporal restrictions, that adhere to real-life pragmatic conventions to a greater or lesser extent. On these platforms, for instance, learners must be able to interpret message tone without physical cues, manage formality and (im)politeness within instant and asynchronous messaging, and even learn to manipulate the nexus between language and medium in order to best achieve their interactional goals (Alcón-Soler, 2017; Nightingale & Safont, 2019; Codina-Espurz & Salazar-Campillo, 2019; Barón et al., 2024).

Furthermore, accounting for contemporary multilingualism (see Singleton & Aronin, 2019) necessitates new approaches to pragmatic competence. For example, in multilingual settings, learners are often required to navigate multiple linguistic frameworks while maintaining appropriate communicative behaviour. Multilingual proficiency not only involves language skills, but also the pragmatic adaptability to fluidly shift between languages, or translanguage. This understanding has led researchers to explore pragmatic development in multilingual settings and to consider how individuals leverage multiple linguistic resources to communicate effectively across varying cultural and linguistic spheres (Alcón-Soler, 2015b; Portolés, 2015; Safont & Portolés, 2016; Martín-Laguna & Alcón-Soler, 2018; Kecskes, 2019; Safont, 2005, 2013, 2022, 2023; Taguchi, 2022; Cenoz & Gorter, 2021; Leonet & Saragueta, 2023; Martín-Laguna, 2023; Guzmán-Alcón, 2023; Portolés & Gayete, 2024).

For all the above reasons, pragmatic competence in contemporary settings must go beyond traditional boundaries to adapt to more complex and varied communicative landscapes. In response to this, the current edited volume, New Directions in Instructional Pragmatics Research, introduces novel avenues for pragmatic learning across diverse educational, digital, and multilingual contexts. This volume builds on existing research by expanding pragmatics to contexts that reflect the increasingly globalized, digital, and multilingual realities that learners face today. The book is organized into four main sections: (i) Pragmatics at School Level, (ii) Pragmatics at Tertiary Level, (iii) Cyberpragmatics, and (iv) Multilingual Pragmatics, each representing new directions in response to shifting educational needs and the evolving landscape of language learning.

Following this introduction, which frames the series of chapters included in the volume, Section I, Pragmatics at School Level, includes three chapters that shed light on the pragmatic needs of young learners and innovative methods for teaching these skills. The section opens with Chapter 1, by Martí, who uses children's literature to teach speech acts, examining how picturebooks, with their unique blend of text and visuals, can serve as an effective medium for enhancing young learners' pragmatic skills. The chapter also provides a model for teacher training, emphasizing the importance of visual and narrative elements in fostering pragmatic awareness. Similarly, Chapter 2, by Martín-Laguna, introduces TBLT to equip pre-service teachers in early childhood education with essential skills for fostering pragmatic routines, and highlighting the role of real-life contextualization in TBLT. The last chapter of this section, Chapter 3, by Guzmán-Alcón, examines the interplay between family socioeconomic status and the effectiveness of CLIL programmes on primary students' pragmatic achievement, highlighting the potential of CLIL to promote equity in education and mitigate the effects of socioeconomic disparities.

Section II, Pragmatics at the Tertiary Level, presents three chapters that focus on developing intercultural competence, awareness of refusals through TV, and collaborative writing in university students. Chapter 4, by Taguchi, investigates how conflict mediation training influences intercultural competence, underscoring how such training fosters empathy, adaptability, and conflict-resolution skills. This study addresses a crucial gap in research by demonstrating how pragmatic training directly enhances students' abilities to manage intercultural interactions. Chapter 5, by Usó-Juan and Martínez-Flor, explores the impact of audiovisual materials, particularly TV series, on students' understanding of L2 pragmatics, specifically refusals. Through a discursive approach, the chapter discusses how audiovisual content exposes students to contextualized language, thus enhancing their awareness and practical application of refusal strategies. In Chapter 6, Martinez-Buffa examines collaborative writing tasks, analysing how multilingual students use their L1 as a resource for negotiating meaning and improving text quality.

Section III, Cyberpragmatics, addresses the growing importance of digital communication in students' lives, with three chapters focusing on technology and the pragmatics of email communication. Chapter 7, by Flöck et al., explores directive feedback strategies in a telecollaborative context among English learners, offering insights into how students navigate digital environments and how these interactions shape their feedback strategies. Chapter 8, by González-Lloret, examines the pragmatics of email requests, dissecting the sociopragmatic nuances and challenges that L2 learners face when expressing politeness and clarity. Furthermore, the last chapter of this section, Chapter 9, by Codina-Espurz and Salazar-Campillo, investigates perceptions of impoliteness in student-professor email interactions, providing insights into how sociopragmatic norms influence students' digital communication skills and highlighting areas where additional support may be beneficial.

The final section, Section IV, Multilingual Pragmatics, advocates for a comprehensive view of pragmatics that reflects the multilingual reality. In Chapter 10, Safont synthesizes findings from studies across age groups and genders in multilingual educational settings, and highlights the need to expand research on pragmatic behaviours and individual differences within multilingual contexts. This chapter challenges the native vs. non-native speaker model, calling for a broader consideration of pragmatics from a multilingual perspective. Chapter 11, by Nightingale, explores relationships between extramural digital media contact, language attitudes, and sociopragmatic awareness in multilingual adolescents in the Valencian Community in Spain. The author finds strong reciprocal relationships between these factors for the minority language in this context. Lastly, Gayete and Portolés close this section with Chapter 12, which explores translanguaging pedagogies, underscoring their positive effects on primary students' pragmatic awareness across Catalan, Spanish, and English. The authors argue for the early integration of multilingual practices, showing how students' full language repertoires can foster pragmatic awareness from a young age.

Overall, the volume New Directions in Instructional Pragmatics Research aims to integrate research and practice across various educational levels and settings. With contributions from established experts and emerging scholars alike, it addresses a wide spectrum for teaching pragmatics, moving from traditional speech acts to contemporary cyber and multilingual pragmatics. This unique blend of perspectives and methodologies offers educators the tools to create more inclusive, pragmatic-sensitive learning environments, making this book a resource to further the development of effective communication skills. In addition, New Directions in Instructional Pragmatics Research aims to bridge the gap between research and classroom application, empowering educators to foster more context-sensitive and pragmatic language use among their students.

References

Alcón-Soler, Eva & Safont, Pilar (eds). 2018. Editors' introduction. Special issue: Mixed method approaches in investigating pragmatic learning. *System*, 75, 1–3.

Alcón-Soler, Eva. 2015a. Pragmatic learning and study abroad: Effects of instruction and length of stay. *System,* 48, 62–74. <https://doi.org/10.1016/j.system.2014.09.001>.

Alcón-Soler, Eva. 2015b. Instruction and pragmatic change during study abroad email communication. *Innovation in Language Learning and Teaching*, 1/9, 34–45.

Alcón-Soler, Eva. 2018. Effects of task supported language teaching on learners' use and knowledge of email request mitigators. In N. Taguchi & Y. Kim (eds) *Task-based approaches to teaching and assessing pragmatics*. Amsterdam: John Benjamins, 56–81.

Alcón-Soler, Eva. 2017. Pragmatic development during study abroad: An analysis of Spanish teenagers' request strategies in English emails. *Annual Review of Applied Linguistics*, 37, 77–92. <https://doi.org/10.1017/S0267190517000125>.

Alcón-Soler, Eva & Martínez-Flor, Alicia (eds). 2008. *Investigating pragmatics in foreign language learning, teaching and testing.* Bristol: Multilingual Matters.

Alcón-Soler, Eva & Sánchez-Hernández, Ariadna. 2019. The role of individual differences on learning pragmatic routines in a study abroad context. In Patricia Salazar-Campillo & Victòria Codina-Espurz (eds) *Investigating the learning of pragmatics across ages and contexts*. Leiden: Brill, 141–164.

Barron, Anne. 2019. Pragmatic development and stay abroad. *Journal of Pragmatics*, 146, 43–53. <https://doi.org/10.1016/j.pragma.2019.05.003>.

Barron, Anne. 2020. Developing pragmatic competence in a study abroad context. In K. P. Schneider & E. Ifantidou (eds) *Developmental and clinical pragmatics*. Boston: De Gruyter Mouton, 429–474. <https://doi.org/10.1515/9783110431056-015>.

Barón, Júlia, Celaya, M. Luz & Martínez-Flor, Alicia. 2024. Multimodal input and L2 pragmatics. An eye-tracking study. In Carmen Muñoz & Imma Miralpeix (eds) *Audiovisual input and second language learning*. Amsterdam: John Benjamins, 126–149.

Bardovi-Harlig, Kathleen. 2018. Pragmatic awareness in second language acquisition. In Peter Garret & Josep M. Cots (eds) *Routledge handbook of language awareness*. Abingdon/Oxon/New York: Routledge, 323–338.

Cenoz, Jasone & Gorter, Durk. 2021. *Pedagogical translanguaging*. Cambridge: Cambridge University Press. <https://doi.org/10.1017/9781009029384>.

Edmondson, Willis J., House, Juliane & Kádár, Daniel Z. 2023. *Expressions, speech acts and discourse: A pedagogic interactional grammar of English*. Cambridge: Cambridge University Press. <https://doi.org/10.1017/9781108954662>.

Gesuato, S., & Cheng, W. (Eds.). (2015). *Teaching, learning and investigating pragmatics: Principles, methods and practices*. Cambridge Scholars Publishing.

Guzmán-Alcón, Irene 2023. *The effect of intensity of content and language integrated learning programmes on students' multilingual writing* [Doctoral dissertation, Universitat Jaume I].

Ishihara, Norilo & Cohen, Andrew D. 2021. *Teaching and learning pragmatics: Where language and culture meet*. New York/London: Routledge.

Kasper, Gabriele & Rose, Kenneth. R. 2002. *Pragmatic development in a second language*. Oxford: Blackwell.

Kesckes, Istvan. 2019. *English as a lingua franca. The pragmatic perspective*. Cambridge: Cambridge University Press.

Leonet, Oihana & Saragueta, Eider. 2023. The case of a pedagogical translanguaging intervention in a trilingual primary school: The students' voice. *International Journal of Multilingualism*, 21/4, 2112–2130. <https://doi.org/10.1080/14790718.2023.2224009>.

Martín-Laguna, Sofía. 2023. Metadiscourse learning trajectories in multilingual learners: A focus on attitude markers and hedges. In Begoña Bellés-Fortuño, Lucía Bellés-Calvera & Ana Isabel Martínez-Hernández (eds) *New trends on metadiscourse: An analysis of online and textual genres*. Cham: Springer, 105–128.

Martín-Laguna, Sofía & Alcón-Soler, Eva. 2018. Development of discourse-pragmatic markers in a multilingual classroom: A mixed method research approach. *System*, 75, 68–80.

Martí, Otilia & Guzmán-Alcón, Irene. 2024. Learner pragmatics in English-medium instruction courses at university: Current research and future avenues. *Applied Pragmatics*. 6/2, 169–182.

Nightingale, Richard & Alcón-Soler, Eva. 2023. Investigating pragmatic development in study abroad contexts. In Carmen Pérez-Vidal & Cristina Sanz (eds) *Methods in study abroad research: Past, present, and future*. Amsterdam: John Benjamins, 265–289

Nightingale, Richard & Safont, Pilar. 2019. Pragmatic translanguaging: Multilingual practice in adolescent online discourse. In P. Salazar-Campillo & V. Codina-Espurz (eds), *Investigating the learning of pragmatics across ages and contexts*. Leiden: Brill, 167–195.

Portolés, Laura. 2015. *Multilingualism and very young learners: An analysis of pragmatic awareness and language attitudes.* Berlin/München/Boston: De Gruyter Mouton. <https://doi.org/10.1515/9781501500022>.

Portolés, Laura & Gayete, Gema. 2024. Enhancing multilingual young students' pragmatic awareness through pedagogical translanguaging. *International Journal of Multilingualism*, *21*, 1– 18. <https://doi.org/10.1080/14790718.2024.2368060>.

Safont, Pilar. 2005. *Third language learners. Pragmatic production and awareness*. Clevedon: Multilingual Matters.

Safont, Pilar. 2013. Early stages of trilingual pragmatic development. A longitudinal study of requests in Catalan, Spanish and English. *International Journal of Pragmatics*, 59, 68–80.

Safont, Pilar & Portolés, Laura. 2016. Pragmatic functions of formulaic speech in three different languages. A focus on early L3 learners of English. *Journal of Immersion and Content-Based Language Education*, 4/2, 225–250.

Safont, Pilar. 2022. 'In English!' teachers' requests as reactions to learners' translanguaging discourse. *Language, Culture and Curriculum*, 35/3, 317–333. <https://doi.org/10.1080/07908318.2021.1979578>

Safont, Pilar. 2023. Multilingual cyberpragmatics in instructional settings. Exploring gender and age effects in Catalan, Spanish and English email requests. *International Journal of Multilingualism*, *21*, 1–23. <https://doi.org/10.1080/14790718.2023.2187811

Salazar-Campillo, Patricia & Codina-Espurz, Victòria (eds). 2019. *Investigating the learning of pragmatics across ages and contexts.* Leiden: Brill.

Sánchez-Hernández, Ariadna & Alcón-Soler, Eva. 2019. Pragmatic gains in the study abroad context: Learners' experiences and recognition of pragmatic routines. *Journal of Pragmatics*, 146, 54–71. <https://doi.org/10.1016/j.pragma.2019.01.017>.

Singleton, D., & Aronin, L. (Eds.). (2018). *Twelve lectures on multilingualism* (Vol. 15). Multilingual Matters.

Taguchi, Naoko (ed.). 2012. *Context, individual differences and pragmatic competence*. Bristol, Blue Ridge Summit: Multilingual Matters.

Taguchi, Naoko. 2014. Pragmatic socialization in an English-medium university in Japan. *International Review of Applied Linguistics in Language Teaching*, 52/2, 157–181. <https://doi.org/10.1515/iral-2014-0007>.

Taguchi, Naoko. 2015. Instructed pragmatics at a glance: Where instructional studies were, are, and should be going. *Language Teaching*, 48/1, 1–50. <https://doi.org/10.1017/S0261444814000263>.

Taguchi, Naoko (ed.). 2019. *The Routledge handbook of second language acquisition and pragmatics*. London/New York: Routledge.

Taguchi, Naoko. 2022. Commentary. *Study Abroad Research in Second Language Acquisition and International Education*, 7/1, 176–180.

Section I
Pragmatics at School Level

Otilia Martí

Teaching Request-Making in the Primary English Language Classroom: A Sociocultural Pedagogical Model with Picturebooks

Introduction

In a time of globalisation, English has become a "near-universal basic skill" (Graddol, 2006: 15) but also a matter of child safety, as captured in Schauer's (2019: 3) concept of *Survival English*. This concept refers to a range of speech acts like requests that should enter the teaching agenda in Primary English Language Teaching (PELT). As she convincingly argues,

> In current textbooks for young learners much emphasis tends to be placed on fruit, vegetables, pets, and colours, as well as basic numbers. However –although useful in some respects– none of these vocabulary items are particularly helpful for children when they find themselves in an emergency situation, such as having been separated from their parents on holiday or finding themselves in even worse situations as a result of having to flee their countries or being trafficked. While the latter circumstances are not frequently addressed in L2 pragmatics publications, they should be because basic speech acts that enable L2 learners to ask for help or to communicate with someone who is in need of help can and should be taught early on (Schauer, 2022: 138–139).

Teaching basic speech acts like requests in the PELT classroom, though, is not an easy task. Rather, it is a challenging endeavour that should go beyond providing young language learners (YLLs) with a set of simple expressions and some "rules of thumb" for selecting the most appropriate one in conformity with native-speaker norms (van Compernolle, 2014).

Admittedly, pragmatic competence has been lately presented as a multidimensional construct encompassing four instructional goals (Taguchi, 2019: 4): (i) knowledge of linguistic forms to understand and produce a speech act (i.e. pragmalinguistics), (ii) knowledge of the sociocultural variables at play when choosing a pragmalinguistic form (i.e. sociopragmatics), (iii) knowledge of how the target speech act is situated in turn-taking (i.e. interactional competence) and (iv) development of learner agency. Given the complexity inherent in this multidimensional construct, it is not surprising that, unlike the detailed guidelines on vocabulary and grammar teaching, the Common European Framework of Reference for Languages (CEFR) has left the role of pragmatic competence mostly underspecified (Sickinger & Schneider, 2014).

The same neglect has been observed in PELT teacher education, where pragmatics training is still lacking with respect to practitioners' metapragmatic awareness and ability to repair pragmatic problems (Glaser, 2018, 2020), their explicit conceptual knowledge, pedagogical knowledge and cultural sensitivity (Ishihara, 2012) or the availability of adequate teaching materials (Cohen, 2016, 2018). As Glaser aptly puts it "a true 'pragmatics change' in teacher education can only come about when conceptual knowledge and awareness is paired with concrete and directly applicable materials and teaching suggestions" (2023: 82). To Bardovi-Harlig (2020: 48), another reason explaining the lack of implementation of pragmatics-focused instruction is the fact that researchers have sometimes proposed *what* to teach but rarely *how* to teach it.

Against this backdrop, the present chapter seeks to contribute to the field of pragmatics pedagogy by providing PELT teachers with an age-appropriate model for teaching requests. In opting for picturebooks as a source of pragmatic input, this study also belongs to the subfield of pragmatics and children's literature (Meibauer, 2017). Inspired by Donato and Adair-Hauck's (2015) PACE model, the adaptation of their story-based approach for dialogic inquiry presented here aims to equip novice and experienced practitioners with a pedagogical framework grounded in Vygotsky's (1978, 1986) sociocultural theory (SCT) of learning.

With the purpose of explaining the rationale behind the suggested model, the next section starts with a review of research on child pragmatic development in second language (L2) request production and comprehension. Once YLLs' instructional readiness is established, the scant empirical evidence available to date on the learning affordances of materials like textbooks or picturebooks, along with the impact of dialogic instructional approaches, will be examined. Finally, the proposed adaptation of the PACE model will be described and exemplified with a selection of picturebooks from Mo Willems' *Elephant & Piggie* stories, a series that might favour children's encounter, awareness and use of the target speech act.

Rationale

Since Ishihara (2010: 946) made a call to investigate age-appropriate second language (L2) pragmatics instruction, aligned with how children learn to be pragmatically competent, a modicum of research with a focus on child requestive behaviour has been conducted. Existing studies in non-immersion instructional settings can be grouped into three main lines of enquiry on the teachability of L2 pragmatics: YLLs' speech act competence, pragmatic input materials and impact of instructional approaches. Next, I will review studies centred on L2 request-making of Primary students, herein defined as learners aged 5/6-11/12, following Enever (2016).

PELT Students' Production and Comprehension of Requests

Requests are speech acts "performed by the speaker [or writer] in order to engage the hearer [or reader] in some future course of action that coincides with the speaker's goal" (Safont, 2008: 42). Such a future course of action may consist of getting information, goods, services or permission for the speaker's or the writer's benefit. In light of the impositive nature of this speech act, appropriate request-making demands considerable pragmalinguistic and sociopragmatic expertise. This has led to the misconception that YLLs are unable to perform or to comprehend this speech act in all its nuances.

However, research on child pragmatic development in first language (L1) acquisition (Cekaite, 2013: 4) has shown that infants aged between 2.6 and 3 can produce unmitigated or indirect requests, depending upon their perception of the interlocutor's status. Despite this early emergence, children's acquisition of pragmatic competence is far from being completed by the end of preschool, as it still develops during the teenage years (Barón, 2015). This also applies to child production and comprehension of L2 English requests. Concerning production, empirical evidence of pragmalinguistic development in requests has been found by Savić (2015) in 58 children studying English as a Foreign Language (EFL) in a Norwegian Primary school, and by Savić, Economidou-Kogetsidis and Myrset (2021) in two groups of 79 Norwegian and 88 Greek Cypriot learners.

To better understand the findings of these two cross-sectional studies, Tables 1.1 and 1.2 offer a selection of the strategies of head acts, "the minimal [units] which can realize a request" (Blum Kulka et al., 1989: 275), according to directness, and the subtypes of external and internal modifiers, added to them.

Table 1.1. Typology of request head acts (adapted from Blum-Kulka & Olshtain, 1984; Trosborg, 1995).

Type	Strategy	Example
Direct	Elliptical statement	*Your pencil*
	Imperatives	*Give me your pencil!*
	Want/need statements	*I want/I need a pencil.*
Conventionally Indirect	Ability	*Can you lend me your pencil?* *Could you lend me your pencil?*
	Willingness	*Will you lend me your pencil?* *Would you lend me your pencil?*
	Permission	*May I borrow your pencil?*
Indirect	Hints	*Do you have a pencil?*

Most examples of modifiers displayed in Table 1.2 are taken from the data collected by Savić (2015) and by Savić, Economidou-Kogetsidis and Myrset (2021).

Table 1.2. Typology of modifiers (adapted from Blum-Kulka et al., 1989; Woodfield & Economidou-Kogetsidis, 2010).

Type	**Sub-type**		**Examples**
INTERNAL	**Lexical/ phrasal downgraders**	Politeness markers:	Can you *please* bring some snacks to the party?
		Openers:	*Do you think* you could bring some snacks, like a bag of chips?
		Understaters/Hedges:	Can I get *some* soup?
		Downtoners:	Can you *maybe* help with the cookies?
	Intensifiers		*Now, really…*
EXTERNAL	**Alerters**	Attention getters:	*Hello, excuse me, look!, listen!*
		Address terms:	*Titles/first names, teacher, dad, mum, mate, dude…*
	Supportive moves	Grounders:	Can you buy me this kite *because it's my birthday?*
		Disarmers:	*I know that it's school time but* can I please borrow a mobile phone to phone my dad?
		Preparators:	*See, this is a kite.* Can I get this?
		Imposition-minimisers:	Can I get any of the papers? *Doesn't matter what colour it is.*
		Sweeteners:	*The dinner was really good,* so I was wondering if I could eat here another day.
		Thanking:	*Thank you for inviting us.* Can we come again for another delicious dinner?

As to the realisation of head acts –see Table 1.1–, the 848 requests obtained by Savić (2015) from two role-play scenarios, performed in pairs by 18 second-graders (aged roughly 8), 20 fourth graders (aged roughly 10) and 20 sixth-graders (aged roughly 12), evince a lower frequency of direct request head acts with increasing age and proficiency level. While the second graders still resort to direct head-act strategies – pointing, naming and want statements– accompanied by conventionally indirect requests (beginning with the modal verb *can*), the fourth graders prefer conventionally indirect requests, headed by *could* and *would*. A wider variety of head acts, with *if* clauses and non-conventional indirect requests or hints, only appear in the sixth graders' requests.

The second developmental pattern concerns the range of modifiers or adjuncts to the head acts, which also increases with age. Significantly, the politeness marker *please* is the only internal modifier employed by the youngest pupils to soften their head acts, devoid of any alerters or supportive moves. In turn, the fourth graders' modifying strategies are characterised by an overgeneralisation of the downgrader *please* and the first occurrences of external and internal modification, mainly by means of attention getters such as *excuse me* or *hello* and address terms like first names or titles (e.g. *teacher*). Once again, the oldest group's pragmalinguistic repertoire is the one showing more internal modifiers, with the inclusion of openers (i.e. *Do you think. . .?*) or downtoners (i.e. *maybe*). In relation to external modifiers, the sixth graders favour, on the one hand, informal address terms like first names, nicknames or *dude* and, on the other hand, supportive moves like disarmers or preparators.

The first pragmalinguistic developmental pattern identified by Savić (2015) is confirmed in Savić, Economidou-Kogetsidis and Myrset's (2021) study, even though participants, 79 Norwegian (NLs) and 88 Greek Cypriot (GCLs) EFL learners aged 9–13, are a year older and the main data collection instrument is not a role-play but a video-based oral discourse completion task (VODCT). Indeed, direct strategies such as elliptical statements, imperatives and want statements significantly decrease with age and proficiency, whereas conventionally indirect head acts also increase (Savić et al., 2021: 23).

This linear development in request head act strategies is more noticeable in the case of GCLs because conventional indirectness amounts to only 55.9 % of the request head acts produced by the youngest group of 9 year olds. In contrast, their age peers in Norway realise 75 % of their request head acts as conventionally indirect ones with the modal verb *can*. Both trends might respond to two opposing politeness orientations, within which direct requestive strategies are the preferred pragmalinguistic forms to attend to the positive-face demands in terms of solidarity and involvement operating in L1 Greek. Alternatively, conventionally indirect strategies headed by the modal verb *can*—a cognate of the Norwegian modal verb *kan*– are a pragmatic feature characteristic of a languageculture that favours parsimony and avoids verbosity (Savić et al., 2021: 19).

Other areas of divergence are found, first, in modal verbs other than *can*, which are *would* in GCLs 11-year-olds' requests or *may* and *could* in NLs 11-year-olds' and, second, in the higher occurrence of understaters/hedges or sweeteners present in NLs 13-year-olds' external modifiers. It is also noteworthy that Norwegian 9-year-olds externally modify their request head acts and never employ direct strategies like pointing, a requestive wordless behaviour documented by Savić (2015) in the performance of Norwegian 8-year-olds. The evidence available on PELT students' pragmalinguistic development, then, seems to indicate that 8-year-olds/9-year-olds are the two age groups whose requestive behaviour would certainly benefit from pragmatics-focused instruction.

All in all, a picture of YLLs' instructional readiness would be incomplete without considering their ability not only to produce but also to understand requests. Comprehension of this speech act brings to the fore the notion of *pragmatic awareness*, defined by Alcón and Safont as a "conscious, reflective, explicit knowledge about pragmatics" (2008: 193). Albeit closely related to *metapragmatic awareness*, these two terms should not be used interchangeably. As rightly posited by McConachy, pragmatic awareness turns into metapragmatic awareness when the former "goes beyond knowledge of specific pragmatic norms" and shows "a broader capacity for reflection on pragmatic decision making and interactional effects" (2018: 28). In the same line, following McConachy (2013), Myrset and McConachy conceive metapragmatic awareness as "the ability to articulate one's conscious understanding of pragmatic meanings within and across languages and cultures" (2022: 309). Keeping these caveats in mind, Myrset and Savić regard metapragmatic awareness as "the ability to verbalize reflections on linguistic forms, contextual features and/or their interplay" (2021: 165).

Previous literature on multilingual YLLs' comprehension and appraisal of requests in instructional settings has documented a high degree of pragmatic awareness even in preliterate children (e.g. Portolés, 2015; Portolés & Safont, 2018). However, to the best of my knowledge, research investigating YLLs' metapragmatic awareness is sparse and has focused thus far on upper Primary Education learners from the age of nine onwards. Verbalisations of children's appraisals of requests, at the age of 9 (third graders), 11 (fifth graders) and 13 (seventh graders), have been elicited and analysed by Myrset and Savić (2021). Reports on those verbalisations show that Norwegian Primary students can reason about their own request pragmalinguistic forms, produced in a previous task, in terms of degree of directness and addition of internal and external modifiers. For instance, to the question "What is important to think about when we ask for something in English?", some of the participants' responses are: " 'to be polite', 'to say *please*', to say *can I* and not *give me*', 'to smile', 'to show respect', 'intonation' and 'where you are' " (Myrset & Savić, 2021: 179).

The level of sophistication of these metapragmatic reflections about linguistic and contextual features grows with age. In fact, whilst third graders' reasonings mostly refer to pragmalinguistic choices, favouring conventionally indirect requests with the modal verb *can*, fifth graders introduce sociopragmatic aspects leading to the formulation of their own metapragmatic rules. This is the case of 11-year-old Oscar who holds that one does not need to be very polite in those urgent situations where the cost of the request is very low because the requested object is at hand, as when an astronaut is on the moon and needs a tank because he has no air. In his own words, *"he can't say 'please can you give me another tank', because he can't breathe. Then [. . .] it would take less time if he just said 'give me a tank, I'm running out of air' "* (Myrset & Savić, 2021: 180).

In another study by Savić and Myrset (2022), 79 Norwegian Primary students, from the third, fifth and seventh grades, consider the (in-)appropriateness of direct, conventionally indirect requests and hints. Their metapragmatic appraisals of requests seem to mirror the strategies they have at their disposal when request-making (see Savić, 2015; Savić et al., 2021). Actually, the group of third graders mostly comment on linguistic aspects related to the request head act and identify politeness with conventional indirect requests headed by the modal verb *can* and the addition of the marker *please*. Further, 9-year-olds remain unaware of the function played by alerters or by supportive moves, two external types of modifiers they never perform. The negative appraisal of direct requests starts diminishing in the fifth graders' contributions, where attention is paid to intonation (equating loudness with directness) and supportive moves like grounders or thanking are also noticed. Finally, a wider repertoire of modal verbs (e.g. *may* versus *can*) and modifiers –with openers like *Do you think* I can?– is the focus of the seventh graders' metapragmatic reflections.

From a sociopragmatic perspective, the oldest students are the only ones reflecting upon the impact of contextual constraints such as the interlocutor's age and familiarity or the place where the exchange takes place –e.g. ordering food at a fast food restaurant allowing for more directness than requesting stationary from the teacher in class. As a common trait, the authors remark the overgeneralisation of *please* present in the three age groups' comments and possibly derived from a partial understanding of its function, which Savić and Myrset view as "a springboard for creating a more nuanced understanding of linguistic and contextual variability" (2022: 136).

Apart from the above, more empirical evidence with the potential of informing pragmatics instruction in the PELT classroom is found in Savić and Myrset (2021). In a chapter entitled "But in England they're certainly very polite, so you mustn't forget that", the authors describe the interpretative frameworks underlying the metapragmatic reflections of the same 79 Norwegian students in Savić and Myrset's (2022) study. These interpretative frameworks fall into the following categories: perceived feelings of the addressee, hypothetical stories and lived experiences, mostly invoked by the younger group of 9 year olds, or L1 cultural assumptions and stereotypical views of the target language (TL) and its speakers.

Such stereotypical views, apparent in the metapragmatic reflections of 11- and 13-year-olds, are rooted in the belief that the English are more polite than Norwegians or in their perception that the manners of British upper classes, like drinking tea with the pinky finger up, are the quintessence of politeness. As none of these interpretative frameworks, however simplistic, "display essentialist and ethnocentric views" (Savić & Myrset, 2021: 55), they are not considered as an obstacle to promote intercultural understanding in the PELT classroom. On the contrary, with careful teacher guidance and collaborative dialogue (Savić, 2021), they are seen as a starting point for raising YLLs' awareness of intracultural and intercultural variations.

Before moving into the teaching approaches that might dispel some of the aforementioned stereotypes, next I will summarise the investigations about the pragmatic input on request-making to which PELT students are exposed in materials like textbooks and picturebooks.

Pragmatic Input Materials: Textbooks and Picturebooks

In Jakupčević and Portolan Ćavar's (2021) study of textbooks used in Croatian schools for YLLs aged 9–12, requests are absent from the materials for fourth graders, exclusively centred on greetings. Moreover, the amount of input on request-making greatly varies from one textbook to the other and is embedded in dialogues without metapragmatic information or pragmatics-focused practice. In contrast, Schauer's (2019: 154–156) analysis of the pragmatic input included in four German textbook series for third and fourth graders reveals that requests are over-represented, amounting to 74 % of all speech act occurrences. Also of note are, first, the imbalance observed with respect to responses to requests, representing 11 % of all speech act instances and, second, the dominance of direct request strategies. These reduce YLLs' exposure to speech act pairs (i.e. requests and request responses) and conventional indirectness.

Remarkably, conventional indirectness features strongly in three EFL textbook series, also published in Germany but for older students aged 10/11 to 15/16, where learners are advised to use:

> (a) the modal verbs *may* and *can* to ask politely for permission or to request something
> (b) *please* to utter a request politely
> (c) *sorry* and *excuse me* as polite forms to address or interrupt somebody [. . .]
> (h) With phrases like *Could you. . . Would you. . .*and *Please* you can change the register from casual to polite
> [. . .]
> (t) If you don't know which register to use (formal? informal?), it is better to be more formal, i.e. more polite. Using language that is too informal is impolite in the UK and the US (Limberg, 2016: 281–282).

In presenting some pragmalinguistic forms as inherently polite and in equating formality to politeness, there is the risk of misapplying these guidelines as maxims or "rules of thumb" (van Compernolle, 2014). This oversimplification of conventional indirectness could help to account for some of the stereotypes, described above, like the negative perception of directness or the overgeneralisation of *please* in the performance and comprehension of requests (Savić, 2015; Savić et al., 2021; Savić & Myrset, 2022). The onus is therefore placed on the teacher to ensure that PELT students will understand that "language choices are subject to socio-cultural constraints and that politeness is not automatically communicated with specific words or phrases" (Limberg, 2016: 285).

Still, textbooks are not the only materials implemented in the PELT classroom. Accordingly, Schauer (2019: 159–165) compares the provision of pragmatic input in textbooks and in picturebooks, a literary genre that, as Egoff states, "represents the most diverse, *the most didactic*, and the most debated of all forms of present-day children's literature" (1981: 248, emphasis mine). Quantitatively speaking, the provision of authentic request-making input is poorer than expected. In fact, the top speech acts found in the 22 picturebooks examined are the same already identified in textbooks, namely, requests, responses to requests and greetings. Requests account for 62 % of all speech act occurrences and 94 % of their head acts are direct with only three examples of permission and none of the ability strategies.

However disappointing, these quantitative findings do not necessarily invalidate the use of picturebooks. Indeed, according to Faya Cerqueiro (2022), when a direct style predominates and the narrator's voice is kept to a minimum, as is the case of Steve Antony's *Mr Panda*'s stories she explores, even preschoolers' receptive pragmatic repertoire may be widened. In any event, as can be seen in the next sub-section, the benefits of using picturebooks depend, to a great extent, on the PELT practitioner's didactic skills to maximise their learning affordances.

Impact of Dialogic Teaching Through Picturebooks

Among the sparse literature on pragmatics instruction with YLLs (for a comprehensive review, see Myrset, 2021: 37–42), two dialogic interventions on requests are addressed to Primary students –i.e. from 5/

6 to 11/12 years. Both studies, conducted by Ishihara (2013) and by Ishihara and Chiba (2014), involve three Japanese 9-year-old boys learning English in Tokyo and a group of five children, two 9-year-old boys and three girls aged 7 or 12, belonging to Japanese families temporarily residing in Hong Kong. Without falling into unwarranted generalisations, these two small-scale experiments may shed light on how picturebooks "can provide the rich sociocultural contexts that are crucial in learning pragmatics" (Ishihara, 2013: 137). The interactional data obtained during three pragmatics-focused lessons (a total of 120 minutes, spread out over six weeks in Tokyo, and 180 minutes, divided into three sessions in Hong Kong) offer some insights into the use of picturebooks.

On the plus side, the first insight gained is that YLLs are able to derive sociopragmatic meaning from the visual clues present in picturebooks –including drawings and font size–, either spontaneously or with the teacher's guidance. For example, 9-year-old Shota infers that *How do you do?*, an expression unknown to him, must be polite because the character who utters it "*is lowering his hat like this* (gestures) [. . .] *Like magicians hold their hats too. Which is, yes, it's polite language!*" (Ishihara, 2013: 140). Secondly, the recursive narrative structure of picturebooks allows the teacher to stop on a given page and ask students what they would say in each situation. Thirdly, the use of children's L1 (i.e. Japanese) does not only facilitate YLLs' participation but also reduces the cognitive demands of metapragmatic discussions. Lastly, instructional materials such as a formality judgement tasks (FJTs), discourse completion tasks (DCTs) or student-generated visual discourse completion tasks (SVDCTs) prove to be valuable in enhancing and assessing participants' metapragmatic awareness.

On the minus side, only the children living in Hong Kong (Ishihara & Chiba, 2014: 99–100), a city where exposure to English is higher, produce conventionally indirect requests of the ability type –i.e. *can I/you, could I/you, may I*– in combination with *please*. Conversely, the Tokyo data indicate an overreliance on *please* as the main politeness marker elicited, regardless of the situation. This unequal impact on learning outcomes, favouring meta-pragmatic awareness over production, leads Ishihara to conclude that isolated and short-term pragmatics-focused interventions in informal settings are insufficient and that "continued and recurrent pragmatics instruction incorporated into regular language instruction" (2013: 146) is needed.

The PACE Model

The easiness with which it can be implemented in larger mainstream classes is one of the advantages of the PACE model, defined by Donato and Adair-Hauck as "a dialogic approach to the teaching of grammar using cultural stories as the centerpiece of a lesson in standards-based foreign language instruction" (2015: 206). Despite its focus on grammar, there are three reasons to believe that this model –whose acronym stands for **P**resentation, **A**ttention, **C**o-construction and **E**xtension– is well suited to teaching L2 pragmatics to YLLs. First, the functional perspective it adopts is highly compatible with pragmatics, as it aims at understanding how, for instance, the subjunctive gains meaning in the context of the speech act of advice-giving (Donato & Adair-Hauck, 2015: 211). The second reason is that the PACE model is SCT-informed with Vygotskyan principles like meaning-centred instruction, human and material mediation with a focus on literary works or learners' L1(s) as scaffolding tool(s). Such principles, as shown by Ishihara (2013) and by Ishihara and Chiba (2014), can be feasibly applied to the PELT classroom. The third reason is that, when adapted to pragmatics instruction, the PACE model has the potential to depart from other pedagogical frameworks, harshly criticised by van Compernolle (2014: 8) because of their transmission of "rule-of-thumb-based knowledge" about pragmalinguistic forms and socio-pragmatic factors.

In avoiding teacher-fronted explanations of *a priori* pragmalinguistic and sociopragmatic knowledge, the PACE model follows a constructivist approach. Constructivism is more in tune with children's cognitive development and how they learn language holistically, without analysing abstract language forms and "through opportunities to talk things through with others, usually adults" (Pinter, 2017: 5). A dialogic co-constructed and problem-solving procedure like the PACE model, then, might lead to children's L2 pragmatic development, understood here as unassisted performance and comprehension of request-making. Essentially, as outlined by Vygotsky, "the only good kind of instruction marches ahead of development and leads it. It must be aimed not so much at the ripe, but at the ripening functions" (1986: 188).

Text Selection

Prior to designing a PACE learning situation, the selection of an age-appropriate story, where the target pragmatic features are salient and meaningful, must be ensured. Particular care should also be taken to choose texts that are within YLLs' zone of proximal development (ZPD). In Vygostky's terms, the ZPD refers to the distance existing between the "actual developmental level as determined by independent problem solving and the level of potential development as determined through problem solving under adult guidance or in collaboration with more capable peers" (1978: 86). The ZPD in child request-making considered hereafter is drawn from the literature reviewed above.

This literature suggests that PELT students from the ages of eight or nine onwards would greatly benefit from pragmatics-focused instruction insofar as, even in Norway, a setting favourable to Extramural English with a languaculture closer to the TL, production and comprehension of requests suffer from several shortcomings. In truth, second graders still realise requests through direct strategies –i.e. imperatives, elliptical or want statements–, the modal verb *may* does not consistently appear until the age of 11, third graders are unsure about the role of alerters, *please* is overgeneralised and sociocultural variables such as familiarity or age only figure in seventh graders' metapragmatic reflections. Along with Savić and Myrset (2022: 136), the aforementioned shortcomings can be seen as "a springboard for creating a more nuanced understanding of linguistic and contextual variability" (2022: 136). Accordingly, the texts chosen belong to three picturebooks from Mo Willems' *Elephant & Piggie* stories, a series that is very rich in speech act input, generally, and in requests in particular.

Mo Willems (1968, Des Plaines, Illinois, USA) is an awarded author and illustrator, whose successful career began as a writer and animator on *Sesame Street.* This experience is mentioned when he talks about the *Elephant & Piggie* series thus:

> One of the greatest joys in my career has been the ability to make the Elephant and Piggie easy readers [. . .] Back at *Sesame Street*, the writers were required to attend child-development seminars, some of which involve learning about how kids learn to read, a topic that really interested me. Later, it was fascinating watching my daughter decode shapes into letters, then letters into words, followed by words into story (Willems, 2013: 252).

Seemingly, those child-development seminars paid off, because the masterful way Willems uses colours in letter bubbles and font size does not only facilitate early independent reading but also conveys the characters' emotions. Starring a male elephant called Gerald, who is indecisive and constantly worrying, and a female pig called Piggy, a spirited character full of joy and curiosity, the episodically organised 25 stories revolve around their friendship, with its ups and downs. Readers are also told about the everyday dilemmas the two protagonists face and the different moods they pass through, when meeting each other to play or in their encounters with other animals. While letter bubbles are coloured depending on who speaks –grey for Gerald, pink for Piggy, golden for Birds or light blue for Penguin–, the font size gets larger or smaller to express either loudness in moments of excitement or a whispering voice in moments of sadness and uncertainty.

Thanks to these compelling visual resources, the narrator is made redundant and dialogues come to the fore, allowing us to see request-making in action. Table 1.3 specifies the requestive behaviour to which heed will be paid and the pedagogical purposes guiding this selection.

Table 1.3. Selected picturebooks, requestive forms and pedagogical purposes.

Picturebook title	Request act sequence	Pedagogical purposes
***1. There Is a Bird on Your Head!* (2007)**	1 Gerald (G): Piggie! 2 G: Is something on my head? 3 Piggy (P): Yes. 4 P: There is a bird on your head. [. . .] 9 P: Now there are two birds on your head. [. . .] 16 P: They are making a nest! [. . .] 24 P: You have three eggs on your head. [. . .] 35 G: **I do not want** three baby chicks, two birds, and a nest on my head! 36 P: Where do you want them? 37 G: SOMEWHERE ELSE! 38 P: Why not ask them to go somewhere else? 39 G: Ask them? 40 P: Ask them! 41 G: Okay. I will try asking. 42 G: **Excuse me, birds. Will you please go somewhere else?** 19 Birds (B): No problem. 20 G: It worked! 21 B: Bye! 22 G: Now there are no birds on my head! 23 G: Thank you, Piggie! Thank you very much! 24 P: You are welcome. . .	–Target pragmalinguistic forms: the conventional indirect **willingness strategy** *Will you?*, internally modified with *please* and externally modified with two alerters. –Sociocultural variables: perceived high cost of the requested action and interlocutor low familiarity. –Interactional features of the request with a beginning (*I do not want. . .*) and an ending point (*Bye!*). –Adjacency pairs: requests and request responses (*No problem*).

***2. Watch Me Throw the Ball!* (2009)**	1 P: La, la, la! 2 P: A ball! 3 G: You found my ball! 4 P: This is your ball? 5 G: Yes. I threw it from way over there! [. . .] 7 G: I am very good at throwing. 8 P: Wow. . . 9 P: **May I throw your ball?** 10 G: You want to throw my ball? 11 P: Yes! 12 G: Do you know the secret to throwing? 13 P: Sure. "Have fun." 14 G: FUN!?! 15 G: Throwing this ball is not easy! [. . .] 18 Got it. **May *I* try now?** 19 G: Yes. Maybe one day you can throw like me. But— 20 P: **STAND BACK!** 21 P: **THE PIG IS THROWING!**	–Target pragmalinguistic forms: the unmodified **permission strategy** *May I?,* reiterated with the intensifier *now* and the emphasised *I* pronoun, showing the requester's impatience *versus* the imperative *stand back*, modified with a grounder *The pig is throwing*. –Sociocultural variables: perceived high cost of the requested object (i.e. the ball) and interlocutor high familiarity. –Interactional features of the reiterated request.

Continued

Table 1.3. *Continued*

Picturebook title	Request act sequence	Pedagogical purposes
3. Should I Share My Ice Cream? **(2011)**	1 Penguin (Pe): Ice cream! Get your cold ice cream for a hot day! 2 G: Oh, boy! Ice cream! 3 G: **One ice cream, please.** 4 Pe: Here you go! 5 G: Oh, boy! Oh, boy! 5 G: I *love* ice cream! 6 G: **Wait!** 7 G: Piggie loves ice cream, too. 8 G: Piggie is my best friend. 9 G: Should I share my ice cream with her?	–Target pragmalinguistic forms: elliptical statement *One ice cream*, internally modified with *please*. –Sociopragmatic variables: perceived low cost of the requested good and client-server relationship (low familiarity). –Interactional features of requests in brief service encounters.

Steps in the PACE Model

The acronym PACE results from the four steps developed by Donato and Adair-Hauck "for integrating focus on form in the context of interesting cultural stories" (2015: 214). This four-step model builds a whole learning situation that can spread out over several sessions. In the adaptation to pragmatics teaching put forward hereafter, Willems' selected picturebooks are approached as three episodes of the same story-line, each one showing a motive to perform a request (i.e. action in number 1, object in 2 and service in 3). Ultimately, the purpose is to problematise the idea that direct requests are impolite by default and conventional indirect requests with *can* and *please* are inherently polite and formal, two misconceptions detected in YLLs' metapragmatic appraisals (Savić & Myrset, 2021, 2022) and in textbooks for upper Primary and lower Secondary education (Limberg, 2016). Dispelling these misconceptions would entail raising PELT students' awareness of how and why certain pragmalinguistic forms, including unmodified direct request head acts, are appropriately used in a particular context, depending on two sociocultural variables: the perceived cost of complying with the request from the requestee's perspective, on the one hand, and the social distance or familiarity between interlocutors, on the other.

The ageless animal characters, devoid of status, prevent us from tackling other sociocultural variables like age or power. In return, the clear conversational sequences make request-making more transparent. For example, in picturebook 1, we see how Gerald's initial request ("I do not want three baby chicks, two birds, and a nest on my head!") is realised, thanks to Piggy's suggestion ("Why not ask them to go somewhere else?"), by means of an internally and externally conventional indirect question ("Excuse me, birds. Will you please go somewhere else?"), to which the birds immediately comply ("No problem [. . .] Bye!"). This shift from a direct want-statement to an indirect willing strategy allows us to see effective request-making in action.

Step P: Presentation

To start the cycle, Donato and Adair-Hauck (2015: 223) advocate "interactive storytelling", rather than just teacher story-reading. As they make clear: "storytelling needs to be a social interactive event [...] a collaborative listening experience. During storytelling, both the teacher and learners engage in the meaning-making event" (Donato & Adair-Hauck, 2015: 225). To that aim, practitioners should resort to comprehensible input techniques –e.g. gestures, mime, sound effects, props or child-directed speech–, whereas YLLs cannot remain passive and, for instance, may act out the scenes by participating in Total Physical Response activities. Willems' picturebooks are susceptible to be dramatised, during or after the presentation, and the quality of their illustrations enables the teacher to use them no only as visual aids but also as "mental" scaffolds (Eitel & Scheiter, 2015: 166). Other ways to promote student engagement, enlisted by Donato and Adair-Hauck, are "learner repetitions of key phrases [...], thumbs up/down comprehension checks" or invitations to predict "what will happen next" (2015: 215).

Step A: Attention

While the goal of step **P** was ensuring comprehension, step **A** is the shortest stage, lasting just some minutes, with only part of a teaching session needed to draw students' *attention* to the pragmalinguistic forms on focus. As summarised by Donato and Adair-Hauck, joint attention between the practitioner and the learner "can be established explicitly and directly through various mediational means, such as printed text with enhancements or questions that direct attention" (2015: 217). Given that second/third graders may still be low-literate, practitioners are strongly advised to accompany the main requestive move(s), underlined or presented in italics or bold font –see Table 1.3–, with images taken from the picturebook(s). These images will help YLLs to better understand the context and the interlocutors' attitudes towards a given request.

Step C: Co-Construction

It is at this point when the teacher's role as provider of "responsive instructional assistance" (Donato & Adair-Hauck, 2015: 209) takes centre stage. The aim here is to enhance YLLs' metapragmatic awareness, defined earlier as "the ability to articulate one's conscious understanding of pragmatic meanings within and across languages and cultures" (Myrset & McConachy, 2022: 309). Hence, the challenge is twofold. For one thing, preventing that classroom discussions "degenerate into an interrogation on the one hand or a teacher-fronted explanation on the other" (Donato & Adair-Hauck, 2015: 219). For another, creating the conditions for YLLs "to verbalize [their] reflections on linguistic forms, contextual features and/or their interplay" (Myrset & Savić, 2021: 165).

Consequently, children's reflections to co-construct explanations on the interplay between pragmalinguistic forms and sociopragmatic variables can be aided by (i) asking "teacher questions that are well chosen, clear and direct" (Donato & Adair-Hauck, 2015: 217), (ii) incorporating PELT students' L1(s) and life experiences or (iii) designing tasks where both questions and YLL's linguistic and cultural backgrounds are put at the service of collaborative discussions. Of particular interest for a pragmatics-focused PACE model is the implementation of a discussion webbing or the Emoticon and the Ranking circle tasks, designed by Myrset and Savić (2021) as data elicitation techniques.

A discussion webbing with Willems' picturebooks would include teacher questions like "if you had the birds on your head, what would you say in your L1(s) to ask them to move?", "and in English?", "should Piggy use "please" when asking Gerald's permission to throw his ball?", "why/why not?", "what would you say to buy an ice-cream on the street in your L1(s)?", "and in English?" Complementarily, the Emoticon and the Ranking circle are two metapragmatic appraisal tasks. The former is an individual activity that invites students to decide whether a request is *nice, so-so* or *not so nice,* by sticking a post-it note on a smiley, a neutral or an angry face emoticon (Myrset & Savić, 2021: 176). The latter starts with a general question (i.e. "What is important to think about when we ask for something in English?"), followed by a discussion, performed in groups, intended to elicit YLLs' metapragmatic ideas. Once these are elicited, each group has to reach an agreement to place the raised ideas on a three-concentric circles diagram in increasing order of importance, with the inner circle in yellow accommodating the most important metapragmatic issues and the outer circle in blue, the least important ones (Myrset & Savić, 2021: 176). Both tasks can double, first, as instructional tasks and, second, as assessment instruments, to ascertain the extent to which the intended pedagogical purposes have been achieved.

Step E: Extension

The 4-step cycle closes with YLLs carrying out a number of activities taking as many sessions as the teacher deems necessary. Whilst in Step **C**, the objective was developing children's logical thinking, now is the time to boost their creativity by writing and/or performing their own texts. With low-literate students, multimodal and multilingual responses should be favoured. Creating scripts for Readers Theatre or student-generated visual discourse completion tasks (SVDCTs), successfully implemented by Myrset (2021) and by Ishihara (2013), respectively, appear as feasible options. Other ideas proposed by Donato and Adair-Hauck are suggesting a new ending to the story, retelling it in a different setting or time, writing a poem, creating a song or designing a film poster for the story (2015: 225–226).

Final Thoughts

This study set out to respond to Glaser's call for "concrete and directly applicable materials and teaching suggestions" (2023: 82), in the case of request-making, one of the most recurrent and well-researched speech acts. The effectiveness of the adaptation of Donato and Adair-Hauck's (2015) PACE model to instructional pragmatics for YLLs presented earlier is yet to be determined. Further research should confirm whether this sociocultural pedagogical framework really works in the PELT classroom. In the meantime, this chapter adds to the relatively new subfield of pragmatics and children's literature (Meibauer, 2017) with a teaching proposal that, following Schauer, may be helpful for those practitioners with no expertise in pragmatics, who "would benefit from accessible research that describes which books could be used for teaching which speech acts", as well as for "teachers already familiar with pragmatics [who] would also benefit from research outlining the pragmatic potential of individual books" (2022: 150–151).

Acknowledgements

As a member of the LAELA (Lingüística Aplicada a l'Ensenyament de la Llengua Anglesa) research group at Universitat Jaume I (Castelló, Spain), I would like to acknowledge that this study is part of the research project PID2020-117959GB-I00 funded by MCIN/AEI/10.13039/501100011033. Additional funding has been granted by Projectes d'Innovació Educativa de la Unitat de Suport Educatiu, from Universitat Jaume I, 51020/24.

References

Alcón, Eva & Safont, Pilar. 2008. Pragmatic awareness in second language acquisition. In Jasone Cenoz & Nancy H. Hornberger (eds) *Encyclopedia of language and education* (2nd ed., Vol. 6: *Knowledge about Language*). Amsterdam: Springer, 193–204.

Bardovi-Harlig, Kathleen. 2020. Pedagogical linguistics: A view from L2 pragmatics. *Pedagogical Linguistics*, 1/1, 44–65. <https://doi.org/10.1075/pl.19013.bar>.

Barón, Júlia. 2015. "Can I make a party, mum?" The development of requests from childhood to adolescence. *ATLANTIS*, 37/1, 179–198.

Blum-Kulka, Shoshana & Olshtain, Elite. 1984. Requests and apologies: A cross-cultural study of speech act realization patterns (CCSARP). *Applied Linguistics*, 5/3, 196–213. <https://doi.org/10.1093/applin/5.3.196>.

Blum-Kulka, Shoshana, House, Juliane & Kasper, Gabriele. 1989. *Cross-cultural pragmatics: Requests and apologies.* Norwood: Ablex Publishing Corporation.

Cekaite, Asta. 2013. Child pragmatic development. In Carol A. Chapelle (ed.) *The encyclopedia of applied linguistics*. Oxford: Blackwell Publishing, 1–7.

Cohen, Andrew D. 2016. The teaching of pragmatics by native and non-native language teachers: What they know and what they report doing. *Studies in Second Language Learning and Teaching*, 6/4, 561–585. <https://doi.org/10.14746/ssllt.2016.6.4.2>.

Cohen, Andrew D. 2018. *Learning pragmatics from native and non-native language teachers*. Bristol: Multilingual Matters.

Donato, Richard & Adair-Hauck, Bonnie. 2015. PACE: A story-based approach for dialogic inquiry about form and meaning. In Judith Shrum & Eileen W. Glisan (eds) *Teacher's handbook: Contextualized foreign language instruction* (5th ed.). Boston: Cengage Learning EMEA, 206–230.

Eitel, Alexander & Scheiter, Katharina. 2015. Picture or text first? Explaining sequence effects when learning with pictures and text. *Educational Psychology Review*, 27/1, 153–180. <http://dx.doi.org/10.1007/s10648-014-9264-4>.

Enever, Janet. 2016. Primary ELT: Issues and trends. In Graham Hall (ed.) *The Routledge Handbook of English Language Teaching*. London: Routledge, 353–366. <https://doi.org/10.4324/9781315676203-30>.

Egoff, Sheila A. 1981. *Thursday's child: Trends and patterns in contemporary children's literature*. Chicago: American Library Association.

Faya Cerqueiro, Fátima. 2022. The role of picturebooks in the acquisition of pragmatic competence: Analysis of Mr Panda. In Raúl Navarro Olivas & Eugenio Cortés (eds) *Habilidades comunicativas y didáctica de la L2*. Madrid: Dykinson, 145–156.

Glaser, Karen. 2018. Enhancing the role of pragmatics in primary English teacher training. *Glottodidactica: An International Journal of Applied Linguistics,* 45/2, 119–131. <https://doi.org/10.14746/gl.2018.45.2.06>.

Glaser, Karen. 2020. Assessing the L2 pragmatic awareness of non-native EFL teacher candidates: Is spotting a problem enough? *Lodz Papers in Pragmatics*, 16/1, 33–65. <https://doi.org/10.1515/lpp-2020-0003>.

Glaser, Karen. 2023. Teachers' awareness, knowledge and attitudes towards instruction in L2 pragmatics. In Alicia Martínez-Flor,

Adriana Sánchez-Hernández & Júlia Barón (eds) *L2 pragmatics in action: Teachers, learners and the teaching-learning interaction process*. Amsterdam: John Benjamins Publishing Company, 63–87. <https://doi.org/10.1075/lllt.58.03gla>.

Graddol, David. 2006. *English next: Why global English may mean the end of 'English as a Foreign Language'*. Plymouth: British Council. Retrieved from: <https://www.teachingenglish.org.uk/sites/teacheng/files/pub_english_next.pdf>.

Ishihara, Noriko. 2010. Instructional pragmatics: Bridging teaching, research and teacher education. *Language and Linguistics Compass*, 4/10, 938–953. <https://doi.org/10.1111/j.1749-818x.2010.00242.x>.

Ishihara, Noriko. 2012. Critical narratives for teaching pragmatics: Application to teacher education. *The European Journal of Applied Linguistics and TEFL*, 1/2, 5–17.

Ishihara, Noriko. 2013. Is it rude language? Children learning pragmatics through visual narratives. *TESL Canada Journal*, 30/7, 135–149. <https://doi.org/10.18806/tesl.v30i7.1157>.

Ishihara, Noriko & Chiba, Akiko. 2014. Teacher-based or interactional? Exploring assessment for children's pragmatic development. *Iranian Journal of Language Testing*, 4/1, 84–112.

Jakupčević, Eva & Portolan Ćavar, Mihajla. 2021. An analysis of pragmatic content in EFL textbooks for young learners in Croatia. *Language Teaching Research*, 28/1, 114–137 <https://doi.org/10.1177/1362168820986936>.

Limberg, Holger. 2016. "Always remember to say *Please* and *Thank you*": Teaching politeness with German EFL textbooks. In Kathleen Bardovi–Harlig & J. César Félix-Brasdefer (eds) *Pragmatics and language learning* (Vol. 14). Honolulu: University of Hawai'i, 265–299.

McConachy, Troy. 2013. Exploring the meta-pragmatic realm in English language teaching. *Language Awareness*, 22/2, 100–110. <https://doi.org/10.1080/09658416.2011.644795>.

McConachy, Troy. 2018. *Developing intercultural perspectives on language use: Exploring pragmatics and culture in foreign language learning*. Bristol: Multilingual Matters.

Meibauer, Jörg. 2017. Pragmatics and children literature. In Raquel Giora & Michael Haugh (eds) *Doing pragmatics interculturally: Cognitive, philosophical, and sociopragmatic perspectives.* Berlin/Boston: De Gruyter Mouton, 371–388.

Myrset, Anders. 2021. *From Act to Action: (Meta)pragmatic instruction with young EFL learners in Norway.* Stavanger: University of Stavanger.

Myrset, Anders & McConachy, Troy. 2022. Incorporating pragmatics into primary English language teacher education. In David Valente & Daniel Xerri (eds) *Innovative practices in early English language education.* London: Palgrave Macmillan, 305–327. <https://doi.org/10.1007/978-3-031-12922-3_15>.

Myrset, Anders & Savić, Milica. 2021. 'If an astronaut were on the moon…': Eliciting metapragmatic data from young L2 learners. *Applied Pragmatics*, 3/2, 163–196. <https://doi.org/10.1075/ap.19027.myr>

Pinter, Annamaria. 2017. *Teaching young language learners* (2nd ed.). Oxford: Oxford University Press.

Portolés, Laura. 2015. *Multilingualism and very young learners: An analysis of pragmatic awareness and language attitudes.* Berlin/Boston: De Gruyter Mouton.

Portolés, Laura & Safont, Pilar. 2018. Examining authentic and elicited data from a multilingual perspective. The real picture of child requestive behaviour in the L3 classroom. *System*, 75, 81–92. <https://doi.org/10.1016/j.system.2018.03.012>.

Safont, Pilar. 2008. The speech act of requesting. In Eva Alcón Soler (ed.) *Learning how to request in an instructed language context.* Bern: Peter Lang, 41–64.

Savić, Milica. 2015. "Can I very please borrow it?": Request development in young Norwegian EFL learners. *Intercultural Pragmatics*, 12/4, 443–480. <https://doi.org/10.1515/ip-2015-0023>.

Savić, Milica. 2021. Co-constructing metapragmatic understandings: How young EFL learners talk about making requests. *The European Journal of Applied Linguistics and TEFL*, 10/2, 153–176.

Savić, Milica, Economidou-Kogetsidis, Maria & Myrset, Anders 2021. Young Greek Cypriot and Norwegian EFL learners: Pragmalinguistic development in request production. *Journal of Pragmatics*, 180/, 15–34. <https://doi.org/10.1016/j.pragma.2021.04.006>.

Savić, Milica & Myrset, Anders. 2021. 'But in England they're certainly very polite, so you mustn't forget that': Young EFL learners making sense of pragmatic practices. In Troy McConachy & Anthony J. Liddicoat (eds) *Teaching and learning second language pragmatics for intercultural understanding.* London: Routledge, 40–59.

Savić, Milica & Myrset, Anders. 2022. 'Hey, can I loan your yellow pencil?' Young Norwegian EFL learners' metapragmatic appraisal of requests. In Nicola Halenko & Jiayi Wang (eds) *Pragmatics in English language learning*. Cambridge: Cambridge University Press. <https://doi.org/10.1017/9781108894241.006>

Schauer, Gila A. 2019. *Teaching and learning English in the primary school: Interlanguage pragmatics in the EFL context*. Cham: Springer. <https://doi.org/10.1007/978-3-030-23257-3>.

Schauer, Gila A. 2022. Teaching L2 pragmatics to young learners. A review study. *Applied Pragmatics,* 4/2, 137–158. <https://doi.org/10.1075/ap.00006.sch>.

Sickinger, Pawel & Schneider, Klaus Peter. 2014. Pragmatic competence and the CEFR: Pragmatic profiling as a link between theory and language use. *Linguistica,* 54/1, 113–127. <https://doi.org/10.4312/linguistica.54.1.113-127>.

Taguchi, Naoko. 2019. *The Routledge handbook of SLA and pragmatics*. New York: Routledge.

Trosborg, Anna. 1995. *Interlanguage pragmatics: Requests, complaints and apologies*. Berlin: Mouton de Gruyter.

Van Compernolle, Rémi A. 2014. *Sociocultural theory and L2 instructional pragmatics*. Bristol: Multilingual Matters.

Vygotsky, Lev S. 1978. *Mind in society: The development of higher psychological processes*. Cambridge, MA: Harvard University Press.

Vygotsky, Lev S. 1986. *Thought and language*. Cambridge, MA: MIT Press.

Willems, Mo. 2007. *There is a bird on your head!* New York: Hyperion.

Willems, Mo. 2009. *Watch me throw the ball!* New York: Hyperion.

Willems, Mo. 2011. *Should I share my ice cream?* New York: Hyperion.

Willems, Mo. 2013. *Don't pigeonhole me! Two decades of the Mo Willems sketchbook*. New York: Disney Editions.

Woodfield, Helen & Economidou-Kogetsidis, Maria. 2010. "I just need more time": A study of native and non-native students' requests to faculty for late submission. *Multilingua,* 29/1, 77–118. <https://doi.org/10.1515/mult.2010.004>

Sofía Martín-Laguna

Integrating Pragmatic Expressions in Young Learners' Classrooms: A Task-Based Proposal for Pre-Service Teachers

Introduction

Second language[1] (L2) pragmatics involves two dimensions, i.e. pragmatics and L2 research. Crystal (1997: 301) defines pragmatics as "the study of language from the point of view of users, especially of the choices they make, the constraints they encounter in using language in social interaction and the effects their use of language has on other participants in the act of communication". Pragmatics involves two dimensions, i.e. pragmalinguistics and sociopragmatics (Leech, 1983; Thomas, 1983). Pragmalinguistics refers to the linguistic resources used to convey pragmatic functions (e.g. directness and indirectness, routines, or linguistic forms to intensify or soften communicative acts). In turn, sociopragmatics addresses the social perceptions and conventions to perform pragmatic functions (e.g. in terms of the interlocutors' social distance, social power, their rights and obligations and degree of imposition) (see Thomas, 1983; Kasper & Rose, 2001). L2 pragmatics examines how learners develop pragmatic competence, which is the ability to use language norms and principles appropriately in context (Taguchi, 2019). Pragmatics is an essential component of L2 communicative competence, helping to prevent communication breakdowns and negative perceptions of the

1 Following Taguchi (2019), L2 pragmatics refers to both L2 and foreign language (FL) learning contexts.

L2 speaker (Gass & Selinker, 2008). In English as a Foreign Language (EFL) contexts, most interaction occurs within the classroom, and teachers play a crucial role in fostering learners' pragmatic development by guiding classroom discourse and making methodological and content choices. Training EFL teachers in pragmatic skills is thus vital (Glaser, 2018), but courses for teachers of young learners (YLs) have often overlooked this aspect (Edelenbos et al., 2006; Enever, 2014; Dausend, 2017; Kubanek, 2017). In this chapter, YLs will be considered children aged between 3 and 13 years old (see Schauer, 2022a for a discussion).

Classroom settings should be treated as professional environments with context-specific pragmatic norms (Edmondson et al., 2023). As Nikula (2002: 447) puts it, they must be seen "as social contexts in their own right and with their own pragmatic constraints which may not correspond to those of everyday discourse in other settings". This implies that training courses must equip in-service and pre-service teachers of YLs with the pragmatic skills necessary for effective classroom interaction. A recurrent pragmatic resource that teachers need to master in classroom discourse are classroom pragmatic expressions, e.g. *Let's check attendance*.

Incorporating real-life contexts into language teaching is central to task-based approaches (Ahmadian & Long, 2022), making them effective for teaching pragmatics (González-Lloret, 2019; Taguchi & Kim, 2018). While some studies have applied a task-based approach to teach pragmatics, they have primarily examined learners' performance. There is a need for research on how a task-based approach can prepare pre-service teachers for effective classroom management. This chapter presents a task-based proposal to develop classroom pragmatic expressions in pre-service teachers of YLs.

The chapter starts with an overview of the literature on pragmatics in teacher education, examining the teachers' perspective in YLs' EFL classrooms, and classroom pragmatic expressions in classroom discourse. Then, a task-based teaching proposal is presented. Finally, concluding remarks and limitations are discussed.

Theoretical Background

Pragmatics in Teacher Education

A large body of research has evidenced that pragmatic instruction is beneficial to promote pragmatic learning (see Taguchi, 2015, and Taguchi & Youn, 2022 for overviews). Researchers have proposed approaches to enhance learners' pragmatic competence (e.g. Alcón-Soler & Guzmán, 2010; Codina-Espurz & Salazar-Campillo, 2019; Martínez-Flor & Usó-Juan, 2006; Usó-Juan & Martínez-Flor, 2021, 2022, among others), which stress the importance of developing learners' pragmalinguistic and sociopragmatic awareness before production. In this regard, Usó-Juan and Martínez-Flor (2021) proposed a set of awareness-raising questions for pragmalinguistic analysis, such as *Is the interactant's first turn a request, an invitation, an offer or a suggestion?* or *How is the refusal realised? (i.e. direct strategies, indirect strategies or a combination of both)*. Regarding sociopragmatic variables, they adapted Hymes' (1974) SPEAKING framework, which focuses on contextual analysis. This framework covers eight components critical to understanding and constructing conversations: Setting (physical circumstances), Participants (speakers and audience), Ends (purposes), Act sequence (form and order of events), Key (tone), Instrumentalities (style of speech), Norms (interaction rules), and Genre (speech event type).

Most pedagogical models for teaching pragmatics have been designed for general EFL learners, overlooking their specific pragmatic needs. Recently, some scholars have turned their attention to teachers (e.g. Glaser, 2023; Myrset & McConachy, 2024; Savvidou & Economidou-Kogetsidis, 2019; Schauer, 2022a, 2022b; Usó-Juan & Martínez-Flor, 2020; see also the volume edited by Martínez-Flor et al., 2023), but the inclusion of pragmatics in teacher training has not received much attention yet. Existing research suggests that training teachers in pragmatic dimensions is both possible and beneficial (Eslami & Eslami-Rasekh, 2008; Bagherkazemi & Arefkal, 2021; Vásquez & Fioramonte,

2011; Povolná, 2012; Ngai & Janusch, 2018). Teachers improve their knowledge and awareness of pragmatics through instruction and find it valuable (Chavez de Castro, 2005; Cohen et al., 2023; Martínez-Flor, 2023), though integrating research-based pragmatic insights into their teaching practice can be challenging (Ishihara, 2011). One challenge is that non-native teachers may lack confidence in pragmatic aspects compared to linguistic components such as grammar and vocabulary (Hsie & Chuang, 2021; Cohen, 2016, 2018; Karatepe & Civelek, 2021), often relying on their first language (L1) pragmatics to teach the L2 (Cohen, 2016, 2018). Another challenge is related to limited availability of suitable classroom resources for teaching pragmatics. Thus, teachers' workload, curricular constraints and restricted time for materials development prevent inclusion of pragmatics in the classroom (Glaser, 2023; Hsie & Chuang, 2021; Karatepe & Civelek, 2021).

The research above refers to teachers' knowledge, attitudes and beliefs about how they approach general pragmatic aspects in their teaching. However, effective communication in the classroom is essential for target language development, requiring alignment with pragmatic conventions in natural classroom discourse, but primary English language teacher training often neglects pragmatic abilities (Glaser, 2018).

To develop a pedagogical approach, some scholars have proposed guidelines for enhancing teachers' pragmatic competence. Myrset and McConachy (2024) advocate for raising awareness across three dimensions: pragmatics, flexible language use to facilitate pragmatic learning, and multilingual and intercultural awareness. They suggest using teachers' narratives of communicative experiences as a pedagogical tool to scaffold pragmatic awareness and reflect on appropriate language use. Additionally, they recommend using teachers' L1 strategically to deepen discussions on contextually appropriate language use and social relationships. A flexible use of available languages is seen as an opportunity to scaffold pragmatic knowledge and to enhance multilingual and intercultural awareness. Another critical aspect is encouraging pre-service teachers to creatively express pragmatic functions, a skill that does not come out naturally and requires training through critical reflection (Myrset & McConachy, 2024). Additionally, Lacorte (2021) emphasises integrating the following dimensions in a pragmatics-focused teacher education programme: (i) raising awareness through pragmatic input, (ii) analysing and reflecting on pragmatic input, and (iii) applying analysis and reflection to pedagogical activities.

L2 pragmatics has recently turned its attention to task-based approaches (see Taguchi & Kim, 2018). Although generally included within Task-Based Language Teaching (TBLT), two main task-based perspectives have been distinguished: a strong form known as TBLT and a weaker form known as Task-Supported Language Teaching (TSLT) (Ellis, 2017). Both approaches share the concept of tasks as everyday activities that offer real-life contexts for communication (Barón et al., 2020a). Criteria for defining tasks include (i) a primary focus on meaning, (ii) a gap to be filled, (iii) learners' reliance on their own linguistic and non-linguistic resources, and (iv) a clearly defined communicative outcome (Ellis & Shintani, 2013). The main difference lies in how TBLT and TSLT manage attention to form (Ellis, 2017). In TBLT, the primary focus is communication to achieve the task outcome, and attention to form is secondary. TSLT directs attention to the specific target form providing explicit instruction before task performance, and uses tasks to practice language elements taught through a traditional syllabus structure. As Ellis (2017) puts it, TBLT is experiential (i.e. learning-by-doing), while TSLT concerns transmission (i.e. learning-to-do). In some task-based approaches, pedagogical tasks are used to prepare learners for real-life communication. These tasks maintain "authenticity, a focus on meaning, contextualised language use, and real-life outcomes" (Kim et al., 2023: 6), although they may not always replicate real-life contexts. Tasks are therefore suitable for teaching pragmatics as they facilitate language use for achieving social-interpersonal functions.

Research on the intersection between pragmatics and tasks is still emerging (Taguchi & Kim, 2018). Studies comparing different approaches to teaching pragmatics have found task-based approaches to be more effective in enhancing learners' interactional skills (Kim et al., 2023; Barón et al., 2020a). Additionally, research has explored how learner interaction during collaborative tasks contributes to pragmatic learning (e.g., Alcón-Soler, 2018; Martín-Laguna & Alcón-Soler, 2013; Martín-Laguna, 2014). This research emphasises the role of teachers' pragmatic awareness in supporting learner development to foster pragmatic learning. For example, Alcón-Soler (2018) examined interactions between learners and teachers during tasks, highlighting the need for teachers' pragmatic awareness to support learners' development. However, existing research has predominantly paid attention to learners' performance, and the teachers' perspective has remained mostly unnoticed.

Pragmatics in YLs' EFL Classrooms: The Teachers' Perspective

Over the past two decades, early FL teaching has become widespread, with most curricula making FL instruction compulsory in schools globally (Edelenbos et al., 2006). English is typically chosen for YLs due to its role as a lingua franca, given that most European countries are non-English speaking (Glaser, 2018). This shift has created a demand for well-trained teachers capable of teaching EFL to YLs. These teachers, often non-native English speakers, face unique challenges as they instruct children and beginners simultaneously (Glaser, 2018). Despite variability in learners, contexts, and resources (Enever, 2016), teachers must recognise the importance of interaction, peer work, and physical movement in L2 pragmatics development (Myrset & McConachy, 2024). Since teachers are the primary input source for YLs (Cenoz & Lindsay, 1996), their pragmatic choices significantly impact these learners. Insufficient pragmatics training may result in inadequate input, affecting the pragmatic awareness and proficiency of future language learners and teachers (Glaser, 2018).

Pragmatic aspects are crucial in the YL classroom from early stages (Glaser, 2018). Despite increased exposure to English through digital media, EFL input opportunities remain limited, relying mainly on teaching materials and teacher talk. Textbooks and materials often lack varied speech act content and do not always reflect real interactions (see Schauer, 2022a for a review of L2 teaching materials for YLs' pragmatics instruction; Glaser, 2020). Teacher talk usually provides a limited range of communicative situations and registers (Nikula, 2002). Therefore, teachers are vital in YLs' L2 pragmatic development, both in selecting materials and modelling FL use in the classroom.

Teachers often lack pragmatic awareness, which can impact their students' learning. Glaser (2018) illustrates this with examples from teacher education, such as teachers' misuse of forms of address, indicating that insufficient pragmatic knowledge may be passed on to learners. She identifies three main reasons for the omission of pragmatics in YLs' English language teaching contexts: (i) pragmatics is seen as less essential compared to vocabulary, pronunciation, or grammar; (ii) teachers' lack of pragmatic awareness and skills due to their own EFL education not covering pragmatics; and (iii) inadequate teaching materials (Glaser, 2014). Through communicative functions such as giving instructions and explanations, allocating turns, providing feedback, and dealing with discipline, the teacher manages the classroom, facilitates learning opportunities, and transforms the lesson into a social and cognitive event (Glaser, 2018). It is crucial to help pre-service teachers in YLs' EFL classrooms develop their pragmatic competence as a source of input for learners, particularly in classroom discourse.

Pragmatics in Classroom Discourse: A Focus on Pragmatic Expressions

Classroom discourse can be defined as any kind of discourse that takes place in the classroom[2]. It is characterised by (i) being a transactional event, (ii) following a predictable pattern, (iii) being monologic, and (iv) including pragmatic expressions associated with it.

First, discourse in instructional settings entails structured interactions that serve both cognitive (information exchange) and social (social cohesion) purposes (Hall, 1993). This can be seen in the distinction between transactional and interactional talk (Brown & Yule, 1983), which often overlap during communication. Dalton-Puffer (2007) illustrates these concepts with real-world examples: a telephone enquiry typically follows a transactional script, while casual conversation at a dinner party tends to be interactional, focusing on social bonding rather than a specific agenda. Classroom discourse is predominantly transactional (Dalton-Puffer, 2007), driven by educational objectives while incorporating interactional elements such as side talk and personal exchanges during breaks.

Second, classroom discourse follows a predictable pattern. It has prestructured, conventional, and routinised elements that make evident the extent to which lessons are similar or different from other speech events

2 Due to limitations of space, this chapter focuses on L2 and FL classrooms. L1 classroom discourse is addressed only when compared to the former contexts.

(Dalton-Puffer, 2007: 25). These structured elements, categorised as *scripts* and *roles*, outline expected behaviours and interaction sequences within classroom settings. According to Dalton-Puffer (2007), *scripts* are recurring action sequences in everyday experiences, such as "shopping groceries" or "ordering at restaurant", that set expectations for the sequential flow of interactions; *roles* define the patterns of participation in everyday experiences, outlining the expected and acceptable behaviors for individuals in specific positions or performing certain activities. For example, a typical lesson can be divided into phases such as an opening phase, an instructional phase and a closing phase (Mehan, 1979). Lemke (1989: 50–51) elaborated this sequence suggesting the following basic lesson script: (i) pre-lesson activities (e.g., setting up desks, wiping board), (ii) getting started (bids come from the teacher), (iii) preliminary activities (e.g., taking attendance, announcements, business, collect homework, review), (iv) main lesson (new thematic content that usually begins with triadic dialogue), (v) dissolution (bids come from the students, e.g., packing their things), and (vi) post-lesson activities (e.g., chatting with the students, tidying up). These are examples of recurring situations that form patterns, which build the expectation of the discourse community of teachers and learners. Thus, classroom discourse has characteristics to be considered a genre following Swales' (1990: 58) definition:

> A genre comprises a class of communicative events, the members of which share some set of communicative purposes. These purposes are recognized by the expert members of the parent discourse community (. . .). In addition to purpose, exemplars of a genre exhibit various patterns of similarity in terms of structure, style, content and intended audience.

Genre analysis uses rhetorical *moves* to describe organizational patterns. A *move* is a part of discourse "that performs a specific communicative function [. . .] but also contributes to the overall communicative purposes of the genre" (Connor et al., 2007: 23). Moves are semantic and functional units that have distinct linguistic boundaries that can be objectively identified. Those that occur frequently in a genre are conventional, but if they are not so frequent, they are considered optional. They may contain elements that, put together, realise the move, which are called *steps* (Swales, 1990). Swales (1981) initially used genre analysis to describe rhetorical moves in research articles, but this perspective can be applied to the understanding of classroom discourse. In this regard, Dalton-Puffer (2007: 41–42) notes that classroom discourse is "far too complex and multi-facetted to seriously count as *one genre* of any kind (. . .) [but as] a 'genre colony' (maybe called 'instructional genres') held together by a common but very general communicative purpose". For example, classroom assemblies are characteristic of pre-school lessons, but are not present in university seminars. However, both instructional genres may share some common steps in the move beginning the lesson (e.g. greetings or getting down to work). It must be noted that, while classroom interactions often follow structured scripts or moves, there is also room for negotiated interaction (Griffin & Mehan, 1981), where participants deviate from the expected pattern. Classrooms are dynamic environments where multiple actions occur simultaneously (Dalton-Puffer, 2007). The sequential stages outlined above may oversimplify this complexity. Ehlich and Rehbein (1986) propose a structure for classroom discourse distinguishing between main discourse (teacher-controlled) and parallel discourse (student-controlled). Parallel discourse includes discussions among students related to the main topic, such as seeking clarification, as well as unrelated side conversations that contribute to social cohesion, sometimes involving the teacher.

Third, classroom discourse is predominantly monologic. It can be categorised into instructional discourse, and discourse organising instruction and learning (Dalton-Puffer, 2007). Christie (2000) refers to these two dimensions as "instructional register" and "regulative register". Instructional discourse deals with content, while regulative register includes (i) instructions related to pedagogical activity and the lesson topic, and (ii) broader organisational aspects, such as managing physical conditions and addressing personal needs within the learning environment (Dalton-Puffer, 2007). Other scholars, such as Ellis (1992) and Ernst (1994), add a social dimension to classroom discourse, highlighting goals related to content delivery, management, and social cohesion.

Fourth, while moves refer to discourse organization, communicative functions in moves are linguistically performed by pragmatic expressions. In oral discourse, each move may involve several speech act categories. The general term pragmatic expressions has been previously used in research to include several speech act realizations in conversation (Barón, 2023). Thus, classroom pragmatic expressions are defined here as the pragmalinguistic elements that realize moves in classroom discourse which may involve different speech acts, and are mediated by sociopragmatic variables.

Finally, research on pragmatic dimensions of classroom discourse highlights various challenges. Many teacher candidates feel uncertain and tend to use direct and abrupt language. For instance, Glaser (2018) identified inappropriate expressions such as *No, that's wrong* in response to student errors. She noted German trainee teachers' overuse of the modal verb *should*, influenced by their native language. In a Spanish context, Barón et al. (2020b) found that teachers predominantly used imperatives in both L1 and EFL pre-primary lessons, possibly due to perceptions of YLs' limited L2 proficiency and L1 transfer.

Following Schauer's (2022a) suggestion to integrate pragmatic content into teacher training programs, this chapter emphasises the importance of teacher talk as a primary input source in EFL contexts. Research reviewed above shows the need to train teachers specifically in the use of classroom pragmatic expressions for effective classroom management. Classroom pragmatic expressions are the ultimate means through which teachers *do* things with the language in classroom discourse, which is the essence of task-based pragmatic instruction (Youn, 2018). In the next section, a task-based proposal for training teachers of YLs is presented.

Teaching Proposal

Prior to explaining the proposal for teaching classroom pragmatic expressions, some terms must be clarified. The main task consists in pre-service teachers teaching an art lesson, first as a pedagogical task in their university class, and then in the real world, i.e. a school, to actual pupils. The content of the lesson is an art workshop (Tullet, 2019), where the script is adapted for the use of the corresponding classroom pragmatic expressions in a school context. In this teaching proposal, the task-based approach adopted is TSLT, because the task is central to the proposal but learners are pre-taught the target pragmatic expressions they need in order to perform the task.

Pre-service teachers are the author's university students and are considered the learners in this teaching proposal. The teacher is the university lecturer teaching this proposal, while school teachers are in-service teachers in the school where the task is performed. The pupils are YLs, pre-school children to whom the final task is aimed.

Target Learners and Context

This teaching proposal is primarily aimed at pre-service teachers in YLs' education degrees (i.e. undergraduates in Pre-School and Primary Education degrees) enrolled in an English course for teachers in an EFL university context. Their L1s are Spanish, Catalan, or both. They are expected to have at least an A2 or B1 English proficiency level according to the Common European Framework of Reference for Languages. However, those with higher proficiency levels can also benefit across various dimensions, as the complexity of pragmatic expressions can be tailored to different learner levels.

Needs Analysis

Task-based approaches, either TBLT or TSLT, begin with a needs analysis to identify relevant communicative tasks (Gilabert & Malicka, 2021; Youn, 2018). The starting point of this needs analysis was to identify the real needs of in-service teachers who were already working in order to prepare pre-service teachers for their future jobs. The needs analysis aimed to: (i) identify moves that in-service teachers perform in English, (ii) determine language needs for these moves for in-service teachers, (iii) assess pre-service teachers' familiarity with classroom pragmatic expressions, (iv) analyse how classroom language was presented in the coursebook (Hughes & Moate, 2008), and (v) propose a real-world task for this teaching proposal. Additionally, the proposal was motivated by the increasing demand for pre-service teachers to potentially teach content subjects in English, such as Arts and Crafts in many schools, due to programmes such as Content and Language Integrated Learning (CLIL), English-Medium Instruction, and Erasmus +.

Data were triangulated from three different sources: (i) in-service teachers, (ii) pre-service teachers, and (iii) the coursebook. First, classroom observations of 4 English teachers in Spanish primary and pre-school education informed the analysis of in-service teachers' language needs, revealing challenges in using English for classroom management (regulative register) despite their advanced overall proficiency. Interviews with these teachers indicated they often lacked context-specific expressions and relied on expressions translated from Spanish or Catalan, or they just used those languages. Teachers brainstormed situations and expressions that they would say in the L1 in which they did not feel confident in English. In the interview, teachers were also asked to suggest a practical task similar to teaching a lesson that pre-service teachers could perform with real pupils. One teacher mentioned that her school had an art project, titled 'Women Artists', for 4-year-olds. She suggested that pre-service teachers could go to her school and teach an art lesson by adapting a workshop from Hervé Tullet's (2019) book, *Art Workshops for Children*, for a classroom context with these young EFL learners.

Second, a questionnaire was used to assess pre-service teachers' (N=14) awareness of classroom pragmatic expressions. The questionnaire was a modified version of the multilevel Vocabulary Knowledge Scale (VKS) (Wesche & Paribakht, 1996) by Alcón-Soler and Sánchez-Hernández (2017). The author adapted it to include classroom pragmatic expressions. It presented 10 expressions (*Are you ready?, Can I talk to you in the hallway?, Please raise your hand!, Thumbs up!, Move places!, Be careful!, Stop bothering your classmate!, Put away that toy!, Let's check attendance!, Good job!*), and elicited responses ranging from recognition to understanding and contextual use. Responses highlighted pre-service teachers' familiarity with direct translations from Spanish or Catalan but also revealed uncertainties, as illustrated in Example 1 below (translated from Spanish):

(1) (Student 13)
Pragmatic expression: Let's check attendance!
– Familiarity with the expression:
Answer: (c) I have seen or heard this expression before but I don't know what it means.
– The expression *Let's check attendance* means...
Answer: *Let's check*: I know that means that we are going to correct [exercises]. I do not know about *attendance*.
– The expression *Let's check attendance* is used when...
Answer: -

Third, the coursebook *Practical Classroom English* (Hughes & Moate, 2008) is, to our knowledge, the only one available in the market dealing specifically with classroom pragmatic expressions. It evolved from an original handout on classroom pragmatic expressions in 1975 and has been further elaborated in several republications. It is based on observation reports and lesson recordings from different countries. It has been devised as a coursebook but also as a work for reference. The analysis of the coursebook focused on two aspects: (i) how pragmatic expressions were presented and (ii) how they were taught. The analysis revealed that the coursebook (i) included comprehensive lists of classroom pragmatic expressions but lacked metapragmatic explanations, and (ii) provided situations to practise the expressions, although most of them were exercises.

Although the results from the needs analysis outlined above cannot be generalised, they provided the author with insights into aspects to consider in the proposal based on real needs. The needs analysis revealed an authentic task for the teaching proposal, i.e. teaching an art lesson. The content of the lesson was given by Tullet's (2019) book, but the script had to be adapted to be taught in a YLs' classroom context with 4-year-olds, considering the necessary moves and classroom pragmatic expressions. The target pragmatic expressions are explained in the next section.

Target Pragmatic Expressions

The proposal focuses on three conventional moves in instructional genres from the coursebook (Hughes & Moate, 2008), i.e. beginning, running, and ending the lesson, associated with optional steps as shown in Table 2.1. Table 2.1 also provides examples of classroom pragmatic expressions taught in the teaching proposal to realise those moves, but a closed list is not included here because communicative functions in moves and steps can be conveyed by a variety of classroom pragmatic expressions and there is variability across learning contexts (e.g. American vs. British English). Learners were provided with a more exhaustive list of examples for reference in the coursebook (Hughes & Moate, 2008).

Table 2.1. Moves, steps and examples of classroom pragmatic expressions (adapted from Hughes & Moate, 2008).

Conventional moves	**Optional steps**	**Examples of pragmatic expressions**
Beginning the lesson	Entering the classroom	*Let's go in!*
	Everyday greetings	*Good afternoon, everyone.*
	Meeting a new class	*Perhaps you are wondering who I am.*
	Taking the register	*Let's see if everyone is here.*
	Dealing with lateness	*You are late. We started ten minutes ago.*
	Getting down to work	*All right. It's time to start our English lesson.*
Running the lesson	Starting something new	*Let's move on./Let's do another exercise.*
	Making things clear	*Is everything clear?*
	Sequencing activities	*Firstly, let's run through your homework. To continue, could you take out your workbooks? To finish with, you can do some reading.*
	Checking progress	*Any problems?*
	Stopping	*Ok, everybody. Two more minutes./Have you finished?*
Ending the lesson	Checking the time	*What's the time? We have five more minutes.*
	Setting homework	*For your homework, please do exercise 24.*
	Stopping work	*We'll have to finish now. Today we've practised asking the time.*
	Making announcements	*Just a minute, please. I have something to tell you.*
	Saying goodbye	*Bye, everyone! See you next class!*
	Clearing the class	*Go out quietly, please! Take all your things with you.*

The TSLT Proposal

The main task in the TSLT proposal was teaching an art lesson. The teaching proposal has three phases: Pre-task, Task, and Post-task. The Pre-task phase explores elements needed for the main task. The Task phase implies preparing the task in the classroom to train learners for real-life communication by writing the art lesson script and rehearsing it with classmates. It involves a pedagogical task. The Post-task phase consists in performing the task. In other words, it transforms the pedagogical task into a real-world task, i.e. teaching the art lesson to real pupils in a school setting. This TSLT proposal is to be done in eight 2-hour sessions: Pre-task (2 sessions), Task (3 sessions), and Post-task (3 sessions) (see Table 2.2).

Table 2.2. Phases of the TSLT proposal.

Phase	**Step**	**Task objective**
Pre-task phase		**Exploring task elements**
	Step 1	Raising sociopragmatic awareness of instructional genres
	Step 2	Raising pragmalinguistic awareness of moves in instructional genres
	Step 3	Scaffolding multilingual and intercultural awareness
	Step 4	Exploring input
	Step 5	Guiding output
Task phase		**Preparing the task**
	Step 6	Setting the context
	Step 7	Setting the task
	Step 8	Planning the task (art lesson script)
	Step 9	Rehearsing the task (art lesson)
	Step 10	Reporting the task
Post-task phase		**Performing the task**
	Step 11	Addressing weaknesses
	Step 12	Performing the task in the real world
	Step 13	Reflecting on self-performance

Pre-task Phase

Pre-task activities aim to engage pre-service teachers in instructional genres and prepare them to understand pragmalinguistic and sociopragmatic dimensions in classroom discourse.

Step 1. Raising Sociopragmatic Awareness of Instructional Genres

In Step 1, pre-service teachers watch videos from two TV series depicting two instructional genres (e.g. a university lecture vs. a school lesson for YLs) (for examples of the use of audiovisual materials to teach metapragmatic awareness, see Usó-Juan & Martínez-Flor, 2021). This is followed by a whole-class discussion to raise sociopragmatic awareness of instructional genres with YLs compared to other instructional genres. The discussion is guided by awareness-raising questions that focus on sociopragmatic issues. Sociopragmatics, which involves language use in context and society, aligns with the concept of genre. The questions, based on the SPEAKING framework (Hymes, 1974), have been adopted by Usó-Juan and Martínez-Flor (2021) and reflect Swales' (1990) genre definition elements such as communicative purpose, audience, and patterns of similarity (see Table 2.3). These dimensions range in a continuum from genre-related to purely sociopragmatic aspects.

Table 2.3. Questions for raising sociopragmatic awareness of instructional genres.

Focus	**Term in definition of genre**	**Awareness-raising questions**	**Emphasis in the continuum**
Genre	Communicative event	What type of communicative situations have you seen in the videos? How do you know?	+genre –socio-pragmatics
Setting	Communicative event	Where are the interactants having this conversation?	
Participants	Intended audience	Who are the interactants? What is the social relationship between them?	

Table 2.3. *Continued*

Focus	**Term in definition of genre**	**Awareness-raising questions**	**Emphasis in the continuum**
End	Communicative purpose	What is the communicative purpose of this conversation?	
Act sequence	Structures, patterns of similarity	What kind of conventions or rituals can you identify in the video that are specific to this communicative situation?	
Key (style)		What clues let us know the tone of communication or feelings of the speakers?	
Norm		Can interactional norms for politeness be observed in the conversation?	
Instrumentalities		Is the language used in this conversation polite, casual, or in-between?	– genre + socio-pragmatics

Step 2. Raising Pragmalinguistic Awareness of Moves in Instructional Genres

In Step 2, pre-service teachers first raise awareness of classroom moves and steps and then learn the corresponding pragmalinguistic strategies. The teacher leads a whole-class discussion to identify typical lesson moves or steps in instructional genres (see Table 2.4) and provides metapragmatic information about moves and steps (see Dalton-Puffer, 2007). Together, they brainstorm moves and steps within moves and compare differences across contexts (e.g. university vs. primary education). After identifying moves, they discuss pragmalinguistic elements for each step, and in small groups, pre-service teachers brainstorm associated classroom pragmatic expressions. This may not be an exhaustive list.

Table 2.4. Sample questions for raising pragmalinguistic awareness of moves in instructional genres.

Focus	**Awareness-raising questions**
Moves and steps	What lesson routines can you identify? General ones are called moves, and specific routines within moves are called steps.
Moves and steps	Think about the learning contexts in both videos. To what extent are moves and steps expected to be the same across contexts? Which ones would be different or new in a school context?
Moves and steps	Think about a school context. Which moves and steps are obligatory and which ones are optional?
Pragmalinguistic elements	Can you think of classroom pragmatic expressions associated to each step?

Step 3. Scaffolding Multilingual and Intercultural Awareness

In Step 3, we must consider the linguistic and pragmatic backgrounds that pre-service teachers bring to the classroom. Teachers' experiences influence them (Glaser, 2018) and using these as pedagogical tools can enhance multilingual and multicultural awareness (Myrset & McConachy, 2024). Table 2.5 presents sample questions for whole-class discussions to scaffold multilingual and intercultural awareness of pragmatic expressions in instructional genres.

Table 2.5. Sample questions for scaffolding multilingual and intercultural awareness.

Would you use the equivalent expressions in your L1/L2 in the same situation?
Which pragmatic expressions did your English language teachers use to perform these moves?
What was your reaction?
What changes would you make?

Step 4. Exploring Input

In Step 4, input-based tasks are used to provide a more comprehensive list of classroom pragmatic expressions in context for each step within a move, while Step 2 consisted in brainstorming moves, steps and pragmatic expressions. Pre-service teachers watch a video about a lesson for YLs and identify the steps in the video and pragmatic expressions associated with the steps. They also discuss which pragmatic expressions clearly mark transitions between moves (see Table 2.6).

Table 2.6. Sample questions for input-based tasks.

Pragmalinguistic elements	Which pragmatic expressions can be used in each step?
Pragmalinguistic elements	How does each move sequence start and end?

Step 5. Guiding Output

In Step 5, output-based tasks involve guided practice using written discourse-completion tasks (DCTs) with different sociopragmatic factors. The number of DCTs depends on the time available and on the learners' needs, but the situations must cover the three conventional moves, i.e. beginning, running and ending the lesson.

In the DCTs, pre-service teachers are given classroom scenarios considering Brown and Levinson's (1987) sociopragmatic variables (+ /– power, social distance and degree of imposition). Since all scenarios involve teacher-student interactions, it was considered that some sociopragmatic variables remain constant (+ teacher power, medium social distance), while context changes affect the degree of imposition and the appropriate pragmalinguistic strategies. Example 2 illustrates two situations at the beginning of the lesson with different degrees of imposition: Situation 1 involves a high degree of imposition due to repetitive misbehaviour, while Situation 2 has a lower degree. Each DCT corresponds to one of three lesson sequence parts: beginning, running, or ending the lesson.

(2) Situation 1 (+ degree of imposition)
You go into the classroom. The class is very noisy today. It takes you 10 minutes to calm it down. Once you do it, there is a knock at the door and Will appears. It is the third time he is late this week. He leaves the door open. What would you say?

Situation 2 (– degree of imposition)
You go into the classroom. A moment later there is a knock at the door and Will appears. It is the first time he is late. You invite him in. What would you say?

Task Phase

Task phase activities aim to prepare and rehearse the art lesson task as a pedagogical task in pre-service teachers' university classroom as if teaching YLs.

Steps 6 and 7. Setting the Context and the Task

Context is crucial in both TSLT and pragmatics. In Steps 6 and 7, the teacher explains the context, which is inseparable from the corresponding task. Figure 2.1 provides a sample context and task based on the invitation from a school teacher who participated in the needs analysis to teach an art lesson in her school.

INSTRUCTIONS: AN ART LESSON TASK

A local school is starting a project on 'Women Artists' with 4-year-olds. You have been invited to do the kick-off activity for the project in February. School teachers have suggested that you could teach an art lesson based on the art workshop "A field of flowers" from the book *Art Workshops for Children* by Hervé Tullet. You must adapt the script for 4-year-olds considering the lesson's beginning, running and ending stages and the necessary pragmatic expressions.

Figure 2.1: Sample context and task worksheet.

Additionally, pre-service teachers and their teacher have a meeting with the school teacher(s) where art lesson is going to be given in order to specify the guidelines: the procedure, aspects to consider with pupils and school spaces for the day of the art lesson in the school. Sample guidelines as a result of such a meeting are provided in Figure 2.2.

For the beginning stage, pupils wait in the playground while pre-service teachers arrange tables and supplies. Then, pre-service teachers meet pupils in the playground, and use warm-up activities to introduce themselves, group pupils and proceed to the classroom.

For the running stage, pre-service teachers teach the art lesson to groups of 8 4-year-old pupils.

For the ending stage, pre-service teachers plan for clearing the class and washing pupils' hands.

When working with 4-year-olds, it is important to include phrases to encourage and praise pupils (e.g. Good job!), give clear instructions, mimic actions and exaggerate gestures.

Figure 2.2: Sample guidelines.

Step 8. Planning the Task (Art Lesson Script)

In Step 8, pre-service teachers write the art lesson script in small groups as part of the planning. They can refer to the coursebook (Hughes & Moate, 2008) for support classroom pragmatic expressions.

Step 9. Rehearsing the Task (Art Lesson)

After writing the lesson script, in Step 9, pre-service teachers perform the art lesson task in small groups. This is an authentic pedagogical task that takes place in their university classroom and serves as a rehearsal for teaching the art lesson in a real school. Pre-service teachers take turns acting as school teachers and pupils, swapping roles so that everyone experiences both. Those acting as pupils are given action cards to simulate classroom issues raised in the needs analysis, such as a pupil bothering another classmate, for the teachers to manage. The teacher and classmates can take notes on the pre-service teachers' performance as teachers. Interaction can be recorded for further analysis in Step 10.

Step 10. Reporting the Task

In Step 10, pre-service teachers evaluate their own performance as teachers (self-assessment) through written reports. They are asked to reflect on task performance and achievement. Questions on task performance address a set of factors adapted from Cohen (2012: 256) (see Table 2.7). There is also peer and teacher assessment in written reports, adapting the questions with an asterisk (*) in Table 2.7. For giving more accurate feedback in the reports, audio or video recordings of performance can be used if available. Scaffolded modelling is provided if needed (Usó-Juan & Martínez-Flor, 2022). The phase concludes with a whole-class discussion with the teacher to pinpoint weaknesses that occur repeatedly and need reinforcement.

Table 2.7. Sample questions for self-assessing factors in task performance and task achievement.

Dimensions	**Factors**	**Questions**
Task performance	Negative transfer of pragmatic behaviour in their L1	To what extent has your L1 influenced your performance?
	Limited FL grammatical ability, fluency, pronunciation	* What aspects related to grammar, fluency and pronunciation need to be improved or reinforced?
	The effect of instruction or instructional materials	To what extent have the preparatory sessions contributed to your performance?
	Resistance to target language norms for pragmatic behaviour	Are there pragmatic expressions in English that you do not use because you do not feel comfortable with them?
	Pragmatic expressions and moves to be revised and reinforced	* Which stages and expressions in the lesson need to be revised and reinforced?
Task achievement		* Generally speaking, do you consider that you have been able to perform the task, i.e. teaching a lesson?

Post-task Phase

Post-task activities aim to address weaknesses, perform the task in a real-world setting, and self-reflect on performance.

Step 11. Addressing Weaknesses

In Step 11, weak points from Step 10 are addressed through rephrasing or reformulation exercises, rehearsing difficult moves, or pronunciation drills based on previous performance.

Step 12. Performing the Task in the Real World

In Step 12, pre-service teachers visit a real school to conduct the art lesson task with actual pupils (4-year-olds). This is the same school where the in-service teacher, who recommended the art lesson task during the needs analysis, works.

Step 13. Self-reflecting on Performance

In Step 13, pre-service teachers reflect on their own task experience. They examine issues from pedagogical, motivational, language learning, pragmatic learning perspectives, as well as overall task achievement (see Appendix 1).

Concluding Remarks

Classroom discourse is a complex phenomenon (Dalton-Puffer, 2007), with specific conventions and variations linked to each distinct oral genre within instructional genres, influenced by language contexts and cultures. Mastering pragmatic expressions for classroom management is challenging for many pre-service teachers due to limited knowledge of pragmatics and of the target language culture. Training pre-service teachers on pragmatic aspects related to their future professional context is crucial, as teachers serve as input sources and decision-makers of classroom materials. In so doing, it is paramount to incorporate authentic language use, central to TSLT and for L2 pragmatics.

On that account, this chapter presents a TSLT proposal for teaching pragmatic expressions in classroom discourse to pre-service teachers. It integrates pre-task, task and post-task activities aimed at (i) raising pre-service teachers' awareness of pragmalinguistics, sociopragmatics and genre, (ii) providing input opportunities, (iii) offering output opportunities from pedagogical to authentic tasks, and (iv) enhancing others and self-reflection and assessment on task performance. The proposal is a valuable example of how to apply TSLT in an EFL context where

English is not the societal language. Considering the learners' needs as pre-service teachers, it suggests an authentic task that they will have to perform in their future careers, which is carried out as a pedagogical task in their university classroom and as a real-world task in a school. The proposal is also relevant for in-service EFL and CLIL teachers across education levels, since moves and classroom pragmatic expressions can be adapted to these contexts.

Despite the pedagogical benefits of the proposed task-based approach, there are some limitations worth considering. One limitation is that the proposal addresses main discourse (teacher-controlled). However, classroom discourse is complex and cannot be captured linearly through stages, as multiple discourses occur simultaneously (Ehlich & Rehbein, 1986). Thus, classroom discourse also involves parallel discourse (student-controlled), for example, in learners' discussions and aside conversations (Ehlich & Rehbein, 1986). In line with Dalton-Puffer (2007), main classroom discourse has been chosen for practicality reasons, since the difficulty to capture parallel discourse for research purposes makes it an under researched area, and because the target learners for this proposal were pre-service teachers. Another limitation is that the proposal takes a monolingual perspective focusing only on FL classroom discourse, leaving aside the fact that real-world EFL classrooms are multilingual environments where teachers often use learners' L1(s) and translanguaging strategies (Martí-Arnándiz & Portolés, 2019; Portolés & Martín-Laguna, 2012). While the use of additional languages in classroom discourse is not questioned, this proposal has built on previous research (Barón et al., 2020b; Hsie & Chuang, 2021; Cohen, 2016, 2018; Karatepe & Civelek, 2021) and on a needs analysis to taylor the FL practical needs of pre-service teachers.

Acknowledgements

As a member of the LAELA (Lingüística Aplicada a l'Ensenyament de la Llengua Anglesa) research group at Universitat Jaume I (Castellón, Spain), I would like to acknowledge that this study is part of the research project PID2020-117959GB-I00 funded by MCIN/AEI/10.13039/501100011033. Additional funding has been granted by Projectes d'Innovació Educativa de la Unitat de Formació i Innovació Educativa 51020/24. My gratitude goes to two anonymous reviewers for helping me improve this chapter. Any errors remain my own.

Appendix 1. Post-task. Step 13. Questions for Self-reflection on Task Performance

Perspective		
Pedagogical		1. What have you experienced with this methodology based on performing authentic tasks compared to what you are used to doing in class to learn English?
		2. Do you think this methodology helps the teacher connect with learners and interact? Why? Can you provide examples from your experience?
Motivational	Intrinsic motivation	3. Did you enjoy the art lesson in the school? Describe how you felt.
		4. How did you feel about English and learning English before the art lesson in the school? Do you think the art lesson in the school changed your attitude towards English and learning this language? In what way?
	Extrinsic motivation	5. Do you think the art lesson in the school was useful for you as a future teacher? Could you mention specific aspects (linguistic or not) for which you think it was useful?
Language learning		6. Do you think this methodology has helped you become more confident in speaking, and more spontaneous when speaking English?
		7. Do you think this methodology has helped you feel more confident about teaching English to children in the future?

Pragmatics learning	Pragmalinguistics	In the art lesson in the school, you used classroom management expressions such as the following: – Are you ready? – Let's go! – Stop! – Hands up! – Move places! – Be careful! – Well done! – You are doing it very well! 8. Do you think the art lesson in the school and preparation have helped you incorporate these expressions into your oral discourse more spontaneously?
	Sociopragmatics	9. Do you think these expressions associated with the classroom context would be appropriate in another context outside the classroom? 10. In what communicative situation or context would you change any of them to express the same meaning and why? Choose some examples and explain.
	General questions	11. What did you like most about the whole process (preparation sessions and art lesson in a school)? 12. What did you like least about the whole process (preparation sessions and art lesson in a school)? 13. What would you have liked to do that we did not do? 14. Rate from 0 to 5 your performance in the art lesson. Explain why.

References

Ahmadian, Mohammad J. & Long, Michael H. (eds). 2022. *The Cambridge handbook of task-based language teaching.* Cambridge: Cambridge University Press.

Alcón-Soler, Eva. 2018. Effects of task-supported language teaching on learners' use and knowledge of email request mitigators. In Naoko Taguchi & Youjin Kim (eds) *Task-based approaches to teaching and assessing pragmatics.* Amsterdam: John Benjamins, 55–81.

Alcón-Soler, Eva & Guzmán, Josep. 2010. The effect of instruction on learners' pragmatic awareness: A focus on refusals. *International Journal of English Studies,* 10/1, 65–80.

Alcón-Soler, Eva & Sánchez-Hernández, Ariadna. 2017. Learning pragmatic routines during study abroad: A focus on proficiency and type of routine. *Atlantis,* 39/2, 191–210.

Bagherkazemi, Marzieh & Arefkal, Maryam. 2021. Impact of an awareness-raising workshop on the pragmatic awareness and attitudes of high school English language teachers in Iran. *English Teaching & Learning*, 46, 1–18.

Barón, Júlia. 2023. A task-supported language approach to teaching L2 pragmatics. In Alicia Martínez-Flor, Ariadna Sánchez-Hernández & Júlia Barón (eds) *L2 Pragmatics in action. Teachers, learners and the teaching-learning interaction process.* Amsterdam: John Benjamins, 319–339.

Barón, Júlia, Celaya, M. Luz & Levkina, Mayya. 2020a. Learning pragmatics through tasks. When interaction plays a role. *Applied Pragmatics*, 2/1, 1–25.

Barón, Júlia, Roquet, Helena, Evnitskaya, Natalia & Navarro, Noelia. 2020b. Pragmatics in teacher talk: The case of pre-primary education. *English Language Teaching*, 13/8, 168–177.

Brown, Penelope & Levinson, Stephen C. 1987. *Politeness. Some universals in language usage.* Cambridge: Cambridge University Press.

Brown, Gillian & Yule, George. 1983. *Discourse analysis.* Cambridge: Cambridge University Press.

Cenoz, Jasone & Lindsay, Diana. 1996. English in primary school: Teaching a third language to eight years olds in the Basque country. *Cuadernos de Filología Inglesa,* 5/1, 81–102.

Chavez de Castro, Maria Cristina Lana. 2005. Why Teachers Don't Use Their Pragmatic Awareness. In Nat Bartels (ed.) *Applied linguistics and language teacher education. educational linguistics.* Boston: Springer, 281–293.

Christie, Frances. 2000. The language of classroom interaction and learning. In Len Unsworth (ed.) *Researching language in schools and communities: Functional linguistic perspectives*. London: Cassell, 184–203.

Codina-Espurz, Victòria & Salazar-Campillo, Patricia. 2019. Openings and closing in emails by CLIL students: A pedagogical proposal. *English Language Teaching*, 12/2, 57–67.

Cohen, Andrew D. 2012. Comprehensible pragmatics: Where input and output come together. In Mirosław Pawlak (ed.) *New perspectives on individual differences in language learning and teaching.* Berlin: Springer, 249–261.

Cohen, Andrew D. 2016. The teaching of pragmatics by native and non-native language teachers: What they know and what they report doing. *Studies in Second Language Learning and Teaching,* 6/4, 561–585.

Cohen, Andrew D. 2018. *Learning pragmatics from native and nonnative language teachers.* Bristol: Multilingual Matters.

Cohen, Andrew D., Knight, Stephanie W. P. & Sykes, Julie M. 2023. Teachers gaining awareness of L2 pragmatics by means of an asynchronous professional development module. In Alicia Martínez-Flor, Ariadna Sánchez-Hernández & Júlia Barón (eds) *L2 pragmatics in action. Teachers, learners and the teaching-learning interaction process.* Amsterdam: John Benjamins, 31–61.

Connor, Ulla, Upton, Thomas A. & Kanoksilapatham, Budsaba. 2007. Introduction to move analysis. In Douglas Biber, Ulla Connor & Upton, Thomas (eds) *Discourse on the move. Using corpus analysis to describe discourse structure*. Amsterdam: John Benjamins, 23–41.

Crystal, David. 1997. *English as a global language.* Cambridge: Cambridge University Press.

Dalton-Puffer, Christiane. 2007. *Discourse in Content and Language Integrated Learning (CLIL) classrooms*. Amsterdam: John Benjamins Publishing.

Dausend, Henriette. 2017. Theory and practice in primary English teacher education. In Eva Wilden & Raphaela Porsch (eds) *The professional development of primary EFL teachers. National and international research*. Münster & New York: Waxmann, 109–125.

Edelenbos, Peter, Johnstone, Richard & Kubanek, Angelika. 2006. *The main pedagogical principles underlying the teaching of languages to very young learners. No. EAC 89/04, Lot 1 study*. Brussels: European Commission, Education and Culture, Culture and Communication Multilingualism Policy.

Edmondson, Willis. J., House, Julianne & Kádár, Daniel. Z. 2023. *Expressions, speech acts and discourse. A pedagogic interactional grammar of English*. Cambridge: Cambridge University Press.

Ehlich, Konrad & Rehbein, Jochen. 1986. *Muster und Institution. Untersuchungen zur schulischen Kommunikation*. Tübingen: Narr.

Ellis, Rod. 1992. Learning to communicate in the classroom: A study of two learners' requests. *Studies in Second Language Acquisition*, 14, 1–23.

Ellis, Rod. 2017. Task-based language teaching. In Shawn Loewen & Masatoshi Sato (eds) *The Routledge handbook of instructed second language acquisition*. London/New York: Routledge, 108–125.

Ellis, Rod & Shintani, Natsuko. 2013. *Exploring language pedagogy through second language acquisition research*. New York: Routledge.

Enever, Janet. 2014. Primary English teacher education in Europe. *ELT Journal*, 68/3, 231–242.

Enever, Janet. 2016. Primary ELT: Issues and trends. In Graham Hall (ed.) *Routledge handbook of English language teaching*. London/New York: Routledge, 353–366.

Ernst, Gisela. 1994. Talking circle: Conversation and negotiation in the ESL classroom. *TESOL Quarterly*, 28, 293–322.

Eslami, Zoreh R. & Eslami-Rasekh, A. 2008. Enhancing the pragmatic competence of non-native English-speaking teacher candidates (NNESTCs) in an EFL context. In Eva Alcón-Soler & Alicia Martínez-Flor (eds) *Investigating pragmatics in foreign language learning, teaching and testing*. Clevedon: Mutlilingual Matters, 178–197.

Gass, Susan M. & Selinker, Larry. 2008. *Second language acquisition: An introductory course* (3rd ed.). New York: Routledge.

Gilabert, Roger & Malicka, Aleksandra. 2021. From needs analysis to task-based design: Methodology, assessment and programme evaluation. In N. P. Sudharshana & Lina Mukhopadhyay (eds) *Task-based language teaching and assessment.* Singapore: Springer, 93–118.

Glaser, Karen. 2014. *Inductive or deductive? The impact of method of instruction on the acquisition of pragmatic competence in EFL.* Newcastle: Cambridge Scholars Publishing.

Glaser, Karen. 2018. Enhancing the role of pragmatics in primary English teacher training. *Glottodidactica*, 45/2, 119–131.

Glaser, Karen. 2020. Pragmatikvermittlung im Englischunterricht der Primarstufe: Der Sprechakt' Begrüßen' in Lehrplänen und Lehrwerken. [Teaching pragmatics in Primary EFL: The speech act of greetings in curricula and text books.] In Holger Limberg & Karen Glaser (eds) *Pragmatische Kompetenzen im schulischen Fremdssprachenunterricht.* Bern: Peter Lang, 199–248.

Glaser, Karen. 2023. Teachers' awareness, knowledge and attitudes towards instruction in L2 pragmatics. In Alicia Martínez-Flor, Ariadna Sánchez-Hernández & Júlia Barón (eds) *L2 Pragmatics in Action. Teachers, learners and the teaching-learning interaction process.* Amsterdam: John Benjamins, 63–87.

González-Lloret, Marta. 2019. Task-based language teaching and L2 pragmatics. In Naoko Taguchi (ed.) *The Routledge handbook of SLA and pragmatics*. New York: Routledge, 333–352.

Griffin, Peg & Mehan, Hugh. 1981. Sense and ritual in classroom discourse. In Florian Coulmas (ed.) *Conversational routine.* The Hague: Mouton, 187–213.

Hall, Joan Kelly. 1993. The role of oral practices in the accomplishment of our everyday lives: The sociocultural dimension of interaction with implications for the learning of another language. *Applied Linguistics*, 14/2, 145–166.

Hsie, Ming-Hung & Chuang, Hsueh-Hua. 2021. Investigating pre-service English teachers' beliefs of sociolinguistic instruction in EFL classes in Taiwan. *TESOL and Technology Studies*, 2/2, 16–28.

Hughes, Glyn S. & Moate, Joséphine. 2008. *Practical classroom English*. Oxford: Oxford University Press.

Hymes, Dell. 1974. *Foundations in sociolinguistics: An ethnographic approach*. Philadelphia: University of Pennsylvania Press.

Ishihara, Noriko. 2011. Co-constructing pragmatic awareness: Instructional pragmatics in EFL teacher development in Japan. *TESL-EJ*, 15/2, 1–7.

Karatepe, Çiğdem & Civelek, Mustafa. 2021. A case study of EFL teachers' views on material adaptation for teaching pragmatics. *RumeliDe Journal of Language and Literature Studies*, 23, 894–910.

Kasper, Gabrielle & Rose, Kenneth. R. 2001. *Pragmatics in language teaching*. Cambridge: Cambridge University Press.

Kim, Youjin, Kang, Sanghee, D'Arienzo, Meredith & Taguchi, Naoko. 2023. Comparing traditional and task-based approaches to teaching pragmatics: Task design processes and learning outcomes. *Language Teaching Research*, 2/2, 1–24.

Kubanek, Angelika. 2017. 25 years of 'new' young learner classrooms. Insights and challenges for teacher education. In Eva Wilden & Raphaela Porsch (eds) *The professional development of primary EFL teachers. National and international research*. Münster: Waxmann, 27–44.

Lacorte, Manel. 2021. Pragmatics and teacher education. In Dale A. Koike & César Félix-Brasdefer(eds) *The Routledge handbook of Spanish pragmatics: Foundations and interfaces*. New York: Routledge, 468–484.

Leech, Geoffrey. 1983. *Principles of pragmatics*. London: Longman.

Lemke, Jay L. 1989. *Using language in the classroom*. Oxford: Oxford University Press.

Martí-Arnándiz, Otilia & Portolés, Laura. 2019. Is teacher talk for very young learners pragmatically tuned? Directives in two EAL classrooms. In Patricia Salazar-Campillo & Victòria Codina-Espurz (eds) *Investigating the learning of pragmatics across ages and contexts*. Leiden/Boston: Brill Rodopi, 87–122.

Martín-Laguna, Sofía. 2014. Raising learners' attention to refusals during Focus on Form interaction: Does the interlocutor matter? In Ana Díaz Galán, María del Carmen Fumero Pérez, María del Pilar Lojendio Quintero, Sally Burgess, ulalia Sosa Acevedo & Antonio Cano Ginés (eds) *Comunicación, Cognición, Cibernétic@. Actas del XXXI Congreso Internacional de AESLA*. La Laguna, Spain: Universidad de La Laguna, 368–379.

Martín-Laguna, Sofía & Alcón-Soler, Eva. 2013. The effect of proficiency and interlocutor on learners' performance during refusal focused tasks. In Àngels Llanes Baró, Lirian Astrid Ciro, Lídia Gallego Balsà & Rosa M. Mateu Serra (eds) *Lingüística Aplicada en la era de la globalización = La Lingüística Aplicada en l'era de la globalització = Applied Linguistics in the Age of Globalization.* Lleida: Publicacions de la Universitat de Lleida, 80–87.

Martínez-Flor, Alicia. 2023. Teachers' awareness and beliefs towards corrective feedback in L2 pragmatics. In Alicia Martínez-Flor, Ariadna Sánchez-Hernández & Júlia Barón (eds) *L2 pragmatics in action. Teachers, learners and the teaching-learning interaction process.* Amsterdam: John Benjamins, 113–144.

Martínez-Flor, Alicia, Sánchez-Hernández, Ariadna & Barón, Júlia (eds). 2023. *L2 Pragmatics in Action. Teachers, learners and the teaching-learning interaction process.* Amsterdam: John Benjamins.

Martínez-Flor, Alicia & Usó-Juan, Esther. 2006. A comprehensive pedagogical framework to develop pragmatics in the foreign language classroom: The 6Rs approach. *Applied Language Learning*, 16/2, 39–64.

Mehan, Hugh. 1979. *Learning lessons: Social organization in the classroom.* Harvard MA: Harvard University Press.

Myrset, Anders & McConachy, Troy. 2024. *Incorporating pragmatics into primary English language teacher education.* In David Valente & Daniel Xerri (eds) *Innovative practices in Early English language education.* New York: Springer, 305–327.

Ngai, Phyllis & Janusch, Sandra. 2018. Professional development for TESL teachers: A course in transcultural pragmatics. *TESL-EJ*, 22/3, 1–26.

Nikula, Tarja. 2002. Teacher talk reflecting pragmatic awareness. *Pragmatics. Quarterly Publication of the International Pragmatics Association (IPrA)*, 12/4, 447–467.

Paribakht, T. Sima & Wesche, Marjorie Bingham. 1993. Reading comprehension and second language development in a comprehension-based ESL program. *TESL Canada Journal.* 11/1, 9–29.

Portolés, Laura & Martín-Laguna, Sofía. 2012. Code switching in classroom discourse: A multilingual approach. In Eva Alcón-Soler & Pilar Safont (eds) *Discourse and language learning across L2 instructional settings.* Leiden: Brill Rodopi, 295–317.

Povolná, Renata. 2012. Pragmatic awareness in teacher education. *Acta Academica Karviniensia.* 12/1, 148–158.

Savvidou, Christine & Economidou-Kogetsidis, Maria. 2019. Teaching pragmatics: Nonnative-speaker teachers' knowledge, beliefs and reported practices. *Intercultural Communication Education*, 2/1, 39–58.

Schauer, Gila A. 2022a. Teaching L2 pragmatics to young learners. A review study. *Applied Pragmatics*, 4/2, 137–158.

Schauer, Gila A. 2022b. Intercultural competence and pragmatics in the L2 classroom: Views of in-service EFL teachers in primary, secondary, and adult education. In Troy McConachy & Anthony J. Liddicoat (eds) *Teaching and learning second language pragmatics for intercultural understanding*. New York: Routledge, 173–198.

Swales, John M. 1981. *Aspects of article introductions*. Birmingham, England: University of Aston.

Swales, John M. 1990. *Genre Analysis: English in academic and research settings*. Cambridge: Cambridge University Press.

Taguchi, Naoko. 2015. Instructed pragmatics at glance: Where instructional studies were, are, and should be going. *Language Teaching*, 48/1, 1–50.

Taguchi, Naoko 2019. Second Language Acquisition and Pragmatics. An Overview. In Naoko Taguchi (ed.) *The Routledge handbook of second language acquisition and pragmatics* New York: Routledge, 1–14.

Taguchi, Naoko & Kim, Youjin (eds). 2018. *Task-based approaches to teaching and assessing pragmatics*. Amsterdam: John Benjamins.

Taguchi Naoko & Youn, Soo Jung. 2022. Pragmatics: Assessing learning outcomes in instructional studies. In Laura Gurzynski-Weiss & Youjin Kim (eds) *Instructed second language acquisition research methods*. Amsterdam: John Benjamins, 149–180.

Thomas, Jenny. 1983. Cross-cultural pragmatic failure. *Applied Linguistics*, 4/2, 91–112.

Tullet, Hervé. 2019. *Art workshops for children*. New York: Phaidon Press Limited.

Usó-Juan, Esther & Martínez-Flor, Alicia. 2020. Teacher pragmatic awareness in English as an international language. In Zia Tajeddin & Minoo Alemi (eds) *Pragmatics pedagogy in English as an International Language*. New York: Routledge, 44–58.

Usó-Juan, Esther & Martínez-Flor, Alicia. 2021. Fostering learner's (meta)pragmatic awareness through film analysis. *Language Value*, 14/1, 85–111.

Usó-Juan, Esther & Martínez-Flor, Alicia. 2022. Using audiovisual material to teach refusals from a discursive perspective: A research-based proposal. *Complutense Journal of English Studies*, 30, 53–66.

Vásquez, Camilla & Fioramonte, Amy. 2011. Integrating pragmatics into the MA-TESL program: perspectives from former students. *TESL-EJ*, 15/2.

Youn, Soo Jung. 2018. Task-based needs analysis of L2 pragmatics in an EAP context. *Journal of English for Academic Purposes*, 36, 86–98.

Irene Guzmán-Alcón

Pragmatic Outcomes in English: The Role of Socioeconomic Status and CLIL

Introduction

The significance of Content and Language Integrated Learning (CLIL) has been growing since the 1990s, propelled by the efforts of the European Community, and in harmony with the EU's language policy, which aims for every EU citizen to be proficient in two additional languages apart from their mother tongue. Although the potential of CLIL was soon acknowledged as an approach to foster multilingualism (Marsh, 2002), debates have arisen regarding the necessity to differentiate CLIL from other educational approaches, such as Content-Based Instruction or immersion programmes (Cenoz et al., 2014). In addition, although Dalton-Puffer et al. (2014) highlight key features that distinguish CLIL (the employment of major or minor international lingua franca, with English being the most common in Europe; CLIL's function as an adjunct rather than a substitute for foreign language teaching; and its execution through content-based classes), these traits can be applied in varied ways, and prompted a wide range of studies in the early 21st century, ranging from investigating language learning outcomes to the development of pedagogical practice through theory-based interventions (Dalton-Puffer et al., 2022).

Considering the increasing interest in CLIL, this study builds on previous research that has examined CLIL's effectiveness across different educational subjects and levels, particularly those dealing with the socioeconomic status of students' families. More specifically, this research aims to unravel how the family's socioeconomic status interacts with CLIL programmes and whether it affects student pragmatic achievement.

Literature Review

So far, previous research on CLIL has analysed the benefits of CLIL versus non-CLIL programmes (Pladevall-Ballester & Vallbona, 2016; Agustín-Llach, 2017; San Isidro & Lasagabaster, 2018). However, CLIL under different intensities of CLIL programmes has not been much investigated (Guzmán-Alcón, 2023; Hidalgo-Villarreal, 2024; Guzmán-Alcon, in press). Previous studies that have explored the effect of intensity of CLIL programmes, have dealt with English proficiency improvements (Merino & Lasagabaster, 2017; Llinares & Naashat-Soby, 2023; Guzmán-Alcón, 2023). For instance, Merino and Lasagabaster (2017) investigated how intensity of CLIL sessions influenced English learning among 393 secondary students, reporting significant effects on English proficiency from those in higher intensity programmes. More recently, Llinares and Nashwa-Sobhy (2023) analysed the written work of CLIL students who responded to a prompt about the Women's Movement, assessing differences in their use of cognitive discourse function. Their findings indicated that students with greater English exposure performed better in knowledge transfer. Furthermore, Guzmán-Alcón (2023) explored the impact of different intensities of CLIL programmes (High, Medium, and Low) on students' communicative appropriateness in writing. A total of 392 primary students participated in the study, completing a written task on water pollution in Science. The findings highlighted that the number of CLIL hours played a crucial role, with significant differences observed between High- and Medium-intensity CLIL programmes compared to Low-intensity ones. Similarly, Arias-Hermoso and Imaz-Agirre (2023) examined trilingual writing among secondary students in a Basque immersion programme, exploring relationships between students' compositions in Basque, Spanish, and English. The study revealed that multilingual learners demonstrated similar writing processes across languages, suggesting that both immersion and CLIL models are effective in fostering competence in multiple languages. Together, these studies underscore the importance of programme intensity and exposure in enhancing multilingual writing skills. More recently, Hidalgo and Villareal (2024) explored low- and high-intensity CLIL programmes with a standard English as a foreign language programme in primary schools. Their study focused on the receptive skills of 11-year-olds, and the findings revealed that high-intensity CLIL programmes significantly improved listening and reading proficiency compared to lower-intensity programmes.

Despite the positive effects of the CLIL programmes, CLIL has also been criticised. One major critique is that while CLIL aims to foster multilingualism in public education centres and promote equality (Marsh, 2002; Egger et al., 2012; Hüttner & Smit, 2014; García & Leiva, 2014; Lorenzo, 2019; Lorenzo et al., 2021; Llinares & Evnitskaya, 2021) it unintentionally perpetuates inequality within the educational system to a certain extent (Martín-Rojo, 2013; Bruton, 2013; Paran, 2013; Dallinger et al., 2018; Van Mensel et al., 2020). The issue does not appear to be inherent to CLIL itself, but rather stems from its implementation, which can be influenced by family socioeconomic status.

Previous studies that have explored the relationship between socioeconomic status and students' achievements reported inconclusive results. Some investigations have shown that the socioeconomic status of the family plays a significant role in students' achievement (Anghel et al., 2016; Fernández-Sanjurjo et al., 2017; Pérez-Cañado, 2018; Tompkins, 2022). For instance, Anghel et al. (2016) explored bilingual students' achievement at the secondary level. Data were collected by means of a written exam and a questionnaire that included a series of socioeconomic background items. Results indicated that parental educational level affected students' outcomes. In other words, students whose parents had only completed lower-secondary education performed more poorly in the exam than those with university degrees, higher-secondary education, or vocational training. Similarly, Fernández-Sanjurjo et al. (2017) investigated a total of 709 primary learners in year six from diverse social backgrounds who were enrolled in public schools. Data were collected by means of a science test and a questionnaire measuring participants' economic background. Results indicated that students from less favoured socioeconomic backgrounds obtained significantly lower scores than those from more privileged settings. Along the same lines, "Pérez-Cañado (2018) investigated the effects of CLIL on language outcomes across different educational levels, with a particular focus on the role of socioeconomic status. A total of 2,024 students from 53 schools in three Spanish regions participated in the study. Data were collected by means of an English test and a questionnaire to explore the impact of socioeconomic status based on parents' educational level. Findings from the study showed that socioeconomic status played a significant role, with students whose parents had higher education performing better in English.

Similarly, Tompkins (2022) explored the potential differences in socioeconomic status and English high-exposure and low-exposure programmes at a bilingual (Spanish/English) secondary school. Data were collected by means of a cultural and economic capital questionnaire. The findings revealed that students from the lowest and highest socioeconomic status backgrounds were predominantly grouped in the low-exposure and high-exposure tracks, respectively. In the low exposure track, CLIL and English teachers used English less frequently, and students demonstrated lower levels of intrinsic motivation. For students with lower English proficiency—often from lower socioeconomic status backgrounds—the opportunities to benefit from the cultural and economic capital associated with English proficiency might have been limited due to fewer meaningful learning experiences.

In contrast, other studies reported no significant difference between students' achievement and parents' socioeconomic status. For instance, Rascón-Moreno and Bretones-Callejas (2018) examined the influence of parental education level on student performance in CLIL and non-CLIL contexts, among primary and secondary students in Andalucia. Data were collected by means of a questionnaire. The results showed that in CLIL contexts, student performance was not influenced by parental education level, unlike in non-CLIL contexts where a difference was observed based on the parents' educational level. The researchers noted that the better language and content attainment of bilingual students was not clearly attributable to the socioeconomic background to which they belonged. Along the same line, Lorenzo et al. (2021) explored the differences between CLIL bilingual education and traditional monolingual education regarding student equity. A sample of over 3,800 students representing four levels of socioeconomic status was selected through stratified random sampling and analysed using correlational methods. The focus was on their Spanish L1, English L2, and history performance across CLIL and non-CLIL schools. The findings revealed that CLIL education might have promoted equity, as all CLIL students achieved similarly high results regardless of their socioeconomic status. In contrast, in non-CLIL settings, students from higher socioeconomic backgrounds consistently performed better.

Given the mixed results reported above, and the need to conduct further research on the intersection of CLIL programmes and the socioeconomic status of the family, the present study aims to explore family socioeconomic status, based on parents' employment, and its impact on students' pragmatic achievement, taking into account the content and comprehensibility of students writing, its coherence and cohesion and its linguistics adequacy. Additionally, we seek to identify which predictors—family socioeconomic status or CLIL programme—most significantly influence students' pragmatic achievement.

With this in mind, two research questions were formulated:

RQ1: Research Question 1: Does family socioeconomic background impact students' pragmatic achievement?

RQ2: Research Question 2: Does family socioeconomic background predict students' pragmatic achievement in CLIL programmes?

Method

Participants and Data Sources

The sample consisted of 270 primary students from three different state schools in the Valencian Community. Unlike other regions such as Madrid, Asturias, and Andalucia, where enrollment in a bilingual programme depends on family choice, in the Valencian Community, the main criterion for school assignment is proximity to the centre. Thus, the three public schools selected for the present study were located in different areas. They all follow a multilingual educational programme (two co-official languages, English as a foreign learning and a CLIL programme). The schools vary in language programmes and in family socioeconomic status. Thus, the school with a High CLIL programme had 14 sessions per week of CLIL, with 46.67 % of the time dedicated to language and content instruction. It was considered an example of a High-intensity CLIL programme because it represented a high percentage of hours dedicated to CLIL in the Valencian Community. The school with a Low CLIL programme had 6.67 % of hours of CLIL. This is an example of a Low-intensity CLIL programme, since it is the type of school with the lowest percentage of time dedicated to CLIL in the Valencian Community. Finally, the school with a Medium CLIL programme had 13.67 % of hours of CLIL, and it was considered a Medium-intensity CLIL programme, as it represents an intensity level between the categories mentioned above, although not necessarily an intermediate point.

A total of 99 participants were enrolled in High CLIL, 55 in Medium CLIL, and 116 participants were enrolled in Low CLIL. Regarding the students' characteristics, 50 % (n = 50) of them were male, and 49.5 % were female (n = 49). They were students of Year 6, the last year of Primary Education in the Valencian Community. Their mean age was 10.5, ranging from 10 to 11 years old. Moreover, a Cambridge assessment test was used to measure students' English proficiency. According to the Common European Framework of Reference for Languages (CEFR), participants in the present study obtained an A2 level. This level signifies that students can understand and use everyday expressions and engage in simple communicative exchanges on familiar and routine matters. Students with an English proficiency level higher or lower than A2 were excluded from the study.

Data were collected through a written task and a questionnaire. The written task was designed to be as authentic as possible and related to a topic students had already covered in their Science subject. The task was conducted during class time in CLIL science sessions, where English was the language of instruction. The questionnaire was adapted from Lasagabaster and Huguet (2007), and administered after the written task to gather participants' personal information (including gender, nationality, and age), exposure to English beyond the classroom, and family socioeconomic background, which was considered in terms of parents' employment, and it is the variable analysed in the present study.

Procedure and Data Analysis

Participants completed the written task and a questionnaire within a standard classroom setting, with a maximum time limit of twenty minutes. The data collection adhered to ethical standards; all students voluntarily participated and provided informed consent. To maintain anonymity, each participant's responses were coded with a unique number. The data collection process was consistent across all schools. Participants listened to a twenty-minute explanation of water pollution in English given by the researcher, followed by a twenty-minute session to complete the written task in English. In total, 270 written tasks were analysed. Each writing task was coded according to a taxonomy adapted from Kuiker and Vedder (2018) and Jacob et al. (1989). The taxonomy was used to measure the content and comprehensibility of the text, its coherence and cohesion, and its linguistic adequacy. Each writing task was scored on a scale from 0 to 5, based on the categories in the taxonomy. The students' writing scores were considered an indicator of students' pragmatic achievement in writing.

Participants also filled out a background questionnaire (15 minutes). It is generally assumed that higher education leads to better employment opportunities and, consequently, a higher income. In the present study, in line with Tompkins (2022), parents' occupation was considered the indicator of family socioeconomic status. Thus, adopting the National Statistics Institute's (INE) Occupation Classification (https://www.ine.es/daco/daco42/discapa/tar1.pdf), family socio-economic background was categorised using the following scale: Housewives (HW), Unemployed (UNP), Unskilled Workers (USW) for individuals without educational qualifications, Skilled Workers (SW) for those with education but not a university degree,

Technicians and Professionals (TAP) for those with a university degree, and Managers (MG) for individuals with a university degree holding positions such as CEOs or directors of institutions. Categories were assigned points from 1 for the highest income to 6 for lowest positions. Furthermore, to examine the relationship between CLIL programmes and family socioeconomic background, statistical analysis tests were conducted using SPSS (version 27). Since the data was not normally distributed, non-parametric tests were employed. Spearman's correlation test was used to explore the relationship between students' achievement and their families' socioeconomic status, considering both the mother's and father's occupations. It is worth pointing out that in the present study no same-sex or nonparental families participated in the study. In other words, all families were formed by a male and a female. Additionally, a hierarchical regression analysis was performed to determine whether the primary predictor of students' achievement was the family's socioeconomic status or the fact of participating in a CLIL programme. In this case, both fathers and mothers' occupations were considered; they were categorised, according to the occupation classification mentioned above, and added to have a one single variable of the family socioeconomic status.

Results

To address our first research question, which examined the impact of family socioeconomic background on students' pragmatic achievement, it is essential to highlight variation in family employment across schools. Figures 3.1 and 3.2 illustrate the professional status of parents, categorised by gender and school.

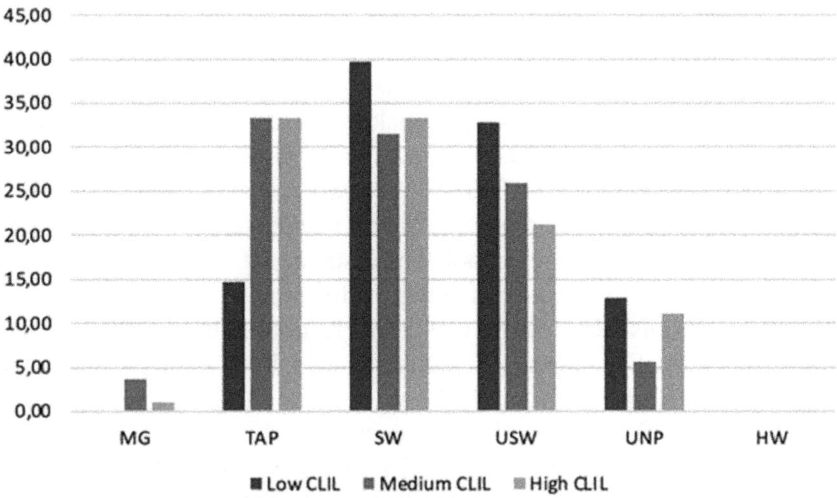

Figure 3.1: Fathers' professions at each school.
Note. Housewives = HW; Unemployed = UNP; Unskilled Workers = USW; Skilled Workers = SW; Technicians and Professionals = TAP; Managers; MG

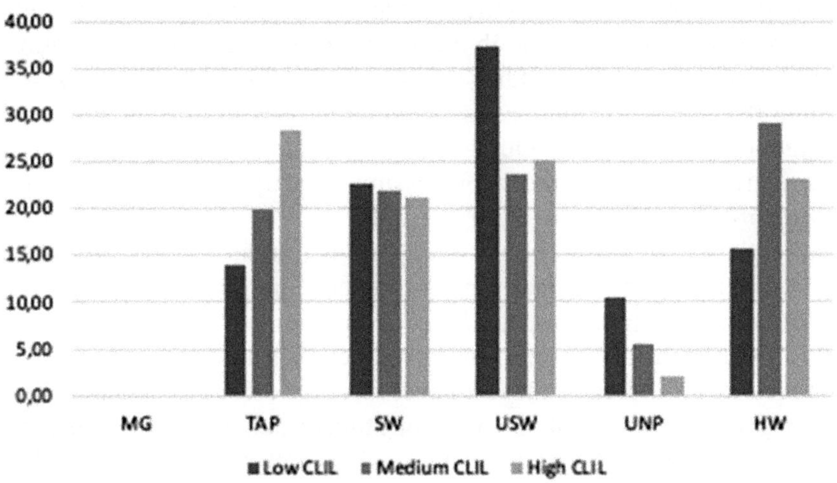

Figure 3.2: Mothers' professions at each school.
Note. Housewives = HW; Unemployed = UNP; Unskilled Workers = USW; Skilled Workers = SW; Technicians and Professionals = TAP; Managers; MG

As depicted in Figures 3.1 and 3.2 findings on parental occupation indicate that Skilled Workers (SW) and Unskilled Workers (USW) categories represent nearly 60 % of the occupations for both parents overall. For mothers, the Unskilled Workers (USW) category is the most prevalent at 30.11 %, while for fathers, Skilled Workers (SW) is more common at 35.68 %. Notably, the Housewives (HW) category accounts for almost 11 % for women. These occupational distributions also vary by school. For instance, at Low CLIL, Skilled Workers (SW) is the dominant category for men at 39.66 %, while at the other schools, the Technicians and Professionals (TAP) category exceeds 33 %. For women, Technicians and Professionals (TAP) is over 20 % at High CLIL and 28 % at Medium CLIL, whereas at Low CLIL, Unskilled Workers (USW) reaches 37.39 %. Additionally, at Low CLIL, the Unemployment (UNP) category exceeds 10 % for both men and women. However, at Medium and High CLIL, the highest percentages of Housewives (HW) are found among women, at 29.09 % and 23.23 %, respectively.

The descriptive data analysis provides an overview of the socioeconomic characteristics of the sample, which is crucial for interpreting the results of our research questions. The Spearman's correlation coefficient was used to address Research Question 1, which investigated the impact of family socioeconomic background on students' pragmatic achievement. Our findings revealed a significant positive correlation between fathers' professional occupations and students' pragmatic achievement, $r(268) = 0.408$, $p < .001$, indicating that higher levels of professional occupations among fathers are associated with better pragmatic performance. Similarly, a positive low correlation was found for mothers' occupations, $r(268) = 0.276$, $p < .001$. Although this correlation is weaker than the one reported for fathers, it still indicates that higher levels of professional occupations among mothers are linked to better student achievement. Thus, we can claim that our findings related to Research Question 1 revealed a significant relationship between parents' professional occupations and students' pragmatic performance in writing, suggesting that fathers' professional occupations contribute positively to students' academic success, with a more pronounced effect observed from fathers' occupations.

Building on these insights, our Research Question 2 explored the interplay between CLIL programmes and family socioeconomic status. Thus, a hierarchical multiple regression analysis was conducted to examine the extent to which scores in pragmatic achievement can be attributed to family socioeconomic status or to the CLIL programme implemented in the school. These variables were introduced hierarchically to assess their respective contributions, considering the Low CLIL programme as the reference group.

Table 3.1 shows the standard multiple regression model coefficients for students' pragmatic achievement. The regression included the variables of family socioeconomic status and CLIL programme. Model 1, including High CLIL (HCLIL), led to a statistically significant value of 0.197 ($F (1, 268) = 65.608$, $p < 0.001$; adjusted $R^2 = 0.194$). Model 2, adding Medium CLIL, also led to a positive increase in R^2 of 0.445 ($F (2, 267) = 106.972$, $p < 0.001$; adjusted $R^2 = 0.441$). Model 3 leads to a further increase in R^2 of 0.520 ($F (7, 262) = 95997$, $p < 0.001$; adjusted $R^2 = 0.514$). Model 3 was preferred to the other two, considering that it explained a greater variability of the scores as shown by the R2 value.

Table 3.1. Hierarchical multiple regression predicting the effect of school programme and socioeconomic status on writing scores.

	Model 1		**Model 2**		**Model 3**	
Predictor	B	β	B	β	B	β
Constant	7.023		3.741		11.226	
H.CLIL	7.007	0.443	10.289	0.651	9.697	0.614
M.CLIL			10.204	0.540	9.846	0.521
SS					−2.031	−0.276
R^2	0.197		0.445		0.542	
F	65.608		106.972		44.257	
ΔR^2	0.194		0.248		0.075	
ΔF	65.608		119.361		41.552	

Note. $p < 0.001$

Note: M.CLIL= Medium CLIL; H.CLIL= High CLIL; SS= Socioeconomic Status

In addition, the standardised coefficients, included in Table 3.1, enabled us to establish the relative weight of the variables of family socio-economic background and CLIL programme on the dependent variable, total scores in pragmatic achievement (see column β in each model of Table 3.1). As shown in Model 3, the variable High CLIL shows a significant positive relationship with the dependent variable ($\beta = 0.614$, $p < 0.001$). Additionally, the variable Medium CLIL also demonstrates a positive but slightly weaker effect ($\beta = 0.521$, $p < 0.001$). On the contrary, the variable of family socioeconomic status does not show significant relationships with the scores in pragmatic achievement. In other words, the variable CLIL programme (labelled as High CLIL and Medium CLIL), with higher standardised coefficients, seems to be the most influential predictor of students' pragmatic achievement in writing. However, it is important to note that a significant amount of variance remains unexplained. Model 2 shows a goodness of fit of 0.445 and Model 3 0.520. Thus, although CLIL programmes seem to be the main predictor of students' writing, approximately 47 % of the variance is still unaccounted for.

To sum up, our findings related to Research Question 2 show that, regardless of the number of CLIL hours, the presence of CLIL programmes in a school is a more crucial predictor of students' pragmatic achievement than the socioeconomic background of the families. In all the programmes (High, Medium and Low) the CLIL program has a greater impact on students' writing than the family socioeconomic status. It is true that scores are higher in High and Medium CLIL programmes than in the Low CLIL programme, but, even in the Low CLIL programme, the fact of participating in a CLIL programme has a greater impact than the family socioeconomic status. This suggests that CLIL programmes can contribute to greater equity in the educational field.

Discussion

The present study provides evidence of the influence of family socio-economic background and CLIL programmes on primary students' pragmatic achievement in writing. Our findings reveal that the father's employment has a greater impact on students' writing than the mother's. In addition, the study also presents new insights into the interplay between family socioeconomic status and CLIL programmes, suggesting that CLIL programmes are a stronger predictor of students' writing performance than family socioeconomic status.

Our results are consistent with those of Anghel et al. (2016) and Fernández-Sanjurjo et al. (2017), who also found that family socioeconomic background influences students' learning outcomes. However, while Anghel et al. (2016) focused on secondary students and assessed socioeconomic status using parents' educational level, our study extends these findings to primary students and considers parents' employment. Our results are also in line with those reported by Fernández-Sanjurjo et al. (2017), who identified significant differences in primary students' achievement based on family socioeconomic background, although they focused on English proficiency rather than writing. Moreover, our findings corroborate Pérez-Cañado's (2018) and Tompkins' (2022) studies that found a positive correlation between students' language learning and family socioeconomic background. However, while Pérez-Cañado (2018) focused on the parents' educational level at the primary and secondary school level, and Tompkins (2022) examined the role of family socioeconomic status at the secondary school level, the present study focused on the impact of parents' employment on primary students' pragmatic achievement in writing.

In addition, our findings show that the school environment, particularly CLIL programmes, may play a more significant role than family background in shaping student achievement. These findings are in line with those reported by Rascón-Moreno and Bretones-Callejas (2018) and Lorenzo et al. (2021). The difference lies in the fact that while Rascón-Moreno and Bretones-Callejas (2018) considered the influence of parental education level on student performance, we focused on parental employment and its impact on students' pragmatic achievement, and Lorenzo et al. (2021) focused on secondary students, while we considered primary learners. Our results, in line with García and Leiva (2014), Hüttner and Smit (2014), and Lorenzo et al. (2021), indicate that CLIL programmes can contribute to equity in education. Our findings also challenge earlier research that positioned family socioeconomic status as the primary determinant of student success, and suggest that school policies, particularly the adoption of CLIL programmes, can be a powerful tool to mitigate the disadvantages associated with lower socioeconomic status.

Finally, our results underscore the critical importance of educational environment and instructional quality in shaping students' achievement. Our results show that schools implementing CLIL programmes, regardless of their students' socioeconomic backgrounds, appear to foster pragmatic achievement. However, it is crucial to recognise that a significant portion of the variance in student achievement remains unexplained, indicating that other factors, including unmeasured aspects of socioeconomic status or whether same-sex or nonparental families might also be influential.

From this perspective, future research needs to be conducted on other factors, not considered in this study, that may be impacting students' achievement. Moreover, there is a need to explore the long-term impact of CLIL programmes on students from different socioeconomic backgrounds. Additionally, understanding how specific school policies can be leveraged to reduce educational disparities and promote equity are needed to be investigated in the context of CLIL. In the same vein, studies that examine the effectiveness of various educational interventions across CLIL programmes could provide deeper insights into how schools can better support students from lower socioeconomic backgrounds.

Conclusion and Pedagogical Implications

The study explored the influence of family socioeconomic background and the effectiveness of CLIL programmes on students' pragmatic achievement. Findings from the study showed that the professional occupation of parents significantly had an impact on student performance. However, the study also revealed that CLIL programmes have a more substantial predictive power on student pragmatic achievement compared to family socioeconomic background. CLIL was shown to be a significant positive predictor of success in pragmatic achievement, suggesting that the educational environment and the instructional quality in CLIL programmes might have a more pronounced impact on student success than socioeconomic factors, and in so contribute to equity in the educational field.

These findings have important implications for educational policies. Given the significant influence of paternal occupations, it becomes essential to design educational interventions that provide targeted support for students from lower socioeconomic backgrounds, where paternal influence is less conducive to academic achievement. Those initiatives could include mentoring, tutoring, or financial assistance to mitigate disparities caused by socioeconomic factors. Moreover, policymakers and educational leaders might consider increasing investments in teacher training, enhancing the availability of CLIL programmes across schools, and integrating CLIL into the curriculum. By supporting innovative teaching methods like CLIL, policymakers can significantly improve educational outcomes across diverse student populations. This may facilitate that all students, regardless of their background, have access to high-quality educational experiences supporting their academic and personal development.

Acknowledgements

As a member of the LAELA (Lingüística Aplicada a l'Ensenyament de la Llengua Anglesa) research group at Universitat Jaume I (Castellón, Spain), I would like to acknowledge that this study is part of the research project PID2020-117959GB-I00 funded by MCIN/AEI/10.13039/501100011033. Additional funding has been granted by Projectes d'Innovació Educativa de la Unitat de Suport Educatiu 51020/24.

References

Agustín-Llach, María Pilar. 2017. The effects of the CLIL approach in young foreign language learners' lexical profiles. *International Journal of Bilingual Education and Bilingualism*. 20/5, 557–573. <https://doi.org/10.1080/13670050.2015.1103208>.

Anghel, B., Cabrales, A., & Carro, J. M. (2016). Evaluating a bilingual education program in Spain: The impact beyond foreign language learning. *Economic Inquiry, 54*(2), 1202–1223. https://doi.org/10.1111/ecin.12305

Arias-Hermoso, Roberto & Imaz-Agirre, Ainara. 2023. Exploring multilingual writers in secondary education: Insights from a trilingual corpus. *European Journal of Applied Linguistics*. Advance online publication. <https://doi.org/10.1515/eujal-2023-0022>.

Bruton, Anthony. 2013. CLIL: Some of the reasons why and why not. *System*, 41/3, 587–597. <https://doi.org/10.1016/j.sys tem.2013.07.001

Cenoz, Jasone, Genesee, Fred & Görter, Durk. 2014. Critical analysis of CLIL: Taking stock and looking forward. *Applied Linguistics,* 35/3, 243–262. <https://doi.org/10.1093/applin/amt011>.

Dallinger, Sara, Jonkmann, Kathrin & Hollm, Jan. 2018. Selectivity of content and language integrated learning programmes in German secondary schools. *International Journal of Bilingual Education and Bilingualism,* 21/1, 93–104. <https://doi.org/10.1080/13670 050.2015.1130015>.

Dalton-Puffer, Christiane, Hüttner, Julia & Llinares, Ana. (2022). CLIL in the 21st century: Retrospective and prospective challenges and opportunities. *Journal of Immersion and Content-Based Language Education*, 10/2, 182–206. <https://doi.org/10.1075/jicb.21021.dal>.

Dalton-Puffer, Christiane, Llinares, Ana, Lorenzo, Francisco & Nikula, Tarja. 2014. "You Can Stand Under My Umbrella": Immersion, CLIL and bilingual education. A response to Cenoz, Genesee & Görter (2013). *Applied Linguistics*, 35/2, 213–218. <https://doi.org/10.1093/applin/amu010>.

Egger, Gerlinde, Lechner, Christine & Ward, Sean 2012. Introduction. In Gerlinde Egger & Christine Lechner (eds) *Primary CLIL around Europe. Learning in two languages in primary education.* Marbug: Tectum Verlag, 11–12.

Fernández-Sanjurjo, Javier, Fernández-Costales, Alberto & Arias Blanco, José Miguel. 2017. Analysing students' content-learning in Science in CLIL vs. non-CLIL programmes: Empirical evidence from Spain. *International Journal of Bilingual Education and Bilingualism*, 22/6, 661–674. <https://doi.org/10.1080/13670 050.2017.1294142>.

García, Ofelia & Leiva, Camila. 2014. Theorising and enacting translanguaging for social justice. In Adrian Blackledge & Angela Creese (eds) *Heteroglossia as practice and pedagogy*. Dordrecht: Springer, 199–216. <https://doi.org/10.1007/978-94-007-7856-6_11>.

Guzmán-Alcón, Irene. (In press). The role of hours of CLIL exposure in primary multilingual science writing. In Ainara Imaz-Agirre & Roberto Arias-Hermoso (eds) *Insights into disciplinary literacies: Multilingual perspectives across educational levels*. Bristol, Blue Ridge Summit: Multilingual Matters.

Guzmán-Alcón, Irene. 2023. *The effect of intensity of content and language integrated learning programmes on students' multilingual writing* [Doctoral dissertation, Universitat Jaume I].

Hidalgo, María Ángeles & Villarreal, Izaskun. 2024. Intensity matters in CLIL: Evidence from primary school learners' receptive skills. *System*, 125. <https://doi.org/10.1016/j.system.2024.103402>

Hüttner, Julia & Smit, Ute. 2014. Content and language integrated learning: The bigger picture. A response to: A. Bruton. 2013. CLIL: Some of the reasons why . . . and why not. *System*, 41/2013, 587–597, 44, 160–167. <https://doi.org/10.1016/j.system.2014.03.001>.

Jacobs, H., Zinkgraf, S., Wormuth, D., Hearfiel, V., & Hughey, J. (1981). *Testing ESL Composition: A Practical Approach*. Longman Higher Education.

Kuiken, F., & Vedder, I. (2018). Assessing functional adequacy of L2 performance in a task-based approach. In N. Taguchi & Y. Kim (Eds.), *Task-Based Language Teaching* (pp. 266–285). John Benjamins. https://doi.org/10.1075/tblt.10.11

Lasagabaster, D., & Huguet, Á. (2007). *Multilingualism in European bilingual context*. Multilingual Matters.

Llinares, Ana & Nashaat-Sobhy, Nashwa 2023. CLIL students' academic language performance on a non-curricular topic: A comparison between high-exposure and low-exposure groups. *English Teaching and Learning*, 47/3, 337–358.

Llinares, Ana & Evnitskaya, Natalia. 2021. Classroom interaction in CLIL programs: Offering opportunities or fostering inequalities? *TESOL Quarterly*, 55/2, 366–397. <https://doi.org/10.1002/tesq.607>.

Lorenzo, Francisco. 2019. *Educación Bilingüe en Andalucía. Informe de Gestión, Competencias y Organización*. <http://DOI:10.13140/RG.2.2.14996.76167>.

Lorenzo, Francisco, Granados, Adrián & Rico, Nuria. 2021. Equity in bilingual education: Socioeconomic status and content and language integrated learning in monolingual Southern Europe. *Applied Linguistics*, 42/3, 393–413. <https://doi.org/10.1093/applin/amaa037>.

Marsh, David. 2002. *CLIL/EMILE: The European dimension: Actions, trends and foresight potential*. Jyväskylä: University of Jyväskylä: UniCOM, Continuing Education Centre.

Martín-Rojo, Luisa. 2013. (De) capitalising students through linguistic practices. A comparative analysis of new educational programmes in a global era. In Alexandre Duchêne, Melissa Moyer & Celia Roberts (eds) *Language, migration and social inequalities*. Bristol, Blue Ridge Summit: Multilingual Matters, 120–148. <https://doi.org/10.21832/9781783091010-007>.

Merino, Jon Ander & Lasagabaster, David. 2017. CLIL as a way to multilingualism. *International Journal of Bilingual Education and Bilingualism*, 21/1, 79–92. <https://doi.org/10.1080/13670050.2015.1128386>.

Paran, Amos. 2013. Content and language integrated learning: Panacea or policy borrowing myth? *Applied Linguistics Review*, 4/2, 317–342. <https://doi.org/10.1515/applirev-2013-0014>.

Pladevall-Ballester, E. & Vallbona, A. 2016. CLIL in minimal input contexts: A longitudinal study of primary school learners' receptive skills. *System*, 58, 37–48. <https://doi.org/10.1016/j.system.2016.02.009>.

Pérez-Cañado, María Luisa. 2018. CLIL and educational level: A longitudinal study on the impact of CLIL on language outcomes. *Porta Linguarum Revista Interuniversitaria de Didáctica de las Lenguas Extranjeras*, 29, 51–70. <https://doi.org/10.30827/Digibug.54022>.

Rascón-Moreno, Diego & Bretones-Callejas, Carmen M. 2018. Socioeconomic status and its impact on language and content attainment in CLIL contexts. *Porta Linguarum Revista Interuniversitaria de Didáctica de las Lenguas Extranjeras*, 29, 115–135. <https://doi.org/10.30827/Digibug.54025>.

San Isidro, Xavier & Lasagabaster, David. 2018. The impact of CLIL on pluriliteracy development and content learning in a rural multilingual setting: A longitudinal study. *Language Teaching Research*, 23/5, 584–602. <https://DOI:10.1177/1362168817754103>.

Tompkins, Forrest Lea. 2022. Socioeconomic status, English exposure and CLIL motivation in high and low exposure CLIL groups. *CLIL Journal of Innovation and Research in Plurilingual and Pluricultural Education*, 5/1, 41–52. <https://doi.org/10.5565/rev/clil.67>.

Van Mensel, Luk, Hiligsmann, Philippe, Mettewie, Laurence & Galand, Benoît. 2020. CLIL, an elitist language learning approach? A background analysis of English and Dutch CLIL pupils in French-speaking Belgium. *Language, Culture and Curriculum*, 33/1, 1–14. <https://doi.org/10.1080/07908318.2019.1571078>.

Section II

Pragmatics at Tertiary Level

Naoko Taguchi

Teaching Intercultural Competence Through Conflict Mediation Training[3]

Introduction

In the current global society, the importance of intercultural competence is widely acknowledged in both international and domestic contexts. There has been a keen interest in higher education to produce graduates who can function effectively in a global society (IIE, 2021; Rogers, 2021). Correspondingly, many universities situate intercultural learning as part of their strategic plans, implementing it through general education requirements, foreign language courses, and study abroad programs. Hence, intercultural competence, broadly defined as "a complex of abilities needed to perform effectively and appropriately when interacting with others who are linguistically and culturally different from oneself" (Fantini, 2006: 12), is an important mission of higher education today. Yet, teaching intercultural competence is a challenging task because of a large number of dimensions involved in the construct (Leung et al., 2014; Spitzberg & Chagnon, 2009). In addition, those dimensions are called for differently according to different contexts. Acknowledging this, Dervin (2006) proposed the term proteophilic competence as an alternative to intercultural competence, emphasizing the fluid nature of that competence. Someone who is interculturally

3 This is part of a larger study that examined the effect of conflict mediation training using multiple data sets (survey data, performance data, participants' situation analyses and reflections). Som parts of the methods and findings appear in Taguchi (2023).

competence in one situation maybe not be so in another situation. Hence, proteophilic competence—understanding people as individuals who identify with a variety of groups rather than one particular group—is an important part of intercultural learning.

A number of resource books provide guidance on how to teach intercultural competence (e.g., Griffith et al., 2016; Liddicoat, 2011). Instructional tasks given in those books are wide-ranging, including film and literary text analysis, role-plays and simulations, cultural image-making, analysis of cultural artifacts, and interviews with cultural informants. One approach that has been under-represented is teaching how to mediate intercultural conflicts. According to Jackson (2020), intercultural conflict mediation calls for a specific set of knowledge and skills such as cultural knowledge, knowledge of others' assumptions and feelings, adaptability to the situation, and effective communication. These skills likely underlie the construct of intercultural competence that involves a body of personality traits, attitudes, and abilities (Leung et al., 2014). However, almost no studies have investigated whether teaching intercultural conflict mediation can actually improve students' intercultural competence. Yet, such a study can be informative for teachers who seek evidence on effective approaches to intercultural competence training.

The present study, conducted as part of a college-level course on intercultural communication, examines the potential link between conflict mediation training and development of intercultural competence. The study develops original instructional materials on conflict mediation strategies and implements them in a classroom. The materials' effectiveness (i.e., students' intercultural development) is evaluated based on students' use of conflict mediation strategies in a simulation task and their responses to a standardized survey assessing intercultural competence.

Background

Intercultural Competence

Over the last few decades, considerable effort had been made to determine what constitutes intercultural competence. As a result, a number of definitions, frameworks, and assessment measures of intercultural competence have emerged in the field (for a review, see Deardroff, 2006; Leung et al., 2014; Spitzberg & Chagnon, 2009). This body of literature has uncovered knowledge, personal traits, attitudes, and abilities that are particularly effective in intercultural settings. While existing definitions are diverse, several core elements persist, including flexibility and openness to new ideas, intercultural empathy, understanding of cultural similarities and differences, and minimal ethnocentrism.

Existing frameworks often emphasize the multidimensionality of intercultural competence. For instance, Byram (1997) presents a framework involving five dimensions. The first dimension, attitudes, refers to personal qualities that help relativize the self and value others. The second dimension, knowledge of self and others, refers to understanding cultural rules and practices. The third dimension, skills of interpreting and relating, involves the ability to interpret and relate to events from another culture. The fourth dimension, skills of discovery and interaction, includes one's ability to learn about a new culture. The last dimension, critical cultural awareness, is about drawing on one's own and other cultures to make a decision. Byram's framework serves as a basis for the Intercultural Competence Assessment (INCA, 2004), which contains a survey assessing ambiguity tolerance, flexibility, communicative awareness, knowledge discovery, respect for otherness, and empathy (k=21; three-point Likert scale).

Aside from INCA, several measures have incorporated the multidimensional approach. Van Odenhoven and Van der Zee's (2000) survey instrument is particularly relevant to this study. They created the Multicultural Personality Questionnaire (MPQ) designed to assess five components of intercultural competence: cultural empathy, open-mindedness, social initiative, emotional stability, and flexibility. Cultural empathy means the capacity to understand others' feelings and perspectives, while open-mindedness and flexibility help people accept cultural differences and adapt to new cultures. Social initiative involves willingness to participate in intercultural interactions, while emotional stability helps people stay calm in stressful intercultural settings. These components are assessed with 91 seven-point Likert-scale items. Validity and reliability of the MPQ have been established in numerous studies. In Van Odenhoven and Van der Zee (2002), the MPQ significantly predicted participants' adjustments to an international business school in a different country. In Van Odenhoven and Van der Zee (2003) involving 102 expatriates in Taiwan, the dimension of emotional stability predicted cultural adjustment most, while dimensions of social initiative, cultural empathy, and flexibility were significant predictors for other areas (e.g., psychological well-being). In the context of Saudi Arabia, Alghizzi and Alshahrani (2022) found that students at higher academic levels in an English-medium university had higher cultural empathy and open-mindedness.

While validity and reliability of the MPQ are clear, the self-report survey-based assessment has a limitation in that it can only assess participants' *perceived* intercultural competence, not their actual performance in intercultural settings. In fact, the current assessment practice is overwhelmingly survey-based (Griffith et al., 2016). A number of surveys with different item formats—Likert-scale items, multiple-choice questions, and forced choices—have been created to assess intercultural competence, and assessment of participants' performance in navigating intercultural encounters has been extremely limited. While survey-based measures are practical, allowing large-scale data collection in one sitting and a quick data analysis, surveys can only generate indirect data about participants' intercultural competence. Survey results may not offer a direct picture of participants' intercultural competence because participants respond as they think they would do in imaginary situations. In addition, they may present responses that are perceived ideal in others' eyes (social desirability) or they might have different interpretations of survey statements, skewing results.

Considering these limitations, performance-based assessments eliciting students' actual verbal and nonverbal behaviors may provide a more direct picture of their intercultural competence. For example, students can do a simulation of intercultural communication. They can place themselves in a setting involving people from different cultures. They can decide how to act in such a situation while considering how the situation is going to unfold. Such an assessment task can provide students with lifelike intercultural experiences. Behaviors observed during the task could be a reasonable representation of what they can do in a real-life situation, adding to the ecological validity of assessment tasks.

More importantly, a performance-based measure can be combined with a survey-based measure so we can gain a more comprehensive understanding of students' intercultural competence. Combining both assessment methods allows us to evaluate different aspects of their competence. The survey-based method can assess students' perceptions about their personality traits, attitudes, and imagined behaviors in intercultural settings. As such, the method can reveal students' general awareness of intercultural behaviors that are not affected by performance constraints (e.g., nervousness coming from talking spontaneously). On the other hand, the performance-based method can reveal how students can actually manage an intercultural situation in a specific task. Verbal and nonverbal skills observed in their performance may reflect their intercultural competence.

Since a single assessment method has its own limitations, it is important to use multiple assessments to gain better and stronger inferences about students' competence. Inferences drawn from test results become stronger with more evidence. Multiple assessments combined can reinforce each other's results and interpretations about students' intercultural competence. The INCA project (2004) mentioned in the previous section is an example of such a mixed methods approach. The project developed a battery of measures, including forced-choice survey items, open-ended questions, and role-plays. Critical dimensions of intercultural competence—empathy, ambiguity tolerance, respect for otherness, and communication awareness—were addressed in all measures to ensure coherence in the target constructs assessed. Following the INCA project, the present study is another attempt to assess intercultural competence using multiple methods—perception-based (survey) and performance-based (simulation role-play)—to gain a fuller understanding of students' intercultural competence.

Teaching and Assessing Intercultural Competence

Assessment of intercultural competence has various goals. Multilingual corporations may assess employees' intercultural competence to inform workplace policies and practices. Universities might assess students' intercultural competence at pre- and post-sojourn to document impact of study abroad programs. Business sectors might assess expatriates' intercultural competence to better prepare them for cultural adjustments and job performance in a foreign country. Among many goals available, one common goal of intercultural assessment is to improve course design and curriculum development. To integrate global learning within a local context, many universities offer a course designed to promote students' intercultural communication and global engagement. Such courses typically cover topics such as theories of intercultural competence, verbal and non-verbal communication processes, intercultural transitions, intercultural conflict mediation, identity, and intercultural relationships. It is important for those courses to adopt objective assessment measures to document learning outcomes so instructors can communicate the value of their courses with various stakeholders.

Despite this importance, the current literature on teaching intercultural competence has been largely limited to materials development and curriculum design, showcasing activities and tasks that can be used in a classroom (Byram et al., 2001; Huber & Reynolds, 2014; Liddicoat, 2011; Wagner et al., 2018). Existing instructional materials draw on a variety of approaches including experiential learning, cooperative learning, and project-based learning (Huber & Reynolds, 2014). Some activities involve role-plays and simulations based on hypothetical intercultural scenarios, while others involve analyses of cultural artifacts such as films, texts, and images. Still others include ethnographic activities in which students are sent to the community to discover cultural practices and the meaning behind them through observations and interviews. While these activities can inform teachers about how to teach intercultural competence, without separate objective measures of learning outcomes, their effectiveness is yet to be known.

Several studies have implemented a pre-post design to document learning outcomes of intercultural training at the university level. Garrette-Rucks (2016) taught intercultural competence to 13 students in a second-semester French course in a U.S. university. Pre-post survey results showed that, after 16 weeks of instruction involving reading, discussion, and discovery of French cultural practices, students' intercultural sensitivity increased. They also overcame stereotypes about French people and culture. In Mu and Yu's (2023) study, 33 Chinese students in a Business English course were guided through intercultural learning processes of noticing, comparing, and reflecting on cultural behaviors using role-plays and other activities. Pre-post survey data revealed a significant improvement in knowledge of cultural distinctions and value systems. Interview and journal data showed that students demonstrated interests in cultural perspectives and products, understood the importance of effective intercultural communication, and developed intercultural awareness. Other studies used virtual reality (VR) technology to develop materials for intercultural training. Using 360-degree VR simulations, Akdere et al. (2021) exmined how students in a U.S. university interacted with their imagined couterparts in Latin America. Survey results revealed participants' increased cultural knowledge and intercultural sensitivity, but there was no increase in ambiguity tolerance and comfort with difference. Finally, in Shadiev et al.'s (2020) study, college students in China and Uzbekistan discussed their local culture using 360-degree videos illustrating local scenes. Pre-post survey results showed increase in cultural knowledge and awareness, attitude, and skills.

As summarized above, several studies used a pre-post design to assess the effects of intercultural training in a classroom. However, measures of learning outcomes are largely confined to ready-made surveys, assessing students' perceived skills and abilities. Very few studies have used a performance-based measure to assess students' actual skills of intercultural interaction. Hence, although existing findings have shown what students think they can do after instruction, they have not revealed what they can actually do. To fill this gap, the present study uses both a survey and performance measure to assess the impact of intercultural training on students' development.

Another gap found in the existing literature relates to approaches to intercultural training and instruction. While previous studies implemented a variety of activities to teach intercultural competence (e.g., role-plays, simulations, image creations, reading and discussion), those activities were mainly restricted to understanding practices of a specific cultural group (e.g., China, Uzbekistan, Latin America, France). What is limited is a culture-generic approach of teaching general skills of intercultural communication that are applicable to wider cultural settings. The present study intends to compensate for this limitation by teaching all-purpose conflict mediation strategies in intercultural settings. Since working across cultures has become the norm, intercultural conflicts occur in everyday situations. Hence, it is critical to learn skills to resolve situations of conflict effectively. This study addresses this important need.

Intercultural Conflict Mediation

According to Wilmot and Hocker (2010), a conflict is "an expressed struggle between at least two independent parties who perceive incompatible goals, scarce resources, and interference from others in achieving their goals" (p. 11). A conflict often occurs between individuals coming from different cultures because of different cultural values and norms. Hence, solving an intercultural conflict is a process of re-negotiating and re-constructing knowledge, norms, and ideologies toward the goal of establishing a common ground.

Ting-Toomey (2012) contends that we need to be equipped with "necessary and sufficient knowledge to deal with culture-based conflict communication issues competently" (p. 279). Core competencies of conflict mediation entail cultural knowledge, attentiveness to the other's assumptions and emotions, constructive communication skills, and flexibility (Ting-Toomey, 2012). Building on these, Jackson (2020) demonstrates several strategies for effective conflict mediation. For example, a conflict mediator needs to look for a common ground among people in conflict and listen to them attentively. While listening, it is important to understand both parties' perspectives without taking one side. Ultimately, a mediator's job is to generate workable solutions that are acceptable to both parties. During the process, a mediator has to be mindful of their language use to show empathy and respect to people in conflict.

The goal of this study is to teach and assess these skills of conflict mediation as a foundation of intercultural competence. The study adopts a one-sample pre-post design by comparing college students' intercultural competence before and after they complete a training on intercultural conflict mediation. The assessment of learning outcomes combines two measures: a survey (MPQ, Van der Zee and Van Oudenhoven, 2000) and a role-play. By combining instruction and assessment, this study investigates how critical components of intercultural competence—perspective-taking, empathy, emotional stability, flexibility, and effective communication—can be taught and assessed using intercultural conflict mediation as a foundation.

Research Questions

1. Does conflict mediation training help improve college students' intercultural competence as assessed using a perception-based survey?
2. Does conflict mediation training help improve college students' intercultural competence as assessed using a performance-based role-play task?

Methods

Participants

Participants were 22 students enrolled in an upper-level course on intercultural communication at a U.S. university (4 male and 18 female students; mean age of 22). There were 10 seniors, eight juniors, one sophomore, and three graduate students. Of 22, five students were international students from China, Taiwan, Germany, and Saudi Arabia, and the rest were Americans. Their length of residence in the U.S.A. ranged from one semester to two years. No American students had lived outside of the U.S.A. for more than a month.

Intercultural Conflict Mediation Training

Conflict mediation training was provided as part of the regular coursework over two class sessions (75 minutes each). The goal of the training was to teach Van Odenhoven and Van der Zee's (2000) five dimensions of intercultural competence defined as follows:

1. Social initiative: Tendency to approach social situations actively and take initiative
2. Cultural empathy: Ability to identify with others' feelings, thoughts, and behavior

3. Open-mindedness: Ability to be open to different values and norms
4. Emotional stability: Ability to remain calm in stressful situations
5. Flexibility: Ability to adjust behavior to new and unknown situations

These dimensions were taught in the context of conflict mediation. *Social initiative* was taught as willingness to step into a conflict between two people with different cultural backgrounds and present a solution. *Cultural empathy* and *open-mindedness* were taught as ability to acknowledge both people' perspectives rooted in different cultural values. *Emotional stability* and *flexibility* were taught as ability to speak calmly and logically while mediating a conflict.

In the first class session, the instructor (the researcher) provided a lecture on how to manage intercultural conflict. She presented Jackson's (2020) conflict mediation strategies with examples (e.g., listen attentively, try to understand both sides of an issue, generate mutually agreeable solutions). After that, students read a scenario illustrating an intercultural conflict situation. They analysed the cultural background of two individuals who are in conflict and discussed how their views and positions might stem from their cultural norms. Then, they watched a two-minute video illustrating the conflict situation. While watching, they were asked to identify the main problem, explain the parties' perspectives, and come up with a solution. Appendix A provides the handout used in the first class session.

The second class session started with a review of the conflict situation. Then, students watched a video illustrating a conflict resolution between a boss and her employee. The students were instructed to watch the video and identify the strategies used by the boss to solve a conflict. Using a video, the instructor presented five conflict mediation strategies, which align with Van Odenhoven and Van der Zee's (2000) five dimensions of intercultural competence as illustrated below:

1. Initiative: Recognizing the problem explicitly and initiating mediation (social initiative)
2. Empathy: Expressing empathy and understanding explicitly (cultural empathy)
3. Perspective-taking: Acknowledging people's perspectives (open-mindedness, flexibility)

4. Solution: Presenting a solution with specific action plans (social initiative)
5. Clarity: Speaking clearly and calmly (emotional stability)

These strategies were presented to the students. After that, students practiced the strategies by role-playing the situation of conflict. They took turns playing the role of a conflict mediator. Then, the instructor provided a rubric reflecting Van Odenhoven and Van der Zee's (2000) framework (see the next section) so students could self-assess their role-play performance. Appendix B presents a handout used in the second class session.

Assessment of Intercultural Competence

The students' intercultural competence was assessed before and after the conflict mediation training to see whether the training had any effect on their intercultural development. Two types of assessment were used: perception-based and performance-based.

Perception-Based Assessment

The perception-based assessment involved administering the multicultural personality questionnaire (MPQ) developed by Van der Zee and Van Oudenhoven (2001). MPQ assesses traits and attitudes that determine typical behaviors in intercultural settings. MPQ is supported by high reliability in a number of studies (Leone et al., 2005). MPQ has 91 Likert-scale items assessing five characteristics of intercultural competence that were targeted during training (see the previous section). Participants were asked to read statements describing these characteristics and selected their answers on a five-point scale ranging from (1) 'totally not applicable to me' to (5) 'completely applicable to me'. Participants completed the questionnaire twice, before and after the instruction, and changes in their responses were compared. Sample items are below:

Social initiative: knows how to act in social settings
Cultural empathy: is able to voice other people's thoughts
Open-mindedness: is fascinated by other people's opinions
Emotional stability: has ups and downs
Flexibility: likes to work on my own

Performance-Based Assessment

The performance-based assessment involved a role-play of intercultural mediation. In order to make the assessment realistic, immersive virtual reality (VR) was used to structure the role-play. Participants first read a scenario describing a conflict between two people with different cultural backgrounds. Then, they watched a 360-degree video illustrating the conflict scene. A professional writer developed a play script based on the scenario. Two theater majors at a U.S. university acted out the script, which was recorded using a VR camera to produce a 360-degree video clip (about 2 minutes in length). The video was loaded into a VR headset (Oculus Go). Participants put on a VR headset to watch two people acting out a conflict in a 360-degree environment. After an argument, the two actors in the video turned to face the participant and then froze. Participants were asked to talk to the people when the video froze. Participants' speech was video-recorded on a computer. Figure 4.1 presents a screenshot of the VR video, while Figure 4.2 presents a participant performing the task.

Figure 4.1: Screenshot of a 360-degree video of a conflict situation (post-test).

Figure 4.2: Picture of a participant performing the mediator role in the conflict mediation task.

Two parallel versions of the VR task were created and used before and after the training to reduce the practice effect. The two conflict situations (see Appendix C) were developed based on input from international students at a university.

Participants' video-recorded speech and demeanors were evaluated using a rubric encompassing five areas: initiative, solution, empathy, perspective-taking and clarity (Table 4.1). These areas correspond to Van Oudenhoven and Van der Zee's (2001) five dimensions of intercultural competence (Table 4.2). The dimension of *social initiative* was reflected in the area of *Initiative,* indicating if participants stepped in to mediate the conflict situation and presented a clear solution that benefits both parties. The dimensions of *cultural empathy* and *open-mindedness* were reflected in the areas of *empathy* and *perspective-taking* (whether participants explicitly acknowledged both parties' perspectives using emphatic language such as "I understand . . ."). *Emotional stability* and *flexibility* were reflected in the areas of clarity, which focused on participants' ability to speak clearly and logically while mediating a conflict.

Table 4.1. Performance assessment rubric (Taguchi, 2023, p. 116).

	Initiative	*Solution*	*Empathy*	*Perspective-taking*	*Clarity*
4	Initiated the mediation actively and showed involvement	Solution was provided with useful details and specifics	Explicitly recognized the addressees' feelings	Explicitly acknowledged perspectives of both parties	Spoke clearly and logically
3	Initiated the mediation but not very active	Solution was provided with some details	Recognized the addressees' feelings but only sparsely	Addressed perspectives of both parties but only sparsely	Spoke somewhat clearly and logically
2	Initiated the mediation but not involved	Solution was provided but it was vague and lacking details	Showed minimum understanding of the addressees' feelings	Addressed the perspective of only one party	Speech was not very clear/logical; used emotional language
1	Did not initiate the mediation	No solution was provided	Did not recognize the addressees' feelings at all	Did not address the addressees' perspectives at all	Speech was disorganized and hard to follow

Using the rubric, two fluent speakers of English rated all the samples. During the initial norming session, both raters analysed the scoring rubric carefully and rated a few samples together. After that, they independently rated remaining samples, and their scores were compared. Interrater reliability was .83. When their ratings differed by two points, the raters discussed their rating to reach a consensus. When there was a discrepancy of one point, an average score was assigned.

Data Analysis

To answer the first research question, participants' responses to the MPQ were tallied separately for the pre- and post-training session and compared. To answer the second research question, a composite score of their conflict mediation performance was compared between the pre- and post-tests. Due to the small sample size, the nonparametric test of the Wilcoxon signed-rank test was used to compare the pre-post difference for both questions.

Results

Results of the Perception-Based Assessment

The first research question asked whether students improve their intercultural competence after the conflict mediation training as assessed with Van Oudenhoven and Van der Zee's (2001) MPQ. Table 4.2 presents descriptive statistics of students' responses to the MPQ before and after the training. The Wilcoxon signed-rank test revealed a significant gain from pre to post-test, Z=2.93, p=.003. The effect size was medium, r=.62.

Table 4.2. Descriptive statistics of MPQ scores.

	Mean	**SD**	**95 % CI [lower**	**upper]**
Pre-MPQ				
Social initiative	55.46	6.26	52.84	58.08
Cultural empathy	68.82	6.79	65.9	81.66
Open-mindedness	67.18	6.79	64.34	71.02
Emotional stability	51.18	3.05	49.91	52.45
Flexibility	52.91	3.57	51.42	54.40
Total score	295.55	19.50	287.40	303.70
Post-MPQ				
Social initiative	51.91	7.50	48.78	55.04
Cultural empathy	69.32	7.95	66.00	75.64
Open-mindedness	67.32	7.09	64.36	70.28
Emotional stability	62.59	3.47	61.14	64.04
Flexibility	54.32	4.11	52.60	56.04
Total score	334.00	21.88	324.90	343.10

Note. N=22. k=91. Each item had a five-point Likert scale. Range for the total score: 91–455.

When individual dimensions are concerned, a significant difference was found in two areas: emotional stability and social initiative. Participants improved on emotional stability after the conflict mediation training, Z=4.11, p=.0001 (r=.88). In contrast, participants' social initiative decreased significantly, Z=-3.55, p=.0001 (r=.76).

Results of the Performance-Based Assessment

The second research question asked whether students improve their intercultural competence after the conflict mediation training as assessed with a role-play task in a virtual environment. Their performance was scored in five areas reflecting Van Oudenhoven and Van der Zee's (2001) five dimensions of intercultural competence (see Table 4.1). Table 4.3 presents descriptive statistics of students' performance scores before and after the training. The Wilcoxon signed-rank test revealed a significant difference between the pre- and post-test total score, Z=.397, p= .0001. The effect size was relatively large (r=0.85), indicating that the participants made a substantial gain after the training.

Table 4.3. Descriptive statistics of performance scores (Taguchi, 2023, 117).

	Mean	**SD**	**95 % CI [lower**	**upper]**
Pre-test				
Initiative	2.61	0.90	2.23	2.97
Solution	1.84	0.86	1.48	2.20
Empathy	1.84	0.93	1.45	2.23
Perspective-taking	2.05	1.08	1.60	2.50
Clarity	2.82	0.99	2.41	3.23
Total score	11.16	3.31	9.78	12.54
Post-test				
Initiative	3.73	0.59	3.48	3.98
Solution	3.61	0.60	3.36	3.86
Empathy	3.30	0.90	2.92	3.68
Perspective-taking	3.57	0.79	3.20	3.86
Clarity	3.72	0.67	3.46	3.98
Total score	17.93	2.68	16.81	19.05

Note. N=22. Each dimension was rated on a four-point scale, ranging from 1 to 4 (see Table 4.2). Range for the total score: 4–20.

All five dimensions showed significant gains from pre- to post-test with slight differences in effect sizes. The largest gain was found in the dimension of Solution, $Z = 3.95$, $p = 0.0001$, $r = 0.84$, followed by the dimension of Initiative, $Z = 3.56$, $p = 0.0001$, $r = 0.76$. The dimensions of Empathy ($Z = 3.49$, $p = 0.0001$, $r = 0.74$) and Perspective-taking ($Z=3.48$, $p = 0.0001$, $r = 0.74$) showed similar gains. The dimension with least gain was found in Clarity, $Z = 3.23$, $p = 0.001$, $r = 0.69$.

At pre-test, the participants' solution typically acknowledged the concerns of only one party (not both). Their solution was also somewhat lacking details or concrete plans (mean=1.84). The score almost doubled at post-test (mean=3.61). The following excerpts from Participant 14 illustrate this dramatic improvement. The pre-test scenario was about a German student and a Japanese student having an argument over class participation (see Appendix C). The German student wants the Japanese student to contribute more to a group discussion, while the Japanese student prefers to remain quiet and take notes. At pre-test, Participant 14 said that both students should be more aware of each other's expectations coming from their previous experience, but did not provide concrete means for achieving this (Excerpt 1). Quality of a solution improved after the training. The post-test situation illustrated a conflict between an American student (Andrew) who is often late for a group project meeting and a Japanese student (Mika) who wants to start a meeting on time. Participant 14 presented a concrete solution directed to both people, along with a convincing justification as to why the solution is beneficial for them (Excerpt 2).

(1) Participant 14, pre-test
So, I think with that in mind is– it is a better foundation to– [pause] have a better class discussion where we are– where you guys are more level and aware of what each expects of each other while keeping in mind what people are used to and what they are most comfortable with.

(2) Participant 14, post-test
So, Andrew, would you consider possibly, um, making time or setting alarms maybe with, um, when class is over so you know when to meet with your four group members, or your three group members, so that you guys can have one meeting on time together to establish who is doing what. And then from there, Mika, would it be okay if instead of meeting multiple times altogether to do each task that has already been assigned, maybe after the initial meeting where you all know what you're doing, you can work from home, or just separately in general, to get what you need to be done so Andrew doesn't feel like he has to be at every single meeting that's hard for his schedule.

Along with the area of Solution, participants showed a large gain in Initiative. At pre-test, they were less involved in the conflict situation, taking on an observer role and appearing detached from the situation. This is illustrated in Excerpt 3 (pre-test). When starting a mediation, Participant 16 objectively presented her observation by using the pronoun "I". However, at post-test (Excerpt 4), she switched to the pronoun "we" to situate herself as part of the group. By using the inclusive "we", it became clear that finding a solution is a shared goal among people involved, including herself. The way she started out the mediation ("we can all stand to take a deep breath") also indicates her involvement and initiative in mediating the conflict.

(3) Participant 16, pre-test
Um well if the assignment is to discuss the event and opinions on it I do think it can be valuable to do that especially um outside perspectives can help to both build empathy and understand history as it relates to the entire world.

(4) Participant 16, post-test
Um I think that we can all stand to take a deep breath and take a second. We don't necessarily need to exclude someone from the group. Um I think there's a way that we can find a solution that works for everyone.

In the area of Empathy, the participants' gains were notable in their use of explicit emphatic expressions. For example, Participant 21 received a score of 1 for Empathy at pre-test, but at post-test she used expressions such as "I understand" to show empathy to the students in conflict, leading to a full score of 4 at post-test (Excerpt 5). Critically, the empathy was directed to both parties, acknowledging the value of both perspectives, which also contributed to her gains in the area of Perspective-taking.

(5) Participant 21, post-test
And I understand from your perspective, Mika, that you value being on-time and working as a group altogether, and a benefit of that is that you really care about each person in your group. As well as I understand your point, Andrew, that you, even though you come in late sometimes, you still know what your responsibilities are for the group project and you know that you're going to do them on-time.

Smaller gains found in Clarity compared with other areas could be that the participants were relatively competent in this area before the training, achieving the highest mean (2.82) among all five areas. Since

Clarity was assessed on the general area of communication (i.e., ability to speak clearly and logically without emotional language use), not specific to intercultural competence, the participants were probably already competent in this area, leaving less room to improve compared with other areas.

Discussion

This study, which was conducted as part of the undergraduate course on intercultural communication, developed a training on intercultural conflict mediation and assessed the effectiveness of the training. Training and assessment tasks were developed based on Van Oudenhoven and Van der Zee's (2001) five dimensions of intercultural competence. *Social initiative* addresses willingness to step in and mediate a conflict actively, while *cultural empathy*, *flexibility*, and *open-mindedness* are defined as understanding others' feelings and acknowledging perspectives of all parties involved. Finally, *emotional stability* refers to the ability to speak clearly and logically even in a stressful conflict situation.

Results showed that students improved their intercultural competence after the training sessions. There was a significant gain in both students' survey responses and conflict mediation performance in a virtual intercultural setting (total scores). The findings indicate that the domain of intercultural conflict mediation can be used effectively to improve students' intercultural competence. The ability to mediate intercultural conflicts draws on several core elements of intercultural competence. Since a conflict situation is context-specific, mediators need to have culturally-relevant knowledge in conflict behavior differences, increase self-awareness and other-awareness of cultural norms underlying the conflict, acknowledge others' perspectives and feelings, and manage emotional challenges with competent communication skills (Ting-Toomey, 2012). By practicing these aspects of conflict mediation, students can develop intercultural competence in a classroom. The present findings go beyond the existing studies that documented the effectiveness of instruction using perception-based data alone (e.g., survey responses, reflection data) (Akdere et al., 2021; Garrette-Rucks, 2016; Mu & Yu, 2023; Shadiev et al., 2020). Students' intercultural performance can also improve as a result of focused training.

The findings expand the scope of the current literature on teaching intercultural competence. Beyond already-existing approaches and materials (Liddicoat, 2011; Wagner et al., 2018), teachers can introduce conflict mediation as a critical area of intercultural management and teach Jackson's (2020) conflict mediation strategies to manage a conflict. This study adapted Jackson's (2020) strategies: listening emphatically, addressing both sides of an argument, and guiding through workable solutions and communicating them effectively. Activities and tasks targeting these strategies helped to boost students' intercultural competence even in a relatively small amount of time (two class sessions).

While the effectiveness of conflict mediation activities was evident in overall scores, when we turn to individual areas, results are less conclusive. Among five areas assessed with the survey, only one area—emotional stability—showed a significant improvement. Emotional stability refers to the ability to stay calm even in a stressful situation. It is assessed with survey items reflecting emotional states (e.g., feeling nervous) and personality traits (e.g., being afraid of failing, being able to function in unfamiliar settings). It is possible that conflict situations presented during training gave participants exposure to stressful settings. Tools given to manage such an intense setting, along with step-by-step practice on how to manage the setting, probably helped them remain stable under pressure. The survey also assessed one's ability to manage a problematic situation as shown in statements like "considers problems as solvable" and "has a solution for every problem". Since a major part of the conflict mediation practice was finding a compelling solution, it is possible that the training promoted participants' confidence in problem-solving, leading to increased scores on the dimension of emotional stability.

In contrast, the dimension of social initiative declined significantly after the training. It is puzzling why this particular aspect regressed. Data on participants' reasoning behind their responses (e.g., interview) is necessary to explore this unexpected finding, which, unfortunately, this study did not collect. Yet, one important thing to note is that the survey items addressing this dimension were concentrated around initiating contacts with others and being social (e.g., "makes contacts easily", "is inclined to speak out", "easily approaches other people", "knows how to act in social settings"). Since this dimension was about being proactive in social settings, it was largely unrelated to the conflict mediation training that taught how to take initiative in mediating a specific argument. Hence, in essence, it is not unsurprising that the students did not show a gain in the general area of social initiative.

Supporting this interpretation, the performance data (virtual role-play) revealed a significant gain on the assessment criterion of Initiative, approaching the perfect score after the training (3.74 out of 4.00). After the training, the students were able to initiate the mediation actively and signaled their involvement, as indicated in their use of in-group language (e.g., inclusive "we", suggestions marked with "Let's"). These strategies of Initiative were taught during the training sessions. Hence, we can say that the students gained in the precise area of initiative addressed during training but not in social initiative in general. This discrepancy between the two data sets indicates that intercultural training targeting a particular area (i.e., conflict mediation) may not sufficiently cover all constructs of intercultural competence. Students can improve on certain skills and strategies they learned and they can demonstrate their improvement in a similar task, as shown in significant gains found across all five criteria of performance data. Yet, their learning may not easily transfer to broader and more general areas of intercultural competence, as evidenced in a significant gain found in only one area (emotional stability) in the survey data.

Limitations and Future Directions

There are several limitations in this study, which need to be addressed in future research. Given a small sample size and a relatively homogenous population (students at a U.S. university), generalizability of the present findings should be examined in a future study involving a larger population of diverse participant nationalities, educational settings, and age groups. The narrow focus on the instructional topic (i.e., intercultural conflict mediation) can be expanded in future research to address wider topics including intercultural collaboration, teamwork, and cultural adjustments. When deciding on a topic, it is critical to connect core elements of intercultural competence to skills and knowledge enhanced using the topic so instruction is grounded on theories. Specifically, as found in the current results (i.e., lack of gains in the Initiative dimension of the MPQ), the theoretical construct of intercultural competence is often broad and may not align perfectly with specific skills and knowledge of intercultural competence practiced in class. Hence, it is important that teachers and researchers carefully examine the alignment between the theoretical constructs and activities/tasks that intend to tap on the constructs. Finally, multiple methods used to assess instructional outcomes were found useful in this study since they revealed complementary data, and this practice should continue in the future. The confounding results coming from the perception and performance-based assessment can inform teachers as they reflect on what aspects of intercultural competence benefit from instruction and what aspects do not. While this study did not collect data on students' accounts, future research can solicit student feedback to improve instruction.

In conclusion, intercultural competence is an invaluable asset in the 21st century. Teachers across disciplines (e.g., linguistics, foreign languages, communication studies, psychology, and business) have responsibility in educating the next generation who can navigate intercultural settings skillfully. Researchers should commit to this global mission and continue to explore effective approaches and materials for instructional intercultural learning.

Appendix A: Conflict Mediation Training, Session 1 Handout

Intercultural conflict occurs because of a number of reasons including: different expectations, uncertainty about the other's way of thinking and behaving, (non)linguistic barriers, face needs, and different perceptions of a conflict. Jackson (Chapter 9) provides six suggestions for managing intercultural conflict situations:

1. Be aware of your own goals and those of others. Look for **common grounds** or overlapping between your aims and those of the other person.
2. **Listen attentively** before responding. Conflicts can escalate when we do not listen to each other. Don't be emotional. Try to be patient and attend to what others are saying.
3. When misunderstandings and conflict arise, try to **understand both sides of an issue**, and to be **open to different perspectives**. Together, you and the other people may synthesize your ideas and come up with a creative third perspective or resolution that is mutually acceptable.
4. Be sensitive to **face and identity needs**. Make use of positive facework strategies and demonstrate respect for the other person's identities and position.
5. Avoid personal attacks, offensive or abusive language, name calling, and emotional overstatements in conflict situations.
6. Generate possible solutions to the conflict instead of focusing on the difficulties. **Be proactive.** Try to negotiate **a solution that is mutually acceptable**.

Keep these suggestions in mind when you look at a sample intercultural conflict situation.

This situation reflects a problem between two Marketing Directors at an international corporation. Mateo, a Mexican man, has been transferred to the company's branch in New York to help Sarah, the Director there. Read the background and perspectives of Mateo and Sarah.

****

Background: Mateo has been working in his company in Mexico City for five years. His understanding of market patterns has led the company to a strong success, with increasing profits and an brand familiarity among her local population. Corporate has asked Mateo to transfer to New York City where profits have begun to stay the same despite different ideas attempted by Sarah, the local Director. Sarah has worked in New York City for 10 years and is resistant to foreign ideas.

Mateo's perspective: I am young in the field. I have only been working for five years in a company in Mexico City since graduating from a university with business major. But I have had great successes and my company's management has recognized this. The company wants me to keep doing what I have been doing in the past, so I don't see a reason to change or adapt very much. I know New York will be very new and I am excited for the different culture, but this does not mean that I need to change my work strategy. Part of what makes my success is separating work from home. By keeping my ability to relax at home, I can perform at my very best at work. Sarah doesn't understand this. She works late most days even though I leave once the day has ended. She has also begun to call me at home. Sometimes I ignore these calls so I can stay relaxed.

Sarah's perspective: New York is my home. I was born and raised here, and I understand the culture here very well. I have been working in advertising for my entire career and the company has always had high profits in my career. We are going through a period when profits are remaining the same, but this is not due to my work; this is simply what happens from time to time. The company has brought in a Mexican man, Mateo, who has never left her country before. I do not understand how he is supposed to help. I am doing everything I can to increase profits, and that will mean working more hours than normal. Sometimes this is required from the company to achieve better results. Mateo has not been willing to do this, and I don't think he understands that this is required in New York. I need him to take her new position as seriously as I do.

****

Part 1 Answer the following questions.

1. Who are they? Where are they from? What roles do they play? What do they have as a common goal?
2. What are Mateo and Sarah's perspective toward work? How are their perspectives related to their goals? Do you think their cultural backgrounds influence their perspectives? How?

Mateo's perspective	**Sarah's perspective**

3. Whose perspective do you agree with, Mateo or Sarah? Why?
4. Take the perspective you don't agree with and explain why. Think about the perspective from the person's standpoint and list 2–3 benefits of this perspective.

Part 2 Watch a video about a conflict between Mateo and Sarah and answer the questions.

1. What was the main problem portrayed in the video? Describe the issue objectively.
2. Identify Mateo's feelings and his perspective. Explain why his perspective makes sense.
3. Identify Sarah's feelings and her perspective. Explain why her perspective makes sense.
4. What are some possible solutions to the problem?

Appendix B: Conflict Mediation Training, Session 2 Handout

Part 1

Watch a video between a boss and her employer on a conflict. Identify the strategies below used by Stacy (employer) while mediating a conflict/problem with Brandon (employee).

1. Recognizing the problem explicitly
2. Acknowledging people's perspectives; Expressing empathy & understanding
3. Specifying the goal of the talk
4. Introducing a solution
5. Adding specific details to the solution so it becomes achievable
6. Presenting the immediate action plan toward a solution
7. Encouraging and assuring positive outcomes

Part 2

1. Review the intercultural conflict situation from last class (Mateo & Sarah). Work with a partner and discuss the points below.
   - o Mateo and Sarah's backgrounds
   - o Focal issue in the conflict (details)
   - o Mateo's perspective and its strengths
   - o Sarah's perspective and its strengths
   - o Common goals
2. Watch a video illustrating the conflict between Mateo and Sarah. Come up with a solution that can benefit both parties. Share your solution with your partner.

   ____

   ____

3. Here is the end of the video. Continue the dialogue with your turn. What do you say to Mateo and Sarah? <u>Incorporate the strategies you identified in Part 1.</u>

   MATEO: It does not matter, Sarah! I do everything I need to do during the day. If there was a big problem at night, I would fix the problem. But the video is not a big problem. You are making this sound like a big problem, but it is not.

SARAH: This will lead to bigger problems. When you are not willing to work more often, you are making the problem worse.

MATEO: No I am not! You work too often. You do not need to fix every problem when it happens. Some problems can wait! This video can wait!

SARAH: No, Mateo! This cannot wait!

YOU: ____

____

____

Part 3 Let's role play the scene in group of three (Mateo, Sarah, and you—mediator). Mateo and Sarah responds to the mediator.

Part 4 Self-evaluate your response using the rubrics below. Which areas are you competent in? Which areas do you need to work further?

	Initiative	**Solution**	**Empathy**	**Perspective-taking**	**Clarity**
4	Initiated the mediation actively and enthusiastically	Solution was provided with useful details and specifics	Explicitly recognized the addressees' feelings	Explicitly acknowledged perspectives of both parties	Spoke clearly, logically, and calmly
3	Initiated the mediation but not very active	Solution was provided with some details	Recognized the addressees' feelings but only sparsely	Addressed perspectives of both parties but only sparsely	Spoke somewhat clearly, logically, and calmly
2	Initiated the mediation but not involved	Solution was provided but it was vague lacking details	Showed minimum understanding of the addressees' feelings	Addressed perspective of only one party	Speech was not very clear/ logical; used emotional language
1	Did not initiate the mediation	No solution was provided	Did not recognize the addressees' feelings at all	Did not address the addressees' perspectives at all	Speech was disorganized, hard to follow; too emotional

Appendix C: Performance-based Assessment Task Scenarios

Pre-test

Misako is taking a class in European history at an international university in Japan. The class watched a video on the fall of the Berlin Wall in 1989. After that, Misako is placed in a group with Kat, a German student. The professor asked the group to discuss the video. Misako doesn't want to say anything because she is not used to discussing ideas in class. In Japanese classes, students just listen and take notes. Kat is frustrated with Misako's silence because he wants to know what Misako thinks about the video.

Post-test

Mika is a Japanese student studying information technology at an international university in Japan. There are many group projects in the class. Mika has been placed into a group with Andrew, an American student from New York City. The group hasn't made progress on their assignment. Andrew is often late for group meetings. Mika thinks he is not responsible enough for the project. Andrew, on the other hand, thinks that it is OK to be late for meetings as long as he completes the work assigned to him.

References

Akdere, Mesut, Acheson, Kris & Jiang, Yeling. 2021. An examination of the effectiveness of virtual reality technology for intercultural competence and development. *International Journal of Intercultural Relations*, 82, 109–120.

Alghizzi, Talal Musaed & Alshahrani, Tahani Munahi. 2022. An investigation of multicultural personality traits of EFL learners in English as a medium of instruction setting: A case of Saudi Arabia. *Frontiers Psychology*, 13.

Byram, Michael. 1997. *Teaching and assessing intercultural communicative competence.* Philadelphia: Multilingual Matters.

Byram, Michael, Nichols, Adam & Stevens, David. 2001. *Developing intercultural competence in practice.* Bristol, Blue Ridge Summit: Multilingual Matters.

Deardorff, Darla K. 2006. Identification and assessment of intercultural competence as a student outcome of internalization. *Journal of Studies in International Education*, 10, 241–266.

Dervin, Fred. 2006. Quality in intercultural education: The development of proteophilic competence. *EU-Bildung 2010, Regionalveranstaltung fur Wien, Niederösterreich und Burgenland. BM: BWK, Stadtschulrat fur Wien,* 75–87.

Fantini, Aqeel. 2006. Exploring and assessing intercultural competence. Retrieved February 15, 2012, from <https://digitalcollections.sit.edu/cgi/viewcontent.cgi?article=100&context=worldlearning_publications>

Garrett-Rucks, Paula. 2016. *Intercultural competence in instructed language learning: Bridging theory and practice.* Charlotte, NC: IAP-Information Age Publishing Inc.

Griffith, Richard L., Wolfeld, Leah, Armon, Brigitte K., Rios, Joseph & Liu Ou Lydia. 2016. *Assessing intercultural competence in higher education: Existing research and future directions*. ETS.

Hocker, Joyce L. & Wilmot William W. 2010. *Interpersonal conflict.* New York: McGraw-Hill.

Huber, Josef & Reynolds, Christopher. 2014. *Developing intercultural competence through education.* Council of Europe Publishing.

INCA, LdVII. 2004. Intercultural Competence Assessment (INCA). Retrieved on January 10, 2022 from <www.incaproject.org>

International Education Exchange (IIE). 2021. *Open Doors 2021: Report on international educational exchange.* New York City, NY, United States. IIE.

Jackson, Jane. 2020. *Introducing language and intercultural communication.* London/New York: Routledge.

Leone L, Van der Zee KI, Van Oudenhoven JP, Perugini M, Ercolani AP. 2005. The cross-cultural generalizability and validity of the Multicultural Personality Questionnaire. *Personality and Individual Differences, 38*(6), 1449–1462.

Leong, Chang Hoong. 2007. Predictive validity of the multicultural personality questionnaire: A longitudinal study on the socio-psychological adaptation of Asian undergraduates who took part in a study-abroad program. *International Journal of Intercultural Relations*, 31, 545–559.

Leung, Kwok, Ang, Soon & Tan, Mei Ling. 2014. Intercultural competence. *Annual Review of Organizational Psychology and Organizational Behavior*, 1, 489–519.

Liddicoat, Anthony J. 2011. Language teaching and learning from an intercultural perspective. In Eli Hinkel (ed.) *Handbook of research in second language teaching and learning* (Vol. 2). London/ New York: Routledge , 837–855.

Mu, Yuting & Yu, Baohua. 2023. Developing intercultural competence in college business English students: A study of innovative teaching in China. *International Journal of Intercultural Relations*, 92, 1–12.

Rogers, Alice. 2021. *Internationalizing the campus at home.* IIE.

Shadiev, Rustam, Wang, Xueying & Huang Yueh Min. 2020. Promoting intercultural competence in a learning activity supported by virtual reality technology. *International Review of Research in Open and Distributed Learning*, 21, 157–174.

Spitzberg, B. H., & Chagnon, G. (2009). Conceptualizing intercultural communication competence. In D. K. Deadorff (Ed.), *The SAGE handbook of intercultural competence* (pp. 2–52). Thousand Oaks, CA: Sage.

Taguchi, Naoko. 2023. Using immersive virtual reality for the assessment of intercultual conflict mediation. *Language Learning & Technology*, 27/3, 108–126.

Ting-Toomey, Stella. 2012. Understanding intercultural conflict competence: Multiple theoretical insights. In Jane Jackson (ed.) *The Routledge handbook of language and intercultural communication*. London/New York: Routledge, 279–295.

Van der Zee, Karen. I. & Van Oudenhoven, Jan Pieter. 2000. The multicultural personality questionnaire: A multidimensional instrument of multicultural effectiveness. *European Journal of Personality*, 14/4, 291–309.

Van der Zee, Karen I. & Van Oudenhoven, Jan Pieter. 2002. Predicting multicultural effectiveness of international students: The multicultural personality questionnaire. *International Journal of Intercultural Relations*, 26, 679–694.

Van der Zee, Karen I. & Van Oudenhoven, Jan Pieter. 2003. Study of the adjustment of Western expatriates in Taiwan ROC with the multicultural personality questionnaire. *Asian Journal of Social Psychology*, 6, 159–170.

Wagner, Manuela, Perugini, Dorie Conlon & Byram, Michael. 2018. *Teaching intercultural competence across the age range: Theory and practice*. Bristol, Blue Ridge Summit: Multilingual Matters.

Esther Usó-Juan and Alicia Martínez-Flor

How Do Advanced EFL Learners Apply Refusal Strategies? Monitoring Refusal Production and Perceptions of Pragmatic Instruction

Introduction

Successful communication in a target language (TL) goes beyond mere grammatical correctness and lexical accuracy; it requires an intricate understanding of pragmatics. Pragmatic competence denotes the ability to understand and apply language within various social contexts, encompassing not only literal word meanings but also implied connotations, intentions, and sociocultural norms associated with language use (Taguchi, 2011). Bardovi-Harlig and Mahan-Taylor (2003) highlight notable disparities in pragmatics among language learners, irrespective of their first language (L1) background or proficiency level, when explicit instruction is lacking. This variability in pragmatic proficiency is often attributed to pragmatic failure, which encompasses various challenges learners face in using language appropriately for communicative purposes. Pragmatic failure, as delineated by Thomas (1983), occurs when there are discrepancies between learners' intended meaning and their linguistic expression, leading to hindered communication and unintended outcomes. One salient aspect of pragmatic failure is negative transfer, wherein learners inadvertently apply the pragmatic norms of their L1 to the TL, resulting in communication strategies that may prove unsuitable or inefficient in achieving communicative goals (Kasper, 1992).

Even advanced-level language learners may exhibit discrepant levels of pragmatic competence despite their linguistic proficiency

(Bardovi-Harlig & Harford, 1990; Codina, 2013). Nonetheless, studies addressing the development of pragmatics among advanced second/foreign language (L2) learners remain relatively scarce in the existing literature (Taguchi, 2017; Xiao, 2018). Expanding upon this unexplored area concerning advanced pragmatic competence, this chapter aims to contribute to the field of interlanguage pragmatics (ILP). Specifically, it seeks to delve into the application of refusal strategies among advanced English as a Foreign Language (EFL) learners both prior to and following instruction in pragmatics. Furthermore, the study explores learners' perceptions of such instructional intervention. The choice to focus on refusal strategies in this investigation is based on the intricate nature of refusals. This speech act involves discretely balancing one's assertion of autonomy with the preservation of interpersonal relationships and social harmony (Alcón-Soler & Guzmán, 2013). A direct refusal might come across as confrontational, whereas an excessively indirect approach risks ambiguity or misunderstanding. Consequently, instruction on refusal strategies for advanced EFL learners is not only relevant but also necessary for their communicative success within diverse cultural and social contexts. Hence, the chapter starts with a review of instructional pragmatics research on refusals to contextualise the study and identify gaps. Subsequently, it outlines the methodological framework, presents and discusses results, and concludes with a synthesis of findings, accompanied by reflections on study limitations.

Theoretical Background

Instructional Research on Refusals: Methodological Features

Refusals fall under the classification of commissive acts as described by Searle (1976) because they commit the refuser to (not) performing an action. Within conversational dynamics, refusals form part of adjacency pairs, following requests, invitations, suggestions or offers. They contrast acceptance or agreement, posing a threat to the listener's face by contradicting expectations, often necessitating indirect strategies with mitigating techniques and temporal delays within and across conversational turns. Refusals are intricately involved in negotiation processes, employing face-saving maneuvers to mitigate conflicts (Gass & Houck, 1999). They serve multiple functions: avoiding offense, negotiating resolutions, and preserving participants' face (Eslami, 2010). Salazar et al. (2009) present a taxonomy of refusal strategies, drawing from Beebe et al.'s (1990) coding system, divided into semantic formulas and adjuncts. Semantic formulas encompass direct (bluntness, negation of proposition) and indirect strategies (plain indirect, reason/explanation, regret/apology, alternative, disagreement/dissuasion/criticism, statement of principle/philosophy, avoidance). Adjuncts include expressions such as positive opinion, willingness, gratitude, agreement, and solidarity/empathy, which accompany refusals without constituting refusals themselves.

Given the complexity and cultural variations of refusal speech acts, pragmatic instruction is essential to assist learners in navigating these complexities. Many studies on pragmatic intervention incorporate the essential components for pragmatic development, namely authentic input, output opportunities, and feedback mechanisms (Martínez-Flor & Usó-Juan, 2020). These studies also employ various pedagogical strategies that include: (i) consciousness-raising dimensions, (ii) cultural issues, (iii) discursive elements, (iv) explicit metapragmatic explanations, (v) implicit-based techniques, and (vi) audiovisual-based activities. These salient methodological aspects are subsequently elaborated upon when teaching refusals.

The first methodological feature suggests incorporating consciousness-raising aspects for the development of refusals (Farrokhi & Atashian, 2012; Usó-Juan, 2013; Flores-Salgado & Halenko, 2022). For instance, Flores-Salgado and Halenko (2022) investigated the impact of explicit instruction on learners' production and perception of refusal strategies. Their study included an experimental and a control group of lower-intermediate English learners. The experimental group received ten hours of explicit instruction based on Usó-Juan's (2010) five-step approach: L1 exploration, L2 exploration, awareness-raising, language practice, and learner feedback. Results showed significant improvements in pragmalinguistic skills for the experimental group, including producing a greater variety of refusals, distinguishing between direct and indirect refusal situations, and using mitigated indirectness more effectively. They also demonstrated a heightened awareness of sociopragmatic aspects in different communicative contexts.

The second instructional aspect highlights the importance of focusing on cultural issues to improve the learning of appropriate refusal strategies. Following task-based principles, Bacelar Da Silva (2003) investigated the effects of explicit instruction on refusal production among low-intermediate English learners. The treatment session lasted fifty-five minutes and comprised three stages. Initially, learners engaged in awareness-raising activities, viewing video segments depicting invitation/refusal scenarios from the sitcom *Friends* and completing cross-cultural awareness exercises. Next, an inductive presentation clarified semantic formulas and modifiers. The final phase involved learners planning and executing role-plays, followed by comprehensive corrective feedback. In contrast, the control group participated in a video-based activity without explicit instruction on refusals. Results showed improved pragmatic proficiency among learners in formulating refusals, along with increased awareness of significant cultural disparities between the American culture depicted in the selected scenes and tasks, and the learners' own culture.

The third methodological aspect supports the inclusion of discursive elements to explore the conversational dynamics of refusals, enhancing learners' understanding of how this speech act is collaboratively constructed. Alcón-Soler and Guzmán (2013) conducted a study using scenes from the TV series *Stargate* for a structured four-step intervention across six two-hour sessions. The treatment involved: (i) identifying refusal instances, (ii) explaining speech act sets, (iii) recognising and comprehending refusal sequences, and (iv) actively negotiating learners' use of refusals. Post-instructional improvements were observed in learners' awareness and production of appropriate refusals. Additionally, learners showed increased ability to navigate the non-compliant nature of refusals during extended conversational exchanges and to sequence them within their discourse turns.

The fourth instructional aspect suggests that explicit instruction, including metapragmatic explanations followed by focused practice, enhances the acquisition of refusals in instructional settings (Farahian et al., 2012; Farrokhi & Atashian, 2012; Haghighi et al., 2019; Ling-li & Wannaruk, 2010; Shirinbakhsh et al., 2016). For example, Farahian et al. (2012) assessed the impact of explicit instruction on intermediate English learners' proficiency in executing refusals, using a control group design. The intervention entailed: (i) teaching the function and contextual usage of refusals, (ii) exposing learners to authentic refusal models, (iii) structuring exercises for formulating refusals, (iv) integrating refusals into communicative activities, and (v) providing corrective feedback. Significant improvements in refusal skills were observed immediately and two weeks post-instruction in the experimental group compared to the control group. Similarly, Haghighi et al. (2019) found that integrating metapragmatic explanations within inductive teaching surpassed deductive methods for teaching refusal strategies to intermediate EFL learners. In their study, they compared the effectiveness of the flipped classroom model with the conventional approach in teaching refusals.

The fifth methodological approach involves using implicit-based techniques. Ahmadian (2020) compared the effectiveness of explicit and implicit teaching methods for learning refusal strategies among upper-intermediate EFL learners. Participants received twelve hours of refusal-focused instruction, with groups assigned to explicit, implicit, and control conditions. The explicit group received detailed descriptions, examples, and feedback, while the implicit group received input enhancement and recasts (i.e. confirmation checks). The control group had no refusal-related activities. Results indicated notable enhancements in both the production and comprehension of refusal strategies across the instructional groups, with explicit instruction demonstrating a marginally superior effectiveness. However, implicit instruction also had beneficial effects, sustained in both groups during a delayed post-test two months later.

Finally, the sixth methodological aspect involves the efficacy of employing audiovisual materials like TV series (Bacelar Da Silva, 2003; Alcón-Soler & Guzmán, 2013) or film data (Usó-Juan, 2013) for pragmatics-focused instruction. For example, Usó-Juan (2013) assessed the efficacy of teaching refusal strategies to lower-intermediate EFL learners. The intervention comprised three two-hour sessions, encompassing six stages. The initial two phases introduced foundational pragmatics concepts and analysed L1 refusal data. The next two stages provided learners with explicit metapragmatic insights into refusals using film data from *A Walk to Remember*. The final stages afforded learners opportunities to practice refusals and receive feedback. Post-instructional analysis revealed significant improvements in learners' ability to produce diverse refusal strategies adeptly applied across varying social scenarios.

Aim of the Study

The literature reviewed in the previous section has underscored the effectiveness of diverse teaching frameworks and methodological features in the teaching of refusal strategies within instructional contexts. However, it is pertinent to note that the scope of these studies has been limited to learners at low-intermediate, intermediate, or upper-intermediate levels. This gap in research reveals the absence of interventional studies targeting learners at advanced proficiency levels. Building on Taguchi's (2017) recognition of this underexplored domain concerning advanced pragmatic competence, this study seeks to contribute to the field of ILP by providing a comprehensive investigation into the pedagogy of teaching refusal strategies to advanced EFL learners.

The primary aim of this study is to examine how advanced EFL learners apply refusal strategies within the framework of pragmatic instruction. By monitoring the production of refusals, as well as exploring the learners' perceptions of the instructional approach, this research seeks to shed light on the intricate dynamics of refusal communication among advanced language learners. The following research questions (RQs) guide this investigation:

RQ1: Is there a difference in refusal production, considering social status and social distance, between the advanced EFL learners in the experimental group and those in the control group?

RQ2: How do advanced EFL learners in the experimental group perceive the pragmatics training aimed at learning refusals?

Method

Participants

The study involved a final cohort of 38 Spanish-speaking EFL learners, averaging 21.3 years in age, selected from intact classes based on demonstrated advanced proficiency in English. 23 participants were excluded due to insufficient English proficiency (n=10), non-compliance (n=2), or incomplete data (n=11). These individuals were enrolled in an English major program at a university in Spain and were categorised into two distinct groups for comparative analysis: an experimental group comprising 17 learners and a control group consisting of 21 learners.

The experimental group underwent a structured six-hour intervention across three weeks aimed at enhancing proficiency in English refusals, seamlessly integrated into an academic course exploring fields such as Law, Tourism, and Medicine. Guiding this group was one of the researchers, who brought her expertise in pragmatics-centered pedagogy. Conversely, the control group received standard EFL instruction as part of a general English course, taught by an instructor specialising in English linguistics rather than pragmatics. Before the study began, all students provided written consent to voluntarily participate. The research adhered to the ethical standards of the Universitat Jaume I's Ethics Committee, receiving approval on 4th April 2022 (Project Reference: CD/24/2022).

Data Collection Instruments

The study employed a pre-test post-test design, incorporating a control group, to evaluate the effectiveness of the instructional method. It assessed observed changes within and between the experimental and control groups. Three research instruments were employed: (i) an English proficiency test to establish learners' advanced English proficiency, (ii) a pre-test and a post-test to measure learners' pragmatic production of refusals, and (iii) a perception questionnaire for the experimental group to evaluate their perceptions of and motivation towards pragmatics instruction.

English Proficiency Test

At the outset of the study, all participants took a standardised placement test (UCLES, 2001) to determine their advanced proficiency level corresponding to C1 on the Common European Framework of Reference for Languages (CEFR) scale. This comprehensive test incorporated cloze and multiple-choice assessments, integrating evaluations of grammar, vocabulary, and pragmatics.

Pre-test and Post-test

A written Discourse Completion Test (DCT) was used to gather data at both the pre-test stage (one week before the instructional treatment) and the post-test stage (one week after the instructional treatment). The DCT consisted of four scenarios prompting learners to formulate responses in the form of refusals to requests across diverse situations (Martínez-Flor & Usó-Juan, 2011). Learners were instructed to enact refusal behaviours assuming the role of university students and responding as they would naturally in analogous situations. These scenarios were situated within contexts familiar to the learners: the university setting (situations 1, 3, and 4) or at the cinema (situation 2). Additionally, the scenarios were crafted to account for the social status between the person making the request and the one refusing, as well as the social closeness or distance between them (Brown & Levinson, 1987). Specifically, the social status of the requester was represented with two values: low (scenarios 1 and 4) and high (scenarios 2 and 3). Similarly, the social distance between the individuals involved was categorised into two levels: acquaintances (scenarios 1 and 3) and strangers (scenarios 2 and 4). For further details, Table 5.1 provides an overview of the refusal scenarios.

Table 5.1. Refusal scenarios included in the DCT (adapted from: Martínez-Flor & Usó-Juan, 2011).

Scenarios	**Social Status**	**Social Distance**
Situation 1. A 4th-year student refuses to participate in an interview for a class project with a 1st-year student.	low	acquaintance
Situation 2. A student refuses to sell his/her cinema ticket to a well-dress middle-aged man.	high	stranger
Situation 3. A student refuses to help his/her lecturer carry some books to his/her office.	high	acquaintance
Situation 4. A graduate student refuses to sign for a political cause for an unfamiliar undergraduate student.	low	stranger

Perception Questionnaire

Following the post-test, learners in the experimental group completed a questionnaire designed to evaluate their perceptions of the pragmatic instruction. Using a 4-point Likert scale (1=disliked; 2=neutral; 3= liked; 4=strongly liked), participants rated three key aspects: (i) overall satisfaction with the lessons, (ii) effectiveness of audiovisual materials in learning pragmatics and cultural nuances, and (iii) enjoyment of analysing audiovisual scenes. The questionnaire encouraged learners to provide justifications for their ratings, allowing for deeper insights into their perspectives. It also included an open-ended query prompting participants to elaborate on enjoyable activities and suggest enhancements for the instructional approach. To ensure that responses were as unbiased as possible, participants were assured that their feedback was crucial for improving the instructional approach and would be used solely for research purposes. By combining structured Likert scale responses with qualitative feedback, the questionnaire aimed to comprehensively capture participants' viewpoints and experiences.

Instructional Treatment

The instructional treatment administered to the experimental group followed the structure of the one devised by Usó-Juan and Martínez-Flor (2022) to enhance learners' proficiency in handling refusals at a discourse level. This structured treatment unfolded across three distinct two-hour sessions, delineated into three stages: pre-watching, while-watching, and post-watching. In the pre-watching stage, learners embarked on *Step 1*, delving into the "multi-layered" construct of pragmatics (Taguchi, 2019). This step entailed an exploration of form-function-context mapping, interaction skills, and agency within the context of refusals. This was followed by *Step 2*, where learners engaged in discussions using transcripts from scenes of the TV series *Grey's Anatomy*, thereby focusing deeper on these dimensions. This TV series was chosen to enhance learners' professional communicative skills, focusing on contexts like Medicine, aligned with course objectives.

Transitioning to the while-watching stage during Session 2, learners undertook *Step 3*, which involved a meticulous contextual analysis of refusal dialogues extracted from the aforementioned TV series (Usó-Juan & Martínez-Flor, 2021). Here, the use of the SPEAKING model (Hymes, 1974) guided learners in examining crucial elements of the scenes, such as Setting, Participants, Ends, Act sequence, Key, Instrumentalities, Norm, and Genre. Building upon this analysis, *Step 4* prompted learners to scrutinise the array of pragmalinguistic expressions employed in refusals, with a particular emphasis on developing a discursive comprehension of refusal strategies.

Finally, the post-watching stage in Session 3 introduced learners to *Step 5*, wherein they actively participated in the co-construction of refusals through structured dialogic tasks and freer role-playing scenarios. This interactive engagement aimed to reinforce learners' practical application of refusal strategies within contextualised settings. Concluding the instructional framework in *Step 6*, learners engaged in a reflective self-assessment of their pragmatic ability. This phase encouraged learners to critically evaluate factors such as negative transfer from their L1, potential overgeneralisation of English norms, proficiency in English grammar, the influence of instructional materials, and potential resistance towards adopting English pragmatic behaviour. After this self-evaluation, learners participated in peer feedback sessions facilitated by the instructor, where metapragmatic guidance further enriched their understanding of the nuanced dimensions of refusals as jointly constructed speech acts.

Data Collection Procedure

As depicted in Table 5.2, the data collection procedure of this study involved 5 distinct sessions designed to assess the impact of the instructional intervention on English refusals within the experimental group as compared to the control group. During session 1, both the experimental and control groups underwent a proficiency test and a pre-test, each lasting 30 minutes. These initial assessments provided baseline data on the participants' language proficiency and their preliminary understanding of English refusals.

In the next three 120-minute sessions, the experimental group received the instructional intervention, while the control group did not. This group remained engaged solely in general English instruction without a specific emphasis on pragmatics. Session 2 focused on pre-watching activities, encompassing *Step 1*, which delved into teaching the pragmatics of refusals, and *Step 2*, where refusals were discussed within contextual frameworks. Building upon this foundation, Session 3 centred on while-watching activities. Here, *Step 3* involved analysing the contextual nuances of refusals, while *Step 4* entailed a detailed examination of the language employed in refusals. These activities aimed to immerse the experimental group in practical applications, reinforcing their understanding within specific communicative contexts. Session 4 dealt with post-watching activities. Within this session, *Step 5* involved collaborative efforts in co-constructing refusals, followed by *Step 6*, where refusals were assessed and refined. These activities were crafted to consolidate the experimental group's learning and application of English refusals strategies.

The intervention concluded in Session 5, during which both the experimental and control groups took a 30-minute post-test to evaluate their proficiency in English refusals following the instructional intervention. Additionally, only the experimental group completed a 30-minute perception questionnaire, providing insights into their perceptions and experiences with the instructional sessions.

Table 5.2. Summary of the data collection procedure.

Sessions	**Data Collection Procedure**	**Group**
Session 1	Proficiency test (30 minutes) Pre-test (30 minutes)	EG +CG EG +CG
Session 2	Instructional session: Pre-watching (120 minutes) Step 1 + Step 2	EG
Session 3	Instructional session 2: While-watching (120 minutes) Step 3 + Step 4	EG
Session 4	Instructional session 3: Post-watching (120 minutes) Step 5 + Step 6	EG
Session 5	Post-test (30 minutes) Perception questionnaire (30 minutes)	EG +CG EG

Note. EG stands for experimental group and CG for control group.

Data Analysis and Statistical Procedure

The 304 refusal sequences derived from the diverse communicative scenarios (38 learners x 4 situations x 2 times) underwent a linguistic analysis to address RQ1. Salazar et al.'s (2009) taxonomy, discerning direct, indirect, and adjuncts to refusals, guided the classification of these refusal strategies. Moreover, data from the learners' perception questionnaire, addressing RQ2, were subjected to quantitative assessment using a Likert scale, complemented by qualitative exploration. Both researchers reviewed the entire analysis to ensure accuracy, and differences were carefully discussed and resolved.

Quantitative data were submitted to the Statistical Package for the Social Sciences (SPSS) software version 22.0. The descriptive analysis of the data encompassed the construction of frequency distributions to illustrate the occurrence of values alongside their corresponding percentages, as well as the computation of means and standard deviations to characterise central tendencies and the variability within the dataset. The paired discrete quantitative data (pre-test values and post-test values within each group) were compared using the Wilcoxon test. Statistical differences were considered significant at $p \leq 0.05$.

Results and Discussion

Advanced Learners' Application of Refusal Strategies

RQ1 aimed to investigate differences in refusal production, considering social status and social distance, between advanced EFL learners who underwent explicit instructional intervention and those in the control group. The refusal data were classified into fourteen distinct refusal strategies based on participants' responses in pre-test and post-test assessments. Table 5.3 displays the distribution of these strategies, including direct strategies, indirect strategies, and adjuncts, among the experimental and control groups across various situations in both pre-test and post-test stages.

Table 5.3. Refusal strategies employed by the experimental (n=17) and control group (n=21).

	Experimental Group				**Control Group**			
	Pre-test		**Post-test**		**Pre-test**		**Post-test**	
Strategies and Adjuncts	***f***	**%**	***f***	**%**	***f***	**%**	***f***	**%**
Direct Strategies								
1.Bluntness	2	1.34	0	0	1	0.47	2	1.01
2. Negation of proposition	25	16.78	23	9.83	16	7.58	22	11.06
Total Direct Strategies	**27**	**18.12**	**23**	**9.83**	**17**	**8.05**	**24**	**12.07**
Indirect Strategies								
3. Plain indirect	3	2.01	2	0.85	0	0	3	1.51
4. Reason/Explanation	50	33.56	90	38.46	78	36.97	66	33.17
5. Regret/apology	36	24.16	55	23.50	70	33.17	72	36.18
6. Alternative								
• Option	8	5.37	20	8.55	18	8.53	10	5.03
• Time	6	4.03	8	3.42	10	4.74	9	4.52
7. Disagreement/Criticism	1	0.67	1	0.43	0	0	0	0
8. Statement of principle	0	0	4	1.71	1	0.47	2	1.01
9. Verbal Avoidance								
• Hedging	0	0	0	0	0	0	1	0.50
• Change topic	0	0	0	0	0	0	0	0
• Joking	0	0	0	0	0	0	0	0
• Sarcasm	1	0.67	0	0	0	0	0	0
Total Indirect Strategies	**105**	**70.80**	**180**	**76.02**	**177**	**83.88**	**163**	**82.92**

Continued

Table 5.3. *Continued*

	Experimental Group				Control Group			
	Pre-test		Post-test		Pre-test		Post-test	
Strategies and Adjuncts	*f*	%	*f*	%	*f*	%	*f*	%
Adjuncts to refusals								
10. Positive opinion	0	0	3	1.28	0	0	1	0.50
11. Willingness	10	6.71	15	6.41	8	3.79	9	4.52
12. Gratitude	1	0.67	2	0.85	5	2.37	1	0.50
13. Agreement	0	0	0	0	0	0	0	0
14. Solidarity/Empathy	6	4.03	11	4.70	4	1.90	1	0.50
Total Adjuncts to Refusals	**17**	**11.41**	**31**	**13.24**	**17**	**8.06**	**12**	**6.02**
Total Strategies	**149**	**100**	**234**	**100**	**211**	**100**	**199**	**100**

Note. Due to rounding, percentages may not sum up to 100 %.

In the post-test phase, the experimental group used more strategies (n=234) compared to the pre-test (n=149), while the control group slightly decreased their usage (post-test: n=199; pre-test: n=211). Analysing the Direct Strategies, both groups preferred using the *negation of proposition* strategy over *bluntness* in both stages (EG: pre-test 25 cases to 2; post-test 23 to 0; CG: pre-test 16 to 1; post-test 22 to 2). However, the experimental group reduced the usage of the *negation of proposition* strategy from pre-test (n=25) to post-test (n=23), whereas the control group slightly increased it (pre-test: n=16; post-test: n=22). These results suggest a shift in strategy preference, with the experimental group refining their refusal strategies after the intervention, while the control group maintained their original approach to refusal communication throughout the study.

Among the indirect strategies, *reason/explanation* strategies were most prevalent in both the experimental and control groups, followed by *regret/apology* and *alternative* strategies. However, notable differences emerged between the two groups. In the experimental group, there was a significant increase in *reason/explanation* strategies from pre-test (n= 50) to post-test (n=90), while in the control group, a slight decrease was observed (pre-test: 78; post-test: 66). Similarly, *regret/apology* strategies increased notably in the experimental group (pre-test: 36; post-test: 55) but only slightly in the control group (pre-test: 70; post-test: 72). *Alternative* strategies, such as *option* and *time*, also showed distinct patterns. In the experimental group, *option* strategies increased (pre-test: 8; post-test: 20) as did *time* strategies (pre-test: 6; post-test: 8), whereas they decreased in the control group. Overall, the experimental group exhibited a more pronounced shift towards using these strategies more frequently after instructional intervention compared to the control group, which showed minor fluctuations or decreases in usage. The remaining strategies—namely *plain indirect, disagreement/criticism, statement of principle*, and *verbal avoidance*—were relatively infrequent in both the pre-test and post-test phases. However, it is noteworthy that statement of principle strategies emerged in the post-test phase of the experimental group (n=4).

Looking at adjuncts to refusals, in the pre-test, the experimental group primarily employed the *willingness* strategy (n=10), followed by expressions of *solidarity/empathy* (n=6) and *gratitude* (n= 1). Interestingly, instances of *positive opinion* and *agreement* were absent. In the post-test, the *willingness* strategy remained prominent (n=15), and there was an increased use of *solidarity/empathy* (n=11) and *gratitude* (n=2), along with new expressions for *positive opinion* (n=3). However, no instances of *agreement* strategies were found. Similarly, the control group relied on the *willingness* strategy (n=8) as the main adjunct to refusals in the pre-test, followed by *gratitude* (n= 5) and *solidarity/empathy* (n=4), with no instances of *positive opinion* or *agreement*. Minimal changes were observed in the post-test frequencies of expressions of *gratitude, solidarity/empathy*, and *positive opinion*, while *agreement* strategies remained negligible, with no instances observed.

In summary, the experimental group showed significant shifts in refusal strategies, notably adopting new approaches such as the *statement of principle*, along with increased use of *reason/explanation, regret/apology, alternative* (*option* and *time*), and diverse adjuncts. This suggests an enhanced capacity for navigating complex social interactions. Conversely, the control group exhibited stable patterns with minor fluctuations in strategy usage across the pre-test and post-test phases.

Tables 5.4 and 5.5 depict the results of the Wilcoxon signed-rank test for pair samples, comparing the means of the refusal strategies used in the pre-test and post-test phases for the experimental and control groups, respectively, across the four situational contexts.

Table 5.4. Wilcoxon test results for distribution of refusal strategies in pre-test and post-test in the experimental group (n=17) across situations (n=4).

Strategies and Adjuncts	**Pre-test**		**Post-test**			
	M	*SD*	*M*	*SD*	*Z*	*p*
Direct Strategies						
Situation 1	0.35	0.493	0.24	0.437	−0.707	0.480
Situation 2	0.24	0.437	0.18	0.393	−0.447	0.655
Situation 3	0.24	0.437	0.29	0.470	−0.447	0.655
Situation 4	0.76	0.437	0.65	0.606	−0.707	0.480
Indirect Strategies						
Situation 1	1.76	1.437	2.71	1.160	−1.895	0.050*
Situation 2	1.76	0.903	2.88	0.781	−3.020	0.003*
Situation 3	1.76	0.752	2.94	0.748	−3.270	0.001*
Situation 4	0.88	1.054	2.06	1.029	−2.419	0.016*
Adjuncts to refusals						
Situation 1	0.35	0.493	0.59	0.507	−1.633	0.102
Situation 2	0.35	0.493	0.24	0.437	−0.816	0.414
Situation 3	0.12	0.332	0.35	0.493	−1.633	0.102
Situation 4	0.18	0.393	0.65	0.702	−2.530	0.011*

$*p \leq 0.05$

Table 5.5. Wilcoxon test results for distribution of refusal strategies in pre-test and post-test in the control group (n=21) across situations (n=4).

Strategies and Adjuncts	**Pre-test**		**Post-test**			
	M	*SD*	*M*	*SD*	*Z*	*p*
Direct Strategies						
Situation 1	0.19	0.402	0.33	0.577	−0.905	0.366
Situation 2	0.05	0.218	0.14	0.478	−0.816	0.414
Situation 3	0.14	0.359	0.29	0.561	−0.905	0.366
Situation 4	0.43	0.507	0.38	0.498	−0.378	0.705

Table 5.5. *Continued*

Strategies and Adjuncts	**Pre-test**		**Post-test**			
	M	*SD*	*M*	*SD*	*Z*	*p*
Indirect Strategies						
Situation 1	2.38	0.590	2.14	0.793	−1.127	0.260
Situation 2	2.10	0.700	1.95	0.740	−0.812	0.417
Situation 3	2.29	0.644	2.10	0.539	−2.000	0.064
Situation 4	1.67	1.155	1.62	0805	−0.121	0.904
Adjuncts to refusals						
Situation 1	0.33	0.483	0.33	0.483	0.000	1.000
Situation 2	0.14	0.359	0.05	0.218	−1.000	0.317
Situation 3	0.14	0.359	0.14	0.359	0.000	1.000
Situation 4	0.19	0.402	0.05	0.218	−1.324	0.180

$^*p \leq 0.05$

Regarding Direct Strategies, a scarcity of instances was employed in both the experimental and control groups with a preference shown towards the *negation of the proposition* (see Table 5.3). No statistically significant differences were observed in both the experimental group (Z = -0.707, p = 0.480; Z = -0.447, p = 0.655; Z = -0.447, p = 0.655; Z = -0.707, p = 0.480 for Situations 1, 2, 3, and 4, respectively) and the control group (Z = -0.905, p = 0.366; Z = -0.816, p = 0.414; Z = -0.905, p = 0.366; Z = -0.378, p = 0.705 for Situations 1, 2, 3, and 4, respectively) across situations. These results indicate a parallelism in the use of direct refusal strategies between the two groups, portraying a tendency of minimal reliance on direct strategies among the advanced proficiency learners, irrespective of the instructional treatment. These findings echo earlier studies, such as Codina (2013) and Bella (2014), which underscore the inclination of advanced language learners to employ more indirect and contextually nuanced strategies as their language proficiency advances, facilitating effective communication of refusals. Although the use of the *negation of proposition* was not prevalent, Example (1) illustrates the application of this refusal strategy employed by learner #3 in the experimental group. In this situation the requester has a low status level and the interactants are acquaintances.

(1) A 1st-year student requests a 4th-year student to participate in an interview for a class project (Situation 1).

Pre-test: I am sorry. I can't right now.
[regret+negation of proposition]

Post-test: Sorry! I'm full of work at the moment. Perhaps we can have the interview another day.
[regret+reason+alternative]

In Example (1), the pre-test response presents a straightforward expression of regret, coupled with the negation of the proposition. However, the post-test response reveals a progression in refusal strategies. Instead of simply denying the proposition, the learner now incorporates regret, provides a reason for the unavailability, and suggests an alternative arrangement. This shift towards a more nuanced and contextually sensitive approach reflects the learners' enhancement in their ability to convey refusals effectively, especially when maintaining interpersonal relationships is a priority.

With regard to the use of Indirect Strategies, significant increases in the employment of indirect strategies across all four scenarios were observed in the experimental group from the pre-test to the post-test phase ($Z = -1.895$, $p = 0.05$; $Z = -3.020$, $p = 0.003$; $Z = -3.270$, $p = 0.001$; $Z = -2.419$, $p = 0.016$ for Situations 1, 2, 3, and 4, respectively). Conversely, within the control group, no statistically significant shifts from the pre-test to the post-test phase were detected in the use of indirect strategies. Consistent with previous research findings on refusals among English language learners with lower proficiency levels (Codina, 2013; Taguchi, 2013), the predominant strategy employed by advanced EFL learners was the provision of a *reason/explanation* for their inability to comply with a request. Particularly noteworthy was the prevalent pattern mode of refusal which combined expressions of *regret* with the presentation of a *reason/explanation*.

However, following the instructional phase and aligning with earlier studies focusing on instructional interventions concerning refusals (Alcón-Soler & Guzmán, 2013; Flores-Salgado & Halenko, 2022), learners not only increased the frequency of their use of indirect strategies but also diversified their repertoire to include strategies such as offering *alternatives* or articulating *statements of principle*. Regarding the former, the act of offering to comply with the request by modifying the option or time could potentially aid in preserving face, thereby mitigating the refusal to avoid conflict (Taguchi, 2013). For the latter, instances were common in Situation 4, wherein the learner was led to refuse by appealing to personal convictions when asked to provide his/her signature in support for a political cause. This use of *statement of principle* serves as a strategic means for learners to assert their autonomy and values, aligning their refusal with deeply held beliefs. By framing their refusal in this manner, learners not only maintained a sense of personal integrity but also conveyed a respectful yet firm decline, demonstrating an advanced level of sociopragmatic competence in refusal strategies (Codina, 2013).

Moreover, the fact that there were limited instances of *plain indirect*, *disagreement* or *verbal avoidance* was somewhat expected for two reasons. First, the instructional focus of the intervention likely encouraged learners to explore more nuanced strategies, steering them away from relying solely on straightforward indirect refusals or simple disagreement. Second, in accordance with Codina's findings (2013), the absence of instances related to verbal avoidance in the post-instructional data could be attributed to the nature of the data collection instrument. The use of a DCT necessitates students to provide written responses, thereby eliminating the option of verbal avoidance tactics. Examples (2) and (3) provide insight into the responses of learner #1 within the experimental group across situations 2 and 3. These scenarios involve interactions with requesters of high social status. However, while Example (2) involves interactions between strangers, Example (3) depicts interactions with acquaintances.

(2) A well-dressed middle-aged man politely requests a student to sell him the last available ticket for a film (Situation 2).

Pre-test: Sorry, I can't give you my ticket. I got it first.
[*regret+negation of proposition+reason*]

Post-test: I'm sorry, sir, but I've been waiting for this movie for a long time, and I really want to see it. Could you please understand?
[*regret+reason+reason+empathy*]

(3) A lecturer requests a student in his class to help him carry some books to his office (Situation 3).

Pre-test: I'm afraid I won't be able to help you with the task. Sorry!
[*plain indirect+regret*]

Post-test: I would be delighted to help you, but I regret to say I have another class in five minutes. I hope you understand.
[*willingness+regret+reason+empathy*]

In Example (2), the pre-test response represents a straightforward refusal to give the last available cinema ticket to a well-dressed middle-aged man, employing a combination of regret, negation of the proposition, and a reason for their decision. However, in the post-test the response reveals a noticeable shift towards a more polite and empathetic approach. Here the learner expresses regret for not being able to comply, provides reasons for his/her strong desire to see the film, and appeals to the requester's understanding with empathy. This change reflects an enhanced ability to consider the requester's perspective and convey the refusal more politely, especially given the requester's perceived higher social status as a stranger.

In a similar vein, the pre-test response in Example (3), while conveying regret, presents a rather straightforward refusal without much elaboration. The use of "I'm afraid" adds a slight degree of formality, but the refusal lacks context or empathy towards the lecturer's request. However, the post-test response demonstrates the student's enhanced ability to navigate social status within the academic hierarchy. The student begins with an expression of willingness to assist, acknowledging the lecturer's authority and the significance of the request. Following this, the student then presents a clear reason for their inability to help, mentioning a conflicting commitment with another class. The inclusion of "but I regret to say" maintains a polite and respectful tone while conveying the reason for refusal. Additionally, the student concludes displaying empathy towards the lecturer's position. In both examples, the post-test responses illustrate learner #1's progression towards a more considerate, polite, and empathetic approach in refusing requests, particularly when interacting with individuals of higher social status. These changes reflect an enhanced ability to consider the requester's perspective, convey refusals with tact, and maintain respectful interpersonal relations in diverse social contexts.

In analysing the use of Adjuncts to refusals, a significant difference was observed in the experimental group in Situation 4 ($Z = -2.530$, $p = 0.011$). This indicates a significant enhancement in the learners' sociopragmatic repertoire after the instructional intervention, demonstrating a skill in strategically using a variety of adjuncts to manage refusal situations. However, no statistically significant differences were detected within the control group across the four situations. Although post-instructional data revealed a preference for *willingness,* consistent with previous studies focusing on refusals among learners with lower proficiency levels of English (Codina, 2013; Usó-Juan, 2013), the expansion of the learners' repertoire of adjuncts attests to their advanced sociopragmatic competence. Specifically, and consonant with findings from native speakers' data (Bella, 2014), learners frequently employed expressions of solidarity/empathy.

Nonetheless, the absence of the adjunct of *agreement* suggests a nuanced understanding of the eliciting act among learners, as posited by Alcón-Soler and Guzmán (2013). The DCT scenarios, including requesting an interview when you do not have time (Situation 1), seeking the last cinema ticket when eager to attend a film (Situation 2), requesting assistance with carrying books amidst scheduled classes (Situation 3), or soliciting a signature for a political cause from an unfamiliar individual (Situation 4), could potentially be perceived as unfair by learners. In such contexts, expressions of gratitude might have been understood as ironic, diverging from the expected social norms. This strategic deployment of *agreement* adjuncts not only underscores the learners' awareness of sociolinguistic nuances but also their capacity to tailor responses to meet the demands of specific contextual settings, thereby exemplifying an advanced level of communicative competence in social interactions. Example (4) illustrates the responses of learner #12 within the experimental group in Situation 4, where the requester holds a low social status, and the interactants are strangers.

(4) An undergraduate student requests a graduate student for his/her signature for a political cause (Situation 4).

Pre-test: I don't have time for this. Sorry!
[*reason+regret*]

Post-test: Thank you for thinking of me, but I prefer not to sign petitions for causes I'm not fully informed about. However, I appreciate your efforts in raising awareness for important issues like this.
[*gratitude+statement of principle+positive opinion*]

The pre-test response in Example (4) provides a brief and direct refusal, citing lack of time and expressing regret. This initial response may appear dismissive due to its brevity. However, the post-test response demonstrates a significant improvement in the refusal strategy. The learner begins by expressing gratitude for the request, then politely declines by stating a personal principle of not signing petitions without full information. Furthermore, the learner acknowledges and appreciates the requester's efforts to raise awareness for the cause. This shift indicates a more nuanced and respectful approach in refusing the request, showing an understanding of the importance of the cause despite declining to participate. This evolution suggests an improved ability to handle refusals, especially in situations involving individuals of lower social status who are strangers.

These findings affirm RQ1. Wilcoxon tests revealed a significant enhancement in the use of indirect refusal strategies across all scenarios, with a particularly notable increase in adjuncts to refusals in Scenario 4 for the experimental group. In contrast, the control group exhibited no significant changes. The strategic use of refusal strategies and adjuncts by learners in the experimental group not only highlights their awareness of sociolinguistic nuances but also shows their capacity to tailor responses to meet the demands of specific contextual settings, showcasing advanced communicative competence. The provided examples illustrate their progression from basic to socially aware responses, showcasing improved navigation of social hierarchies and fostering positive interpersonal relations while refusing requests.

Advanced Learners' Perceptions of the Instructional Method

RQ2 sought insights from advanced EFL learners in the experimental group regarding their perceptions of the instructional treatment, specifically targeted at learning refusal strategies. The analysis of learner evaluations concerning key aspects of the pragmatic instruction yielded valuable insights into their perceptions. Firstly, in terms of overall satisfaction with the lessons, the majority of participants expressed a high level of contentment. Specifically, 52.94 % of the learners (9 out of 17) rated their satisfaction as a 4, indicating a pronounced affinity for the instructional content. Moreover, 47.06 % of the cohort (8 out of 17) rated their satisfaction as a 3, denoting a favourable disposition towards the instructional materials. Notable themes emerged from the learners' feedback, exemplified by the comments provided. For instance, in Example (5), Learner #1 underscored the engaging and well-structured nature of the lessons, which contributed to an enhanced understanding of refusals. Additionally, Learner #5's comment emphasised the necessity of acquiring diverse refusal strategies, highlighting the limitations of formulaic responses such as "No, thank you" or "I'm sorry, but no" across varying social contexts. The impact of language tone and wording on the reception of refusals was also noted as a point of interest. Furthermore, Learner #6 discussed the value of the lessons in navigating hierarchical interactions, citing personal challenges in such situations.

(5) Learner #1: Yes, I liked them a lot. They were well-structured and engaging, which made learning about refusals and pragmatics interesting.

Learner #5: Yes, I liked the lessons because I realised that sticking to the same formulas of "No, thank you" or "I'm sorry, but no" aren't always suitable for all contexts. These lessons helped me learn different refusal strategies that are more adaptable to different social situations. It was interesting to see how small changes in wording or tone can make a big difference in how a refusal is received.

Learner #6: I found these lessons to be really valuable. Personally, I struggle with saying 'no' to people higher in the hierarchy, so learning about refusal strategies was particularly helpful for me.

Secondly, moving to the perceived effectiveness of integrating audiovisual resources to learn pragmatics and cultural aspects, the data indicated a strong trend towards positive evaluations. The overwhelming majority of learners, comprising 88.24 % of the cohort (15 out of 17), rated the effectiveness as a 4, emphasising the valuable role of audiovisual materials in understanding pragmatics and cultural nuances. Conversely, a smaller percentage, 11.76 % (2 out of 17), rated this aspect as a 3, suggesting a slightly lower perception of effectiveness. Echoing these findings, learners' comments in Example (6) further underscored the positive impact of these materials. Learner #7 expressed the significant benefits, describing how the use of audiovisual aids allowed for a vivid understanding of cultural aspects, enhancing engagement with the learning process. Similarly, Learner #13 highlighted the effectiveness of audiovisual resources in learning pragmatics, noting a refreshing departure from traditional methods. Learner #15 emphasised the indispensable nature of audiovisual aids, stating they provided a dynamic understanding of language and essential non-verbal communication aspects crucial in understanding refusals.

(6) Learner #7: Absolutely, using audiovisual materials was incredibly beneficial. It allowed us to see the cultural aspects in action, making the learning experience more engaging.

Learner #13: I found that using audiovisual materials was very effective for learning about pragmatics. It provided a fresh change from the usual routine of following a textbook and participating in typical role-plays.

Learner #15: Yes, I believe using audiovisual material was essential. It provided a dynamic way to understand not only the language but also the non-verbal communication aspects that are crucial in understanding refusals.

Thirdly, in the evaluation of the enjoyment derived from analysing audiovisual scenes, all learners (100 %) unanimously rated this aspect as a 4, indicating a positive response to this component of the pragmatic instruction. This unanimous agreement among the learners reflects their satisfaction with the incorporation of audiovisual input in the learning process. For instance, in Example (7), Learner #8 found the exercise intriguing, noting that analysing scenes provided valuable insights into the practical use of language in real-life scenarios, facilitating its application in personal conversations. Learner #11 compared analysing audiovisual scenes to solving a puzzle, showing satisfaction in unravelling meanings and intentions behind characters' actions. Similarly, Learner #17 expressed appreciation for the activity, emphasising its dual role of being both enjoyable and informative. This learner noted that the engagement with the scenes contributed significantly to a deeper comprehension of the diverse ways of saying 'no' in English.

(7) Learner #8: Yes, it was an interesting exercise. Analysing the scenes allowed us to see how language is used in real-life situations, making it easier to apply in our own conversations.

Learner #11: I really enjoyed it. It was like solving a puzzle, trying to figure out the meanings and intentions behind the characters' words and actions.

Learner #17: Absolutely! It was both fun and informative. The scenes were engaging and analysing them helped in developing a deeper understanding of the different ways refusals are communicated in English.

Finally, concerning the open-ended question soliciting insights into enjoyable activities and proposals for lesson enhancements, valuable glimpses into the perspectives of the learners were observed. In detailing engaging activities, learners offered diverse viewpoints, as exemplified in Example (8). Some learners emphasised the stimulating nature of analysing language refusals (Learner #11) while others highlighted the enriching discussions using transcripts from *Grey's Anatomy* (Learner #12) and the interactive dialogic tasks during the post-watching stage (Learner #15).

(8) Learner #11: I really enjoyed looking at the language details. It was interesting to see how small changes in words can change what we mean when refusing.

Learner #12: The discussions we had using transcripts from Grey's Anatomy were fascinating. It was so interesting to analyse the dialogues of the characters and to understand the tactful ways they refused things.

Learner #15: I found the dialogic tasks in the post-watching stage to be quite enjoyable. It was fun to construct refusals with other learners and see the different approaches other learners took.

Turning to proposals for enhancing the instructional lessons, a notable proportion of learners expressed satisfaction with the array of activities provided, as illustrated in Example (9). Nevertheless, suggestions for further refinement emerged. Specifically, participants recommended the incorporation of a broader selection of audiovisual materials drawn from diverse cultural contexts (Learner #3). Additionally, they proposed the development of supplementary online interactive resources tailored to individual student needs (Learner #9), alongside initiatives to foster real-life language practice beyond the classroom environment.

This included advocating for language exchange programs as valuable opportunities for practical application (Learner #10).

(9) Learner #3:	I missed the inclusion of audiovisual materials from different cultural contexts. This would enhance our understanding of how language is used in various social settings.
Learner #9:	It would be beneficial to have more interactive online resources for self-study. Additional interactive online exercises could help reinforce the concepts we learned in class.
Learner #10:	It might be quite interesting to have chances for real-life practice outside of class. Maybe joining online language exchange partners could be an excellent opportunity to apply our pragmatic skills in real conversations.

In response to RQ2, participants in the experimental group expressed high satisfaction with the pragmatics intervention, particularly in four areas: overall satisfaction, effectiveness of audiovisual materials, enjoyment of film analysis, and feedback on preferred activities and enhancements. They appreciated the engaging nature of the lessons and recognised the importance of diverse linguistic resources for navigating refusal contexts. The integration of audiovisual materials was well-received, providing a refreshing learning experience. Analysing film scenes was enjoyable and informative, offering practical examples for real-world application. Suggestions for enhancements included incorporating a wider range of audiovisual materials and developing tailored online resources for self-study, indicating a desire to deepen understanding of pragmatics and cultural nuances in English communication. Taken collectively, these findings underscore the positive reception and perceived efficacy of teaching pragmatics among advanced EFL learners in the experimental group. They align with previous studies on pragmatic instruction, wherein learners also engaged in the completion of a perception questionnaire. These investigations have examined various speech acts such as compliment responses (Alsuhaibani, 2022), refusals (Flores-Salgado & Halenko, 2022) and a combination of different speech acts (Kim, 2016; Noonkong et al., 2017), underscoring the relevance of these pedagogical methodologies for language instructors.

Conclusions

This study delved into the effects of pragmatic instruction on the application of refusal strategies among advanced EFL learners, monitoring their performance both before and after the instructional intervention. Additionally, the study explored the perceptions of these learners regarding the provided pragmatic instruction. The findings revealed a significant enhancement in the experimental group, characterised by a transition from basic pre-test responses to more intricate and socially aware post-test responses. This shift demonstrates a strategic adjustment and underscores the learners' increasing competence in employing sociolinguistic strategies to address potential face threats inherent in contexts where a refusal is performed. In contrast, the control group demonstrated stable patterns with minor fluctuations, indicating minimal changes in their refusal strategy preferences. Furthermore, the study indicated a favourable reception and perceived effectiveness of the instructional approach among learners in the experimental group. Particularly noteworthy was their appreciation for the integration and analysis of audiovisual materials, which facilitated an expansion of their pragmalinguistic repertoire in refusal strategies and their awareness of sociopragmatic considerations.

However, several limitations should be noted. Firstly, the use of a DCT to assess learners' application of refusal strategies may not fully capture the nuances of real-life interactions, potentially leading to responses that differ from those in authentic situations. Secondly, the reliance on self-reported questionnaires introduces the possibility of social desirability bias, which may restrict the depth of understanding and only capture surface-level experiences. Future research should consider employing more diverse data collection methods to gain a more comprehensive view of the impact of pragmatic instruction on learners' use of refusal strategies, as well as their perceptions of pedagogical approaches in L2 pragmatics. Furthermore, given that studies in pragmatics frequently show positive outcomes from any form of instruction compared to no instruction, it would be beneficial to conduct future studies incorporating a third group with a different instructional approach. Comparing different teaching methods could provide valuable insights into which strategies are the most effective for enhancing students' pragmatic skills and understanding.

Acknowledgements

This study is part of the research project PID2020-117959GB-I00 funded by MCIN/AEI/10.13039/501100011033. Additional funding has been granted by Projectes d'Innovació Educativa de la Unitat de Suport Educatiu 51020/24.

References

Ahmadian, Mohammad Javad. 2020. Explicit and implicit instruction of refusal strategies: Does working memory capacity play a role? *Language Teaching Research*, 24, 163–188.

Alcón-Soler, Eva & Guzmán, Josep Roderic. 2013. The effect of instruction on learners' use and negotiation of refusals. In O. Martí-Arnándiz & P. Salazar-Campillo (eds) *Refusals in instructional contexts and beyond*. Amsterdam, New York: Rodopi, 41–6.

Alsuhaibani, Zainab. 2022. Developing EFL students' pragmatic competence: The case of compliment responses. *Language Teaching Research*, 26/5, 847–866.

Bacelar Da Silva, Antonio José. 2003. The effects of instruction on pragmatic development: Teaching polite refusals in English. *Second Language Studies*, 22/1, 55–106.

Bardovi-Harlig, Kathleen & Hartford, Beverly S. 1990. Congruence in native non-native conversations: Status balance in the academic advising sessions. *Language Learning*, 40/4, 467–501.

Bardovi-Harlig, Kathleen & Mahan-Taylor, Rebecca. 2003. T*eaching pragmatics*. Washington, DC: United States Department of State.

Beebe, Leslie, Takahashi, Tomoko & Uliss-Weltz, Robin. 1990. Pragmatic transfer in ESL refusals. In R. Scarcella, E. Andersen & S. Krashen (eds) *Developing communicative competence in a second language*. New York: Newbury House, 55–73.

Bella, Spyridoula. 2014. Developing the ability to refuse: A cross-sectional study of Greek FL refusals. *Journal of Pragmatics*, 61, 35–62.

Brown, Penelope & Levinson, Stephen C. 1987. *Politeness: Some universals in language use*. Cambridge: Cambridge University Press.

Codina, Victòria. 2013. The role of proficiency in the production of refusals. In O. Martí-Arnándiz & P. Salazar-Campillo (eds) *Refusals in instructional contexts and beyond*. Amsterdam, New York: Rodopi, 121–146.

Eslami, Zohreh R. 2010. Refusals: How to develop appropriate refusal strategies. In A. Martínez-Flor & E. Usó-Juan (eds) *Speech act performance: Theoretical, empirical and methodological issues*. Amsterdam: John Benjamins, 217–236.

Farahian, Majid, Rezaee, Mehrdad & Gholami, Afshin. 2012. Does direct instruction develop pragmatic competence? Teaching refusals to EFL learners of English. *Journal of Language Teaching and Research*, 3/4, 814–821.

Farrokhi, Farahman & Atashian, Soheil. 2012. The role of refusal instruction in pragmatic development. *World Journal of Education*, 2/4, 85–93.

Flores-Salgado, Elizabeth & Halenko, Nicola. 2022. 'Learning to Say "No" in Different Ways.' Tracking EFL learner performance and perceptions of pragmatics instruction in Mexico. In N. Halenko & J. Wang (eds) *Pragmatics in English language learning*. Cambridge: Cambridge University Press, 173–199.

Gass, Susan & Houck, Noël. 1999. *Interlanguage refusals: A cross-cultural study of Japanese-English*. Berlin: Mouton de Gruyter.

Haghighi, Hamzeh, Jafarigohar, Manoochehr, Khoshsima, Hooshang & Vahdany, Fereidoon. 2019. Impact of flipped classroom on EFL learners' appropriate use of refusal: Achievement, participation, perception. *Computer Assisted Language Learning*, 32/3, 261–293.

Hymes, Dell. 1974. *Foundations in sociolinguistics: An ethnographic approach*. Philadelphia: University of Pennsylvania Press.

Kasper, Gabriele. 1992. Pragmatic transfer. *Second Language Research*, 8/3, 203–231.

Kim, Hyekyeng. 2016. An Investigation into EFL learners' perception towards L2 pragmatic instruction. *Theory and Practice in Language Studies*, 6, 452–462.

Ling-li, Duan & Wannaruk, Anchalee. 2010. The effects of explicit and implicit instruction on English refusals. *Chinese Journal of Applied Linguistics*, 33/3, 93–109.

Martínez-Flor, Alicia & Usó-Juan, Esther. 2011. Research methodologies in pragmatics: Eliciting refusals to requests. *Estudios de Lingüística Inglesa Aplicada*, 11, 47–87.

Martínez-Flor, Alicia & Usó-Juan, Esther. 2020. Teaching speech acts in a second language. In K. P. Schneider & E. Ifantidou (eds) *Developmental and clinical pragmatics*. Berlin/Boston: Mouton de Gruyter, 269–299.

Noonkong, Uraiwan R., Damnet, Anamal & Charttrakul, Kanjana. 2017. Enhancing Thai Engineering students' complaints and apologies through Pragmatic Consciousness-raising Approach (PCR). *Advances in Language and Literary Studies*, 8, 92–99.

Salazar, Patricia, Safont, Pilar & Codina, Victoria. 2009. Refusal strategies: A proposal from a sociopragmatic approach. *RœL: Revista Electrónica de Lingüística Aplicada*, 8, 139–150.

Searle, John R. 1976. The classification of illocutionary acts. *Language in Society*, 5, 1–24.

Shirinbakhsh, Salva/Rasekh, Eslami Abbass & Mansoor, Tavakoli. 2016. Metapragmatic instruction (6Rs) versus input-based practice: A comparison of their effects on pragmatic accuracy and speed in the recognition and oral production of English refusals. *The Language Learning Journal*, 46/4, 514–537.

Taguchi, Naoko. 2011. Teaching pragmatics: Trends and issues. *Annual Review of Applied Linguistic*, 31, 289–310.

Taguchi, Naoko. 2013. Refusals in L2 English: Proficiency effects on appropriateness and fluency. In O. Martí-Arnándiz & P. Salazar-Campillo (eds) *Refusals in instructional contexts and beyond*. Amsterdam, New York: Rodopi, 101–119.

Taguchi, Naoko. 2017. Interlanguage pragmatics. A historical sketch and future directions. In A. Barron, Y. Gu & G. Steen (eds)

The Routledge handbook of pragmatics. New York: Routledge, 153–167.

Taguchi, Naoko. 2019. Second language acquisition and pragmatics: An overview. In N. Taguchi (ed) *The Routledge handbook of second language acquisition and pragmatics.* London, New York: Routledge, 1–14.

Thomas, Jenny. 1983. Cross-cultural pragmatic failure. *Applied Linguistics*, 4/2, 91–112.

University of Cambridge Local Examinations Syndicate (UCLES). 2001. CAMBRIDGE IELTS with answers 2—*Examination papers from University of Cambridge local examinations syndicate.* Cambridge University Press.

Usó-Juan, Esther. 2010. Requests: A sociopragmatic approach. In A. Martínez-Flor & E. Usó-Juan (eds) *Speech act performance: Theoretical, empirical and methodological issues.* Amsterdam: John Benjamins, 237–256.

Usó-Juan, Esther. 2013. Effects of metapragmatic instruction on EFL learners' production of refusals. In O. Martí-Arnándiz & P. Salazar-Campillo (eds) *Refusals in instructional contexts and beyond.* Amsterdam, New York: Rodopi, 65–99.

Usó-Juan, Esther & Martínez-Flor, Alicia. 2021. Fostering learners' (Meta)pragmatic awareness through film analysis. *Language Value*, 14/1, 85–111.

Usó-Juan, Esther & Martínez-Flor, Alicia. 2022. Using audiovisual material to teach refusals from a discursive perspective: A research-based proposal. *Complutense Journal of English Studies*, 30, 53–66.

Xiao, Feng. 2018. Advanced-level pragmatics in instructed SLA. In P. A. Malovrh & A. G. Benati (eds) *The Handbook of advanced proficiency in second language acquisition.* Hoboken, NJ: Wiley Blackwell, 463–482.

Ignacio Martinez-Buffa

Learners' Deliberations in Collaborative Writing: Text Quality and L1s Usage

Introduction

The impact of collaboration in foreign language learning has been largely documented (see Storch, 2019 for a review, González-Lloret, 2020). Nonetheless, research on collaborative dialogue has neglected the development of relevant competences such as pragmatic knowledge despite its relevance in the Communicative Competence model (Bachman & Palmer, 1996; Usó-Juan & Martínez-Flor, 2006). As explained by González-Lloret (2021: 199), "it is not only important that learners' [second language] L2 is fluent, accurate, and complex, but it also needs to be appropriate". Research implementing collaborative tasks with the aim of offering learners opportunities to enhance their English as a foreign language (FL) pragmatic knowledge is limited (Taguchi & Kim, 2016; Kim & Taguchi, 2015, 2016). Further research linking collaborative practices and pragmatic development could shed light on the role of student-student interaction in the learning of L2/FL pragmatics. One way to achieve this is by paying attention to pragmatic-related episodes (PREs), that is, "any part of language production where learners talk about the pragmalinguistic forms they are producing and the sociopragmatic factors they are attending to, question their pragmatic language use, or correct themselves or others" (Taguchi & Kim, 2016: 419).

Hence, the current study implements a collaborative writing task eliciting student-student interaction on the use of requests in English. Previous research has reported the benefits of collaborative writing on the final piece of text (Wigglesworth & Storch, 2009; Shehadeh, 2011; Fernandez-Dobao, 2012), but these studies have mainly focused on grammatical accuracy (Storch, 2013). Furthermore, when considering the multilingual experience of learners and the use of their whole language repertoire, little research has been conducted on this matter (Martinez-Buffa & Safont, 2022). In this regard, the aim of this study is twofold: (1) to analyse the effect of collaborative tasks on text quality in terms of pragmatic production and (2) to examine the use of students' L1s when facing pragmatic-related issues.

Collaborative Writing Tasks

A collaborative writing task is defined as "an activity where there is a shared and negotiated decision making process and a shared responsibility for the production of a single text" (Storch, 2013: 3). The implementation of these tasks in the language classroom has been informed by the tenets of the Sociocultural Theory (Vygotsky, 1978) where the interaction between learners is conceived as collaborative opportunities for language development. The emergence of collaborative dialogue, understood as "a dialogue in which speakers are engaged in problem solving and knowledge building" (Swain, 2000: 102), allows for the co-construction of new and deeper knowledge about the language. Furthermore, it can create a space for scaffolding where a more experienced learner can assist a novice in task resolution and language development.

Two major lines of research on collaboration are explored, on the one hand, its impact on text quality and, on the other hand, the role of learners' L1 in student-student interaction. The following subsections further develop these two major research lines.

Effect of Collaboration on Text Quality

Several studies have investigated the impact of working collaboratively as evidenced in language learners' co-written texts. For example, Storch

(2005) compared the text production of 23 adult ESL students working in pairs and individually. The study showed that collaboratively written compositions were shorter, but more grammatically accurate and complex. Storch attributed these findings to the possibility of receiving immediate feedback as offered by the collaborative nature of the task. Similarly, Storch and Wigglesworth (2007) and Wigglesworth and Storch (2009) observed statistically significant differences when measuring the accuracy of jointly and individually written texts. The former contained less errors, but no difference was observed at the level of fluency and complexity. Further support was provided by McDonough et al. (2018) when they observed that their participants' collaborative texts were more accurate than individual texts. In a longitudinal pre-post-test design study conducted by Shehadeh (2011), university EFL students working collaboratively excelled in terms of content, organisation, and vocabulary. Nonetheless, no statistically significant differences were thrown for grammar or mechanisms of the language. This was attributed to the low proficiency of the participants as they were unable to help each other with grammar.

When examining the nature of pairs' collaborative dialogue, language-related episodes (LREs) are the common unit of analysis. Swain and Lapkin (1998: 326) defined LREs as "any part of the dialogue where the students talk about the language they are producing, question their language use, or correct themselves or others". A LRE is "a useful unit for understanding the process and product of L2 learning"' (Swain & Watanabe, 2013: 3). The effect of proficiency on the amount of LREs produced was investigated by Storch and Aldosari (2012) in their study with 60 EFL university students. High-proficiency dyads produced the largest number of LREs, followed by mixed-proficiency and low-proficiency dyads. In addition to this, high proficiency dyads showed a greater focus on language. Storch and Aldosari concluded that attention must be paid when pairing students as such a decision can have an impact on language learning opportunities.

Fernández-Dobao (2012) found that students working in groups produced more LREs, together with their correct resolution, than dyads. Participants were asked to compose a story based on a set of 15 pictures. Once again, collaboration had a positive effect on linguistic accuracy but not on complexity. The results also revealed that group work fostered LREs which were successfully solved. This was appreciated in the final product, that is, a more accurate story. Similarly, McDonough et al. (2016) looked into pair talk in collaborative work. 62 EFL Thai university students composed collaboratively a summary and a problem/solution paragraph. A relationship was found between the amount of LREs and the text quality of the problem/solution paragraph. McDonough et al. (2016) also observed that in the LREs analysed, students mainly employed their L1 to address issues concerning content, organisation and accuracy.

L1 Use in L2 Collaborative Tasks

While for the most part the use of the L1 in the L2/FL classroom can be a controversial issue, some studies on collaboration have described the use of language learners' L1s as a useful resource. Pioneering studies addressing L1 use when tackling L2 cognitively demanding tasks reported its use for metatalk that supported and enhanced L2 development (Behan et al., 1997; Brooks & Donato, 1994). These insights raised an interest for a better understanding of the role and functions of learners' L1 in collaborative dialogue. For example, Antón and DiCamilla (1998) analysed the use of L1 English of five pairs of adults learning Spanish as a foreign language. While engaged in the writing of collaborative essays, participants' interactions were audio recorded. After examining the transcripts, the authors categorised some functions for the use of the L1. On the one hand, the interpsychological functions, referred to the use of the L1 for scaffolding and intersubjectivity. Learners resorted to English to access L2 linguistic forms, generate a space for collective scaffolding, use the language for metalinguistic comments, and evaluate and understand L2 meaning. English L1 also served a social function, that of creating a space to reach intersubjectivity. On the other hand, the intrapsychological functions of L1 included its use for private speech in cognitively demanding tasks. Antón and DiCamilla reflected on the use of the L1 and suggested the need to modify the widespread tendency to discourage its use in the FL classroom.

At the university level, Storch and Wigglesworth (2003) observed students' reluctance to employ their L1 Indonesian or Mandarin Chinese when completing collaborative tasks. However, when L1s were used, they served tasks management and clarification purposes and, in the specific case of a text reconstruction task, they were used for meaning, vocabulary and grammatical clarifications. Storch and Aldosari (2010) also reported reluctance to employ L1 (Arabic) in 36 university EFL students when completing three collaborative writing tasks. However, when the L1 was used, it mainly served task management functions.

When comparing two groups of students at different levels of proficiency in L2 Spanish, DiCamilla and Antón (2012) noticed a stronger reliance on L1 English in low proficiency groups when engaged in collaborative composition writing. Among the main functions of the L1, the authors mentioned content creation and lexical and grammatical problem-solving. Task management and social rapport were also achieved by means of the L1. In the case of high proficiency students, the number of LREs where the L1 was employed was very limited, and in the form of private speech or lexical translation. Yang's (2014) longitudinal study also provided further evidence in relation to L1 use. Through the analysis of multiple sources of data, Yang discussed the role of L1 to mediate collaborative learning. Finally, studying the impact of L1 use on text quality, Zhang (2018) compared two groups of Chinese university students, one working collaboratively in the L1 (n = 18) and the other in L2 English (n = 17). The L1 Chinese group showed more syntactic complexity and error-free clauses. In addition to this, no statistically significant difference concerning fluency and overall text quality was found, implying that the use of the L1 should not be considered detrimental to L2 performance.

Pragmatic Production in Collaborative Tasks

Pragmatic knowledge is oftentimes described through the distinction between pragmalinguistics and sociopragmatics (Leech, 1983; Thomas, 1983). Pragmalinguistic knowledge relates to the linguistic resources needed to convey a specific function, while sociopragmatic knowledge concerns the effect of cultural norms and contextual features on language form. To the best of our knowledge, few studies have directed attention to the relationship between the learning opportunities generated in collaboration and pragmatic development. For example, Taguchi and Kim (2016) considered collaborative dialogue as going beyond just language forms (i.e., LREs), to also include spaces for pragmatic-related discussion that prompts deep levels of cognitive processing. Hence, they operationalised these learning opportunities as pragmatic-related episodes. In their research, Taguchi and Kim examined the interaction of three groups of participants (n = 74) learning L2 English. A 'collaborative group' received explicit instruction on requests head acts and modification devices in order to engage in a dialogue construction task in pairs. An 'individual group' received the same instruction but worked individually and their ideas were said aloud. Finally, a 'control group' received no instruction. Pre-post-tests were implemented to assess the impact of collaboration on the learning of requests. Moreover, dyads' oral interaction was analysed in terms of PREs. Results showed that the collaborative group outperformed the individual and the control group in the appropriate use of request head acts. No difference was observed for modification devices. Furthermore, students working in pairs produced more PREs, with a higher frequency of resolution of such episodes which led to an accurate use of the request head acts. Taguchi and Kim (2016: 432) concluded that collaboration had a positive effect and that "successful task performance led to significantly greater gains of the knowledge of appropriate request head acts". Addressing task complexity as a factor that contributes to pragmatic development, Kim and Taguchi (2015, 2016) implemented simple and complex cognitively demanding collaborative writing tasks. Findings showed that participants working on tasks of higher complexity had more learning opportunities as observed in the frequency of PREs. These groups mainly discussed issues related to sociopragmatic knowledge, request head acts and preparators.

The Study

The current study analyses the impact of collaboration when engaging in PREs on English request-making during a collaborative writing task. Moreover, drawing on the importance of the L1 when understanding FL pragmatic-related issues (McConachy, 2019), attention is paid to the use of learners' whole language repertoire to evaluate the role of their languages in pragmatic-related resolution. The following two research questions are formulated:

RQ1: Is there a relationship between the frequency of PREs in L3/Ln English and text quality when students engage in a collaborative writing task? If so, does the nature of the PREs, pragmalinguistic or sociopragmatic, influence text quality?

RQ2: Do learners' make use of their L1s to address L3/Ln English PREs? If so, what functions do they play?

Participants

As part of a major research project on pragmatic awareness, 30 first-year university students from the bachelor's degree in Mechanical Engineering and the bachelor's degree in Computational Mathematics from Universitat Jaume I took part in the study. They were all taking English for specific purposes. Their age ranged from 17- to 26-year-old with a mean age of 18.70 years (SD = 2.184). Males represented 83 % of participants (n = 25) and females the remaining 17 % (n = 5). In terms of language background, all students lived in a bilingual community where Spanish and Catalan are the two co-official languages. Furthermore, as part of their compulsory education, English is taught and represents participants' L3/Ln. Based on a language-perception questionnaire passed to students, participants' L1s were mainly Spanish (n = 16), and Catalan (n = 9), together with some speakers of Romanian (n = 4) and Arabic (n = 1). Their L2 was either Spanish (n = 15) or Catalan (n = 14), except for one speaking Arabic. English represented the L3 for 25 students and the L4 for five of them. Five participants reported Catalan as an L3, and one as an L4.

Participants' level of proficiency in English ranged from lower intermediate to advanced. Results from the Oxford Quick Placement test (UCLES, 2001) passed the first day of class placed 43 % (n =13) of students in the lower intermediate level, followed by 27 % (n = 8) in the elementary level, 20 % (n = 6) in the upper-intermediate, and finally 10 % (n = 3) in the advanced level. Only 10 % (n = 3) of the participants experienced a stay abroad in an English-speaking country.

Task Procedure

The data was obtained through a collaborative writing task eliciting English request-making in the academic context. Participants were paired up to collaboratively write an email. They were encouraged to choose a partner with whom they shared a more or less similar level of proficiency. This was done to avoid a gap in their language knowledge that could prevent communication or the higher proficiency student taking control over the task. Once formed the 15 dyads, participants were given a written handout with a hypothetical situation, but related to the academic life, containing the prompt for the request email:

> You are in England as part of the Erasmus programme. The first day of class at your new university, you realise that you have enrolled in a subject that you cannot validate when returning to your university. The enrolment period is closed and you cannot change the subject! You decide to email the enrolment manager of your new university to explain the situation and ask for a subject change.

The scenario proposed filled the criteria of far social distance (SD+) between addresser and addressee and of being a high imposition request (R+). Participants were briefly instructed on collaborative writing and the sort of interaction that was expected. They had to collaborate in order to write the final request email. This collaboration had to be done orally and both students were responsible for the decisions made around the final piece of writing. Nonetheless, only one of them was in charge of handwriting the email while they discussed the content and the language of the task. Students were encouraged to interact with each other but not with the other dyads. In addition to this, they could not use dictionaries or any other kind of help. Participants wrote the final email in an average of 10 minutes.

Data Collection and Analysis

During the completion of the task, participants' interaction was audio-recorded. The total corpus consisted of 12,447 words with 2 hours and 32 minutes of pair interaction in the classroom. The recordings were transcribed following the transcription conventions (see Appendix 1) for later analysis in terms of PREs and L1s use. The final outcome of the collaborative task, that is, the email, was rated in terms of pragmatic appropriateness.

Firstly, transcripts were analysed by identifying PREs and, later, classifying them in pragmalinguistic- and sociopragmatic-related categories. Any part of the speech where participants engaged in conversation concerning a pragmatic-related aspect was selected as the unit of analysis. PREs of pragmalinguistic nature were those where students co-constructed or referred to the linguistic resources needed while in sociopragmatic-related episodes, students made explicit reference to the sociological variables (Brown & Levinson, 1978, 1987) and/or the contextual features that shape the email request. The beginning and end of the episode was marked by the emergence of a pragmatic-related problem and its resolution or change of topic. PREs could go from just one turn to several exchanges.

Table 6.1 exemplifies the distinction between pragmalinguistic- and sociopragmatic-related episodes. This distinction frequently overlapped. For example, dyads may exclusively stick to conversation regarding language form (pragmalinguistic) but oftentimes such language form was the initiator of a conversation around sociopragmatic notions. In order to overcome this overlap, PREs were classified as pragmalinguistic-related when the interaction was primarily focused on linguistic forms. On the other hand, PREs were classified as sociopragmatic-related when dyads provided support to the pragmalinguistic form by addressing issues concerning formality, relationships, roles, imposition, context or cultural norms.

Table 6.1. Pragmatic-related episodes: Pragmalinguistic and sociopragmatic distinction.

Pragmatic-related episodes	
Pragmalinguistic-related episode	**Sociopragmatic-related episode**
S29: Eh dear S30: Hello dear? S29: No, I think that hello is not good maybe. Dear only. Ah, don't worry. S29: So, what? S30: Eh, dear eh, enrolment manager, maybe?	S9: If I can... change this subject in a few days... S10: I could? More formal S9: I could... yeah, if you want

PREs frequency was examined in terms of low and high occurrence of episodes. First, the total number of episodes (n = 52) produced by participants was divided by the total number of dyads (n =15). The value obtained, that is 3.4, was taken as the mean for considering low and high occurrence. Hence, low occurrence took place when a dyad engaged in pragmatic-related debate twice or less. On the other hand, three or more PREs in conversation was considered as high occurrence of episodes.

In order to evaluate text quality, an adaptation of the rubric employed by Nguyen et al. (2015) when assessing the production of email requests in the academic setting was used. The rubric consisted of a Likert-scale where 5 was "completely appropriate" in terms of goal, appropriateness, overall discourse, and grammar, vocabulary and punctuation. On the other extreme, 1 stood for "completely inappropriate" where the student failed in communicating the request and showed a lack of awareness of politeness norms. The main researcher and a professor of multilingualism with experience in pragmatics corrected the emails. To measure the level of agreement, a Cohen's Kappa coefficient was run. A perfect agreement was reported (Kappa = 1, $p < 0.000$).

To find a link between the frequency of the PREs and the quality of the emails, a Spearman-ranked correlation coefficient was run. After testing normality, and observing no normal distribution, this non-parametric procedure was chosen as it allows for an examination of the relationship between variables, that is, number and type of PREs and text quality.

Finally, to provide an answer to the second research question, PREs were qualitatively analysed in terms of L1 use as well. In order to do so, any part of the episode where participants employed their L1s in problem-solving was examined in terms of the functions they served: language-related discussion, interpersonal relations and private speech. This classification was based on previous research on functions of the L1 (Antón & DiCamilla, 1998; Storch & Wigglesworth, 2003; DiCamilla & Antón, 2012).

Results and Discussion

Occurance of PREs and Text Quality

The first research question explored the relationship between the number of PREs and text quality. Following a high-low occurrence description, 73.3 % of dyads (n = 11) produced PREs, either of pragmalinguistic and/or sociopragmatic nature, to a high extent, while 26.7 % (n = 4) engaged to a low extent. In line with previous research (Kim & Taguchi, 2015), participants actively produced PREs at a high rate.

In total, 52 PREs were analysed of which 30 concerned pragmalinguistic issues and 22 sociopragmatic notions. As seen in Table 6.2, most dyads engaged in PREs of pragmalinguistic and sociopragmatic nature at a low frequency, with 66.7 % (n =10) and 60 % (n = 9) of pairs respectively. Few dyads interacted at a high frequency, with only 26.7 % (n =4) for pragmalinguistic-related talk and 13.3 % (n = 2) for sociopragmatic-related debate. Finally, 6.7 % (n = 1) did not address pragmalinguistic forms and 26.7 % (n = 4) omitted the contextual features of the communicative situation when collaboratively writing the email request.

Table 6.2. Occurrence of PREs in dyads.

	Dyads with high frequency	**N**	**Dyads with low frequency**	**N**	**Dyads with no occurrence**	**N**
Pragmatic-related episodes (PREs)	73.3 %	11	26.7 %	4	0 %	0
Pragmalinguistic-related episodes	26.7 %	4	66.7 %	10	6.7 %	1
Sociopragmatic-related episodes	13.3 %	2	60 %	9	26.7 %	4

Concerning pragmalinguistic knowledge, students discussed mainly the structure of the request head act, followed by the opening and closing of the email and, finally, modification devices. As for socio-pragmatic knowledge, pairs talked about contextual features that shaped the level of formality of the request and, in a few instances, referred to the level of familiarity with the addressee. These deliberations are interpreted as an interaction that offered opportunities for pragmatic knowledge co-construction. Excerpts 1 and 2 exemplify pragmalinguistic- and sociopragmatic-related talk, respectively. In Excerpt 1, S1 and S2 were talking about the opening of the email and deciding on the best pragmalinguistic structure to employ. In the first line, S1 proposed the structure "dear" and in the following turn, S2 elaborated on that. Disagreement is expressed as he considered that "dear" is used when one knows the name of the addressee. Finally, S2 opted for "Dear mister", an ill-formed to greet a faculty member.

(1) 01 S1: [We start. . . em::: like em::: [dear!
02 S2: [Em::: Dear! Enrolment
03 S1: Dear em::: that's when we know the name
04 S2: Dear mister, mister. . .

On the other hand, in Excerpt 2, students' interaction goes beyond the structure per se. S21 and S22 were finishing their email and S21 referred to "formality" to justify the language form.

(2) 01 S22: Goodbye
02 S21: Goodbye! (laughs) it's not formal. . . eh::
03 S22: You say hello and you say goodbye
04 S21: (laughs) Oh my god! (rereads) um:: have a good day
05 S22: *Yo qué sé*
'What do I know?'
06 S21: Have a nice day, no, have a good day. Have a wonderful. . .

S22 suggested the use of "good bye" to finish their email but S21 laughed at that decision (2). This motivated a change of language form for one that could fit the register (4 & 6). Hence, this episode of sociopragmatic nature showed how S21 connected form with context, that is, an academic email requiring a more formal register. S21' awareness of sociopragmatic norms motivated a change of structure in order to suit the level of formality as required by the academic email. Changes in the pragmalinguistic form were based on the student's reflection upon the contextual features of the communicative situation.

Having illustrated pragmalinguistic- and sociopragmatic-related episodes in interaction, the assessment of the final request emails in terms of text quality was conducted by resorting to the holistic rubric for request email production. Out of the 15 emails, 66.7 % ($n = 10$) were rated as occasionally inappropriate, band 3 on the Likert-scale. 26.7 % ($n = 4$) were evaluated as mostly inappropriate (band 2), and only 6.7 % ($n = 1$) was considered mostly appropriate (band 4). No emails were rated as completely appropriate (band 5) or inappropriate (band 1).

As can be seen, students' pragmatic knowledge concerning request production falls mostly under the category of occasionally inappropriate (band 3). These emails were characterised by an attempt to convey the request but with a lack of proper support for it. In terms of appropriateness, these emails were oftentimes too direct, in line with pragmatic norms of Spanish culture, and the level of formality was problematic. However, good levels of discourse and grammatical knowledge were displayed. The second most frequent category, band 2, mostly inappropriate, featured emails that failed in conveying the request, and the level of directness and formality was inappropriate in relation to sociopragmatic norms. Finally, just one email showed a proper requestive behaviour with an adequate level of directness and appropriateness.

After having counted the occurrences (low vs high) of PREs, classified them according to their nature and assess text quality, a Spearman rank-order correlation was run to account for a relationship. A positive correlation was found between the number of PREs in student-student interaction and the quality of the final email ($r = 0.63$, $p < 0.05$). The magnitude of this correlation was considered large. Therefore, a relationship between the number of PREs and the quality of the final email was found. To further extend the analysis, the frequency of pragmalinguistic- and sociopragmatic-related episodes was also correlated with the mark obtained. Once again, a large, positive correlation was found between pragmalinguistic-related talk and the quality of the outcome ($r = 0.57$, $p < 0.05$). No correlation was observed between sociopragmatic-related talk and text quality. One possible explanation to this is that pragmalinguistic-talk directly reflects on language forms and can be better observed when the final text is assessed. Debates around sociopragmatic notions operate a a more abstract level that goes beyond pure linguistic matters and such discussions cannot always be traceable in the final piece of writing.

To the best of our knowledge, no previous research has dealt with the relationship between the amount of PREs and text quality. Kim and Taguchi (2015, 2016) commented that more frequent instances of PREs led to a greater relation of request mappings. The present research has observed that a high occurrence of PREs in conversation can translate into better requestive behaviour in terms of formality, politeness and appropriateness in the final email. Even though the focus was not pragmatic knowledge, previous studies analysing accuracy on text quality also reported the positive impact of LREs on the final text (Wigglesworth & Storch, 2009; Fernández-Dobao, 2012; McDonough et al., 2016; Mozaffari, 2017).

L1 Use in Pragmatic-Related Episodes

The second research question examined the use of students' other languages when engaged in PREs. Out of the 15 pairs, 73.3 % ($n = 11$) resorted to Spanish to engage in pragmatic-related conversation. More specifically, 36.3 % ($n = 4$) of dyads used Spanish to address exclusively pragmalinguistic aspects of the language, 18.1 % ($n = 2$) to interact at the level of sociopragmatic knowledge, and 45.4 % ($n = 5$) talked about both dimensions when solving the collaborative writing task. Catalan, Romanian or Arabic were not employed in any of the PREs under analysis.

In total, 11 pairs employed Spanish to engage in conversation concerning pragmalinguistic-and/or sociopragmatic-related episodes. A next step in the analysis consisted of examining the role of the L1s in PREs resolution. As seen in previous studies analysing L1 use (Antón & DiCamilla, 1998; DiCamilla & Antón, 2012), students from the current research used Spanish as a mediating device to access target language forms, for metalinguistic talk, for clarification, evaluation and understanding of L3 meaning, and the construction of a social space to foster interpersonal relations. Private speech was also observed. Based on this, PREs were categorised and analysed as follows: (a) Language-related discussion (accessing L3/Ln pragmalinguistic forms, metatalk and understanding and evaluating meaning), (b) Interpersonal interaction and (c) Private speech. This distinction is done for explanatory purposes as it is difficult to untangle the socio-cognitive processes that occur in interaction.

L1 for Language-related Discussion

Dyads resorted to Spanish in order to be able to cognitively access and co-construct the language form needed when dealing with request head acts and modification devices in L3 English. For example, in Excerpt 3, S29 and S30 were focusing on the request head act. They proposed a variety of possible structures to employ by using Spanish.

(3) 01 S29: How do we say? *Em::: quiero pedirle*
'I want to ask you'
02 S30: I... could you... change
03 S29: Em::: I have a... petition?
04 S30: Or I have...
05 S29: *Pero no sé*... demand?
' But I don't know'
06 S30: *O me preguntaba...*
' Or I was wondering...'
07 S29: *¿cómo se llama... el...?* how do we say... em::: um um um... should no.
08 S29: I have... a... request I want or I need to...
09 S30: I need [to change...

The structure S29 intended to produce was formulated in Spanish (1) and after both students provided alternatives, S29 remained unsure and kept trying (5). In the following turn, S30 suggested another alternative, in Spanish, in an attempt to find an answer. In line 7, S29's use of the L1 was understood as a way of accessing the structure they attempted to produce in English. It can be seen how he was trying to retrieve the language form by asking *¿cómo se llama…?* (how do we say…?). The students managed to come up with a request in the form of a need statement. In this case, the use of Spanish to find the right pragmalinguistic form enabled them to solve the PRE.

L1 for Metatalk

Participants employed L1 Spanish in pragmatic-related talk to refer to metapragmatic issues of sociopragmatic and pragmalinguistic nature. For example, in Excerpt 4, S5 used an idiomatic expression to formulate the request (1). S5 opened this episode by resorting to Spanish to suggest a conditional structure. In line 1, the student proposed, as seen in the verb *podríamos*, the use of such pragmalinguistic form. In order to do so, the student used Spanish to employ metalinguistic terminology, *un condiciona*l (1) which most probably could not have been explained using exclusively English. As part of the request, he decided to use an idiomatic expression "it would score a point' (3) which did not consider the readers" negative face and, therefore, it was not the most appropriate choice.

(4) 01 S5: *Un condicional podríamos poner…* It would… It would score a point.
'We could write a conditional [sentence]…'
02 S6: *Punto,* ¿no? It would
'Stop (.)'
03 S5: Score a point
04 S6: *¿Sss qué?*
' Sss what?'
05 S5: *Es como ser un punto a favor*
'It's like to have a point in your favour'

L1 for Understanding and Evaluating Meaning

Some students employed Spanish when facing difficulties at the level of meaning making. In Excerpts 3 and 4, there are some examples of how Spanish was employed to understand meaning. For instance, in

Excerpt 3, S5 used Spanish to evaluate the meaning of the word "hearing" as part of the chosen pragmalinguistic form (4). In Excerpt 4, S5 explained what he meant by "score a point" (5) after his partner asked for clarification. Excerpt 5, further illustrates this L1 use. After proposing the structure (1 & 2) and questioning its appropriateness in terms of formality (3), S21 compared its meaning "in Spanish" (5) and translated the form. After doing so, he concluded that it was a valid choice.

(5) 01 S21: Have a...
02 S22: good day
03 S21: But this is formal?
04 S22: I think:: yes
05 S21: In Spanish *¿que tenga un buen día?* Yeah, we can write that.
Have a good day.

L1 for Interpersonal Relations

As mentioned in previous research (Antón & DiCamilla, 1998; DiCamilla & Antón, 2012), the use of the L1 also serves a social function. By employing L1 Spanish, students create a metaphorical social space to develop not only the language but also a relationship that contributes to the completion of the task. In Excerpt 6, S5 and S6 were deliberating about the meaning of the word "validate" that appeared in the prompt of the task.

(6) 01 S6: Enrolment este, what does it mean? (laughs)
"this"
02 S5: *El jefe, ¿no?*
"The boss, no?"
03 S6: *Pero... no. En plan* enrolment
"But... no. Like"
04 S5: *Será como... como el organizador*
"It must be like... like the organiser."
05 S6: *No pero... a ver...*
"No but... let's see..."

06 S5: *De la Universidad*
"Of the university"
07 S6: (reads instructions) You have enrolled subject that you cannot validate. *Aquí...*
"Here"
08 S5*: Es como cursar... estás... envuelto o como eso.*
"It's like studying... you are... involved or whatever."
09 S6: *A ver es que me sonaba más a: tipo lo de... convalidación o*
"Let's see. It reminds me of: like the thing about... validation *algo así*
or something like that.'
10 S5: *No. Es como que estás cursando una asignatura que no... que*
"No. It's that you are taking a subject that it's not... that
no te sirve de nada cuando vuelva a la universidad.
it's not useful at all when returning to the university.'
11 S6: *Como que, claro. Vas a cursar el... claro...* you cannot
"Like, right. You are taking the... right..."
validate, o sea validate si que es lo de convali... en plan como que...
"I mean" "if the thing about valida... like"
12 S5: *-Validar*
"Validate"

In this interaction, S5 resorted to his L1 in order to assist his partner. After asking for the meaning of "enrolment", S5 offered an explanation in Spanish. The use of the L1 was repeated along the episode (2, 4, 6, 8, 10) and exemplified how S5 was able to guide his partner in the comprehension of the task prompt. This fact does not only exemplify L1 for social use but also for meaning evaluation and understanding (a.3). S6 also employed Spanish but to signal disagreement (3, 5, 10) and to speculate about meaning as seen in the use of *será* (4). As S6 was not able to make his case, he reread the instructions and signalled the part that was problematic by saying *aquí* (7). By using Spanish, he made sure that his partner was able to understand the problem that he was trying to solve. In line 9, S6 made a first attempt to understand "validation" as observed in the use of *convalidación,* the Spanish translation. After much deliberation, S6 made sense of the prompt and found the meaning of the word that was problematic (11). While Spanish was used to engage in cognitive problem-solving, this episode also illustrates its social use. In this sense, this language was employed by S5 as a way to guide S6 along the process of task comprehension. Thanks to the L1, S6 was able to express doubts, recapitulate and finally comprehend the task.

L1 in Private Speech

Lantolf (2000) explained that private speech is characterised by questioning and answering ourselves, telling us to interrupt or continue a certain activity or provide us with feedback. Private speech operates at an individual, private level of cognition. As reported by Antón and DiCamilla (1998), students resort to private speech when engaged in collaborative work to guide themselves through the task. In the current study, instances of private speech by means of L1 Spanish were found. Excerpt 8 provides an example of private speech.

(7) 01 S11: to a new one, *ya, claro, sí.* To a new one (writes) to another one...
"Yeah, of course, yes."
02 S12: To another one
03 S11: Which...I...could
04 S12: could eh:::
05 S11: Validate
06 S12: Validate or any::: or any solution, ¿no? (8)
07 S11: Since, since I cannot do it by myself because the enrollment period is closed... to change anything ¿cómo era? Em::: (5) due to due
'how was it?'
to *es siempre debido a ¿Esto qué es?* due to... due, due to... a...
"Is always due to." "What is this"

S11 and S12 were working on the request head act. Private speech was observed in line 1, where S11 said to himself *ya claro, sí* regarding the structure he was writing. Hence, he was providing feedback to himself. After that, he repeated the structure once again, which signalled how he was in his head debating about this pragmalinguistic form. A few turns later, in line 7, S11 questioned how to continue the sentence by asking to himself *¿cómo era?* Immediately after, he responded with the correct structure "due to" and provided, once again, feedback by saying *es siempre debido*, a translation into Spanish of the target structure. Finally, *¿esto qué es?* introduces again a thinking process around the structure "due to" that marks doubts concerning its use within the sentence.

These results contribute to research on L1 use in the L2 classroom by extending it to L3/Ln English contexts. Their importance lies on considering the multilingual experience of participants as an asset rather than as a constraint. As explained by McConachy (2019: 173):

> (. . .) even when the focus in the classroom appears to be on the L2, learners will implicitly and explicitly engage knowledge of other languages and cultures as a reference point for interpreting the material they are exposed to and constructing comparisons that serve to elaborate the emerging interpretations.

While the use of the L1 in the FL/L2 classroom has been largely documented, the relevance of the current research relies on its focus on pragmatics and its multilingual approach. Few studies have investigated pragmatic knowledge while considering multilingualism as a framework (Safont, 2005; Safont & Alcón-Soler, 2012; Portolés, 2015; Safont & Portolés, 2016; Portolés & Safont, 2018), and even fewer have done it from a sociocultural theory perspective (Taguchi & Kim, 2016; Kim & Taguchi, 2015, 2016).

Conclusion

In the current study, the implementation of a collaborative writing task which elicited request-making promoted student-student interaction around pragmatic-related aspects of the language. A positive correlation was found between the high-frequency occurrence of pragmatic-related talk and a better quality of the final request email. Furthermore, pragmalinguistic-related talk seemed to exert a greater influence on text quality in terms of pragmatic appropriateness. These results contribute to the bulk of research on the relationship between language-related episodes and text quality (Wigglesworth & Storch, 2009; Fernández-Dobao, 2012; McDonough et al., 2016, Mozaffari, 2017) but with a focus on pragmatic-related episodes. In addition to this, the collaborative nature of the writing task allowed participants to co-construct their pragmatic knowledge through active discussion and interpretation of the email request. As seen in previous research, the L1 was employed for the provision of metalinguistic comments, the evaluation and understanding of L3 meaning as well as the construction of a social space and in private speech. These results provide evidence of the importance of students" whole language repertoire to interpret and assess pragmatic-related aspects and the relationship of the language systems in terms of pragmatic connections.

From a pedagogical point of view, these findings seem to suggest that the use of collaborative tasks with a pragmatic focus foster pragmatic-related talk. This dialogue operates at two levels, pragmalinguistic and sociopragmatic, both equally important. Nonetheless, sociopragmatic norms tend to be idealised against monolingual normativity and by engaging multilingual learners in this kind of awareness-raising activities, we promote a space for hypothesis testing and co-construction of new, deeper knowledge. Furthermore, the relevance of learners' whole language repertoire is highlighted by examining the different functions that their L1s have and how they can help in the pragmatic development of L3 English. Therefore, the design of collaborative tasks to foster pragmatic development should be encouraged as it does not only turn beneficial at a cognitive level but at a social one as well.

When considering the implications of this study, its limitations must be acknowledged. To start with, the small sample used in the study prevents generalisations. While it was practical for a closer qualitative examination of learners' L1 use, future research should include a larger number of participants in order to conduct a more in-depth quantitative analysis. Secondly, this study derives from a larger project where multiple collaborative tasks were implemented, but this study just focused on one. Hence, a more pre-post-test design type of research including also different tasks can provide a more accurate and complete picture of PREs and L1 use in L3 English. This study focuses only on one pragmatic aspect, that is, request-making. This line of research could benefit from analysing other speech acts as well as other aspects such as implicatures. Regarding the collaborative nature of the task, the study of other variables like pair type and proficiency could contribute to a better understanding of collaboration and pragmatic learning. Finally, exploring other L1s besides Spanish would also contribute with further evidence around the complexity of L1 use in multilingual contexts.

Appendix 1. Transcription Conventions

S = student
(transcriber's notes)
– cut off speech
(1) pause in seconds
[overlap in speech
::: extension of sound
Other language apart from English

References

Antón, Marta & Dicamilla Frederick J. 1998. Socio-cognitive functions of L1 collaborative interaction in the L2 classroom. *The Modern Language Journal*, 83/2, 233–247.

Bachman, Lyle. F. & Palmer, Adrian S. 1996. *Language testing in practice: Designing and developing useful language tests.* Oxford: Oxford University Press.

Behan, Laurie/Turnbull, Miles & Spek, Jane. 1997. The proficiency gap in late immersion (extended French): Language use in collaborative tasks. *Le Journal de l'Immersion*, 20/2, 41–42.

Brooks, Frank B. & Donato, Richard 1994. Vygotskyan approaches to understanding foreign language learner discourse during communicative tasks. *Hispania*, 77/2, 262–274.

Brown, Penelope & Levinson, Stephen. 1978. Universals in language use: Politeness phenomena. In Esther N. Goody (ed.) *Questions and politeness: Strategies in social interaction.* Cambridge: Cambridge University Press, 56–289.

Brown, Penelope & Levinson, Stephen. 1987. *Politeness: Some Universals in language usage*. Cambridge: Cambridge University Press.

Dicamilla, Frederick. J. & Antón, Marta. 2012. Functions of L1 in the collaborative interaction of beginning and advanced second language learners. *International Journal of Applied Linguistics*, 22/2, 160–188.

Fernández-Dobao, Ana. 2012. Collaborative writing tasks in the L2 classroom: Comparing group, pair, and individual work. *Journal of Second Language Writing*, 21/1, 40–58.

González-Lloret, Marta. 2020. Collaborative tasks for online teaching. *Foreign Language Annals*, 53, 260–269.

González-Lloret, Marta. 2021. Online collaboration through tasks for L2 pragmatic development. In Maria Pilar García-Mayo (ed.) *Working collaboratively in second/foreign language learning*. Berlin: De Gruyter Mouton, 199–226.

Kim, Youjin & Taguchi, Naoko. 2015. Promoting task-based pragmatics instruction in efl classroom contexts: The role of task complexity. *The Modern Language Journal*, 99/4, 656–677.

Kim, Youjin & Taguchi, Naoko. 2016. Learner-learner interaction during collaborative pragmatic tasks: The role of cognitive and pragmatic task demands. *Foreign Language Annals*, 49/1, 42–57.

Lantolf, James. 2000. *Sociocultural theory and second language learning*. Oxford: Oxford University Press.

Leech, Geoffrey N. 1983. *Principles of pragmatics*. London: Longman.

Martinez-Buffa, Ignacio & Safont, Pilar. 2022. Multilingual pragmatic awareness in collaborative writing. *Language Awareness*, 32/3, 421–442.

McConachy, Troy. 2019. L2 pragmatics as 'Intercultural Pragmatics': Probing sociopragmatic aspects of pragmatic awareness. *Journal of Pragmatics*, 151, 167–176.

McDonough, Kim, Crawford, William J. & De Vleeschauwer, Jindarat. 2016. Thai EFL learners' interaction during collaborative writing tasks and its relationship to text quality. In Masatoshi Sato & Susan Ballinger (eds), *Peer interaction and second language learning: Pedagogical potential and research agenda*. Amsterdam: John Benjamins, 185–208.

McDonough, Kim, De Vleeschauwer, Jindarat & Crawford, William. 2018. Comparing the quality of collaborative writing, collaborative prewriting, and individual texts in a Thai EFL context. *System*, 74, 109–120.

Mozaffari, Seyedeh H. 2017. Comparing student-selected and teacher-assigned pairs on collaborative writing. *Language Teaching Research*, 21/4, 496–516.

Nguyen, Thi. T. M., Do, Thi T. H., Nguyen, Anh H. & Pham, Thi T. T. 2015. Teaching email requests in the academic context: A focus on the role of corrective Feedback. *Language Awareness*, 24/2, 169–195.

Portolés, Laura & Safont, Pilar. 2018. Examining authentic and elicited data from a multilingual perspective. The real picture of child requestive behaviour in the L3 classroom. *System*, 75, 81–92.

Portolés, Laura. 2015. *Multilingualism and very young learners: An analysis of pragmatic awareness and language attitudes* (Trends in applied linguistics, TAL, Vol. 20). Berlin: Mouton de Gruyter.

Safont, Pilar & Alcón-Soler, Eva. 2012. Teachability of request act peripheral modification devices in third language learning contexts. In Maria Economidou-Kogetsidis & Helen Woodfield (eds) *Interlanguage request modification: Pragmatics and beyond new series.* Amsterdam: John Benjamins, 275–313.

Safont, Pilar & Portolés, Laura. 2016. Pragmatic functions of formulaic speech in three different languages. A focus on early L3 learners of English. *Journal of Immersion and Content-Based Educations*, 4/ 2, 225–250.

Safont, Pilar. 2005. *Third language learners. Pragmatic production and awareness.* Clevedon: Multilingual Matters.

Shehadeh, Ali. 2011. Effects and Student Perceptions of Collaborative Writing in L2. *Journal of Second Language Writing*, 20/4, 286–305.

Storch, Noemi & Aldosari, Ali. 2010. Learners' use of first language (Arabic) in pair work in an EFL class. *Language Teaching Research*, 14/4, 355–375.

Storch, Noemi & Aldosari, Ali. 2012. Pairing learners in pair work activity. *Language Teaching Research*, 17/1, 31–48.

Storch, Noemi & Wigglesworth, Gillian. 2003. Is there a role for the use of the L1 in an L2 setting? *TESOL Quarterly*, 37/4, 760–770.

Storch, Noemi & Wigglesworth, Gillian. 2007. Writing tasks: The effect of collaboration. In Maria Pilar García Mayo (ed.) *Investigating tasks in formal language learning*. Clevedon: Multilingual Matters, 157–177.

Storch, Noemi. 2005. Collaborative writing: Product, Process, and Students' Reflections. *Journal of Second Language Writing*, 14/3, 153–173.

Storch, Noemi. 2013. *Collaborative writing in L2 classroom*. Bristol: Multilingual Matters.

Storch, Noemi. 2019. Collaborative writing. *Language Teaching*, 52/1, 40–59.

Swain, Merrill & Lapkin, Sharon. 1998. Interaction and second language learning: Two adolescents French immersion students working together. *The Modern Language Journal*, 82/3, 320–337.

Swain, Merrill & Watanabe, Yuko. 2013. Languaging: Collaborative dialogue as a source of second language learning. In Carol A. Chappelle (ed.) *The encyclopaedia of applied linguistics*. Chichester: John Wiley & Sons, 1–8.

Swain, Merrill. 2000. The output hypothesis and beyond: Mediating acquisition through collaborative dialogue. In James P. Lantolf (ed.) *sociocultural theory and second language learning*. Oxford: Oxford University Press, 97–114.

Taguchi, Noemi & Kim, Youjin. 2016. Collaborative dialogue in learning pragmatics: Pragmatic-related episodes as an opportunity for learning request-making. *Applied Linguistics*, 37/3, 416–437.

Thomas, Jenny. 1983. Cross-cultural pragmatic failure. *Applied Linguistics*, 4/2, 91–112.

UCLES (University of Cambridge Local Examinations Syndicate). 2001. *Quick placement test*. Oxford: Oxford University Press.

Usó-Juan, Esther & Martínez-Flor, Alicia. 2006. Approaches to language learning and teaching: Towards acquiring communicative competence through the four skills. In E. Usó–Juan & A. Martínez–Flor (eds), *Current trends in the development and teaching of the four language skills*. Berlin: Mouton de Gruyter, 3–26. <https://doi.org/10.1515/9783110197778>

Vygostky, Lev S. 1978. *Mind in society. The development of higher psychological processes*. Cambridge: Harvard University Press.

Wigglesworth, Gillian & Storch, Noemi. 2009. Pairs vs individuals: Effects on fluency, complexity, and accuracy. *Language Testing,* 26/3, 455–466.

Yang, Luxin. 2014. Examining the mediational means in collaborative writing: Case studies of undergraduate ESL students in business courses. *Journal of Second Language Writing*, 23, 74–86.

Zhang, Meixiu. 2018. Collaborative writing in the EFL classroom: The effects of L1 and L2 use. *System*, 76, 1–12.

Section III
Cyber Pragmatics

Ilka Flöck, Onur Çiçek and Anne Barron

Directives in ELF Peer Feedback

Introduction

Feedback is a central element in many areas of education: Teachers may, for instance, give feedback to their students to improve their language or writing skills, students may give each other peer feedback on their course work, and teacher trainers may provide feedback to future teachers for them to improve their own teaching skills. Feedback has been studied from a variety of perspectives, including ethnographic (didactic) and speech act (language) perspectives. Ethnographic perspectives aim to provide insights into the social and didactic dimensions of peer feedback by highlighting the power structure and institutional roles of the participants as well as other contextual or social factors that can influence the feedback process (cf. e.g. Dippold, 2009; Farr, 2011; Khezrlou, 2023; Swinglehurst et al., 2008). On the other hand, a speech act perspective takes the language as a focal point and focuses on the individual speech acts used within the speech event, such as criticism, praise, suggestions (Batlle & Seedhouse, 2022; Decapua & Findlay Dunham, 2007; Del Bono & Nuzzo, 2021; Hyland & Hyland, 2001; Nguyen, 2008a, 2008b, 2013).

The present study adopts a speech act perspective in the study of feedback and focuses on directive speech acts produced in written peer feedback. While directives are only one of many different components in complex feedback events (among, e.g. positive and negative assessments), they occupy a central role in such events. Whereas previous research has partially shed light on directives in feedback, there is no comprehensive study on such directives to date that is informed by speech act theoretical insights and systematically applies previous findings on directive speech acts to the study of feedback directives. With this paper, we aim at filling this research gap by developing a coding scheme for feedback directives that synthesizes both theoretical insights and empirical findings on a range of directive speech acts. For the development of our coding scheme, we use data from an English as a Lingua Franca (ELF) context to test it in an exploratory analysis. Thus, our research questions are:

1. How can feedback directives be analysed transparently and systematically?
2. Which strategies are used by ELF speakers in their feedback directives and how do their directives compare with native speaker feed-back directives?
3. How do the ELF learners' feedback directives compare with other directive speech acts?

In this paper, we first conceptualise feedback as a complex speech event, then discuss directives in the light of speech-act based theoretical and empirical traditions, before offering a literature review on empirical studies investigating feedback (or components thereof). In our methodology section, we briefly introduce our participant groups, the data collection procedure and our coding scheme before introducing and discussing our initial results.

Theory

Feedback as a Speech Event

Feedback is a complex linguistic phenomenon that may include a number of different individual speech acts, such as providing criticism, praise, or giving the recipient ideas of what could and should be changed (i.e. directive speech acts). The intrinsically complex structure of feedback can also be traced to its institutional situatedness with its related norms and expectations, which in turn are influenced by the purpose, expectations and rules prevalent in a particular situational context

(Copland, 2011, 2012; Vásquez, 2004; Farr & O'Keeffe, 2002). Finally, feedback is produced between interlocutors with pre-defined roles (feedback provider and feedback recipient) and hence is characterised by an asymmetrical power relation. With these characteristics, feedback can be conceptualised as what Levinson (1979: 368, original emphasis) refers to as an "activity type": Activity types are "goal-defined, socially constituted, bounded events with *constraints* on participants, settings, and so on, but above all on the kinds of allowable contributions".

Given its multi-faceted nature and situatedness within a specific context, feedback can furthermore be conceptualised as a speech event (cf. Vásquez, 2004). According to Hymes (1972: 56), speech events are "restricted to activities, or aspects of activities, that are directly governed by rules or norms for the use of speech. An event may consist of a single speech act, but will often comprise several". A speech event differs from a speech act in that it can comprise one or more speech acts and takes place in a specific speech situation. In the present study, our *speech situation* is a classroom, *the speech event* is feedback, and this feedback event may be composed of various *speech acts* (e.g. criticism, praise, directives).

While the concept of a "speech event" highlights the multi-faceted character of feedback events as potentially consisting of a number of different individual illocutions (praise, criticism, advise), the concept "activity type" highlights the situatedness in social or institutional settings with all the constraints that come with such situatedness. These constraints may lead to a number of challenges for ELF or EFL (English as a Foreign Language) speakers, such as a potential lack of awareness of the social/institutional expectations (sociopragmatic perspective) and a potential lack of knowledge of which linguistic structures are suitable or expected in which situation (sociopragmatic/pragmalinguistic perspective).

The concept of a speech event offers a theoretical framework which can capture the complexity of feedback. On an empirical level, a number of individual acts and moves have been identified for feedback and related speech events such as email directives (as in Freytag, 2019). The following list aims at collecting and synthesizing these individual components and offers an overview of the acts and moves that have been identified for feedback. While in our analysis we focus on directive speech acts (strategy 8), it is important to keep in mind that directives do not occur in isolation in feedback events but are embedded in the context of other strategies (in addition to being socially situated).

1. Greeting (Freytag, 2019)
2. Self-introduction (Freytag, 2019)
3. Orientation move (Freytag, 2019)
4. Inquiry about the other's well-being (Tracy & Eisenberg, 1990)
5. Positive prefatory statement (Tracy & Eisenberg, 1990)
6. Negative evaluation/criticism (Nguyen, 2008a)
7. Positive evaluation/praise (Nguyen 2008a, 2008b)
8. Directive (Donaghue 2020; Nguyen 2008a, 2008b; Tracy & Eisenberg, 1990)
9. Positive ending statement (Tracy & Eisenberg, 1990)
10. Farewell move (Tracy & Eisenberg, 1990)

In conclusion, as the present study focuses on the multi-faceted nature of feedback and adopts a speech act perspective, feedback is conceptualised as a *speech event* that can include a number of different individual speech acts and an *activity type* that is situated in a specific institutional setting (classroom context). In our analysis, we focus on the linguistic realisation of one particular speech act, viz. directives.

Directive Speech Acts in EIL Feedback

Most studies investigating feedback acknowledge that one component of the complex speech event consists of a speaker providing the addressee with ideas of what to change in their work (Del Bono & Nuzzo, 2021; Nguyen, 2008a, 2008b, 2013; Nguyen & Basturkmen, 2010; Strong & Baron, 2004; Vásquez, 2004). In other words, feedback frequently includes directive speech acts, i.e. linguistic actions in which a speaker directs an addressee to carry out a future action A (Searle, 1969; cf. 8 in the list above). Applied to the case of peer feedback, the feedback giver directs the feedback recipient to change something in their work (and frequently also indicates how to change it). The category of directive speech acts includes a wide range of individual illocutions, ranging from commands, orders, requests to suggestions and advice. Whereas the definition of the overall speech act category of directives is rather straightforward and has not been questioned in the theoretical literature on speech acts and its empirical applications, the delineation of individual directive illocutions is far from being clear-cut (cf. e.g. Flöck, 2016). Different criteria have been employed to distinguish between individual directive illocutions. Speech-act theoretical approaches (such as Fraser, 1974; Hindelang, 1978; Searle, 1969; Wunderlich, 1976) have used the criterion of benefit to delineate requests from suggestions and advice (with requests being in the speaker's and suggestions/advice being in the addressee's interest). While directive speech acts in feedback events can be said to be in the addressee's long-term interest (as the purpose of the feedback is to improve the quality of their work), they may still clash with a recipient's short-term preferences. The criterion of benefit is thus difficult to use and apply in practice in distinguishing between different directive illocutions in feedback.

This difficulty to distinguish between different directive illocutions can also be observed in empirical research on feedback directives: While authors like Nguyen and Basturkmen (2010), Song (2023), Strong and Baron (2004) and Vásquez (2004) identify suggesting and advising as possible directive points in feedback, Nguyen (2008a) also conceptualises directive speech acts in feedback as requests, demands, advice and suggestions. None of these studies have offered systematic structural or contextual criteria for delineating the different illocutions and hence their criteria for coding these acts into different categories remain opaque. More generally, it is questionable whether a systematic delineation is even possible let alone whether it can be implemented validly and reliably in natural data. The question of which specific directive illocutions can be found in feedback events and how they can be distinguished has thus never been and may not be possible to be answered systematically. Thus, instead of relying on *a priori* categories of different directive illocutions, the present study includes all directive speech acts produced in feedback events. In our analysis, we use structural linguistic criteria to differentiate between the different directness levels and realisation strategies employed in these directives.

While a speech act perspective on directives in feedback events sheds light on some of the properties of directives, it cannot account for the social characteristics of this particular speech action. In most investigations of directive speech acts, directive acts are conceptualised as intrinsic face-threatening acts (FTA) in Brown and Levinson's (1987) terms. More specifically, Brown and Levinson (1987: 62) argue that directives primarily threaten the hearer's negative face wants (i.e. their desire to be free in action) but it is conceivable that directives in feedback may also threaten the addressee's positive face wants (i.e. their desire for themselves and their actions to be liked and respected by others) in that directives may be understood as a negative assessment of the feedback recipient's work, and hence function in a similar manner as the act of criticising. The connection between the actions of directing and criticising has been highlighted by a number of authors in the feedback literature (Nguyen & Mushin, 2022; Nguyen, 2008a, 2008b; Nguyen & Basturkmen, 2010; Song, 2023; Strong & Baron, 2004; Tracy et al. 1987; Tracy & Eisenberg, 1990; Vásquez, 2004). Nguyen (2008a, 2008b) even codes the use of directive speech acts as an indirect strategy of criticising. In that sense, it may be helpful to distinguish between the primary and secondary meaning of speech acts. While the primary function of directives is to direct the hearer towards carrying out a future action, a potential secondary function of directives may be to provide a negative assessment (viz. criticism) of the addressee's work. Whereas speech act-based approaches have traditionally focussed on the primary meaning of speech acts, discursive approaches to speech acts have highlighted that speech acts may be used in a number of different functions. Robinson (2004), for instance, finds that explicit apologies are often used as mitigating prefaces for other illocutions (e.g. asking for information) or are used as structural markers of dispreference in dispreferred second pair parts (such as complaints). A similar case can be made for directives in feedback events: While the primary function is to direct the addressee to change aspects of their work, they may at the same time be understood as negative assessments. However, whether addressees perceive them as such can ultimately not be determined based on production data. There are, for instance, some indications that directives in feedback sequences may not automatically be understood as negative assessments due to their specific social and institutional situatedness of the feedback event. In her investigation of how participants negotiate face in feedback events, Copland (2011) finds that participants expect some types of FTAs to happen in feedback and thus do not evaluate them as overly imposing (e.g. providing criticism). However, Copland (2011) does not specifically investigate directives and hence her findings may not be entirely applicable to these speech acts.

Based on the discussions in the current section, the present study focuses on acts with a primary directive function and defines primary directives in feedback speech events as the following:

speech acts in which the feedback giver directs the feedback recipient to carry out a future action by explicitly outlining this specific course of action,
speech actions that may include a number of individual illocutions (suggestions, advice, requests, etc.), which all express directive point,
speech acts which are produced between interlocutors with predefined roles of feedback provider and feedback recipient and hence display an asymmetrical power relation (given the institutional situatedness of the feedback event, cf. Chapter 2.1),
speech acts which potentially threaten the hearer's negative and positive face wants.

To finish our theoretical background section, we give a short overview of the findings of studies which have investigated directives and other related speech acts, such as criticism, in the same speech event: peer feedback. While the studies to be reviewed may differ from our study in their definition and conceptualisation of directives (some use different speech act labels and some attempt such *a priori* categorisations of directive illocutions as critically discussed above), they still provide valuable insights as to how ELF and EFL language users have been found to provide feedback in English.

Directives in (Peer) Feedback: A Literature Review

As outlined in the previous section, the present study focuses on directives in peer feedback events. As previous research focussed on other aspects of the feedback event, feedback directives have frequently been conceptualised as realisation strategies of other speech acts, most notably criticism. Consequently, in such studies, similar but not identical functions (such as criticizing and directing) have been conflated, leading to a diverse and heterogeneous conceptualisation of feedback directives. Hence, findings of studies including feedback directives may not always be comparable in themselves, nor with the present analysis. With this in mind, we focus on only those findings for which at least some comparability is possible. To give the reader a good overview of the research field, we first outline how feedback directives have been conceptualised in previous research before outlining how native speakers and English learners have been found to realise feedback directives.

Feedback Directives as Realisation Strategies for Criticism

Feedback directives have often been conceptualised as realisation strategies for criticism in previous research (Nguyen, 2008a; Nguyen & Basturkmen, 2010; Song, 2023; Tracy et al., 1987; Tracy & Eisenberg, 1990). In a study widely discussed in the feedback literature, Nguyen (2008a) investigates EFL learners' strategies of realising criticism in feedback events. The author conceptualises criticising as an umbrella term for different linguistic actions ranging from negative assessments, disagreements, and warnings, to a number of different directives, such as demanding, requesting, advising, and suggesting. These directives are categorised as indirect realisations of criticism given, as the author argues, that criticism is performed with the intention of guiding the addressee towards improved future behaviour or to express the speaker's discontent or disapproval of the addressee's actions and choices. Within her indirect criticism strategy, Nguyen (2008a) differentiates demands for change, requests for change, advice for change and suggestions for change. Nguyen's (2008a) categorisation of directives differs markedly from established research on requests in that the study conflates distinct directive strategies into seemingly homogenous categories and groups strategies as distinct that are typically treated as instantiations of the same category. This can, for instance, be seen in Nguyen's request for change category where both imperatives and preparatory strategies like *Can you...?* are treated as instantiations of the same category. Furthermore, Nguyen's (2008a) four directive categories are not mutually exclusive as they are not theoretically or structurally defined. While the examples in the demand for change category seem to suggest that the expression of obligation was the criterion for classification, the categorisation of *should* in the advice category contradicts this pattern. Given the lack of structural criteria in Nguyen's (2008a) categorisation of directives, a systematic delineation of directive strategies based on this framework is not possible.

Despite the issues discussed above, Nguyen's (2008a) conceptualisation of directives has been influential in the research field in that a number of authors have adopted a similar approach. Nguyen and Basturkmen (2010), for instance, treat advice about change as a realisation strategy for constructive critical feedback. In a similar vein, Song (2023) codes suggestions and advice for change as strategies of constructive feedback. Nguyen's (2008a) connection (or even conflation) of criticism and directives in feedback events is also visible in Del Bono and Nuzzo's (2021) investigation of criticism and suggestion strategies in intermediate and advanced Italian EFL learners and American English native speakers collaborating in a telecollaborative exchange format.

Furthermore, the conflation of directives with realisation strategies of criticism has led to a lack of focus in the analysis of feedback directives. Song (2023: 79), for instance, analyses head act and modification strategies of critical feedback but does not always systematically distinguish between the two levels of analysis. Hedges (traditionally analysed as modifiers) serve as head act strategies in Song's (2023: 79) framework (alongside direct and indirect strategies). Furthermore, adverbs such as *very* (which are customarily analysed as upgrading modifiers in all frameworks following Blum-Kulka et al., 1989) are treated as direct head act strategies ("strong modal verbs or adverbs"). Similar inconsistencies in speech act categorisation and coding can be found in Del Bono and Nuzzo's (2021: 199) investigation of criticism and suggestion strategies as some of the examples do not correspond to the strategy definitions (e.g. "you could fix that" is coded as an impersonal strategy and not as a possibility strategy). At the same time, Del Bono and Nuzzo (2021) use a modified version of Nguyen's (2008a) coding categories, supplemented with categories from Martínez-Flor's (2005) taxonomy of suggestions, to conceptually differentiate between criticism and suggestions. However, what Del Bono and Nuzzo (2021) term "suggestions" spans a wide range of directives including requests, advice and potentially even orders.

To conclude, the functional overlap between the illocutions of criticising and directing in feedback events (cf. Section 2.2) has led to the conceptualisation of feedback directives as realisation strategies for criticism in previous research. This, in turn, has resulted in directives not being analysed in a systematic and in-depth manner. With the present study, we aim at closing this gap by providing an in-depth analysis of feedback directives that is informed by speech act theory and the findings of empirical studies on directive speech acts.

Feedback Directives in English Native Speaker Groups

There are only a few studies that have investigated the perception and production of feedback strategies (including directives) of native English speakers. Two of the early studies are Tracy et al.'s (1987) and Tracy and Eisenberg's (1990) investigations of the perception of criticism in the feedback produced by American English native speakers. In their study on markers of good and bad feedback, Tracy et al. (1987) find that the level of specificity of the direction provided had an impact on respondents' evaluation of appropriateness. Their index of specificity of suggested change ranges from no direction provided to providing the exact words or phrases to be changed. While high levels of specificity in the direction correlated with respondents' positive evaluation of the feedback instance, redundancy in the directions given and perceived over-specificity of direction led to lower judgement in clarity, and hence more negative evaluations of feedback. Given their focus on criticism, the authors' investigations only provide partial insights about directives in feedback events. Nonetheless, we can conclude from them that feedback recipients expect feedback givers to provide them with specific directions as to what and how to change in their work.

Moving to production, the use of feedback directives among English native speakers has been investigated by Vásquez (2004) and Strong and Baron (2004). While Vásquez (2004) analyses the modification strategies in American English (AmE) feedback advice and suggestions produced in post-observation feedback sessions in a teacher supervision context, Strong and Baron (2004) focus on the realisation of suggestions and their responses in an AmE native speaker group of teacher trainers providing feedback and support for beginning teachers. Strong and Baron (2004: 50) find that suggestion strategies in feedback include the use of performatives (*I suggest...*), expressions of willingness (*You want to...*), "testimonials" (*Many teachers like to...*), interrogative structures (*What do you think about...?*), and indirect strategies like comments (X *would be good.*). The authors find that their participants relied primarily on indirect suggestions with strategies expressing possibility and positive assessment being the most frequent (of the form *I wonder if you could...* and *It would be helpful...*). The second most frequent strategy in their dataset is the use of questions to realise a suggestion (*Will you do* X?) followed by pointing out general rules. While these results are interesting as they provide insights as to which linguistic realisation strategies are used for directives in native speaker feedback, the lack of transparent structural criteria in their coding makes it difficult to compare Strong and Baron's (2004) results to other researchers' findings.

Focussing only on the use of hedging devices in post-observation teacher training interactions at an Irish university, Farr and O'Keeffe (2002) find that the hedge *would* is routinely employed by advisors, especially in first person singular constructions. The authors find that trainers frequently substituted obligation references with *should* with the hedged form *would* in order to make their directives more indirect.

Feedback Directives in EFL Learner Groups

Most of the studies investigating the use of directives in EFL learner populations have conceptualised directives as realisation strategies of criticism. Hence, the lack of systematic focus on directives as discussed earlier (cf. p. 202–204) applies to many studies. Despite these theoretical and methodological issues, they still yield some interesting initial results about EFL learners' use of directives in feedback events. The overall findings of these studies indicate that learners differ from native speakers in their feedback strategies in that they use fewer directives (and hence produce feedback that is not specific enough) and choose different linguistic means to realise their directives.

Nguyen's (2008a) investigation of criticism produced by Vietnamese EFL learners shows learner criticism strategies to be significantly more indirect than those of native speakers. While the learners produced fewer statements of the problem, they used more demands than Nguyen's (2008a) native speaker group. In other words, Ngyuen's learners relied more on directives than on criticism strategies. In addition to differing in the choice of speech act produced, Nguyen's learners also differed from the native speakers in their wording of these acts. Nguyen (2008a: 54–55) reports that her learners used fewer modal past and conditional forms in their suggestions and advice than the native speakers. The author also finds that learners expressed their requests mostly through bare imperatives and want statements. Nguyen also observes that her learners' feedback strategies were generally less complex than native speaker ones.

Similarly, Del Bono and Nuzzo's (2021) results suggest that learners differ from native speakers in their criticism and suggestion patterns. However, the authors report patterns which diverge from Nguyen's (2008a) findings in that their learners produced more negative assessments than directives in feedback events. While their AmE native speakers relied primarily on producing directives that refer to ability (*you could do* X) in giving feedback, the learners predominantly produced negative assessments without a directive. Over time and with exposure to English, this usage pattern shifted slightly and learners started to use more and also different directives: When learners produced directives at the beginning of the observational period, they mainly used need statements (*you need to do* X). At the end of the observational period, Del Bono and Nuzzo's (2021: 199) intermediate and advanced Italian EFL learner group started to produce more impersonal constructions ("*I think it's better to use…*"). Another study that reports differences between learners and native speakers is Song's (2023) investigation of feedback directives in a group of advanced Chinese EFL learners and AmE native speakers. The author finds that their AmE native speaker group relied primarily on what the author calls hedges (a functionally diverse category that also includes ability references). This finding is in line with Del Bono and Nuzzo's (2021) observation that their AmE native speakers used references to ability most frequently. While Song's (2023) Chinese EFL group also displayed a preference for hedges, they used direct strategies markedly less frequently than the English native speakers. In that, the Chinese EFL learners' usage is more similar to their L1 Chinese native patterns, indicating negative pragmatic transfer.

To conclude this literature review, previous studies mostly focussed on the overall speech event of feedback and have often treated directives as a realisation strategy of criticism. This has led to feedback directives not receiving the systematic and in-depth attention that they require, resulting in an unsystematic and, perhaps, idiosyncratic categorization and analysis of directives in feedback events. Irrespective of the limitations in comparability in the coding categories and general theoretical and methodological setup, all studies report that the feedback behaviour in their learner populations differed from that of native speakers. In addition, overall, two dimensions of learner characteristics or divergence from native speakers can be identified from investigations of EFL learners' use of directives in feedback events: (1) the choice of speech act produced (criticism vs. directive), and (2) the linguistic strategies they choose when directing. However, due to the limitations outlined, previous research has not been able to validly and comparably identify the specifics of how learners use directives in feedback strategies. Thus, the objective of this study is to investigate the directives used by language learners in an English as a Lingua Franca (ELF) peer feedback context to develop a coding scheme that can help analyse directives in feedback events systematically.

Methodology

Participants

The participants included 28 university students with various native languages (see Table 7.1 below for an overview). The students were enrolled at three different universities (Leuphana University Lüneburg, Germany; University of Trabzon, Türkiye; and IEP de Fontainebleau, UPEC, France) and took part in a telecollaborative exchange format in which English was used as a lingua franca. Their English proficiency levels, determined by self-assessment reports, ranged from B1–B2 to

C1–C2. There was a slight discrepancy in the proficiency levels between the three groups with the French group being less proficient than the other two groups. Our participants were, on average, 20.9 years old and are comparable with respect to their educational background.

Table 7.1. Informants and dataset.

Group	Native languages	Mean age	C1–C2	B1–B2
Leuphana (Germany)	German, Bulgarian, Finnish, French, Czech	20.3	4	2
Trabzon (Türkiye)	Turkish	21.5	8	1
Fontainebleau (France)	French	21	3	10
Total		*20.9*	*15*	*13*

Data Collection

Peer feedback data collection took place within the curriculum of a Sustainability and Culture course (cf. Birdman et al., forthcoming). Students were required to provide written feedback on an essay produced by an imaginary classmate as part of that student's writing class course assessment. Students were instructed to comment on at least six writing issues. In advance of and in preparation for the task, students together with their instructor had identified several writing issues related to ideas, argumentation, organisation and language use. This preparatory step was taken to avoid potential differences in feedback analytical skills. This task was assigned as homework to be submitted within one week.

The process of data collection for directives involved conducting manual bottom-up searches utilizing a combination of what Jucker (2009) calls a "conversation analytic approach" and "laboratory" methods. While the data collection involved elicitation (making them laboratory in nature), the coding was done in the manner of a conversation analytic approach. This approach entailed systematically examining the written data manually to identify instances of directive speech acts. In addition, to ensure the accuracy and consistency of coding, inter-rater reliability checks were implemented. Any discrepancies were resolved through discussion and consensus of three raters. This rigorous process not only enhanced the reliability of the coding but also informed the development of a synthesized coding scheme. Ultimately, by integrating different insights and ensuring consistency across analyses, the synthesized coding scheme aimed to provide a comprehensive framework for interpreting and categorizing directive utterances within the dataset.

Feedback Directives: Coding Scheme and Data Analysis

In this paper, we aim to develop a systematic coding scheme for the analysis of directives in feedback events. As a starting point, directive strategies identified in previous research were examined for suitability (cf. Table 7.2 below for an overview). These were synthesized and added to ensure content validity, transparency in coding and a systematic analysis based on structural criteria.

Our coding scheme for directives in feedback events is broadly based on Blum-Kulka and House's (1989) distinction of requests into three levels of head act directness: direct, conventionally indirect, and non-conventionally indirect strategies (hints). While in direct requests the speaker's intention is signalled through the linguistic form (e.g. by using imperatives or performatives verbs), there is ambiguity in both types of indirect requests. Blum-Kulka (1989) argues that there are two different types of ambiguity at work, however. Whereas the linguistic resources for conventionally indirect directives are conventionalised, non-conventionally indirect strategies must be inferred by the addressee via contextual cues. Hence, non-conventionally indirect strategies include realisations whose primary function is not a directive. Within feedback, there is thus considerable overlap between non-conventionally indirect strategies and criticism, with negative assessments potentially being classifiable as non-conventionally indirect strategies for directives as they have a secondary directive function (as Nguyen, 2008a, for instance, argues). However, including negative assessments in our hints category would have led to a large and functionally heterogeneous group of strategies in the non-conventional indirectness (hint) category. We opted against this to avoid functional overlap and an indeterminate category of hints. As our database did not include any other strategies in this category, we limit our analysis to direct and conventionally indirect head acts. In sum, what we define and analyse as directives in the present study includes only those acts which clearly delineate a specific course of action (making them primary directives), excluding primary expressions of disagreement, disapproval, or negative assessment in Nguyen's (2008a) terms. That is, of course, not to say that these primary directives cannot at the same time be understood as negative assessments, or criticism in Nguyen's (2008a) terms.

The following excerpt (example 1) from one of our feedback letters illustrates our procedure: The writer produces a negative assessment in lines 2–3 that does not outline any specific course of action. Hence, this negative assessment ("criticism") was not counted as a directive in our study. Only in the last sentence does the writer produce a directive that outlines a specific course of action. Hence, only the last sentence (marked in bold) would be coded as a directive in our database.

(1) You have many extensive examples of the topic—(. . .). However, having many examples can make your essay more superficial in the process of conveying your thoughts. **I would kindly propose concentrating on a small number of convincing arguments that you feel competent in elaborating upon (. . .).**

Table 7.2. Coding categories applied in the present study (and their sources).

	Strategy	Definition	Source
	(A) Mood derivable	S uses an imperative, negative imperative, or elliptical form	Blum-Kulka et al. (1989), Martínez-Flor (2005)
Direct	(B) Performative	S uses a performative verb or nominalised expression	Blum-Kulka et al. (1989), Martínez-Flor (2005), Strong and Baron (2004), Del Bono and Nuzzo (2021)
	(C) Obligation statement	S uses an expression of obligation	Blum-Kulka and House (1989), Martínez-Flor (2005)

Table 7.2. *Continued*

	Strategy	Definition	Source
Conventionally indirect	(D) Want statement	S expresses their desire for H to carry out an action	Blum-Kulka et al. (1989), Breuer and Geluykens (2007), Trosborg (1995)
	(E) Suggestory formulae	S uses a formulaic utterance (in interrogative form) typically associated with the speech act of suggestion	Martínez-Flor (2005)
	(F) Preparatory	S addresses or questions H's ability or the general possibility/probability/ willingness for an action	Blum-Kulka et al. (1989), Breuer and Geluykens (2007), Martínez-Flor (2005), Strong and Baron (2004), Trosborg (1995)
	(G) Positive assessment of future action	S positively evaluates the action they want H to carry out (adjective or verb with positive semantic load)	Martínez-Flor (2005), Strong and Baron (2004)
	(H) Assessment of past action	S assesses H's past decision either positively or negatively and H needs to infer that this has an impact on future actions	not identified in previous research
Convent. indirect	(I) Reflective question	S asks a rhetorical question to instigate reflexion in the addressee	Donaghue (2020), Locher (2013), Nguyen (2008a), Strong and Baron (2004)
	(J) Personal perspective/ account	S outlines that or what they would change if they were in H's position	Del Bono and Nuzzo (2021), Martínez-Flor (2005), Strong and Baron (2004)

In the direct strategies (strategies A-C in Table 7.2), the speaker's intention can be derived directly from the form of the utterance. In mood derivables (A) this information is signalled through the grammatical mood of the utterance, prototypically by using imperative or elliptical structures (example 2). In contrast, the speaker's intention is signalled through the use of a performative verb or nominalised forms in performatives (B). Hence, the speaker explicitly names their intention (example 3). In obligation statements (C), the illocutionary purpose of the utterance is encoded in an expression of obligation. This is typically done with a modal verb (e.g. *have to, must, should, need to, ought to,* etc., as in (4)).

(2) To strengthen your argument, **provide** specific examples or evidence to support this claim and make it more persuasive.[4]
(3) To improve the essay's general arrangement, I kindly **advise** improving the transition between paragraphs two and three.
(4) You **need to** change the subject because roles cannot focus.

In contrast to direct strategies, the directive intention is indirectly conveyed by a different function on the literal level in conventionally indirect requests. For instance, in want statements (D), the speaker expresses their desire for the hearer to make changes to their work, without explicitly indicating that the addressee should carry out the action. Here, the speaker merely communicates their desire or preference ("I'd like to...", Blum-Kulka et al., 1989: 279), leaving the hearer to infer a future action from this statement. In a similar vein, suggestory formulae (E) are realised by a conventional formulaic interrogative utterance typically featuring the forms *Why don't you ...?* or *How about...?*. In preparatory strategies (F), the speaker addresses or questions the hearer's ability to carry out the directive. In that, preparatory strategies refer back to the preparatory condition of requests that the hearer has to be able to carry out an action for an utterance to be understood as a request (Searle, 1969). Request studies such as Blum-Kulka (1989), Trosborg (1995), and Breuer and Geluykens (2007), have added other conditions than the addressee's ability in the preparatory category, including their willingness, general availability or permission, and the non-obviousness of compliance with the request. The typical structure involves a modal verb (*can/could/will/would*) + a verb denoting a course of action to be undertaken (examples 5 and 6).

(5) You **can** also start with an interesting sentence, with a hook at the beginning of your essay.
(6) Perhaps, you **could** change the structure of your text by starting each paragraph with an introductory sentence.

In positive assessments of a future action (G), the speaker assesses the action they want the addressee to carry out positively by using

4 All examples are taken from our database unless we specify otherwise.

an adjective or a verb with a positive semantic load (e.g. *better*, *nice*, *improve*, *benefit,* cf. example 7).

(7) Additionally, the essay would **benefit from** a more structured approach, with clear and well-defined transitions between ideas and paragraphs.

The delineation of preparatory strategies (F) and positive evaluations (G) is not always straightforward as both strategies show similar realisation patterns using modal verbs such as *can*, *could*, or *want to*. However, the semantic meaning conveyed differs slightly in that while the former is concerned with either the speaker's capability to carry out a specific action (A) or the overall likelihood/feasibility of that action, the latter highlights the positive implication that A will bring about when performed. In other words, if the verb or adjective in the directive denotes a positive assessment of the action, the strategy is coded as positive assessment of a future action. If the verb only denotes a future action (without any positive assessment), the strategy is coded as a preparatory. To illustrate this distinction, in (8) and (9) below, the positive semantic load of the verb or adjective is the determining factor in categorizing these examples as 'Positive assessment of future action' whereas in (10) no such positive semantic load is present, instead, we find a verb outlining a future act.

(8)	This could/would be **better**.	→ Pos. assessm. of future A
(9)	You could **benefit** from X.	→ Pos. assessm. of future A
(10)	You could **change/modify** X.	→ Preparatory

In assessments of past action (H), the speaker assesses a past decision either positively or negatively and the hearer needs to infer that this has an impact on their future actions (11). The speaker can also express a missed opportunity, which may be interpreted as a negative assessment (12). In contrast to primary negative assessments (such as *I didn't like your introduction*), the strategies included in this category in our analysis all refer to a specific course of action (e.g. to give examples or evidence, as in example 11).

(11) It **would have been more relevant and accurate** to give examples or evidence, even from your own experience.

(12) For example, **you could have used** the fact that these intelligent machines are automating processes in many areas.

Reflective questions (I) are rhetorical questions intended to instigate reflection in the addressee, and are not meant as a genuine request for information (13). The strategy can be found under the labels "asking/presupposing" (Nguyen, 2008a), "display questions" (Donaghue, 2020), or "interrogatives inviting introspection" (Locher, 2013).

(13) **Wouldn't it be more appropriate** to use other terms such as perfected or reactive?

Finally, in personal perspective/account (J), the speaker outlines what they would do if they were in the addressee's position (14) or offer a personal account or learning outcome of their own (15). This strategy often involves the use of *would* as a modal verb rather than as a hedging device. This strategy has been used under different labels by different authors: While Martínez-Flor (2005) refers to this strategy as 'conditional,' Del Bono and Nuzzo (2021: 199) label this strategy as 'preference'. Irrespective of the label, such strategies highlight the speaker offering a personal perspective or account from their own experience.

(14) **I would use** "affect" or "have an effect on" instead of using "effect" in that sentence.

(15) **A solution for writing paragraphs that a teacher gave me**, to make my writing more explicit, is called the "AEI" method;

In conclusion, this study employs a coding scheme that synthesizes and adds to the realisation strategies identified in empirical studies on a range of directive illocutions and systematizes them based on structural criteria. We hope to make a contribution to the field by doing so.

Results and Discussion

In the following, we present the results of our analysis of feedback directives in 28 letters of peer feedback produced by 28 ELF speakers in a telecollaborative setting. Our ELF participants had not received any kind of pragmatic instruction before writing their peer feedback letters. As outlined earlier in 3.3, our analysis only encompasses those speech acts which have a primary directive function. In turn, all speech acts with a secondary directive function (e.g. negative assessments that are uttered without reference to a future course of action) are not part of our database. While this limits comparability with previous research, a systematic analysis of feedback directives is important to draw attention to the complexities and specifics of this particular speech act.

Overall, the manual bottom-up searches of feedback letters yielded 280 directives for analysis. On average, participants produced 10.0 directives in their feedback letters. Of these, the majority (59.3 %) were realised as conventionally indirect head acts with direct head acts accounting for 40.7 % (cf. Table 7.3 below provides an overview of the frequency distribution of our head act strategies and directness levels). This preference for conventional indirectness has also been reported in studies on requests in non-feedback contexts, where conventionally indirect strategies account for proportions as high as 96.3 % in English as spoken in England (Barron, 2008). The numbers of conventionally indirect directives in the present study are markedly lower than that. This may be due to the register investigated as the social and contextual situatedness of our data in a specific speech event may well have its own conventions of language use. Furthermore, while the requests in Barron's (2008) study (and most other studies on requests) are elicited through production questionnaires, the elicitation element in our data refers to the production of the overall speech event (feedback) rather than the individual speech acts produced. Thus, the type of data used in the present study may have led to higher levels of directness than in questionnaire-based studies. Another reason for diverging patterns may be found in the fact that in contrast to many request studies, our feedback directives were produced by learners (and not native speakers) of English.

Turning to the individual head act strategies employed, our participants showed a preference for three strategies: preparatories, positive assessment of future action, and obligation statements. While performatives and mood derivables were also used with some frequency, other strategies, such as want statements, suggestory formulae, reflective questions, and personal perspective/account were not used at all or were used very infrequently (cf. Table 7.3).

Table 7.3. Frequency distribution of head act strategies in feedback directives.

Directn.	**n**	**%**	**Head act strategy**	**n**	**%**
Direct	114	40.7 %	(A) Mood derivable	24	8.6 %
			(B) Performative	26	9.3 %
			(C) Obligation statement	**64**	**22.9 %**
Convent. indirect	166	59.3 %	(D) Want statement	0	0.0 %
			(E) Suggestory formulae	0	0.0 %
			(F) Preparatory	**78**	**27.9 %**
			(G) Positive assessment of future action	**63**	**22.5 %**
			(H) Assessment of past action	16	5.7 %
			(I) Reflective question	2	0.7 %
			(J) Personal perspective/account	7	2.5 %
	280	100.0 %		280	100.0 %

In the rest of this results and discussion section, we focus on the three most frequent strategies and discuss them in more detail. One of the most frequently used strategies in our sample is the preparatory strategy, which accounts for 27.9 % (n = 78) of all our directive head acts. The high numbers of preparatories are not surprising as most request research finds this strategy to be highly frequent in English requests (cf. Barron, 2008; Blum-Kulka, 1989; Breuer & Geluykens, 2007; Flöck, 2016). However, our numbers for preparatories are lower than in most request studies. Again, this might indicate that while there are some similarities between conversational requests and feedback directives, the norms for feedback directives within our particular speech event may be different.

When looking at the individual strategies used within the preparatory category, our analysis indicates that ability references constitute the most frequent subtype. In our dataset, they account for 96.3 % (n = 75) of all preparatory strategies (cf. Table 7.4 below for an overview), while references to possibility, permission or willingness were rare. The prevalence of ability references in our feedback directives is highly comparable to the patterns found for preparatories in request studies, where ability references also constitute the most frequent subtype of English preparatories (Blum-Kulka, 1989; Flöck, 2016). Again, however, our numbers diverge from those reported in request studies in that the proportion of ability references is much higher in our database compared with request studies. Blum-Kulka (1989: 50), for instance, reports that her Australian English participants used ability references in 66.5 % of all preparatories. While Flöck (2016: 179) finds higher levels in her American and British English requests (70.6 % and 87.7 % respectively) than Blum-Kulka (1989), her relative numbers are still lower than in our database.

Table 7.4. Frequency distribution of preparatory subtypes in feedback directives.

Preparatory	n	%	Strategy	n	%
			You/we could DO X.	37	47.4 %
Ability	75	96.2 %	*You/we can* DO X.	34	43.6 %
			Impersonal	4	5.1 %
Possibility	1	1.3 %	*An idea might be* X.	1	1.3 %
Permission	1	1.3 %	*You may* DO X.	1	1.3 %
Willingness	1	1.3 %	*What you want to* DO is X.	1	1.3 %
	78	*100.0 %*		*78*	*100.0 %*

The overall number of preparatory strategies in our dataset is also comparable to studies focussed on the same speech event. Also focussing on feedback events, Del Bono and Nuzzo (2021) and Strong and Baron (2004: 51–52) find that preparatories (or the strategies that correlate to our preparatories) were among the most frequent strategies employed by their American English native speakers. Del Bono and Nuzzo find possibility references (roughly equivalent to our preparatory strategies) to be used most frequently by American English native speakers (21 % (n=27) of all "suggestions", as they call directives).

What is also striking in our data is the virtual absence of willingness references (n = 1 out of 78), which are routinely used in conversational requests (accounting for 29.4 % in Flöck's, 2016, and 17.7 % in Blum-Kulka's, 1989 database). As willingness references do not seem to occur frequently in other investigations of learner peer feedback (neither Del Bono and Nuzzo, 2021 nor Nguyen, 2008a discuss them), it may be the influence of the feedback event that is responsible for the low numbers of this strategy.

The second strategy frequently employed in our sample is the use of positive assessment of a future action, which accounts for 22.5 % (n = 63) of all directives. Instead of referring to the feedback recipient's ability to carry out a future action, the feedback writer explicitly assesses a future action as positive, indicating the need for change conventionally indirectly. The positive assessment in this strategy can refer to a number of things: it may consist of a general positive assessment (e.g. *It would be good/better to* DO X), or take more specific forms (such as indexing increased quality, understandability, credibility or persuasiveness of the work). In our sample, the most frequent positive assessment strategies included general positive assessments (33.3 %, n=21), references to general beneficialness (12.7 %, n=8), and references to improving the quality of the work (11.1 %, n=7).

Similar to the case of preparatories, Strong and Baron (2004: 51/52) also find positive assessments to be used frequently in their investigation of teacher feedback meetings by their American English native speaker teacher trainers. In contrast, positive assessment of future action is a strategy that is virtually absent in all request studies. This strategy, in conclusion, seems to be a strategy that is specific to directives in the register of feedback. Hence, by also frequently relying on these two strategies in their feedback letters, our learners display knowledge and awareness of the particular norms of this speech event.

Turning to the form of these positive assessments, two patterns can be identified: (1) feedback writers preferred to make specific reference to the feedback recipient by producing personal constructions over impersonal constructions, and (2) they consistently preferred to use hedged over unhedged positive assessments of future action (cf. Table 7.5 below). Hedging in the present study was defined as the presence of a modal particle (*would*, *could,* or *may/might*). While personal second person singular constructions account for 69.8 % (n = 44), impersonal constructions made up 30.2 % (n = 19) of all positive assessment strategies. A similar frequency distribution can be found for hedged vs. unhedged positive assessment strategies (68.3 %, n = 43 vs. 31.7 %, n = 20).

Table 7.5: Head act perspective in positive assessment of future action strategies.

Perspective	n	%	Example	Hedged	n	%
2nd person sg. reference (*you/your*)	44	69.8 %	*I think it would be better if you reduce them to one*	Yes	30	47.6 %
			Maybe you'll benefit from rephrasing the sentence.	No	14	22.2 %
Impersonal	19	30.2 %	*It would be helpful to provide examples for clarity.*	Yes	13	20.6 %
			It is important to focus on a few important aspects of that topic in depth	No	6	9.5 %
	63	*100.0 %*			*63*	*100.0 %*

Similar to the findings in Farr and O'Keeffe (2002), our participants used *would* as a hedging device most frequently but also employed similar strategies such as hedging with the modal past form *could* and modal verbs expressing epistemic modality (*may*, *might*). The preference of hedged over unhedged assessment strategies in our database is also similar to what Farr and O'Keeffe (2002) describe for their corpus-based post-observation teacher training interaction data from an Irish English native speaker context. While the authors report that especially first-person singular structures co-occur with the hedge *would*, we see a more general trend towards the use of hedged forms in second person singular and impersonal constructions in our database. In Farr and O'Keeffe's (2002: 42) data, hedged strategies were so frequent that the authors conclude that hedging "to downtone advice/direction seems to be a typical politeness strategy in this [post-observation feedback] register. It lends a theoretical and global significance to the advice.". The authors even find that hedged strategies with *would* replace all strategies where obligation (*should*) could have been used instead. This pattern was not visible in our ELF learner feedback data as obligation statements account for the third strategy used with high frequency (in fact with the same frequency as the frequently hedged positive assessment of future action strategy).

Obligation statements account for 22.9 % (n = 64) of all directives in our database. With that number, they are employed relatively frequently in our ELF learner population. The substantial number of obligation statements is not surprising given that previous research also finds this strategy to be highly frequent in English learner population. In Nguyen's (2008a) investigation of feedback strategies in a Vietnamese EFL learner population, the learners used more directives expressing obligation than the Australian English native speaker control group, who did not use this strategy at all. Similarly, Del Bono and Nuzzo's (2021) Italian EFL learners used more strategies expressing obligation than their American English native speaker controls. While the English native speakers only used obligation statements (called "need" in Del Bono & Nuzzo, 2021) in 8.5 % (n = 11) of all directives, the learners used them in 26.8 % (n = 57) of all directives at the beginning of the observational period. With that number, their learners' use of obligation statement is comparable to ours. As the use of obligation statements decreased to 13.7 % (n = 13) during their observational period, Del Bono and Nuzzo (2021) conclude that learners approached native speaker norms due to exposure to English. Due to differences in coding and Del Bono and Nuzzo's (2021) small sample size of only four learners and four native speakers, the comparability between our and their study may not always be given. Nevertheless, overall, the comparison of our results with other studies on feedback directives suggests that our learners, like other learner groups, seem to have a stronger preference for obligation statements relative to native speakers.

Compared to studies of requests in English native speaker populations, obligation statements are more frequent in our learner database. Obligation statements are very rare in questionnaire-based request research. Whereas the strategy is more common in naturally occurring requests (accounting for 11.9 %, n = 31 in Flöck's, 2016, American

English and 16.5 %, n = 43 British English request sample), the numbers are still proportionally lower than in our feedback directives. Based on the comparisons with both other feedback directives and with request studies, the high usage of obligation statements thus seems to be a learner feature in this particular register, as the high numbers of our and other studies' learners diverge from both native speaker feedback directives and native speaker conversational requests.

When it comes to the form of obligation statements, our learners opted to use personalised (*You* + modal verb…, e.g. *You should/must/ need to* DO X) forms more frequently than impersonal forms (such as X *needs a change/must be changed.*). While personalised forms account for 75.0 % (n = 48) of all obligation statements, impersonal structures can only be found in the remaining 25.0 % (n = 16) of cases. Table 7.6 below provides an overview of the linguistic strategies found and their frequency distribution. Furthermore, the most frequently used linguistic device expressing obligation was *should* (56.3 %, n = 36). While *need to* was also used occasionally, *must* and *have to* were used rarely.

Table 7.6. Frequency distribution of obligation subtypes in feedback directives.

Type	**n**	**%**	**Linguistic strategy**	**n**	**%**
Personalised	48	75.0 %	*You should* DO X.	31	48.4 %
			You need to DO X.	9	14.1 %
			You have to DO X.	7	10.9 %
			You must DO X.	1	1.6 %
Impersonal	16	25.0 %	X *should be* DO$_{ed}$/Y$_{adjective/\ specific\ change}$	5	7.8 %
			X *needs a change/needs to be* DO$_{ed}$.	4	6.3 %
			It is/would (not) be necessary to DO X.	3	4.7 %
			X *requires* DO$_{ing}$./DO$_{ing}$ *is required.*	2	3.1 %
			X *must* be Y$_{adjective}$	1	1.6 %
			X *has to be* DO$_{ed}$.	1	1.6 %
Total	*64*	*100.0 %*		*64*	*100.0 %*

Conclusion

The present study set out to answer the following research questions:

1. How can feedback directives be analysed transparently and systematically?
2. Which strategies are used by ELF speakers in their feedback directives and how do their directives compare with native speaker feed-back directives?
3. How do the ELF learners' feedback directives compare with other directive speech acts?

On the methodological level (addressing the first two research questions), we have proposed a framework for analysing feedback directives that draws on insights from speech act theory and empirical investigations of a range of directive illocutions. We have argued that feedback directives may include a number of diverse individual pragmatic functions, such as suggesting, advising, warning, etc. As these illocutions cannot be delineated validly both in theory and in practice, we have refrained from an *a priori* categorisation of these actions and have proposed the more inclusive approach of labelling them as 'directives' instead. We have also developed a coding scheme for feedback directives that is informed by, synthesizes, and further develops the relevant coding categories from numerous studies on directives. To ensure concept validity and replicability of results, the coding categories have been defined structurally and the structural criteria underlying our categories have been made transparent.

When it comes to the form of feedback directives (and our second research question), our ELF learners used preparatory strate-gies most frequently, followed by obligation statements and positive evaluations of future actions. In all three strategies, the learners pre-ferred personalised forms over impersonal constructions and positive assessments of future actions occurred in hedged forms most fre-quently. With these patterns of usage, our ELF learners mostly con-verge with native speaker realisation pattern in feedback directives. The only difference between our ELF population and English native speakers in feedback directives can be seen in our learners' overuse of obligation statements. Compared with native speaker feedback direc-tives in previous research, our learners use obligation statements more frequently than native speakers do. As the same pattern has also been described in previous research (cf. Del Bono & Nuzzo, 2021; Nguyen, 2008a; Strong & Baron, 2004), the overuse of obliga-tion statements in feedback directives seems to be a learner feature.

When it comes to our third research question, our results indi-cate that feedback directives produced by ELF learners show complex patterns of convergence with and divergence from other directives produced by native speakers. Our learner feedback directives are simi-lar to the patterns reported for requests (cf. Barron, 2008; Blum-Kulka, 1989; Breuer & Geluykens, 2007; Flöck, 2016) in that prepara-tory strategies occur highly frequently in both directive subtypes. Our learner data further mirror conversational requests in that ability references are the most frequent preparatory substrategy. At the same time, we have observed that there are some differences between our learner feedback directives and the conversational requests investigated in previous research. Whereas our study and feedback studies with English native speakers show high frequencies of positive assessments of future action, this strategy is not found in general request studies. Hence, this strategy likely shows a register-specific pattern in that it is acceptable and expected in feedback directives but not in directives in other registers. Another form of divergence from general request patterns can be found in the use of obligation statements in our learner data. Obligation statements occur with higher frequencies in our learner feedback directives than they do in general request studies. However, this difference does not seem to be correlated with genre (feedback direc-tives vs. requests) but with learner status as obligation statements have been shown to be less frequent in native speaker feedback direc-tives (cf. Del Bono & Nuzzo, 2021; Nguyen, 2008a; Strong & Baron, 2004).

On a final note, the present study delivers a systematic coding scheme based on structural criteria that we hope does justice to the complexities of the individual illocutions. However, going forward, the investigation of the complex speech event of feedback should not be limited to the analysis of feedback directives as feedback directives are only one part of the overall feedback event. Rather, the investigation of feedback directives needs to be supplemented with systematic analyses of other feedback actions and moves (such as negative and positive assessments). In addition, the findings and patterns of the present study need to be explored in greater detail in future scholarship. More specifically, feedback directives might be analysed in a more in-depth manner using our structurally-based coding scheme in contrastive designs to investigate patterns of learner variability (e.g. the influence of proficiency, L1, learning context, such as in English as for foreign, second, international language or lingua franca), the difference between learners and native speakers, and the influence of different instructional designs (e.g. interventional designs or incidental learning). We look forward to manifold studies on such questions.

Acknowledgements

This project is partly funded by the "Stiftung Innovation in der Hochschullehre" within the context of the sub-project "DigiCLIL-Exchange: Integrated teaching of foreign language, intercultural and subject-specific competences", part of the overarching project "Digital Transformation Lab for Teaching and Learning". We would like to express our sincere gratitude to project members, Jodie Birdman, Irina Pandarova and Torben Schmidt and also to telecollaboration partners, Handan Celik and Emilie Vilmen, for their role in developing and/or conducting the Sustainability and Culture course which was instrumental in facilitating the data collection process. Thanks also to Béatrice Miriam Höner for her supporting contribution in data curation.

References

Barron, Anne. 2008. The structure of requests in Irish English and English English. In Klaus P. Schneider and Anne Barron (eds) *Variational Pragmatics: A Focus on Regional Varieties of Pluricentric Languages*. Amsterdam/Philadelphia: Benjamins, 35–67.

Batlle, Jaume & Paul Seedhouse. 2022. Affiliation and negative assessments in peer observation feedback for foreign language teachers professional development. *Applied Linguistics Review*, 13/6, 1077–1101. Berlin: De Gruyter Mouton.

Birdman, Jodie, Handan. Celik, Irina Pandarova, Anne Barron, Nora Benitt & Torben Schmidt. (forthcoming). Connecting sustainability and culture: Building competencies through virtual exchange. In W. Leal, J. Newman & A. Lange (eds) *World sustainability series. North American and European perspectives on sustainability in higher education*. Cham: Springer Nature.

Blum-Kulka, Shoshana. 1989. Playing it safe: The role of conventionality in indirectness. In Shoshana Blum-Kulka, Juliane House & Gabriele Kasper (eds) *Cross-cultural pragmatics: Requests and apologies*. Norwood, NJ: Ablex. 37–70.

Blum-Kulka, Shoshana & Juliane House. 1989. Cross-cultural and situational variation in requesting behaviour. In Shoshana Blum-Kulka, Juliane House & Gabriele Kasper (eds) *Cross-cultural pragmatics: Requests and apologies*. Norwood, NJ: Ablex, 123–54.

Blum-Kulka, Shoshana, House, Juliane & Kasper, Gabriele (eds). 1989. The CCSARP coding manual. In Shoshana Blum-Kulka, Juliane House & Gabriele Kasper (eds) *Cross-cultural pragmatics: Requests and apologies*. Norwood, NJ: Ablex, 273–94.

Breuer, Anja & Ronald Geluykens. 2007. Variation in British and American English requests. A contrastive analysis. In Bettina Kraft & Ronald Geluykens (eds) *Cross-cultural pragmatics and interlanguage pragmatics*. München: Lincom Europa, 107–26.

Brown, Penelope & Stephen C. Levinson. 1987. *Politeness. Some universals in language usage*. Cambridge: Cambridge University Press.

Copland, Fiona. 2011. Negotiating face in feedback conferences: A linguistic ethnographic analysis. *Journal of Pragmatics*, *Negotiating Linguistic Politeness in Japanese Interaction: A Critical Examination of Honorifics*, 43/15, 3832–43.

Copland, Fiona. 2012. Legitimate talk in feedback conferences. *Applied Linguistics*, 33/1, 1–20.

Decapua Andrea & Joan Findlay Dunham. 2007. The pragmatics of advice giving: Cross-cultural perspectives. *Intercultural Pragmatics*, 4/3, 319–42.

Del Bono, Federica & Elena Nuzzo. 2021. Incidental pragmatics learning in telecollaborative exchanges: A case study on criticism and suggestion. *Instructed Second Language Acquisition*, 5/2, 172–201.

Dippold, Doris. 2009. Peer feedback through blogs: Student and teacher perceptions in an advanced German class. *ReCALL*, 21/1, 18–36.

Donaghue, Helen. 2020. "Time to Construct Positive Identities": Display questions in post observation teacher feedback. *Classroom Discourse*, 11/3, 193–208.

Farr, Fiona. 2011. *The discourse of teaching practice feedback: A corpus-based investigation of spoken and written modes*. London: Routledge.

Farr, Fiona & O'Keeffe, Anne. 2002. "Would" as a hedging device in an Irish context: An intra-varietal comparison of institutionalised spoken interaction. In Randy Reppen, Susan Fitzmaurice & Douglas Biber (eds) *Using corpora to explore linguistic variation*. Amsterdam: Benjamins, 25–48.

Flöck, Ilka. 2016. *Requests in American and British English: A contrastive multi-method analysis*. Pragmatics & Beyond New Series. Amsterdam: John Benjamins.

Fraser, Bruce. 1974. *An analysis of vernacular performative verbs*. Bloomington: Indiana University Linguistics Club.

Freytag, Vera. 2019. *Exploring politeness in business emails: A mixed-methods analysis*. Bristol, Blue Ridge Summit: Multilingual Matters.

Hindelang, Götz. 1978. *Auffordern: Die Untertypen Des Aufforderns Und Ihre Sprachlichen Realisierungsformen*. Göppingen: Kümmerle.

Hyland, Fiona & Ken Hyland. 2001. Sugaring the pill: Praise and criticism in written feedback. *Journal of Second Language Writing*, 10/3, 185–212.

Hymes, Dell. 1972. On communicative competence. In: J. B. Pride & J. Holmes (eds) *Sociolinguistics. Selected Readings*. Harmondsworth: Penguin, 269–293.

Jucker, Andreas H. 2009. Speech act research between armchair, field and laboratory: The case of compliments. *Journal of Pragmatics,* 41/8, 1611–35.

Khezrlou, Sima. 2023. Repeated academic writing with synchronous and asynchronous teacher electronic feedback: How are macro and micro aspects affected? In Jingjing Qin & Paul Stapleton (eds) *Technology in Second Language Writing.* Abingdon, Oxon: Routledge, 63–79.

Levinson, Stephen C. 1979. Activity types and language. *Linguistics*, 17/5–6, 365–400.

Locher, Miriam A. 2013. Internet advice. In S. Herring, D. Stein, & T. Virtanen (eds): *Pragmatics of Computer-Mediated Communication* (pp. 339–362). De Gruyter Mouton, 339–362. <https://doi.org/doi:10.1515/9783110214468.339>.

Martínez-Flor, Alicia. 2005. A theoretical review of the speech act of suggesting: Towards a taxonomy for its use in FLT. *Revista Alicantina de Estudios Ingleses*, 18, 167–87.

Nguyen, Ngoc Thi Bich & Ilana Mushin. 2022. Understanding equivocal feedback in PhD supervision meetings: A conversation analysis approach. *Teaching in Higher Education*, 29/6, 1537–1553. <https://doi.org/10.1080/13562517.2022.2068348>.

Nguyen, Thi Thuy Minh. 2008a. Criticizing in an L2: Pragmatic strategies used by Vietnamese EFL learners. *Intercultural Pragmatics*, 5/1, 41–66. <https://doi.org/10.1515/IP.2008.003>.

Nguyen, Thi Thuy Minh. 2008b. Modifying L2 criticisms: How learners do it? *Journal of Pragmatics*, 40/4, 768–91.

Nguyen, Thi Thuy Minh. 2013. Instructional effects on the acquisition of modifiers in constructive criticism by EFL learners. *Language Awareness*, 22/1, 76–94.

Nguyen, Thi Thuy Minh & Helen Basturkmen. 2010. Teaching constructive critical feedback. In Donna Hurst Tatsuki & Noël Houck (eds) *Pragmatics: Teaching speech acts (classroom practice series)*. Alexandria, VA: Teachers of English to Speakers of Other Languages, 125–40.

Robinson, Jeffrey D. 2004. The sequential organization of "Explicit" apologies in naturally occurring English. *Research on Language & Social Interaction*, 37/3, 291–330.

Searle, John R. 1969. *Speech Acts: An essay in the philosophy of language*. Cambridge: Cambridge University Press.

Song, Beibei. 2023. Study of high-proficiency Chinese EFL learners strategy applications in constructive feedback. *Chinese Journal of Applied Linguistics*, 46/1, 71–87.

Strong, Michael & Wendy Baron. 2004. An analysis of mentoring conversations with beginning teachers: Suggestions and responses. *Teaching and Teacher Education*, 20/1, 47–57.

Swinglehurst, Deborah, Jill Russell & Trisha Greenhalgh. 2008. Peer observation of teaching in the online environment: An action research approach. *Journal of Computer Assisted Learning*. 24/5, 383–93.

Tracy, Karen & Eric Eisenberg. 1990. Giving criticism: A multiple goals case study. *Research on Language & Social Interaction*, 24/1–4, 37–70.

Tracy, Karen, Donna Van Dusen & Susan Robinson. 1987. "Good" and "Bad" criticism: A descriptive analysis. *Journal of Communication*, 37/2, 46–59.

Trosborg, Anna. 1995. *Interlanguage pragmatics: Requests, complaints/apologies*. Berlin, New York: De Gruyter Mouton. <https://doi.org/10.1515/9783110885286>.

Vásquez, Camilla. 2004. 'Very Carefully Managed': Advice and suggestions in post-observation meetings. *Linguistics and Education*, 15/1, 33–58.

Wunderlich, Dieter. 1976. *Studien Zur Sprechakttheorie*. Frankfurt am Main: Suhrkamp.

Marta González-Lloret

The Pragmatics of Email Communication: A Synthesis

Introduction

Eva Alcón-Soler's impact in the field of Applied Linguistics is undeniable and the contributions to this volume highlight such an impact. For this chapter, her contributions to the research on L2 pragmatics and email writing (Alcón-Soler, 2013a, 2013b, 2015, 2017, 2018) are especially relevant. Her research in this area was essential for the field of Technology-mediated L2 Pragmatics, with many studies citing her contributions. This chapter aims at synthesizing what we know about the pragmatics of L2 email, highlighting Eva Alcón-Soler's contributions and their impact in the field of Technology-mediate L2 Pragmatics. The chapter addresses first the selection and grouping of existing studies researching L2 email pragmatics. It then presents the results of the studies according to the selected grouping. Finally, conclusions are drawn and new lines of investigation suggested.

The Pragmatics of L2 Email

In today's global communications much of our interaction is situated in and mediated by technologies that highly determine our ways of interacting with others, and therefore, as researchers and L2 instructors. we need to:

1. Understand these forms of communication. As Sykes (2017) states "digital technologies have expanded the possibilities for human interactions in ways that were never before imaginable, further complexifying the teaching and learning of interlanguage pragmatics." (p. 119). Understanding the norms and rules of engagement in digital spaces (sociopragmatics) and the language to interact in appropriate and effective ways (pragmalinguistics) is essential in a world where technology-mediated communications occupy most of our interactions.

2. Develop tasks and instructional materials to help our foreign/second/other language students acquire the pragmatics of different communications. L2 pragmatic instruction for these spaces serves not only to practice and acquire another language, but it can aid our language learners (LLs henceforth) in developing critical and communicative digital literacies, essential for any citizen of our globalized and highly digital world.

Among digital communication tools, email has been one of the most researched computer-mediated interaction tools. This interest in email communication can be attributed first to the fact that email is a pervasive and one of the most employed tools of communication (professional and personal) in the world, with more than 4.48 billion email accounts in 2024 (Ceci, 2024). It could also be that email is still a difficult genre to master, especially for LLs, and even more, for those that have restricted communication with other speakers and little knowledge of the L2 sociopragmatic norms. The hybrid nature of email certainly contributes to this difficulty. Email communication is written and therefore associated with more formal registers, but the language employed can vary from very informal (e.g., a simple heart emoticon for a thank you) to very formal (e.g., a request to a university dean for a salary adjustment).

Each email is a small interaction in which we need to pay conscious attention to the power relation with our interlocutor (i.e., hierarchy), our familiarity (or lack of), our shared background knowledge (e.g., are we both at the same institution, do we share the same culture, the same netiquette rules), whether this is the first email or a follow up, and the pragmatic work that the imposition of the main speech act in the email requires (e.g., a request versus an invitation). As research has shown, the level of directness, structure of an email, and its level of politeness influence how that email is perceived and responded to, and even affect the perceived personality of the sender (Economidou-Kogetsidis, 2016; Hendriks, 2010; Usó-Juan, 2022). It is no wonder that many of us use avoidance strategies when confronted with an email.

In this chapter, I attempt to synthesize what we know up to today about the L2 pragmatic of email communication, highlighting the contributions of Alcón-Soler's work to this research.

Selection Criteria for the Synthesis

Articles and book chapters were included in this review based on four criteria: (1) They were written in English, (2) they were empirical studies, (3) they focused on some aspect of the pragmatics of L2 email writing, and (4) they included LLs. Reviews of literature, unpublished papers, and teaching proposals (e.g., Krulatz & Park, 2015) were not included. A comprehensive search was conducted to include journals with focus on second language learning (e.g., *Applied Linguistics, Foreign Language Annals, System*), pragmatics (e.g., *Journal of Pragmatics, Applied Pragmatics*) and computer-assisted language learning (e.g., *CALICO Journal, LL&T, ReCALL*). Additional searches were conducted using Google Scholar, Semantic Scholar, as well as recent AI tools such as Scite and Research Rabbit. 78 studies were identified and included in this review. In addition, eight studies were added from a recent volume, at the suggestion of one of the reviewers, for a total of 86 studies. The studies were organized according to year of publication, type of study, geographical area, duration of the study, languages, pragmatic focus, participants' characteristics (institution, age, proficiency level), email recipient, type of data, and data collection method.

Chronologically, studies expand from 1996 until 2024 with the majority of the studies clustered at the end of the 1990s and beginning of the 2020s. Figure 8.1 is a visual representation of the timeline. Because the studies all focus on email communication and some aspects of L2 pragmatics, they are strongly interconnected, with a few studies often cited. Figure 8.2 is a visual representation of the studies relationships.

Figure 8.1: Timeline of studies from Research Rabbit (only those found by the tool).

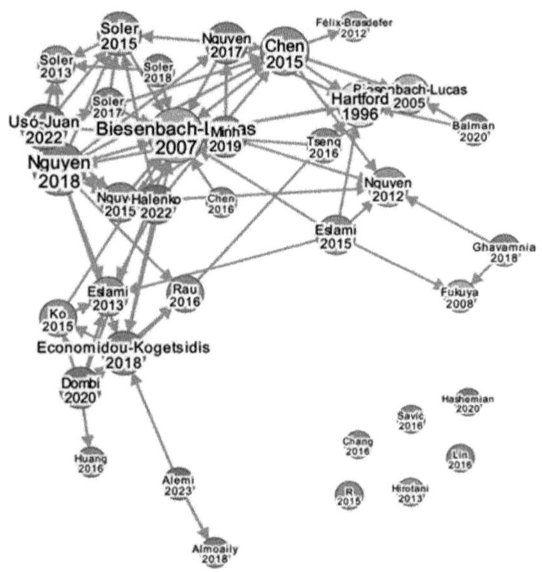

Figure 8.2: Relationship of studies from Research Rabbit (only those found by the tool).

The existing studies can be organized according to the two needs of the field presented above. On one side, non-interventional studies. This group of studies has focused on describing how L2 speakers write emails, how they produce a specific speech act or interactional move (e.g., requests, openings, closings, apologies), or how those emails are perceived by other speakers (e.g., faculty). On the other side, interventional studies which have explored the teachability of L2 emails, investigating different types of interventions and classroom materials to see the LLs' progress of a pragmatic feature (e.g., politeness, requests, sentence final particles).

Of the studies, most are non-interventional and descriptive in nature. Some studies compare two groups of participants, frequently LLs and native speakers (NSs) or LLs of two different proficiencies. These were classified separately as "Comparison" in Figure 8.3 below. Studies that combine recipients' perceptions with description of production were classified as "Combination". Finally, a very small group of studies looked at the development of email production but without any intervention (Developmental). The rest are interventional studies that look at the effect of instruction. Figure 8.3 is an overview of the studies.

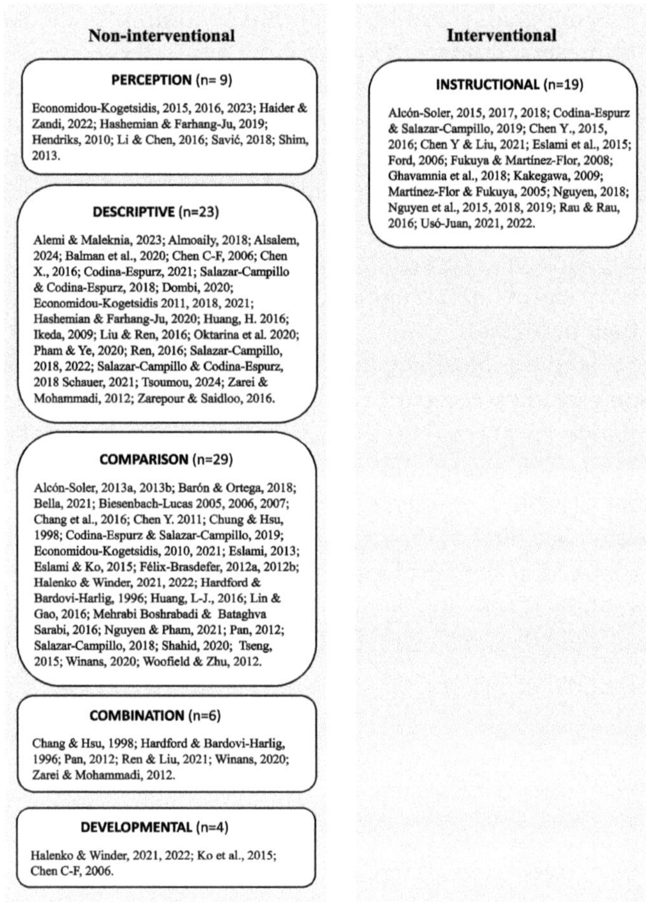

Figure 8.3: Studies included in the synthesis.

The reviewed studies have been conducted in quite a large variety of geographical areas, with a concentration of research in China and Taiwan, Iran, and Spain (see Table 8.1). Figure 8.4 is a visual representation of the geographical concentration of studies.

Figure 8.4: Geographical area of the studies. For study abroad studies, the LLs' country of origin is considered.

Table 8.1. Geographical area of studies. For study abroad studies, the LLs' country of origin is considered.

Country	Perception studies	Descriptive studies	Instructional studies	Total
China	3	11	3	**17**
Cyprus	3	4		**7**
Germany		1		**1**
Greece		1		**1**
Hong Kong		1		**1**
Hungary		1		**1**
Indonesia		2		**2**
Iran	2	9	2	**13**
Netherlands	1			**1**
Norway	1			**1**

Continued

Table 8.1. *Continued*

Country	Perception studies	Descriptive studies	Instructional studies	Total
Saudi Arabia		2		**2**
South Korea	1			**1**
Spain		8	7	**15**
Taiwan		4		**4**
Turkey		1		**1**
UK		2		**2**
United States		8	2	**10**
Vietnam		2	4	**6**
Total	**11**	**57**	**18**	**86**

As for the context of the studies, the great majority are classroom studies or studies that investigate email within an institutional context, mostly a university. A handful of studies differ from this context and investigate the pragmatics of email in virtual exchanges (Huang H, 2016; Kakegawa, 2009) and in study abroad contexts (Alcón-Soler, 2013a, 2013b, 2015, 2017; Bella, 2021; Halenko & Winder, 2021, 2022).

The great majority of participants in the studies are English as a foreign language (EFL) learners, with only three other languages represented; Japanese (Ikeda, 2009; Kakegawa, 2009), Greek (Bella, 2021), and Spanish (Félix-Brasdefer, 2012a, 2012b). In addition, the great majority of participants are adults. Only Alcón-Soler (2013a, 2013b, 2015, 2017) conducted her studies with teenagers, and there are no studies of children. This is understandable since email writing is not a genre in which children usually engage. Since most studies focus on adult university students, the recipients of the emails are mostly university professors/faculty. A few exceptions are Huang H (2016) and Liu and Ren (2016) whose email recipients were learners' peers, Chen X (2016), Xiao and Gao (2016), and Pham and Ye (2020) who investigated emails to international researchers and faculty in other institutions, Chen and Liu (2021) whose recipient was a personnel manager for an internship, and Pham and Ye (2020) who included university staff members.

As for the main focus of research, the great majority of studies focused on email requests, although other speech acts such as apologies, complaints, and suggestions, were also explored (see Table 8.2).

Table 8.2. Main focus of the studies.

Main Focus	Studies
Requests	All except
Apologies	Barón and Ortega, 2018; Chang et al., 2016; Xiao and Gao, 2016
Complaints	Nguyen and Pham, 2021
Suggestions	Fukuya and Martínez-Flor, 2008; Ghavamnia et al., 2018; Martínez-Flor and Fukuya, 2005
Openings & closing/ greetings/self-introductions	Almoaily, 2018 (greetings); Barón and Ortega, 2018; Codina-Espurz, 2021; Codina-Espurz and Salazar-Campillo, 2019; Eslami, 2013; Félix-Brasdefer, 2012a; Halenko and Winder, 2022; Huang, H, 2016; Ko et al., 2015; Mehrabi Boshrabadi and Bataghva Sarab, 2016; Salazar-Campillo, 2018; Salazar-Campillo and Codina-Espurz, 2018; Schauer, 2021 Zarepour and Saidloo, 2016; Savić, 2018
Small talk	Ren and Liu, 2021 (in thanking)
Honorifics/Address forms	Economidou-Kogetsidis, 2018; Ikeda, 2009; Rau and Rau, 2016; Salazar-Campillo, 2022
Politeness (general, strategies, face work)	Codina-Espurz, 2021; Eslami, 2013; Hashemian and Farhang-Ju, 2019; Li and Chen, 2016; Nguyen and Pham, 2021; Savić, 2018; Tsoumou, 2024
Discourse features	Mehrabi Boshrabadi and Bataghva Sarab, 2016
Discourse organization	Huang, L-J., 2016
Other	Alemi and Maleknia, 2023 (request responses); Biesenbach-Lucas, 2005, 2006, 2007 (negotiating, reporting); Chen C-F, 2006 (general); Chen and Liu, 2021 (general); Eslami and Ko, 2015 (assignment submission); Kakegawa, 2009 (sentence final particles); Ko et al., 2015 (small talk); Xiao and Gao, 2016 (Taoci); Nguyen et al., 2015, 2018, 2019 (feedback techniques); Ren, 2016 (maintaining understanding)

Finally, the data collected in the studies is in the great majority naturally occurring data; that is, emails written by students to their faculty. A few investigations used elicited data with the most common form being email role plays or email tasks, that is, participants wrote emails to a determined recipient as a task, but those emails were not necessarily sent. Some authors call this instrument a Discourse Completion Test/ Task (DCT), others just "a task". In some cases (e.g., Hendriks, 2010), LLs' emails served to construct surveys or become part of rating tools. A few studies also made use of questionnaires, surveys, and interviews, mostly in combination with either elicited emails or authentic emails. Table 8.3 shows the studies for these different data collection methods. As a final note, most studies investigating email recipient perception included 2 or more data collection methods. The study that incorporated a larger amount of data collection methods was Savić (2018). The investigation included 201 authentic emails containing requests written to Savić as a faculty member by Norwegian and international students. From those, 20 were selected as prompts for lecture rating (in a 5-point-Likert scale) on their politeness and appropriateness, with a space for optional comments for each email. Afterwards, Savić conducted semi-structured interviews with 10 other faculty, which provided a richness of views of (im)politeness that the questionnaires did not, highlighting the limitations of questionnaires as a data collection method.

Table 8.3. "Data collection methods".

	Descriptive studies	**Interventional studies**
Naturally occurring	**All except**	**All except**
Email roleplay	Alemi and Maleknia, 2023; Chen, X., 2016; Codina-Espurz, 2021; Hendriks, 2010; Ikeda, 2009; Lin and Gao, 2016; Nguyen and Pham, 2021; Ren and Liu, 2021; Tseng, 2015; Zarei and Mohammadi, 2012; Zhu, 2012.	Alcón-Soler, 2018; Chen Y., 2015, 2016; Chen and Liu, 2021; Fukuya and Martínez-Flor, 2008; Ghavamnia et al., 2018; Martínez-Flor and Fukuya, 2005; Usó-Juan, 2021

Table 8.3. *Continued*

		Descriptive studies	Interventional studies
	DCTs (multiple situations)	Pan, 2012; Woofield and Economidou-Kogetsidis, 2010; Zarepour and Saidloo, 2016	Ford, 2006; Eslami et al., 2015; Nguyen, 2018; Nguyen et al. 2015, 2018, 2019; .
	Interviews	Mehrabi Boshrabadi and Bataghva Sarab, 2016; Oktarina et al., 2020; Savić, 2018; Tseng, 2016	Alcón-Soler, 2017
Elicited	Think aloud/ Discussion	Nguyen and Pham, 2021	Chen and Liu, 2021
	Surveys/ Questionnaires	Economidou-Kogetsidis, 2015, 2016; Haider and Zandi, 2022; Hashemian and Farhang-Ju, 2019; Hendriks, 2010; Li and Chen, 2016; Xiao and Gao, 2016; Savić, 2018; Zarei and Mohammadi, 2012; Zhu, 2012	Chen Y, 2016; Fukuya and Martínez-Flor, 2008; Nguyen, 2018
	Rating scales/ Self-assessment	Chang and Hsu, 1998; Economidou-Kogetsidis, 2015, 2016; Haider and Zandi, 2022; Ren and Liu, 2021; Shim, 2013; Winans, 2020	Alcón-Soler, 2018; Usó-Juan, 2021

In the rest of this chapter, I will present a summary of the results of these studies to establish what we know about L2 email pragmatics. research. First, non-interventional studies focusing on email perception are presented, followed by those focusing on email production, both descriptive and comparative in nature. Then the few developmental studies that exist are presented, followed by interventional studies focusing on the impact of instruction.

Studies of L2 Email Perception

About 10% of the studies focus on how LLs' emails are perceived by the recipients, with a few more including recipient perceptions within a larger descriptive study ("Combination" in Figure 8.3). As with the larger body of studies, faculty in the LL's institution were the recipients and raters (see Economidou-Kogetsidis, 2023 for an exception). These studies reveal several key factors influencing how emails are received, and these results are independent of the context and first language (L1) of the LLs writing the emails.

Emails are characterized by direct requests, few downgraders, omitted openings and closings, and incorrect forms of academic titles which may be perceived as impolite and abrupt (Economidou-Kogetsidis, 2011; Shim, 2013; Zarei & Mohammadi, 2012). The perceived politeness of an email is based on more than the use of "please" or "thank you." Request formulation, mitigation devices, acknowledgement of imposition, and true expressions of gratitude are essential (Economidou-Kogetsidis, 2016). A lack of hedging, an overly informal tone, lack of orthographic conventions, absence of grounders, or reasons mitigating the request contribute greatly to negative faculty evaluations (Harford & Bardovi-Harlig, 1996; Savić, 2018).

Direct requests strongly affect the perception of politeness, but it seems to be modified by the entire structure of the email. According to Harford and Bardovi-Harlig (1996), successful emails include elements such as acknowledgement of the imposition on the addressee, presentation of time constraints related to the request, and thorough explanations, while emails are negatively perceived when the learners assume a greater obligation on the part of the faculty to comply. And according to Li and Chen (2016) emails that include a reason first before a request are the best email style. As part of the structure of an email, openings and closings also influence lecturers' perception of politeness and appropriateness (Hashemian & Farhang-Ju, 2019). Zarei and Mohammadi (2012) found that the inclusion of pre-closings in the structure of the email positively influenced perceptions of politeness. This was also supported by Savić (2018) who found negative reactions to the absence of leave-takings in the emails of Norwegian EFL students and also found that greetings were the single most discussed feature in her questionnaires and interviews when referring to politeness and appropriateness. Chang and Hsu (1998) confirmed the importance of the structure of an email. They found that emails that follow an American direct request structure were perceived as more impolite than those with direct requests but a Chinese indirect structure.

An interesting finding from these studies is that raters do not seem to hold homogeneous views on what is polite or appropriate in an email (Economidou-Kogetsidis, 2016; Savić, 2018). Additionally, raters may not be certain of what exactly makes an email polite. Savić's (2018) raters were reluctant to label an entire email as inappropriate or impolite, preferring to describe specific features as such. Likewise, Li and Chen (2016) found that Taiwanese professors had a high degree of tolerance toward nonstandard forms in the emails they rated, which was also found by Hendriks (2010) in a Dutch context. Haider and Zandi (2022) found that faculty characteristics, such as being an expert English speaker, gender, and seniority, influenced their perceptions of email politeness. Senior and non-English speaking faculty were more tolerant of the lack of acknowledgement of imposition. And in a US context, Winans (2020) found that raters still marked learners' requests as polite even when syntactic modifications were lacking, which suggests some variability on how politeness is understood even within the same context.

Studies of L2 Email Production

Most of the studies in this synthesis explore how email is produced by LLs, focusing on various pragmatic aspects. These are the studies in Figure 8.3 under Descriptive and Comparison.

The results of these investigations show that LLs' emails are frequently characterized by directness, lack of e-politeness resources, and inadequate pragmalinguistic competence (Chang & Hsu, 1998; Alcón-Soler, 2013b; Biesenbach-Lucas, 2006; Halenko & Winder, 2021). The emails exhibit limited variance in request strategies, mitigation, and politeness devices (Hartford & Bardovi-Harlig, 1996; Chen C-F, 2006,

2015; Zhu, 2012); verbosity (Chen C-F, 2006; Chang et al., 2016); excessive directness (Alcón-Soler, 2013a; Alsalem, 2024; Chen Y, 2015; Chang et al., 2016; Dombi, 2020; Economidou-Kogetsidis, 2011, 2018, 2021); and incorrect use of address forms (Chen Y; Chen X, 2016; Félix-Brasdefer, 2012a; Ikeda, 2009). In an early study, Biesenbach-Lucas (2007) pointed out that even advanced LLs had issues mitigating disagreement, using appropriate levels of politeness, and understanding power distribution. Recently, Alemi and Maleknia (2023) found that this was the case in their data even when LLs were provided with models.

In contrast, some recent research indicates that LLs are aware of pragmatic context and can produce appropriate emails (Bella, 2021; Savić, 2018; Winans, 2020), they attend to relational goals (Eslami & Ko, 2015), construct a deferent relational identity, and portray themselves as reasonable and appropriate in their email communication (Chen, X., 2016). They even construct new norms to express their identity (Dombi, 2020) such as the use of lowercase letters, emoticons, and the deletion of subjects and determiners (Huang, L-J., 2016). According to Bella (2021), identity may also explain differences between L2 learners' pragmalinguistic choices in, for example, greetings. As Chen C-F. (2006) found in her 2-and-a-half-year longitudinal investigation, the LL's identity in the study changed with time and acculturation into the institutional norms. In addition, LLs are capable of establishing rapport and actively using interpersonal features such as small talk, openings, and closings (Eslami & Ko, 2015; Halenko & Winder, 2022). LLs are also capable of addressing misunderstandings in email by asking direct questions, using confirmation checks and metalinguistic comments to signal a problem, ensuring understanding by building shared knowledge (Ren, 2016). LLs understand the formality of writing to a professor in contrast to writing to a peer (Mehrabi Boshrabadi & Bataghva Sarab, 2016), and, as interviews conducted by Oktarina et al. (2020) demonstrate, they are aware that an email to a faculty member should be formal, simple, and not rambling, and that close attention should be paid to the choice of words.

Several studies have compared L2 email writing with that of expert speakers (either NSs or advanced learners). As expected, there are clear differences between LLs and expert speakers. These studies give us an idea of how different LLs may be from NSs, but we should question whether this is the measure against which LLs should be compared (Davies, 1991, 2003). These studies suggest that LLs use a lot less positive politeness strategies in their emails (Eslami & Ko, 2015). LLs tend to use more formal greetings, more formal strategies, and greater deference compared than NSs (Eslami & Ko, 2015; Hashemian & Farhang-Ju, 2020; Halenko & Winder, 2022; Ko et al., 2015), and their farewell strategies are longer (Salazar-Campillo, 2018; Ko et al., 2015). LLs also include small talk and phatic comments which may reflect their L1 cultural norms and are not always appropriate for the context (Chang et al., 2016; Chen C-F, 2006; Eslami, 2013; Hashemian & Farhang-Ju, 2020; Ko et al., 2015; Ren & Liu, 2021). A final difference is the lack of variety of syntactic modifications and mitigating, elliptical, and formulaic devices (Ko et al., 2015; Winans, 2020; Woofield & Economidou-Kogetsidis, 2010).

Within descriptive and comparative studies of L2 email production, the great majority focus on L2 requests, followed by the study of opening and closing sequences. The results of these will be aggregated below. In addition, several studies (mostly comparative) address the role of the LLs' culture (C1) in the production of L2 emails, as well as their proficiency level, both of which are addressed below. The section closes highlighting Alcón-Soler's contribution to comparative descriptive studies.

L2 Requests in Email Communication

Requests are without a doubt the most investigated speech act within email studies, with a significant percentage of research focusing on either the request itself or the structure of emails containing a request. Although some research suggests that requests are the most frequent speech act in L2 emails (Huang L-J, 2016) others identified low amounts. Pham and Ye (2020), for example, found that only 28 % of the emails by Vietnamese students in their study were requests. Regardless of how much they are produced, it is clear the field has a strong preference for the study of L2 requests.

Different types of requests appear in L2 emails. In Alcón-Soler's (2013a) data, requests for feedback (low-imposition) were the most frequent among LLs, while requests for action (high-imposition) were more common among her expert English speakers. Halenko and Winder (2022) found in their data that requests for information were more frequent than requests for meetings and actions.

There are quite conflicting findings among the existing investigations. Some studies found that requests are most frequently realized through conventionally indirect strategies (Biesenbach-Lucas, 2006; Chen C-F, 2001, 2006; Hashemian & Farhang-Ju, 2020; Pan, 2012), while others found that direct strategies were the most common on their data (Burgucu-Tazegul et al., 2016; Chang & Hsu, 1998; Oktarina et al., 2020; Pham & Ye, 2020). These seemingly contradictory findings could be due to the type of request in the data. As Zarei and Mohammadi's (2012) research showed, indirect strategies were primarily used for requests for action while direct strategies were used for requests for specific information. This seems to suggest that LLs are aware of the different degrees of imposition for different requests, however, it is not so clear whether they can realize them appropriately. For example, Alcón-Soler (2013a) found that LLs use conventional indirect requests for higher-imposition requests, while Balman et al. (2020) found the use of conventional indirect strategies for low-imposition requests. Other studies found query preparatory (e.g., Could you. . .?) the most employed head act strategies in all types of requests, followed by direct strategies using lexical and external mitigators to soften the requestive force (Alsalem, 2024; Hashemian & Farhang-Ju, 2020; Pan, 2012). To muddle the findings even more, Félix-Brasdefer (2012b) found that high-imposition requests often include hint strategies and preparatory strategies, and Alcón-Soler (2013b) found indirect request to be preferred for high-imposition situations (also Balman et al., 2020), while lower-imposition requests tend to be more direct. However, there seems to be more going on than just the differential imposition that some of these studies consider. As Hendriks (2010) shows, even within two parts of the same study with the same participants, clear differences on the effect of power difference and imposition are found, which she attributes to other variables such as the reasonableness of the request or context specific features such as rights and obligations.

Opening and Closing Sequences

The structure of request emails typically includes several main elements: an opening (e.g., greeting, self-identification), the main purpose of the email (i.e., the request), and a closing sequence (e.g., thanking, farewell). As an important part of this structure, openings and closings in L2 emails have generated a strong body of research (12 studies).

Openings and closings are essential for establishing tone, politeness, and formality, and they play a strong role in the appropriateness of an email request. Research indicates that native speakers (NSs) and LLs use different strategies in these sequences. The most frequently used opening strategies include a greeting followed by the recipient's name. The formality of a greeting seems to be highly conditioned by sociocultural and institutional norms. Zarei and Mohammadi (2012) found that Iranian EFL learners tended to use the professor's last name more often than their first name, as did Schauer's (2021) EFL German participants. However, this was not the case in other studies where LLs' greetings in initial email to faculty were seen as too informal and impolite or not appropriate (Almoaily, 2018; Dombi, 2020). However, in a different context (Spain), the most common opening used was a greeting followed by the faculty's first name (70 % of greetings) with the title being used only in rare instances (Salazar-Campillo, 2022). As Salazar-Campillo explains, this is a reflection of the LLs culture.

It is interesting that studies nowadays are still finding large variability of email opening, which indicates that even when email is such a prevalent medium today, the pragmalinguistic choices (and possibly the sociopragmatic norms) are still not clear for L2 writers. As an example, Alsalem (2024) found 13 different types of address, with and without greeting, with the most common, used by only 28 % of the participants.

L2 Proficiency

A few studies have addressed whether language proficiency plays a role in the production of email, but we do not have enough research for solid results yet, especially since the existing research focuses on different pragmatic features. Studies show no significant difference in the perception of offense and the production of general apology strategies between high and low proficiency learners (Xiao & Gao, 2016), in the production of complaints (Nguyen & Pham, 2021), or in the production of small talk (Ren & Liu, 2021). However, when apologizing, lower proficiency learners seem to employ more illocutionary force strategies but fewer upgraders than higher proficiency learners. Additionally, the emails from low proficiency LLs tend to be significantly longer (Xiao & Gao, 2016). When requesting, lower-level LLs use more direct strategies and omitting syntactic and lexical mitigation devices more often (Zhu, 2012). Halenko and Ko (2022) also support the idea that language proficiency plays a role since only 50 % of novice English learners in their data used closings in their emails. Codina-Espurz and Salazar-Campillo (2019) also found qualitative differences in the variety of closing expressions used by LLs with higher proficiency (more English hours of instruction), although at both levels of proficiency students still lacked pragmalinguistic competence and transferred sociocultural norms of greeting from their culture (C1). English majors, who typically have higher English proficiency, use a larger variety of modifiers and have more pragmalinguistic choices than non-English majors (Pham & Ye, 2020). In terms of language use, undergraduate students (with less proficiency) often code-switch, while graduate students maintain more formality in their emails (Huang, 2016). Interestingly, Tseng (2015) found no significant difference in the use of request strategies and politeness devices between low-level (TOEIC scores 350–520) and high-level (TOEIC scores 680–850) learners. Yet, higher proficiency learners displayed a wider range of internal and external modifiers in their requests. Despite their sociopragmatic knowledge, both proficiency levels seemed to lack sufficient pragmalinguistic resources. In summary, we need more research that sheds light on the role that proficiency plays in L2 email communication.

Age and academic level also influence email composition. Graduate students in China, who are generally older, tend to write more formally compared to younger undergraduate students (Huang L-J., 2016). This result was also found by Barón and Ortega (2018) in a completely different context. In their study comparing 18–20-year-olds with 30–40-year-old EFL learners in Cataluña with British speakers of the same age, the authors found differences between the younger and older participants in their openings and use of apologies, although no differences were found between the two age groups of British participants. Their interviews also showed a lack of perceived power differential in the younger group while the interviewee in the older group stated that the situation (apologizing for missing an exam) required more pragmatic work.

The Influence of the L1 Culture

The effect of cultural values on email communication is evident in the reviewed research, even at advanced levels of proficiency (Economidou-Kogetsidis, 2021). Ko et al. (2015) noted that LLs from Asian countries, where formality and respect are conveyed through negative politeness strategies, tend to employ more deferential styles in their emails. Xiao and Gao (2016) highlighted the influence of Chinese cultural practices like *Taoci*, shaping how Chinese students structure their emails and Ren and Liu (2021) also found the types of small talk in Chinese EFL thanking messages to be highly influenced by Chinese culture. Similarly, Oktarina et al. (2020) found that Indonesian students, recognizing the significant social distance between themselves and faculty, reflect their cultural beliefs about respecting elders in their email etiquette. Pham and Ye (2020) observed a large use of 'please' which the LLs seemed to be using as a substitute for the frequent use of honorific markers and markers for downplaying a request in Vietnamese politeness. Tseng (2015), Zarei and Mohammadi (2012), and Zarepour and Saidloo (2016) found similar patterns among Chinese and Iranian students, who incorporate lengthy supportive moves and pre- and post-grounders in their emails, reflecting C1 cultural norms of indirectness and politeness.

In the Vietnam context, Nguyen (2018) found that almost all the EFL learner used aggravators in their email requests, mostly setting expectations for the professor that were rooted in the collectively-oriented Vietnamese culture which places emphasis on values of bonding and intimacy (e.g., meeting at the professor's home, a cafe or restaurant, meeting on a weekend) quite different from most

Anglo-Saxon cultures that prime autonomy and privacy. Finally, Salazar-Campillo (2018) and Codina-Espurz and Salazar-Campillo (2019) observed that the LLs' emails in their studies (young university students around 20 years old) exhibited less hierarchical language use and greater egalitarianism, often addressing professors informally, by first name, as reflection of Spanish society. This was confirmed in a later study (Salazar-Campillo, 2022) focusing on address terms where she found that 50 % of first email messages used the informal address term *tú* which actually increased up to 80 % in following emails, and the fact that the professors from the second message on signed with their first name. Barón and Ortega (2018) confirm this lack of perceived power differential for the same age in the same context (18–20), although in their study, older L2 speakers (30–40) seemed to understand that more politeness was needed in situations of higher imposition. Similar results were found in the low power differential Norwegian academic context (Savić, 2018).

Alcón-Soler's Non-Interventional Research

Within the studies that compared two groups of students, Alcón-Soler published several non-interventional articles (2013a, 2013b) based on data collected from email request to teachers produced by British English teenagers and International English (IESs) speakers of the same age. These studies pushed the investigative field of email requests forward since she was one of the few researchers to investigate email communication in a study abroad context through the analysis of naturally occurring data. The results of these studies showed that these learners in a study abroad setting used more direct strategies and external mitigators, and a limited range of internal modifiers, probably due to the lack of pragmalinguistic knowledge. She also found that both groups of teenagers did not perceive their interaction with their teacher as hierarchical and with social distance, although they did use different forms of address. The results of her second study (2013b) showed that the LLs produced mostly requests for feedback (low-imposition requests) while the British teenagers produced more requests for action and appointments, which are both higher-imposition requests.

Non-Interventional Developmental Studies

Some of the non-instructional studies include longer periods of data collection, however, only three studies are non-interventional and developmental in nature, that is, they look at the evolution of the same group of LLs' email writing for an extended period of time without any instruction (Chen C-F, 2006; Halenko & Winder, 2021, 2022; Ko et al., 2015). It is difficult to judge how time affects development with results from only four studies. Halenko and Winder (2021, 2022) only found small changes in LLs' openings and closings and no change in students' mitigation of requests during the 10 months their LLs spent studying abroad in the UK. Even more, after two years, Ko et al. (2015) did not find much pragmatic development. Contrary, Chen C-F (2006) who followed the development of one Taiwanese student's email practices for two and a half years in the USA found that the student improved her email appropriateness considerably. As Chen C-F (2006) suggests, this was the case because the students' ideas of politeness between student and professor changed through socialization with other PhD Students, which also affected her own identity, both requiring considerable time.

Although the research presented above shows that L2 pragmatics can be acquired implicitly through interaction with other speakers, especially in study abroad contexts where LLs encounter a variety of context and interlocutors (Pérez-Vidal & Shively, 2019), several meta-analyses of the existing research suggest that instruction is effective for L2 pragmatics learning. In addition, explicit instruction is more effective than implicit instruction and this is more the case when the instruction is accompanied by feedback (Plonsky & Zhuang, 2019) and opportunities for practice (Taguchi, 2015). In this line, several of the non-interventional studies reviewed above call for the need to incorporate pragmatic instruction (e.g., Alcón-Soler, 2013b; Aisalem, 2024; Biesenbach-Lucas, 2007; Burgucu-Tazegul et al., 2016; Chang et al., 2016; Codina-Espurz & Salazar-Campillo, 2019; Economidou-Kogetsidis, 2015; Nguyen & Pham, 2021; Rau & Rau, 206; Salazar-Campillo & Codina-Espurz, 2018; Shahid, 2020) and this call has been answered by a group of researchers focusing on the impact of instructional materials and techniques on LLs' L2 pragmatic development.

Instructional Studies

The majority of instructional studies of email have also focused on requests, although a few have investigated suggestions (Fukuya & Martínez-Flor, 2008; Ghavamnia et al., 2018; Martínez-Flor & Fukuya, 2005), sentence final particles (Kakegawa, 2009), strategies (Usó-Juan, 2022), terms of address (Rau & Rau, 2016), and feedback techniques (Nguyen et al., 2015, 2018, 2019). The main difference between non-interventional studies and these interventional studies is the goal of discovering what type of instruction is most effective, either by comparing two or more types of instruction, or by implementing an instructional method and testing LLs gains. Within the first group, the debate of whether explicit or implicit instruction is most effective is reflected in several studies, which produced divergent results.

Type of Instruction

Investigating whether explicit or implicit pragmatic instruction is more effective on the teaching of L2 email writing, Martínez-Flor and Fukuya (2005) and Fukuya and Martínez-Flor (2008) explored the effects of both methods on the production of EFL learners' suggestions (head acts and downgraders). The explicit group watched videos of suggestions and read the scripts, discussed the videos and completed several awareness raising activities. They received explicit instruction on suggestions, completed a multiple-choice test, and they took part in role-plays. The implicit group watched the same videotaped but with captions in boldface, they completed several activities (a listening activity, a reading comprehension of the video scripts (with text enhancement) and engaged in role-plays (with recasting feedback). The results of their studies show no difference between the two types of interaction. In a more recent study, Eslami et al. (2015) matched groups of Iranian EFL learners with an American tutor. The implicit group engaged in (a) consciousness-raising activities using input enhancement (e.g., boldfaced target structures; comparing their own requests to native speakers' requests); (b) DCT production activities; and (c) reflection on their own productions based on recasts and implicit feedback. The explicit group followed the structure described above. Their results revealed that the group that had received explicit instruction outperformed the one that received implicit instruction. The difference in results can be due to the different treatments, or as Ghavamnia et al. (2018) suggest, pragmatic instruction should be better understood by the degree of input enhancement that it incorporates, rather than a dichotomy between implicit and explicit treatments.

One result that seems to be consistent through all the instructional studies (incorporating a control group) is that instruction indeed helps learn L2 pragmatics, and this is true for different pragmatic features. For example, Usó-Juan (2022) found that the teaching of strategies helped LLs produced more concrete subject lines and more complete greetings and closing sequences and helped LLs to mitigate the tone of the email requests using both more conventionally indirect request strategies, and more lexical and syntactic modifiers. Although research has demonstrated that instruction has a positive effect on the learning of L2 pragmatics, some pragmatic features seem to be more responsive to instruction than others (Chen Y, 2015; Nguyen, 2018; Usó-Juan, 2021).

Models of Pragmatic Instruction

One of the main goals of interventional studies seems to be the presentation and discussion of possible models of pragmatic instruction. Although we can find some variations on the types of activities included, most interventional studies include similar patterns of instruction, starting with either examples followed by conscious-raising activities, or the other way around, then metapragmatic explanations, practice, and (some of them) feedback. For example, Codina-Espurz and Salazar-Campillo (2019) suggest a Five Es Approach: 1-Expose (expose learners to examples of real-life pragmatic interactions), 2-Examine (analyse examples to raise awareness either in an inductive or a deductive manner), 3-Enact (LLs produce examples of what they have learned considering different contextual factors), 4- Evaluate (LLs should receive feedback on their production), and 5-Expand (expand the task to other modes of communication, other speech acts, etc.). For readers interested in incorporating pragmatic instruction in class, Chen Y (2016) is possibly the most detailed blueprint for the instruction of L2 email request.

With some variation on the order of the steps, these are the most common steps when instructing L2 pragmatics explicitly:

- Consciousness-raising activities (exposure to real examples, activate prior knowledge) (Chen Y, 2015, 2016; Codina-Espurz & Salazar-Campillo, 2019; Kakegawa, 2009; Eslami et al., 2015; Nguyen, 2018; Usó-Juan, 2022)
- Explicit metapragmatic explanations (Kakegawa, 2009; Chen Y, 2015, 2016; Eslami et al., 2015; Nguyen, 2018; Usó-Juan, 2021)
- Activities such as identifying the target pragmatic feature on emails (Kakegawa, 2009), comparing own email with Ns's email (Chen & Liu, 2021) writing an email with the help of the teacher (Chen, 2015, 2016), discussing inappropriate requests, (Eslami et al., 2015), analyzing contextual variables and produced emails for different scenarios (Nguyen, 2018); reflect on their own email practices (Chen & Liu, 2021; Usó-Juan, 2022)
- Practice writing emails individually (Kakegawa, 2009; Chen Y, 2015, 2016; Usó-Juan, 2022) and providing for their choices of forms (Eslami et al., 2015)
- Feedback (e.g., LLs read their email messages to identify appropriate and inappropriate uses of the target form, and revise their emails based on feedback) (Kakegawa, 2009; Eslami et al., 2015; Nguyen, 2018; Usó-Juan, 2021, 2022)

Focusing on the last step of instruction, feedback, Nguyen and colleagues (2015, 2018, 2019) explored the effects of different corrective feedback techniques on the production of email requests. The results of these studies suggest that feedback indeed affects performance and there seems to be no difference in what type of feedback (i.e., clarification requests, recasts, metapragmatic feedback, or explicit correction) the LLs receive, or whether the feedback came with no revisions, one revision or two revisions. This is without a doubt a line of research that requires much more investigation.

Alcón-Soler's Instructional Research

It is within instructional studies that Alcón-Soler's influence is most prevalent. Following her own suggestion of the need for explicit L2 pragmatic instruction to improve LLs' email competence, Alcón-Soler published two studies (2015, 2017) with Spanish students learning English in a study abroad context. In both studies, 30 English learners received metapragmatic explicit instruction on email requests (four 20-minute sessions) while 30 did not. In the first study, Alcón-Soler (2015) found that that instruction was useful to get students to perform significatively better right away, although at the end of the year both groups were comparable in their production of email requests. The longitudinal nature of the study allowed Alcón-Soler to observe some interesting facts about the learning. Although students started with a tendency to use direct requests, with some external modifiers, after the treatment, the experimental group used a wider range of mitigators, and were able to make explicit reference to what they have learned. They seemed to be aware of the informality of emails but still mitigated their requests and they made greater use of softeners. Alcón-Soler (2017), confirming her previous study, showed immediate benefits from pragmatic instruction in the use of conventionally indirect strategies and internal modifiers. The study also revealed individual variation between the two case studies included in the study. Although both students had gained sociopragmatic knowledge, their pragmalinguistic competence was still different. As a conclusion Alcón-Soler suggests that development is affected by the interaction among pragmatic instruction, language exposure, and individual factors such as learner's perception of request imposition and their desire to be accepted in the community.

Committed to understanding what instructional method best serves L2 pragmatic development, Alcón-Soler (2018) compared two types of explicit metapragmatic teaching intervention: one group engaged in a collaborative group task to write three high-imposition emails, and the other group led by the teacher in the writing of the same emails. The results show short-term improvement for both instructional groups (but not for the control group) on internal mitigators, softeners and syntactic structures, although the effect disappeared by the delayed post-test. No difference was found for the type of instruction or the attention that LLs paid to pragmatic features (measured in amount of pragmatic related episodes). Finally, the qualitative data showed that the collaborative task brought up more metapragmatic discussion about how to construct a high-imposition request via email.

Conclusions

This chapter has presented a synthesis of 86 studies from 18 different countries investigating the pragmatics of L2 writing. Due to the diversity of objectives, pragmatic focus, and research designs, it remains challenging to aggregate the findings into a clear overall picture. And, as it may be now clear to the reader, there is still much we do not know about the topic.

As presented in this synthesis, most studies have focused on requests, possibly because they are a speech act that requires appropriateness to establish and maintain rapport, and because they are frequent in student-faculty communication. While the amount of research is considerable (and growing), there is still a lack of agreement among some results, and the different foci of studies highlight the numerous variables that influence the realization of such act.

It seems that LLs are indeed capable of being polite and constructing themselves as respectful students; however, they may need assistance. Breaking L2 pragmatic rules is viewed as less severe for LLs with obvious linguistic challenges, while for more advanced learners, such breaches may be attributed to their personality (Economidou-Kogetsidis, 2016; Hendriks, 2010; Usó-Juan, 2022). From this research, it also seems clear that L1/C1 pragmatic transfer heavily influences L2 email writing, while it is still not clear what role language proficiency plays.

Instruction, regardless of the method, seems to have a positive effect on learning. Explicit pragmatic instruction seems to be a way to expedite sociopragmatic understanding and acquisition of pragmalinguistic skills that they may not yet possess. However, since most studies employ a variety of techniques for instruction, we do not yet know precisely what helps learning the most. More studies are needed to pinpoint the most effective techniques. When teaching L2 pragmatics, it is impossible to teach all the sociopragmatics and pragmalinguistics of the target language. Even if LLs learn all the sociopragmatic rules and linguistic possibilities to produce a polite and appropriate email, we must remember that, like any other interaction, email communication is co-constructed and subject to recipient interpretation based on their own sociopragmatic rules and understanding of the world. As Savić (2018) and Economidou-Kogetsidis (2011) show, faculty react differently to students' requests. While some may perceive the use of thanking in an email as polite, others may see it as over the top, manipulative, or presupposing the granting of a request. Therefore, it is more efficient to teach students to understand how different contexts change the way we interact and to observe how other speakers interact, that is, teaching them how to handle interactional practices in the communities they may encounter (Sykes & González-Lloret, 2020).

There are many additional lines of research that would help us understand L2 email practices and how to best teach them. For example, it would be interesting to know how much email recipients accommodate LLs' emails and how faculty use pragmatic strategies in their emails to connect with their students. Recent research by Tsoumou (2024) indicates that although LLs are primarily concerned with maintaining their own face in emails, faculty responses also prioritize maintaining connectedness and avoiding classroom conflict, illustrating a nuanced interaction in email communication dynamics between students and faculty. Another possible line of research could be to examine other forms of communication that may be starting to replace email. For example, a study on the use of video for L2 pragmatic learning (Hirotani & Lyddon, 2013) suggest that, even without explicit metapragmatic instruction, video telecollaboration was effective for improving LLs' self-introductions in the L2. Technologies such as video messaging, video posts, and video communities (e.g., YouTube, TikTok) may soon replace written communication genres such as email since they are faster and require less effort, although in specific contexts, such academic contexts and some workplace contexts, email will probably persist. As Lorentz (2024) notes, Gen Z consider themselves, above all, video content creators, indicating a generational shift in online life. As researchers and teachers, we need to consider these advances and adapt our research and our instruction (within our possibilities) to the new generations so we can maintain the relevance of our work and best serve our students.

References

Alcón-Soler, Eva. 2013a. Mitigating e-mail requests in teenagers' first and second language academic cyber-consultation. *Multilingua*, 32, 779–99.

Alcón-Soler, Eva. 2013b. Pragmatic variation in british and international English language users' email communication, a focus on requests. *RESLA*, 26, 25–44.

Alcón-Soler, Eva. 2015. Pragmatic learning and study abroad, effects of instruction and length of stay. *System*, 48, 62–74. <https://doi.org/10.1016/j.system.2014.09.005>.

Alcón-Soler, E. 2017. Pragmatic development during study abroad, an analysis of Spanish teenagers' request strategies in English emails. *Annual Review of Applied Linguistics*. 37, 77–92. <https://doi.org/10.1017/S0267190517000125>.

Alcón-Soler, Eva. 2018. Effects of task-supported language teaching on learning how to mitigate email requests. In Naoko Taguchi & Youjin Kim (eds) *Task-based approaches to teaching and assessing pragmatics. Task-based language teaching*. Amsterdam: John Benjamins, 55–81.

Alemi, Minoo & Maleknia, Zahra. 2023. Politeness markers in emails of non-native English speaking university students. *Russian Journal of Linguistics*, 1/27, 67–87. <https://doi.org/10.22363/2687-0088-33334>.

Almoaily, Mohammad. 2018. Greetings as a politeness strategy in EFL distance learning students' official emails. *Linguistics and Literature Studies*, 6/6, 259–66. <https://doi.org/10.13189/lls.2018.060601>.

Alsalem, Nuha K. 2024. Request strategies in Saudi ESL learners' email communication, a pragmatic analysis. *Journal of Language*

Teaching and Research, 15/2, 540–46. <https://doi.org/10.17507/jltr.1502.22>.

Balman, Rezki P., Sangmok, Lee & Inoue Narahiko. 2020. Request strategies in email communication: The case of Indonesian graduate students in Japan. *Studies in English Language and Education*, 7/2, 379–92. <https://doi.org/10.24815/siele.v7i2.16806>.

Barón, Julia & Ortega, Mireia. 2018. Investigating age differences in e-mail pragmatic performance. *System*, 78, 148–58. <https://doi.org/10.1016/j.system.2018.08.001>.

Bella, Spyridoula. 2021. In search of the missing grade: Egalitarianism and deference in L1 and L2 students' emails to faculty members. In Maria Economidou-Kogetsidis & Milica Savić & Nicola Halenko (eds) *Email Pragmatics and Second Language Learners*. Amsterdam: John Benjamins, 203–26.

Biesenbach-Lucas, Sigrun. 2005. Communication topics and strategies in e-mail consultation, comparison between american and international university students. *Language Learning & Technology*, 9/2, 24–46.

Biesenbach-Lucas, Sigrun. 2006. Making requests in e-mail, do cyber-consultations entail directness? Toward conventions in a new medium. In Kathleen Bardovi-Harlig, Julio César Félix-Brasdefer & Alwiya Omar (eds) *Pragmatics & Language Learning*. Honolulu: NFLRC, 81–108.

Biesenbach-Lucas, Sigrun. 2007. Students writing emails to faculty, an examination of e-politeness among native and non-native speakers of English. *Language Learning & Technology,* 11/2, 59–81. <http://dx.doi.org/10125/44104>.

Burgucu-Tazegul, Assiye, Han, Turgay & Engin, Ali O. 2016. Pragmatic failure of Turkish EFL learners in request emails to their professors. *International Education Studies*, 9/10, 105. <https://doi.org/10.5539/ies.v9n10p105>.

Ceci, Laura. 2024. Number of e-mail users worldwide 2018–2027. *Statista*. https://www.statista.com/statistics/255080/number-of-e-mail-users-worldwide/

Chang, Miao-Hsia, Curran, Jean, Hsu, Yueh-Kuei & Hsu Chih-Chun. 2016. Do Chinese students Waffle in their apologies? An exploration into EFL learners' emails. In Yuan-Shan Chen, Der-Hwa Victoria Rau & Gerald Rau (eds) *Email discourse among chinese using English as a Lingua Franca*. Singapore: Springer, 61–90.

Chang, Yu-Ying & Hsu, Yi-Ping. 1998. Requests on e-mail, a cross-cultural comparison. *RELC Journal*, 29/2, 121–51. <https://doi.org/10.1177/003368829802900206>.

Chen, Chi-Fen Emily E. 2006. The development of e-mail literacy, from writing to peers to writing to authority figures. *Language Learning & Technology*, 10/2, 35–55.

Chen, Xinren. 2016. Emailing requests to international researchers, The construction of identity by Chinese EFL graduate students. In Yuan-Shan Chen, Der-Hwa Victoria Rau & Gerald Rau (eds) *Email discourse among Chinese Using English as a Lingua Franca*. Singapore: Springer, 115–34.

Chen, Yuan-shan. 2015. Developing Chinese EFL Learners' Email Literacy through Requests to Faculty. *Journal of Pragmatics,* 75, 131–49. <https://doi.org/10.1016/j.pragma.2014.05.009>.

Chen, Yuan-shan. 2016. Understanding the development of Chinese EFL learners' email literacy through exploratory practice. *Language Teaching Research,* 20/2, 165–80. <https://doi.org/10.1177/1362168814562014>.

Chen, Yuan-shan & Liu, Chin-Ting. 2021. Reformulation on Chinese EFL Learners' Email Literacy: A Preliminary Exploration. In Maria Economidou-Kogetsidis, Milica Savić & Nicola Halenko (eds) *Email Pragmatics and Second Language Learners.* Amsterdam: John Benjamins, 328, 15–40.

Codina-Espurz, Victòria. 2021. The influence of social distance and power in email politeness in an academic context. *Estudios Interlingüísticos*, 9, 44–59.

Codina-Espurz, Victòria & Salazar-Campillo, Patricia. 2019. Openings and closing in emails by CLIL students, a pedagogical proposal. *English Language Teaching*, 12/2, 57. <https://doi.org/10.5539/elt.v12n2p57>.

Davies, Alan. 1991. *The native speaker in Applied Linguistics*. Edinburgh: Edinburgh University Press.

Davies, Alan. 2003. *The native speaker, myth and reality* (2nd ed.). Clevedon: Multilingual Matters.

Dombi, J. 2020. Email requests in an ELF academic setting, good luck to you, doctor judit. *Applied Pragmatics*, 2/1, 54–79. <https://doi.org/10.1075/ap.18017.dom>.

Economidou-Kogetsidis, Maria. 2011. Please answer me as soon as possible, pragmatic failure in non-native speakers' e-mail requests to faculty. *Journal of Pragmatics*, 43/13, 3193–3215. <https://doi.org/10.1016/j.pragma.2011.06.006>.

Economidou-Kogetsidis, Maria. 2015. Teaching email politeness in the EFL/ESL classroom. *ELT Journal*, 69/4, 415–24. <https://doi.org/10.1093/elt/ccv031>.

Economidou-Kogetsidis, Maria. 2016. Variation in evaluations of the (im)politeness of emails from L2 learners and perceptions of the personality of their senders. *Journal of Pragmatics,* 106, 1–19. <https://doi.org/10.1016/j.pragma.2016.10.001>.

Economidou-Kogetsidis, Maria. 2018. 'Mr Paul, Please Inform Me Accordingly' address forms, directness and degree of imposition in L2 emails. *Pragmatics.* 28, 489–515.

Economidou-Kogetsidis, Maria. 2021. The effect of first language pragmatics on second language email performance: The case of Greek students' email requests. In Maria Economidou-Kogetsidis, Milica Savić & Nicola Halenko (eds) *Email pragmatics and second language learners*. Amsterdam: John Benjamins, 151–78.

Eslami, Zohreh. 2013. Online communication and students' pragmatic choices in English. *Lodz Papers in Pragmatics*, 9, 71–92. <https://doi.org/10.1515/lpp-2013-0005>.

Eslami, Zohreh & Ko, Wei-Hong. 2015. Facework in non-face-threatening emails by native and non-native English speakers. *Russian Journal of Linguistics*, 19, 111–26.

Eslami, Zohreh, Mirzaei, Azizullah & Dini, Shadi. 2015. The role of asynchronous computer mediated communication in the instruction and development of EFL learners' pragmatic competence. *System*, 48, 99–111. <https://doi.org/10.1016/j.system.2014.09.008>.

Félix-Brasdefer, Julio C. 2012a. Email openings and closings, pragmalinguistic and gender variation in learner-instructor cyber consultations. *Utrecht Studies in Language & Communication*, 24, 223–48.

Félix-Brasdefer, Julio C. 2012b. E-mail requests to faculty, e-politeness and internal modification. In M. Economidou-Kogetsidis & H. Woodfield (eds) *Pragmatics & beyond New Series*. Amsterdam: John Benjamins, 87–118. <https://doi.org/10.1075/pbns.217.04fel>.

Ford, Shawn. 2006. The use of pragmatics in e-mail requests made by second language learners of English. *Studies in Language Sciences*, 5, 143–62.

Fukuya, Yoshinori & Martínez-Flor, Alicia. 2008. The interactive effects of pragmatic-eliciting tasks and pragmatic instruction. *Foreign Language Annals*, 41/3, 478–500. <https://doi.org/10.1111/j.1944-9720.2008.tb03308.x>.

Ghavamnia, Maedeh, Abbas, Eslami-Rasekh & Hussein, Vahid Dastjerdi. 2018. The Effects of Input-Enhanced Instruction on Iranian EFL Learners' Production of Appropriate and Accurate Suggestions. *The Language Learning Journal.* 46/2, 114–31. <https://doi.org/10.1080/09571736.2014.972431>.

Haider, Iftikhar & Zandi Hamed. 2022. In my professor's eyes, faculty and perceived impoliteness in student emails. *Lodz Papers in Pragmatics*, 18/1, 197–222. <https://doi.org/10.1515/lpp-2022-0009>.

Halenko, Nicola & Winder, Lisa. 2022. Openings and closings in institutionally-situated email requests. *Study Abroad Research in Second Language Acquisition and International Education*, 7/1, 54–87. <https://doi.org/10.1075/sar.21010.hal>.

Hartford, Beverly S. & Bardovi-Harlig, Kathleen. 1996. 'At Your Earliest Convenience': A study of written student requests to faculty. In Lawrence F. Bouton (ed.) *Pragmatics and language learning*. Urbana Champaign: University of Illinois, 55–69.

Hashemian, Mahmood & Farhang-Ju, Maryam. 2019. Applied linguistics faculty members' perceptions of (im)politeness and (in)appropriateness of l2 learners' e-mail requests. *Journal of Teaching Language Skills*, 38/1. 119–155. <https://doi.org/10.22099/jtls.2019.34578.2729>.

Hashemian, Mahmood & Farhang-Ju, Maryam. 2020. Pragmalinguistic variation in L2 learners' e-requests to faculty, looking at degree of imposition. *Journal of Language Horizons*, 4/1, 105–126. <https://doi.org/10.22051/lghor.2020.30297.1256>.

Halenko, Nicola & Winder, Lisa. 2021. Experts and novices: Examining academic email requests to faculty and developmental change during study abroad. In Maria Economidou-Kogetsidis, Milica Savić & Nicola Halenko (eds) *Email pragmatics and second language learners*. Amsterdam: John Benjamins, 101–26.

Hendriks, Berna. 2010. An experimental study of native speaker perceptions of non-native request modification in e-mails in English. *Intercultural Pragmatics*, 7/2, 221–55. <https://doi.org/10.1515/iprg.2010.011>.

Hirotani, Maki & Lyddon, Paul A. 2013. The development of L2 Japanese self-introductions in an asynchronous computer-mediated language exchange. *Foreign Language Annals*, 46/3, 469–90. <https://doi.org/10.1111/flan.12044>.

Huang, Hsin-chou. 2016. Openings and closings in intercultural email communication, a case study of Taiwanese, Japanese, and Italian students. In Yuan-Shan Chen, Der-Hwa Victoria Rau & Gerald Rau (eds) *Email discourse among Chinese using English as a Lingua Franca*. Singapore: Springer, 185–204.

Huang, Li-Jung. 2016. Discourse organization and features of email writing among EFL students in Taiwan. In Yuan-Shan Chen, Der-Hwa Victoria Rau & Gerald Rau (eds) *Email discourse among Chinese using English as a Lingua Franca*. Singapore: Springer, 37–60.

Ikeda, Keiko. 2009. Advanced learners' honorific styles in emails and telephone calls. In Naoko Taguchi (ed.) *Pragmatic competence*. Berlin: De Gruyter Mouton, 69–100.

Kakegawa, Tomomi. 2009. Development of the use of Japanese sentence-final particles through email correspondance. In Naoko Taguchi (ed.) *Pragmatic competence*. Berlin: De Gruyter Mouton, 301–34.

Ko, Wei-Hong Shuan, Eslami, Zohreh & Burlbaw, Lynn M. 2015. Investigating non-native English speaking graduate students' pragmatic development in requestive emails. *International Journal of Society, Culture & Language*, 3/1, 1–15.

Krulatz, Anna & Park, Koeun. 2015. Fostering pragmatic competence, strategies and materials for email writing. In *Tri-TESOL 2015 Conference Proceedings*, 34–46.

Li, Wang-jing & Chen, Yuan-Shan. 2016. Politeness and effectiveness of English email requests, taiwanese professors' perspectives. In Yuan-Shan Chen, Der-Hwa Victoria Rau & Gerald Rau (eds) *Email discourse among Chinese using English as a Lingua Franca*. Singapore: Springer, 91–111.

Liu, Jianda & Ren, Wei. 2016. Apologies in emails, interactions between Chinese EFL learners and their foreign peers. In Yuan-Shan Chen, Der-Hwa Victoria Rau & Gerald Rau (eds) *Email discourse among Chinese using English as a Lingua Franca*. Singapore: Springer, 205–28.

Lorentz, T. (2024, June 27). The majority of Gen Z describe themselves as video content creators. *The Washington Post*. <https://www.washing-tonpost.com/technology/2024/06/27/genz-video-content-creators-youtube/>

Martínez-Flor, Alicia & Fukuya, Yoshinori. 2005. The effects of instruction on learners' production of appropriate and accurate suggestions. *System*, 33/3, 463–80.

Mehrabi Boshrabadi, Abbas & Bataghva Sarabi, Sepideh. 2016. Cyber-communic@tion etiquette, the interplay between social distance, gender and discursive features of student-faculty email interactions. *Interactive Technology and Smart Education*, 13/2, 86–106. <https://doi.org/10.1108/ITSE-09-2015-0026>.

Nguyen, Minh Thi Thuy. 2018. Pragmatic development in the instructed context, a longitudinal investigation of L2 email requests. *Pragmatics,* 28/2, 217–52. <https://doi.org/10.1075/prag.00007.ngu>.

Nguyen, Minh Thi Thuy, Do, Thi Thanh Ha, Nguyen, Anh Tuan & Pham, Thanh Thuy. 2015. Teaching email requests in the academic context, a focus on the role of corrective feedback. *Language Awareness*, 24/2, 169–95. <https://doi.org/10.1080/09658416.2015.1010543>.

Nguyen, Minh Thi Thuy, Do, Thi Thanh Ha, Pham, Thanh Thuy & Nguyen, Anh Tuan. 2018. The effectiveness of corrective feedback for the acquisition of L2 pragmatics, an eight month investigation. *International Review of Applied Linguistics in Language Teaching*, 56/3, 345–75. <https://doi.org/10.1515/iral-2015-0059>.

Nguyen, Minh Thi Thuy, Do, Thi Thanh Ha, Pham, Thanh Thuy & Nguyen, Anh Tuan. 2019. The effects of corrective feedback with and without revision on enhancing L2 pragmatic competence. *Applied Pragmatics*, 1, 1–25.

Nguyen, Thi Thuy Minh & Pham, Thi Thanh Thuy. 2021. L2 emails of complaints: Strategy use by low and high proficiency learners of English as a foreign language. In Maria Economidou-Kogetsidis, Milica Savić & Nicola Halenko (eds) *Email pragmatics and second language learners.* Amsterdam: John Benjamins, 41–70.

Oktarina, Hanifah, Dewi, Sinta, Imam, Khoirul & Amanda, Putri. 2020. Request strategies in students' requestive emails to faculty, a pragmalinguistic analysis of postgraduate students' emails. *Journal of English Education and Linguistics*, 1/1, 59–71. <https://doi.org/10.56874/jeel.v1i1.49>.

Pan, Cathy. 2012. Interlanguage requests in institutional email discourse. In Maria Economidou-Kogetsidis & Hellen Woodfield (eds)

Interlanguage request modification. Amsterdam: John Benjamins, 119–61.

Pérez-Vidal, Carmen & Shively, Rachel L. 2019. L2 pragmatic development in study abroad settings. In Naoko Taguchi (ed.) *Routledge handbook of SLA and pragmatics*. New York: Routledge, 355–71.

Pham, Minh Thi Thuy & Yeh, Aiden. 2020. Politeness of Vietnamese students in writing request email in English, a course-based and socio-pragmatic study. *International Journal of Language and Literary Studies*, 2/2, 109–28. <https://doi.org/10.36892/ijlls.v2i2.202>.

Plonsky, Luke & Zhuang, Jingyuan. 2019. A meta-analysis of second language pragmatics instruction. In Naoko Taguchi (ed.) *Routledge handbook of SLA and pragmatics*. New York: Routledge, 287–307.

Rau, Der-Hwa Victoria V. & Rau, Gerald. 2016. Negotiating personal relationship through email terms of address. In Yuan-Shan Chen, Der-Hwa Victoria Rau & Gerald Rau (eds) *Email Discourse among Chinese Using English as a Lingua Franca*. Singapore: Springer, 11–36.

Ren, Wei. 2016. Pragmatic strategies to solve and preempt understanding problems in Chinese Professionals' emails when using English as Lingua Franca communication. *International Journal of Bilingual Education and Bilingualism*. 1–14. <https://doi.org/10.1080/13670050.2016.1226749>.

Ren, Wei & Liu, Wenjie. 2021. Phatic communion in Chinese students' gratitude emails in English: Production and perception. In M. Economidou-Kogetsidis, M. Savić, N. Halenko (eds) *Email pragmatics and second language learners*. Amsterdam: John Benjamins, 129–50.

Salazar-Campillo, Patricia. 2018. Student-initiated email communication, an analysis of openings and closings by Spanish EFL learners. *Sintagma, Revista de Lingüística*, 30, 81–93. <https://doi.org/10.21001/sintagma.2018.30.05>.

Salazar-Campillo, Patricia. 2022. Address forms and politeness markers in Spanish students' emails to faculty. *Revista Electrónica de Lingüística Aplicada*, 21/1. 58–73. <https://doi.org/10.58859/rael.v21i1.501>.

Salazar-Campillo, Patricia & Codina-Espurz, Victòria. 2018. Politeness in first and follow-up emails to faculty, openings and closings. In Ariadna Sánchez-Hernández & Ana Herraiz-Martínez (eds)

Learning second language pragmatics beyond traditional contexts. Lausanne, Switzerland: Peter Lang, 85–106. <https://doi.org/10.3726/b14949>.

Savić, Milica. 2018. Lecturer perceptions of (im)politeness and in/appropriateness in student e-mail requests, a norwegian perspective. *Journal of Pragmatics*, 124, 52–72. <https://doi.org/10.1016/j.pragma.2017.12.005>.

Schauer, Gila A. 2021. Email communication in English and in German: A contrastive pragmatic investigation of German university students' emails sent to university staff in their native and foreign language. In Maria Economidou-Kogetsidis, Milica Savić & Nicola Halenko (eds) *Email pragmatics and second language learners*. Amsterdam: John Benjamins, 179–202.

Shahid, Shama E. 2020. Formal email writing convention, differences between native and non-native students. *Journal of NELTA Gandaki*, 3/1–2, 57–72. <https://doi.org/10.3126/jong.v3i1-2.33145>.

Shim, Young-sook. 2013. International faculty perceptions of requestive emails by Korean university students. *Multimedia-Assisted Language Learning*, 16/47, 111–31. <https://doi.org/10.15702/MALL.2013.16.4.111>.

Sykes, Julie & González-Lloret, Marta. 2020. Exploring the interface of interlanguage/(L2) pragmatics and digital spaces. *CALICO Journal*, 37/1, i–xv. <https://doi.org/10.1558/cj.40433>.

Sykes, Julie 2017. Technologies for teaching and learning intercultural competence and interlanguage pragmatics. In Carol A. Chapelle & Shannon Sauro (eds) *The Handbook of technology and second language teaching and learning*. Hoboken, NJ: John Wiley & Sons, Inc, 119–33.

Taguchi, Naoko. 2015. Instructed pragmatics at a glance, where instructional studies were, are, and should be going. *Language Teaching*, 48/1, 1–50. <https://doi.org/10.1017/S0261444814000263>.

Tseng, Chia-Ti H. 2015. 'You Must Let Me Pass, Please!', An investigation of e-mail request strategies by Taiwanese EFL learners. *Journal of ELT and Applied Linguistics/JETAL*. 3/1, 11–28.

Tseng, Chia-Ti H. 2016. E-politeness, an analysis of Taiwanese EFL learners' email discourse on request strategies. *International Journal for 21st Century Education*, 3, 35–62. <https://doi.org/10.21071/ij21ce.v3iSpecial.5707>.

Tsoumou, Jean Mathieu. 2024. Facework in teacher-student email interactions. *Russian Journal of Linguistics*, 28/2, 243–65. <https://doi.org/10.22363/2687-0088-35650>.

Usó-Juan, Esther. 2022. Exploring the role of strategy instruction on learners' ability to write authentic email requests to faculty. *Language Teaching Research*, 26/2, 213–37. <https://doi.org/10.1177/13621688211066997>.

Usó-Juan, Esther. 2021. Long-term instructional effects on learners' use of email request modifiers. In Maria Economidou-Kogetsidis, Milica Savić & Nicola Halenko (eds) *Email pragmatics and second language learners*. Amsterdam: John Benjamins, 71–100.

Winans, Michael D. 2020. Email requests, politeness evaluations by instructors from diverse language backgrounds. *Language Learning & Technology*, 24/2, 104–18.

Woodfield, Helen & Economidou-Kogetsidis, Maria. 2010. I Just Need More Time', A study of native and non-native students' requests to faculty for an extension. *Multilingua. Journal of Cross-Cultural and Interlanguage Communication*, 29/1, 77–118. <https://doi.org/10.1515/mult.2010.004>.

Xiao, Lin & Gao, Yihong. 2016. Intercultural *Taoci* email, new wine in an old bottle. In Yuan-Shan Chen, Der-Hwa Victoria Rau & Gerald Rau (eds) *Email discourse among chinese using English as a Lingua Franca*. Singapore: Springer, 135–62.

Zarei, Gholam R. & Mohammadi, Masoomeh. 2012. E-politeness in iranian english electronic requests to the faculty. *Research in Applied Linguistics*, 3/1, 3–24.

Zarepour, Fatemeh & Saidloo, Masoumeh I. 2016. An analysis of Iranian EFL learners' English written requestive e-mails. *Journal of Language Teaching and Research*, 7/3, 579. <https://doi.org/10.17507/jltr.0703.20>.

Zhu, Wuhan. 2012. Polite requestive strategies in emails, an investigation of pragmatic competence of Chinese EFL learners. *RELC Journal*, 43/2, 217–38. <https://doi.org/10.1177/0033688212449936>.

Victòria Codina-Espurz and
Patricia Salazar-Campillo

Appraisal of (Im)Politeness in Student-Professor Email Communication

Introduction

As a mode of computer-mediated communication (Crystal, 2001), emails have gained popularity since the mid-90s (Gains, 1999). The efficiency and speed of email (Lan, 2000; Crystal, 2001) has contributed to accepting this type of electronic messages as a global tool for communication. Besides the fast nature of email, other advantages have been highlighted, such as the possibility to communicate to several people in different locations at the same time, and the prospect of keeping track of the communication (Waldvogel, 2007). Moreover, the asynchronous nature of email allows for better planning and editing of the communication exchange, which makes email writing more desirable than face-to-face communication (Duthler, 2006). In the academic context, students' communication with their professors via email has become a usual practice in higher education. Students also seem to prefer email writing to face-to-face interaction to make requests dealing with academic matters such as discussing grades, asking for assignment extensions or seeking for feedback (Dürscheid & Frehner, 2013; Níkleva & Núñez, 2013). Bloch (2002) pointed out that, whether for cultural or personality reasons (e.g., anxiety), some students may feel more comfortable interacting via email. However, despite being the most common and frequent way to communicate with professors (Níkleva & Núñez, 2013; Algryani & Al Jardani, 2023), email writing poses some difficulties to students (Bella, 2021). Given the power asymmetry in student-professor interaction, email communication with a faculty member requires higher pragmatic competence than writing to a peer (Chen, 2006). This task becomes even more challenging for L2 learners mainly due to their linguistic and pragmatic limitations and/or lack of familiarity with the TL norms (Chen, 2006; Zhu, 2012). Moreover, Eslami (2013) highlighted the cultural variability of online communication and how email users from different cultural backgrounds may exhibit a variety of discourse styles. As a consequence, an increasing number of studies have analysed pragmalinguistic and sociopragmatic competence in students' emails considering variables such as type of mitigating strategies employed, degree of imposition involved in the emails, power relationships between interlocutors, social status or gender of the sender and/or recipient, among many others (e.g., Félix-Brasdefer, 2012a; Codina-Espurz & Salazar-Campillo, 2019; Bella, 2021). Pragmatic infelicities found in students' direct and unmodified L2 emails may impact negatively on the student's image and the professor's willingness to comply with the request (Economidou-Kogetsidis, 2016).

Recently, a growing number of studies have focused on students' and professors' perceptions on (im)politeness and (in)appropriateness in students' requestive emails. In broad terms, these studies show that perceptions of what is (im)polite in emails tend to diverge between NS lecturers and EFL students (Economidou-Kogetsidis, 2016), among EFL lecturers (Savić, 2018) and even between learners and NSs (Economidou-Kogetsidis et al., 2021), on the grounds that there is no balance between "the importance of email content (reference to choice of compliance, acknowledgement of imposition, student/lecturer time-frames), and form (directness, nature and extent of mitigation, opening/closing moves)" (p. 163).

In light of prior research on different perceptions of (im)politeness in students' emails, the study presented in this chapter attempts to be a further contribution to students' and professors' appraisal of (im)politeness in email communication in the L1 Spanish context. In doing so, we may gain a deeper understanding of what has been traditionally expected in academic email interaction and the actual practice, which seems to be paving the way for a new genre in institutional communication.

Student-professor Email Communication

Students' pragmatic ability in cyberconsultations (i.e., emails) has been the focus of a vast number of studies for the past decades, especially when the students have to interact with their professors in a foreign language. The bulk of the research on email writing has aimed at exploring the strategies and mitigation devices L2 students from various language backgrounds use in their requests to professors (Economidou-Kogetsidis, 2011; Zarei & Mohammadi, 2012; Rahmani & Rahmany, 2014; Alcón-Soler, 2015; Tseng, 2015, 2016; Burgucu-Tazegül et al., 2016; Savić, 2019, to name a few), whereas other studies have addressed differences in production of both content and framing moves between NSs and NNSs in academic contexts (Pan, 2012; Alcón-Soler, 2013; Eslami, 2013; Deveci & Hmida, 2017; among many others).

Most findings on student-professor email communication point to students' pragmatic failure due to their limited pragmalinguistic competence and/or lack of awareness of sociopragmatic variables such as degree of imposition, social distance and power relationships, which should be taken into account in this type of email interaction. In this respect, some studies (e.g., Economidou-Kogetsidis, 2011; Zarei & Mohammadi, 2012; Shim, 2013; Burgucu-Tazegül et al., 2016) point out that the directness of the email requests produced by EFL learners, the use of inadequate mitigation or forms of address, and the omission of a salutation and/or closing rendered learners' email requests as impolite and caused pragmatic failure.

Inappropriate pragmatic choices may impact negatively on the professors' perceptions of the students' emails and thus affect both the transactional and the interactional nature of the email, which serves "to establish and maintain social relationships" (Yule, 2002: 6). This latter aspect has attracted attention in more recent research as some voices have claimed (i.e., Algryani & Al Jardani, 2023) that students may not know how to encode their communicative intent, thus resulting in professors' negative evaluations of the sender (i.e., the student). These negative assessments may stem from students' limited L2 proficiency or knowledge of the L2 culture norms; however, they are not restricted to the L2, as lack of pragmatic ability may also be evident even in the students' L1 (Pinilla, 2020; Robles-Garrote, 2020). A further variable that may contribute to students' pragmatic inadequacies is the tendency to write emails following conventions of chats or social media, which results in lack of accent marks, use of emoticons, errors in punctuation, and so on, as attested by previous research (e.g., Níkleva & Núñez, 2013; Pinilla, 2020; Algryani & Al Jardani, 2023).

In a study on the email writing skills of university students, Níkleva and Núñez (2013) found that punctuation errors were the most common mistakes in learner emails despite students' claim that correct punctuation had to be taken into consideration when writing an email, as it contributed to a better comprehension of the message. Punctuation errors were followed by errors in the use of accent marks, capitalization and lower case letters and morphology. These inadequacies were mainly attributed to the spontaneous nature and the economic use of language which characterizes students' email writing. As the authors argued, their findings seem to corroborate how unaware students are about their own mistakes and the requirements of email writing in academic contexts. In addition, Níkleva and Núñez (2013) maintained that learners need to be aware of instances it may not be appropriate to send a message to a professor, for example, asking for information that is available on the virtual platform or that has been previously provided in class, or using personal email addresses with humorous usernames.

In view of students' pragmatic deficiencies, the need to develop pragmatic awareness seems paramount. As the use of pragmatic norms differs from culture to culture (Codina-Espurz & Salazar-Campillo, 2019; Rodríguez-Velasco, 2023), "L2 learners need to have the necessary tools to identify which pragmalinguistic strategies and politeness conventions can successfully be transferred from their L1 to the L2 and which cannot" (Economidou-Kogetsidis et al., 2021: 173). However, even with typologically close languages, we cannot assume positive transfer from the L1 to the target language, as linguistic similarities do not imply cultural resemblances (Robles-Garrote, 2020). Therefore, learners should be taught to recognize similarities and differences between the L1 and the target language in order to identify whether the sender's communicative intention concurs with the perception of the receiver (Codina-Espurz & Salazar-Campillo, 2019; Robles-Garrote, 2020; Rodríguez-Velasco, 2023). In this sense, recent approaches to promote pragmatic development and awareness have suggested to start teaching pragmatics at an earlier age. For example, in Myrset's (2022) study, teaching pragmatics proved to be beneficial for young Norwegian EFL learners' pragmalinguistic development, which in turn was positive for their sociopragmatic competence.

Markers of (Im)politeness in Students' Emails

A number of markers of (im)politeness (e.g., punctuation, use of emojis/emoticons, etc.) have been addressed in the literature on email communication. In order to compose status-congruent messages and avoid too casual or disrespectful emails, some structural elements should be present. For example, the subject line has to be brief and informative, and should not be left blank (Algryani & Al Jardani, 2023). Email format includes framing moves and content sequences, which mainly provide information, and can also function to construct the student-professor relationship (Bella, 2021). A well-written email should also include different paragraphs (Crystal, 2001) along with salutations and closings, which contribute to more polite emails in a formal setting (Félix-Brasdefer, 2012b; Patrama, 2019; Codina-Espurz & Salazar-Campillo, 2019).

Some other markers relate to grammar and punctuation mistakes, typos or misspelled words, which may render the email sender as careless, unprofessional or even rude, since the asynchronous nature of emails allows for drafting and revision before sending the email. Due to the hybrid character of emails, they may also show traits of oral speech (e.g., contractions), or from instant messaging (e.g., capitalization, emoticons, overuse of punctuation marks, etc.). These features may impact negatively on how students' emails are written and perceived, as wrong grammar or spelling mistakes may be unwelcome by professors (Algryani & Al Jardani, 2023).

In student-professor academic consultations, the degree of imposition of the request may depend on, among other variables, the addressee's time and effort to comply with the demand (Fukushima, 2000). In this sense, requests can be placed along a continuum ranging from low to high imposition (Félix-Brasdefer, 2012b; Economidou-Kogetsidis, 2018). For example, requests for appointment or feedback would be regarded as low, whereas requests for action (e.g., writing a letter of recommendation, changing a grade, etc.) would be considered high in imposition, and thus, more face-threatening. Lack of acknowledgement of imposition and inappropriate address forms are also markers of impolite emails (Bella, 2021), together with absence or insufficient mitigation when requesting. In addition, the use of direct strategies (for example, imperatives) or unhedged demands make emails impolite and abrupt (Burgucu-Tazegül et al., 2016; Níkleva, 2018).

In those languages in which there is a dichotomy between formal (V-form) and informal (T-form) second-person pronouns, such as Spanish, German or French, their choice may denote (im)politeness. Bella and Sifianou (2012) reported that the V-form was mostly used in Greek students' L1 emails to show deference towards the professor. Chejnová (2014) claimed that the informal pronoun was not possible in the Czech university context, thus showing the asymmetrical power relationship between students and professors. More recently, in a study on email requests to faculty members, Salazar-Campillo (2023) found that the V-form was also the most common pronoun employed by Spanish EFL learners. However, inconclusive results have been put forward as to the use of informal and formal pronouns in the Spanish context. Whereas Níkleva and Núñez (2013) reported that nearly 80 % of their participants preferred the V-form to address their professors, Alcón-Soler (2015) indicated a lack of acknowledgement of social distance and power in her participants since they opted for employing the informal pronoun. Alcón-Soler's (2015) findings were further supported by Salazar-Campillo (2023), who found that over 72 % of the students used the T-form in follow-up emails, that is, after the professor's reply, a notable increase from the 50 % in first-contact emails. This shows that there may be a shift towards more egalitarianism (Níkleva, 2018) on the grounds that students seem to favor a more familiar and spontaneous tone in Spanish academic interactions.

An additional marker of (im)politeness refers to emojis and emoticons (i.e., the non-verbal cues which serve to convey nonlinguistic information either emotional or affective), which may be evident in face-to-face interaction, but missing in text-based communication. Dresner and Herring (2010) claim that the main function of these devices is pragmatic, that is, to indicate the illocutionary force of the speech act, and that emoticons "help convey an important aspect of the linguistic utterance they are attached to: What the user intends by what he or she types" (p. 256). In this sense, the authors argue that emoticons do not represent emotions, which tend to be unconsciously displayed in face-to-face communication; rather, emoticons indicate consciously produced intentions and pinpoint "The apparent paradox that emoticons mimic often nonintentional facial expressions, although they are intentionally produced" (Dresner & Herring, 2010: 261). Other functions of emoticons have also been pointed out. For example, Kelly and Watts (2015) maintained that emoticons may act as a form of 'low-cost phatic communication' (n. p.), that is, a means of keeping a conversational connection.

Despite the everyday use of emoticons or emojis, Tang and Hew (2018) claim that the communicative function of these devices and how they affect online interaction may not be as straightforward. These authors suggest that research is needed to understand the intention of the sender and the impact emoticons have on the receiver. In this line, Marder et al. (2019) advanced that the use of emoticons in higher education can become a "double-edged sword" (p. 2274) as university staff may be viewed as friendlier but less competent. Moreover, Vareberg et al. (2023) in a study on how students viewed emojis in a course welcome email the authors emphasized the beneficial effect of emojis in creating student-professor rapport and suggested that "textisms like emojis fuel this relational development when used appropriately for the context" (Vareberg et al., 2023: 6087). Likewise, students who perceived their professor as being approachable and helpful tended to employ more emoticons in their email communication to faculty (Baggia et al., 2022). In another study on emoji use in online student-professor communication in a university context, Crombie (2020) reported that students did not hold any negative perception about the use of these icons, and that emoji omission was mainly the result of uncertainty about the perceived etiquette on how to use them. Her findings also revealed that the meaning and/or the intention of the emojis was not as transparent as initially assumed. Despite the claims on the acceptability of emoticons, given the disparity in their interpretation and the effect on the credibility of the sender (Bartl, 2017), their use has also been disapproved in academic contexts as students' emails with embedded emoticons were regarded as not appropriate (Bakir & Haji, 2019). In a study on professors' evaluations of students' emails, Baggia et al. (2022) found that "students who use emoticons score lower on salutation, self-identification, sign-off, and level of formality" (p. 120), and that emoticons were not well received by professors who expected students' emails to reflect a certain degree of netiquette.

In light of the diverging opinions on use of emoticons, Crombie (2020) argues for changes in the use of such devices when communicating in academic contexts on the grounds that "We need to educate and support students by embracing the tools they appear to be happy to use, rather than risk them thinking that any aspect of their communication is invalid or inappropriate" (p. 38).

Perceptions of (Im)politeness in Students' Emails

Bardovi-Harlig's (2001) early study on perceptions in interlanguage pragmatics claimed that NNSs' and NSs' judgements often differed. In recent years many studies have been carried out on professors' perceptions of students' emails as a result of a general feeling of disrespect or lack of deference in students' requestive emails (Zarei & Mohammad, 2012; Chejnová, 2014; Hashemian & Farhang-Ju, 2019). As claimed by Stephens et al. (2009), overly casual emails may affect student credibility, interpersonal affect, and willingness to comply with the email request. In fact, students' pragmatic choices may impact professors' perception of their emails, especially when students send requestive emails with a high degree of imposition.

Most studies dealing with perceptions of (im)politeness have examined the recipient's perspective and claimed that pragmatic failure provides a poor image of the email sender (Hendriks, 2010; Economidou-Kogetsidis, 2011, 2016). For example, Hendriks (2010) examined how NSs of English perceived differences in request modifications in emails written by Dutch NNSs of English. The author concluded that, although NNS-NS communication was hardly affected, undermodification in email requests provided a less pleasant perception of the L2 sender. Similarly, Economidou-Kogetsidis (2011) claimed that the use of direct strategies by NNS students produced a negative effect on the NS professors. In particular, the use of imperatives was not well received as it rendered the email request as a demand the professors were expected to comply with.

Few studies have addressed the perception of pragmatic deficiencies from the sender's point of view. Alcón-Soler (2013) found differences in perception between British and international teenage students. Both groups of students did not recognize the relationship with their mentor as distant and considered that sending an email to their mentor did not involve a high level of imposition; however, international students, in contrast to their British counterparts, judged email requests as more imposing.

Lewin-Jones and Mason (2014) investigated the attitudes of academic staff and students in email communication. Their study showed that each group seemed to have differing perceptions of emails, especially with respect to style, language and etiquette. The authors pointed out that frustration in student-faculty email communication "is not one-sided" (p. 88) as students also have expectations about appropriate email behavior. Given the negative reactions students' emails may cause, in a study on evaluations of student-professor emails Economidou-Kogetsidis (2023) stated that L2 learners exhibited a low understanding of the sociopragmatic and pragmalinguistic rules and that L2 learners placed more emphasis on formal structural politeness than on the interpersonal goal of the exchange conveyed by the content of the email. The author claimed that learners' limited experience with the power-unequal situation may explain why L2 learners ignored issues such as institutional rights and obligations or acknowledgement of imposition, which tended to be more salient to the professors.

Codina-Espurz (2021, 2022) examined students' elicited English L2 emails addressed to power (un)equal interlocutors. As the author claims, some students reported that they felt empowered to urge their demands if their request fell within the professor's academic obligation, thus perceiving such emails as not too impositive. On the contrary, when the request was addressed to a classmate, students tried to compensate for the imposition by over-mitigating their request in an attempt to avoid risking interpersonal relationships and show empathy towards an equal. Learners' perceptions of their entitlement to pose a request and the professor's obligation to comply have also been tackled in studies on email production. In this line of research, Bella (2021) examined differences between L1 users and L2 learners in email writing when requesting a faculty member to solve a problem about a missing grade in the Greek context. Her findings showed a higher degree of entitlement among NSs in comparison to L2 learners, and she argued that L2 learners, as foreigners, may not be as confident about their rights and obligations. NNSs may lack the sense of "in-groupness", which seems to be present in the NS group (Bella, 2021: 222). In contrast to NNSs, NSs may recognize themselves as members of a community who share a collective identity. However, as Bella (2021) clarifies, NS production should not necessarily be taken as the norm and indeed be considered more appropriate than NNS production, as appropriateness is determined by the receiver's perception of the email request. In the same vein, NS perceptions tend to be considered normative as many studies are devised in terms of an ideal NS rather than taking into account the diversity of language backgrounds of students and professors in the current multilingual and multicultural world (Winans, 2020). To a certain extent, perception of impoliteness is quite subjective: "Impoliteness is very much in the eye of the beholder, that is, the mind's eye." (Culpeper, 2011: 22).

In order to better understand how student emails are perceived in academic contexts, research on (im)politeness has addressed other variables in academic contexts. For example, Haider and Zandi's (2022) study on seniority, age and NS status revealed that senior faculty members were more lenient than junior members toward students' emails; moreover, when comparing the perceptions of NS and NNS of English faculty members, the latter were more tolerant of impoliteness of NNS students' emails in English.

Several studies have addressed professors' reactions to impolite emails. For instance, Aguilar-Roca et al. (2009) stated that the use of an inappropriate salutation (i.e., omitting the title of a professor) greatly contributed to portraying a disrespectful image of the student.

Economidou-Kogetsidis (2016) noted that professors had a negative reaction on the sender's personality and were "less willing to comply with students' email requests" (p. 11). Moreover, Economidou-Kogetsidis (2016) found discrepancies in perception between English NS lecturers and NNS students in their judgements of emails written by EFL students. Learners perceived that, for example, the solely inclusion of a polite marker rendered an email request as polite whereas faculty members considered other elements to be crucial in determining email politeness (e.g., acknowledgement of imposition on the professor, showing gratitude, etc.). The author concluded that NNS learners lacked pragmatic awareness and did not realize the negative consequences of pragmatic failure, namely, the negative impression of the student and the professor's unwillingness to comply with the request. In turn, Burgucu-Tazegül et al. (2016) claimed that professors evaluated too direct and unmitigated emails negatively and that the students' emails received an unfavorable evaluation if framing moves such as greetings or closings were not included. More recently, Hendriks et al. (2023) have also investigated the evaluation of politeness in L1 and L2 emails by L1 and L2 readers. Despite the fact that their findings adhere to previous studies as regards to negative evaluations of undermodified emails, an interesting result shows that the reader was more willing to comply with "an email with less politeness modification than an email with more politeness modification when the writer was an L2 writer" (p. 42). The authors attributed this finding to the fact that the use of fewer modification devices made the L2 writer sound bossy or authoritative, which resulted in the recipient accepting the demand.

Although some studies on perceptions of emails written by NNSs claim that pragmatic inadequacies are frequently found in student-professor interactions, these deficiencies are not exclusive of L2 learners as students also write inappropriate emails in their L1. Níkleva and Núñez (2013) employed an opinion questionnaire to examine email L1 writing abilities of a group of Spanish graduate students. The authors concluded that students were not only unaware of their own mistakes but also unaware of what is (in)appropriate in student-faculty communicative exchanges. Other studies have also examined the inadequacies of L1 emails sent to faculty members (see for example Codina-Espurz & Salazar-Campillo, 2019; Pinilla, 2020). Given the scant research on how students and professors perceive L1 student-faculty emails, the present small-scale study aims to fill the gap related to the need to investigate students' emails written in their L1 (Spanish) and the possible differences in perceptions of students and professors.

The Study

In light of previous research on perceptions of (im)politeness in emails, the present study examines potential differences in students' and instructors' appraisals of L1 Spanish email requests sent by students. More specifically, we aimed to analyse the type of issues our participants as readers focus on when judging the appropriateness of student emails to faculty.

Participants and Data Collection

Twenty Spanish university students (17 females, 3 males) in their 4th year of English Studies and three female Spanish EFL instructors participated in the study. The youngest instructor was 28 years old whereas the other two were 38 years old, with teaching experience ranging from 7 to 14 years.

Participants were asked to assess five L1 Spanish emails which had been sent to one of the researchers. These emails were selected following Petrie's (1999: 24) "emailisms", such as multiple exclamation/interrogation marks, capitalization, or the use of emoticons/emojis, thus resulting in a small sample of emails that varied in terms of appropriateness. The selected emails exhibited a "writing structure" (Del Saz, 2010: 234), that is, they featured an opening, body of the message, closing and signature. Moreover, they were first-contact Spanish requestive emails with different degrees of imposition, either low (i.e., request for information) or high (i.e., request for action). The main characteristics of the emails are presented in Table 9.1.

Table 9.1. Main features of the emails.

Email	Topic/Reguest	Opening*		Body				Closing*
		(a) Salutation (Greeting + Address term) (b) Pleasantry (c) Identification of self	Form of address	Request type	Punctuation	Orthography	Emoticon/ emoji	(a) Preclosing statement (b) Complimentary close (c) Signature
1	Review an exam once the revision period is over	(a) *Hola* (Hello)+ professor's FN** (b) --- (c) Identification of self	T-Form	Action	Exclamation marks following English format Period after greeting	Misspelt verb Lack of stress mark	:)	(a) --- (b) *Gracias* (Thanks) (c) FN+LN
2	Admission (provides phone number for professor to call back)	(a) *Buenas tardes* (Good afternoon) (b) --- (c) ---	V-Form	Information		Wrong verbal form Lack of accent marks Typos		(a) Gratitude/ Appeal (b) --- (c) FN+LNs
3	Information about thesis and placement Name of supervisor	(a) *Hola* (Hello) (b) --- (c) Identification of self	T-Form (plural)	Information	Period missing after the pre-closing Comma missing after the complementary close	Omission of accent marks		(a) Gratitude (b) *Unsaludo* (Regards) (c) FN+LN
4	Information about cancelling the enrollment Information about possibility to switch between online/onsite MA programs	(a) Greeting (*Hola*/Hello) (b) --- (c) ---	Impersonal	Information	Overuse of question and exclamation marks	Omission of accent marks		(a) --- (b) *Gracias* (Thanks) (c) FN+LNs
5	Late submission of an assignment	(a) *Buenos dias* (Good morning)+ professor's FN (b) --- (c) ---	T-Form	Action	Exclamation marks following English format Missing punctuation			(a) --- (b) *Un saludo* (Regards) (c) FN

*Openings and closings are analyzed following Salazar-Campillo and Codina-Espurz's (2018) taxonomy
**FN stands for first name and LN(s) for last name(s)

By means of an open-ended questionnaire, participants were asked to appraise the selected emails on the basis of the following criteria: (1) Email structure (opening, body, closing and signature), (2) Orthographical correctness and use of punctuation, (3) Degree of imposition, (4) Use of second-person pronouns (T-form or V-form), and (5) Use of emoticons ((;)) or emojis (☺).

Results and Discussion

Results are discussed following the five assessment criteria listed above.

Email Structure

According to Whitmell (2014), an email may include a subject line, a salutation (optional), the reason for writing, the main point, the development of point (optional), additional points (optional) and a closing (optional). Likewise, Hashemian and Farhang-Ju (2019) claimed that a well-structured email shows politeness and has to include salutations, openings and closings. In our study, the framing moves of openings and closings were examined following Salazar-Campillo and Codina-Espurz's (2018) taxonomy. According to this taxonomy, openings include (a) Salutation (Greeting + Address term), (b) Pleasantry, and (c) Identification of self, and closings may consist of (a) Preclosing statement, (b) Complimentary close, and (c) Signature.

The majority of the students did not comment on the opening. Only a few (20 %) observed that in emails 3 and 4 the salutation was not separate from the body of the email. This remark is in line with Hashemian and Farhang-Ju (2019), as one of the participants in their study noted that "Greetings should be in a separate line" (p. 138). In Economidou-Kogetsidis' (2015) study, the absence of a salutation was particularly negatively received and described as disrespectful towards the recipient. In our study, the fact that all the emails included a greeting or the full salutation (greeting + address term) could explain why students did not offer any comments in this respect. Contrary to Hashemian and Farhang-Ju's (2019) findings regarding some lecturers' comments about the inappropriate use of Hi/Hello as an opening formula in emails to faculty, the use of *Hola* (Hello) as a greeting did not seem to concern our participants. Since the student-faculty relationship tends to be more familiar in the Spanish academic context, sociopragmatic norms could play a role when judging the appropriateness of the emails (Zhu, 2012).

Few participants referred to the sender's self-identification in the opening. Whereas one student considered that this move was missing, another thought that it was unnecessary as it provided superfluous information. These contradictory views may indicate that students do not have a clear understanding of the structure of the opening.

Openings were not addressed by the instructors either; however, with regards to the body of the emails, the two older instructors commented that the body should not simply consist of an endless list of questions (email 4). Although most of the students did not provide any comments about the body of the email, some discrepancies were found among students who did so, for example, one student reported that the body should be presented as a block whereas another stated that there should be spacing between paragraphs, thus adhering to Crystal's (2001) claims that "Writers are recommended to use a line-of-white between paragraphs" (p. 110). In this case, these students' views seem to follow the conventions of epistolary format in email writing.

With regards to the closings (see Table 9.1), emails 1 and 4 included the complimentary close *Gracias* ("Thanks") as a way of signing off the email; however, some students (20 % in email 1, and 15 % in email 4) did not recognize this expression as a proper closing and stated that the common complimentary close "*Un saludo*" ("Regards") in Spanish was missing. Email 2, in contrast, only featured the pre-closing statement of gratitude and appeal "*Muchas gracias por su atención y espero su respuesta.*" ("Thank you very much for your attention and I'm looking forward to your reply.") to close the email. This statement was accepted as appropriate by 85 % of the participants as a way to close the email even though the more formulaic complimentary close "*Un saludo*" was not present. In this respect, as emails 3 and 5 signed off with "*Un saludo*", students did not raise any concerns. It is interesting to note that in Economidou-Kogetsidis' (2015) study, although thanking the lecturer was appreciated, statement "Thank you in advance" ("pre-closing statement" in Salazar-Campillo and Codina-Espurz's (2018) taxonomy) was received negatively by NS professors of English as it assumes compliance with the request. Moreover, as Economidou-Kogetsidis argues: "such presupposition in hierarchical relationships can be seen as quite inappropriate, even when the request falls within the students' rights and the faculty's obligations" (p. 421).

In L1 English emails, the use of "Thanks" is a preferred farewell formula (Waldvogel, 2007) as well as in L2 English emails (e.g., Economidou-Kogetsidis, 2015; Savić, 2018; Bella, 2021). However, the equivalent *Gracias* in Spanish does not seem to be well received by our students to close an email since they seem to favor the use of a more formal sign-off formula, such as *Regards* ("Un saludo") to show their status-unequal relationship with a professor.

The five emails under analysis featured a signature in the form of sender's first and last name(s) except for email 5, which was signed with only the student's first name. Neither the students nor the instructors focused on this last move, maybe because this element tends to be included in students' emails (Rodríguez-Velasco, 2019; Schauer, 2021).

Orthographic Correctness and Use of Punctuation

Emails 1, 2, 3 and 4 displayed orthographic mistakes although students did not comment on all of them. Issues on punctuation were present in all emails except in email 2. In this sense, the most striking email in terms of punctuation was email 4, which requested information about several MA issues with an excessive use of question and exclamation marks, as the excerpt (1) below shows.

(1) *Hasta cuándo tenemos para anular la matricula al master???? Y cómo he de hacerlo????? Muchas gracias por todo!!!!*
("Until when can we cancel the MA registration???? And how can I do it????? Many thanks for everything!!!!")

The excessive use of exclamation and question marks in this email was ill-judged and interpreted as totally inappropriate by all students (100 %) and the two older instructors, whereas the younger instructor did not address this criterion. Moreover, it is interesting to note that some students ventured to provide an image of the sender by stating "*Me imagino a la típica persona nerviosa, hiperactiva y que no se entera de nada*" ("I can picture the typical nervous, hyperactive person who doesn't get anything"). Actually, one of them even stated how the email affected her as a reader "*Me pone nerviosa la forma que está redactado, inspira desesperación*" ("The way it is written annoys me, he/she must be desperate"). Similar opinions were reported by Hashemian and Farhang-Ju (2019) study on lecturers' perceptions of L2 students' email requests, in which the overuse of question marks was negatively received by faculty. As the authors state, faculty members attributed the use of excessive punctuation to the learner's attempt to express emotions (probably anger). Other studies have also referred to the use of punctuation marks as expressions of emotion in less formal emails (Al-Ali & Sahawneh, 2008) or as attention-grabbing devices (Lan, 2000).

With regards to the rest of the emails under analysis, most students pointed out that the use of interrogation and exclamation marks only at the end of the sentence following an English format was erroneous. The instructors also observed the inappropriate omission of initial interrogation and exclamation marks, which are mandatory in Spanish. To a lesser extent, students indicated the need for revision on the use of commas, verbal forms or accent marks in some emails. Inadequate punctuation marks "make the process of reading hard and can sometimes change the meaning of the text" (Algryani & Al Jardani, 2023: 556). Some students remarked that the senders had not taken the time to review their emails before sending them to their professor. In this sense, many sources of impoliteness could be avoided by simply proofreading an email before sending it, as a way of showing respect to the recipient (Patrama, 2019). Hashemian and Farhang-Ju (2019) reported that language accuracy (i.e., grammatical points, punctuation, spelling, etc.) was the primary (most frequent) criterion lecturers referred to when assessing students' emails as impolite and/or inappropriate. One plausible explanation for neglecting orthography when writing an email could be that electronic communication is viewed as temporary and ephemeral (Níkleva & Núñez, 2013). Therefore, given the asynchronous nature of emails, a careful revision should be considered in order to create "socially desirable messages" (Chejnová, 2014: 179).

Degree of Imposition

The five emails evaluated by the participants varied in the perceived degree of imposition (see Figure 9.1). Emails 2, 3 and 4 requested information and were judged low in degree of imposition, whereas emails 1 and 5 received higher imposition ratings as they required the professor to take some action (to revise an exam in email 1 and to accept a late assignment once the student realizes he/she needs it to pass the course in email 5).

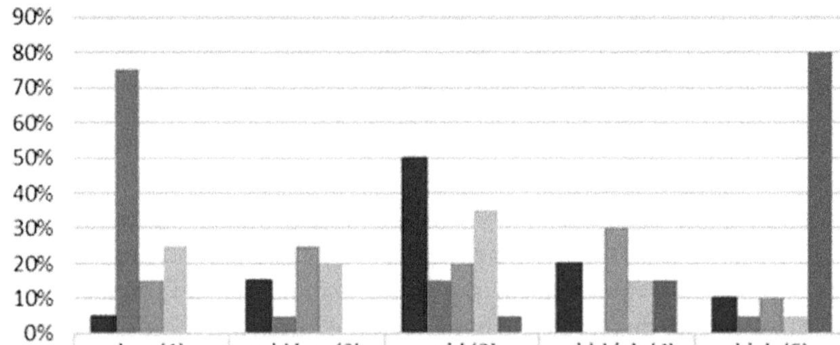

	low (1)	mid low (2)	mid (3)	mid-high (4)	high (5)
email1	5%	15%	50%	20%	10%
email 2	75%	5%	15%		5%
email 3	15%	25%	20%	30%	10%
email 4	25%	20%	35%	15%	5%
email 5			5%	15%	80%

Figure 9.1: Students' ratings on degree of imposition.

The emails requesting for information were assessed as having between a low and mid degree of imposition by 95 % of the students in email 2 and 80 % of the students in email 4; email 3 offered higher variability, since 40 % assessed it as mid-high or high in imposition and another 40 % rated it as low or mid-low. With regard to requests for action, email 5 was perceived the highest in imposition, with a score of 5 by 80 % of the students. Conversely, email 1, also a request for action, was appraised as high in imposition by only 10 % of the students. These results seem to indicate that type of request alone may not suffice to assess degree of imposition, as the differing ratings for emails 1 and 5 (both requests for action) illustrate. In this sense, the qualitative analysis of the data revealed that the students interpreted the directness and boldness of the request in email 5 as playing a crucial role in rating the request as high in imposition. One of the students claimed not to include "*Así me ahorraría la recuperación*" ("Thus, I would be spared from having to retake the exam"), which seems quite audacious of the sender to say, and commented that he/she should have thought how to pose that request and not simply "*Soltar sus pensamientos, sin más*" ("To say something without thinking"). This email received similar reactions from other students who described the sender as "*maleducado, faltando al respeto y lo que es peor, él/ella no es consciente*" ("rude, disrespectful and what's worse, she/he is not aware of that") and showed disbelief about someone daring to write such an email: "*Me cuesta creer que alguien escriba algo así*" ("I find it hard to believe that someone would write something like that"). These comments on email 5 highlight the sender's lack of sociopragmatic knowledge about writing status-congruent emails in an academic context, which may lead to pragmatic failure (Algryani & Al Jardani, 2023; Economidou-Kogetsidis, 2023). Most students agree that this type of request is not appropriate, yet, if made, the sender should at least be "*cuidadoso y educado*" ("thoughtful and polite"). Students felt uneasy with the use of the word "*ahorrar*" ("to spare") in this context and suggested that it would be more acceptable to express a genuine concern for failing the class. Likewise, the two older instructors found this demand totally unwarranted and described email 5 as disrespectful, inappropriate and insolent.

Despite students' and instructors' consensus on the high imposition involved in email 5, some participants held different opinions and rated this email as not too impositive. For example, one student appraised the situation as not being much of a big deal ("*No le costaría tanto*") to refer to the professor's compliance with the request. Similarly, the younger instructor considered that the request could be appropriate if properly justified and highlighted the honesty in which the sender addressed his/her petition in a clear and concise manner. Moreover, this instructor stated that the sender showed responsibility as he/she proposed a solution (i.e., submit a missing assignment) to avoid a more difficult situation (i.e., having to retake the exam).

Use of Second-Person Pronouns

While instructors did not make any reference regarding their preferences for the formal (V-form) or informal (T-form) pronouns, students varied in their opinions. For example, in email 2, in which the V-form was produced, 85 % of the students admitted it was a more appropriate way to address the professor. This may imply that they are aware of the unequal power relationship with their professors and recognise the V-form to show deference. Moreover, as Bjørge (2007) suggested, the choice of a more formal pronoun may also indicate uncertainty about the student-professor relationship, and despite a more informal, egalitarian academic environment such as the Spanish one, the high percentage of students favoring the V-Form may indicate they feel more comfortable with V-forms and perceive them as more appropriate. This preference for the V-form has also been observed in other studies (e.g., Chejnová, 2014; Bella, 2021; Salazar-Campillo, 2023), suggesting a hierarchical and distant relationship between students and professors, since "lecturers prefer to keep their relationship with their students formal" (Hashemian & Farhang-Ju, 2019: 142).

Students did not pay much attention to emails with the T-form (emails 1, 3 and 5), and pointed out there was nothing wrong with using a more familiar form of address ("*No me parece mal tutear*", "I don't think using the T-form is wrong"). These views concur with Vela-Delfa's (2018) claims that there seems to be a tendency to stop using the V-form in student-faculty interactions, especially in computer-mediated communication. Likewise, Pinilla (2020) has also argued that the T-form is a widespread preference among students in the current Spanish university context. Probably, as César-Vera (2015) points out, the Spanish culture is tending towards positive politeness by means of highlighting friendliness and closeness.

Use of Emoticons or Emojis

In our study, emoticons were only present in email 1. In this case, it was used after the student's request to go over the exam with the professor once the review period had expired and within a supporting move to offer the professor the possibility of not complying with the request: "*Si no pudiéramos, lo entenderíamos perfectamente*:)*"* ("If we couldn't (go over the exam), we would perfectly understand:)").

Overall, students regarded the use of emoticons as inappropriate (70 %) or too informal or colloquial for the situation (25 %). Emoticons were thought to indicate overly informal communication, and were judged to be improper as inferred from the following remark "*El alumno incluso utiliza emoticonos*" ("The student even uses emoticons"). However, these non-verbal cues could be acceptable depending on the student-professor relationship, since they may serve to indicate "solidarity, closeness and expressiveness" (Al Rousan et al., 2024: 108) as captured by the following comment "*Pone una cara feliz denotando simpatía*" ("The student adds a happy face showing he/she is nice").

The two older instructors disapproved of the use of emoticons and emojis in emails addressed to a faculty member on the grounds that they indicate too much familiarity in the academic context (Al Rousan et al., 2024). In contrast, the younger instructor did not appear to be bothered by the sender's use of these pictorial representations. This difference in perception, as Baggia et al. (2022) point out, could be attributed to an age factor, as younger generations are more familiar with the use of chats and social media and they may therefore hold different perceptions about what is appropriate in email communication. Other factors such as (in)formality of the relationship between sender and receiver or gender may influence the use of emojis (Shah & Tewari, 2021).

Conclusion

The present study sought to explore students' and instructors' appraisal of (im)politeness in L1 Spanish email requests addressed to a faculty member. Although our results are limited, they reveal insightful perspectives interlocutors display regarding what is (in)appropriate in student-faculty communication.

With regards to the markers of (im)politeness, our findings coincide with previous research on the inappropriateness of excessive punctuation marks to express non-verbal behavior (e.g., Hashemian &

Farhang-Ju, 2019), and on the inclusion of emoticons in academic communication (e.g., Bakir & Haji, 2019). Students seem to hold different opinions regarding whether an email to a faculty member should follow an epistolary format, and appear to be uncertain about the sequences of the opening (e.g., identification of self) and closing (e.g., complimentary close) moves. As for the use of formal or informal address forms, although students regarded both of them as appropriate, the V-form seemed to be favored. Moreover, there appears to be a general consensus among instructors and students that a highly demanding email request is totally unacceptable when the sender fails to employ devices to minimize imposition on the faculty member.

Our exploratory investigation is not without limitations, which mainly refer to the small sample of both participants and emails under analysis and the use of an open-ended questionnaire. To complement data, other data gathering techniques, like retrospective interviews, may have offered additional insights into learners' and instructor's perceptions of and views on email (im)politeness.

Despite the limited number of instructors who appraised the emails in our study, we can foresee some differences in opinions between instructors who differ in age and years of teaching experience. In this sense, Haider and Zandi's (2022) study on seniority and impoliteness in emails revealed a generation difference among faculty and claimed that "the senior faculty show more tolerance despite the potential inclination to be more critical of the impolite behavior of their students" (p. 214). On the contrary, younger instructors were more likely to accept the conventions commonly associated with chats, social media and more informal registers of communication. This latter finding concurs with the youngest instructor in our study, who was more lenient with the oral features included in some emails.

We contend that perhaps we should accept the idiosyncrasies of email writing rather than focusing on the desire to reproduce epistolary conventions in academic settings. As Lan (2000) pointed out, "Email style is shaped by communicative needs and by usage, not by rigid rules. It is organic, evolving and dynamic" (p. 29). Crystal (2001) had also advanced the need to consider the stylistic variations that email writing could display over time and claimed that "The contemporary bias towards informality therefore needs to be kept in perspective" (p. 107).

Future studies that concern variables previously addressed such as students' age (e.g., Barón & Ortega, 2018) gender (e.g., Herring, 2000; Del Saz, 2010) and professors' seniority (Haider & Zandi, 2022) may provide different results on perceptions of (im)politeness. However, and despite these constraints, this study has attempted to provide further insights into perceptions of students' requestive emails written in their L1 by arguing that we may need to consider the dynamic nature of email communication, welcome the strategies learners tend to use in social media (for example, emojis or common abbreviations) and move away from the traditional epistolary format to bring email writing to the current digital era.

Acknowledgements

This study is part of the research project PID 2020-117959GB-I00 funded by MCIN/AEI/10.13039/501100011033. Additional funding has been granted by Projectes d'Innovació Educativa de la Unitat de Suport Educatiu de la Universitat Jaume I (51020/24).

References

Aguilar-Roca, Nancy, Williams, Adrienne, Warrior, Rahul & O'Dowd, Diane. 2009. Two minute training in class significantly increases the use of professional formatting in student to faculty email correspondence. *International Journal for the Scholarship of Teaching and Learning*, 3/1, Article 15. <https://doi.org/10.20429/ijsotl.2009.030115>.

Al-Ali, Mohammed Nahar & Sahawneh, Meera. 2008. An investigation into the generic features of English requestive e-mail messages. *Language for Specific Purposes (LSP) & Professional Communication*, 8/2, 40–65.

Alcón-Soler, Eva. 2013. Mitigating e-mail requests in teenagers' first and second language academic cyber-consultation. *Multilingua*, 32/6, 779–799. <https://doi.org/10.1515/multi-2013-0037>.

Alcón-Soler, Eva. 2015. Pragmatic learning and study abroad: Effects of instruction and length of stay. *System*, 48, 62–74. <https://doi.org/10.1016/j.system.2014.09.005>.

Algryani, Ali & Al Jardani, Khalid Salim. 2023. Email literacy in higher education institutions: A case study on student-instructor email communication at Dhofar University in Oman. *World Journal of English Language*, 13/6, 549–558.

Al Rousan, Rafat Mahmoud, Al-Awawdeh, Nabil, Hassan, Hala & AlRousan, Malak. 2024. "Good Morning, My Dear Dr. ♡" Openings and closings in university students' academic emails. *World Journal of English Language*, 14/6, 99–110.

Baggia, Alenka, Žnidaršič, Anja & Tratnik, Alenka. 2022. Emoticonos en la comunicación por correo electrónico entre estudiantes y profesores. *Comunicar*, 30/73, 119–133. <https://www.scipedia.com/public/Baggia_et_al_2022a>.

Bakir, Salam Nawxosh & Haji, Hadi Hussein. 2019. The use of emoticons among university students: A pragmatic study. *Zanco Journal of Humanity Sciences*, 23/1, 278–290. <https://doi.org/10.21271/zjhs.23.1.19>.

Bardovi-Harlig, Kathleen. 2001. Evaluating the empirical evidence: Grounds for instruction in pragmatics. In Gabriele Kasper & Kenneth Rose (eds) *Pragmatics and language teaching*. Cambridge: Cambridge University Press, 11–32.

Barón, Júlia & Ortega, Mireia. 2018. Investigating age differences in e-mail pragmatic performance. *System*, 78, 148–158.

Bartl, Ramon. 2017. Impact of netiquette on email communication. *Journal of Applied Leadership and Management*, 5, 35–61.

Bella, Spyridoula. 2021. In search of the missing grade. Egalitarianism and deference in L1 and L2 students' emails to faculty members. In Maria Economidou-Kogetsidis, Milica Savić & Nicola Halenko (eds) *Email pragmatics and second language learners*. Amsterdam: John Benjamins, 203–226.

Bella, Spyridoula & Sifianou, Maria. 2012. Greek student email requests to faculty members. In Leyre Ruiz de Zarobe & Yolanda Ruiz de Zarobe (eds) *Speech Acts and politeness across languages and cultures*. Bern: Peter Lang, 89–113.

Bloch, Joel. 2002. Student-teacher interaction via email: The social context of Internet discourse. *Journal of Second Language Writing*, 11, 117–134. <https://doi.org/10.1016/S1060-3743(02)00064-4>.

Bjørge, Anne Kari. 2007. Power distance in English lingua franca email communication. *International Journal of Applied Linguistics*, 17/1, 60–80.

Burgucu-Tazegül, Assigye, Hand, Turganet & Engin, Ali Osman. 2016. Pragmatic failure of Turkish EFL learners in requests emails to their professors. *International Education Studies*, 9/10, 105–115.

César-Vera, Carolina. 2015. La ciber-atenuación de cortesía en el ámbito académico universitario, en Venezuela y en Chile. *Textos en Proceso*, 1/2, 288–310.

Chejnová, Pavla. 2014. Expressing politeness in the institutional e-mail communications of university students in the Czech Republic. *Journal of Pragmatics*, 60, 175–192.

Chen, Chi-Fen Emily. 2006. The development of email literacy: From writing to peer to writing to authoritative figures. *Language Learning & Technology*, 10, 35–55.

Codina-Espurz, Victòria. 2021. The influence of social distance and power in email politeness in an academic context. *Estudios Interlingüísticos,* 9, 48–59.

Codina-Espurz, Victòria. 2022. Students' perception of social contextual variables in mitigating email requests. *The Grove: Working Papers on English Studies,* 29, 57–79.

Codina-Espurz, Victòria & Salazar-Campillo, Patricia. 2019. Student-to-faculty consultation in English, Spanish and Catalan in an academic context. In Patricia Salazar-Campillo & Victòria Codina-Espurz (eds) *Investigating the learning of pragmatics across ages and contexts*. Leiden: Brill, 196–217.

Crombie, Philippa. 2020. Faces, hearths and thumbs: Exploring the use of Emoji in online teacher-student communications in higher education. *Journal of Academic Language & Learning*, 14/1, 30–41.

Crystal, David. 2001. *Language and the internet*. Cambridge: Cambridge University Press.

Culpeper, Jonathan. 2011. *Impoliteness: Using language to cause offence*. Cambridge: Cambridge University Press.

Del Saz, María. 2010. A gender analysis of email communication. *Interlingüística*, 21, 231–239.

Deveci, Tanju & Hmida, Ikhlas Ben. 2017. The request speech act in emails by Arab university students in the UAE. *Journal of Language and Linguistic Studies,* 13/1, 194–214.

Dresner, Eli & Herring, Susan 2010. Functions of the nonverbal in CMC: Emoticons and illocutionary force. *Communication Theory*, 20/3, 249–268.

Dürscheid, Christa & Frehner, Carmen. 2013. Email communication. In Susan Herring, Dieter Stein & Tuija Virtanen (eds) *Pragmatics of computer-mediated communication*. Berlin: Mouton, 35–54.

Duthler, Kirk. 2006. The politeness of requests made via email and voicemail: Support for the hyperpersonal model. *Journal of Computer-Mediated Communication*, 11, 500–521. <https://doi.org/10.1111/j.1083-6101.2006.00024.x>.

Economidou-Kogetsidis, Maria. 2011. "Please answer me as soon as possible": Pragmatic failure in non-native speakers' email request to faculty. *Journal of Pragmatics*, 43, 3193–3215. <https://doi.org/10.1016/j.pragma.2011.06.006>.

Economidou-Kogetsidis, Maria. 2015. Teaching email politeness in the EFL/ESL classroom. *ELT Journal*, 69/4, 415–424.

Economidou-Kogetsidis, Maria. 2016. Variation in evaluations of the (im)politeness of emails from L2 learned and perceptions of the personality of their senders. *Journal of Pragmatics*, 106, 1–19. <https://doi.org/10.1016/j.pragma.2016.10.001>.

Economidou-Kogetsidis, Maria. 2018. "Mr Paul, please inform me accordingly": Address forms, directness and degree of imposition in L2 emails. *Pragmatics*, 28/4, 489–515.

Economidou-Kogetsidis, Maria. 2023. "The language is very formal and appropriate": L2 learners' in/appropriateness evaluations and metapragmatic judgments in student-faculty emails. *Journal of Pragmatics*, 217, 17–32.

Economidou-Kogetsidis, Maria, Woodfield, Helen & Savvidou, Christine. 2021. Non-native EFL teachers' email production and perceptions of e-(im)politeness. *Journal of Politeness Research*, 17/2, 155–187.

Eslami, Zohreh. 2013. Online communication and students' pragmatic choices in English. *Lodz Papers in Pragmatics*, 9, 71–92. <https://doi.org/10.1515/lpp-2013-0005>.

Gains, Jonathan. 1999. Electronic mail—a new style of communication or just a new medium?: An investigation into the text features of e-mail. *English for Specific Purposes*, 1, 81–101. <https://doi.org/10.1016/S0889-4906(97)00051-3>.

Félix-Brasdefer, César. 2012a. Email openings and closings: Pragmalinguistic and gender variation in learner-instruction cyber consultation. In Eva Alcón-Soler & Pilar Safont-Jordà (eds) *Discourse and language learning across l2 instructional settings*. Amsterdam: Rodopi, 223–248.

Félix-Brasdefer, César. 2012b. Email requests to faculty. In Maria Economidou-Kogetsidis & Helen Woodfield (eds) *Interlanguage request modification*. Amsterdam: John Benjamins, 87–118.

Fukushima, Saeko. 2000. *Requests and culture: Politeness in British English and Japanese*. Berlin: Peter Lang.

Haider, Iftikhar & Zandi, Hamed. 2022. In my professor's eyes: Faculty and perceived impoliteness in student emails. *Lodz Papers in Pragmatics*, 18/1, 197–222. <https://doi.org/10.1515/lpp-2022-0009>.

Hashemian, Mahmood & Farhang-Ju, Maryam. 2019. Applied linguistics faculty members' perception of (im)politeness and (in) appropriateness of L2 learners' email requests. *Journal of Teaching Language Skills*, 38/1, 119–155.

Hendriks, Berna. 2010. An experimental study of native speaker perceptions of non-native request modification in emails in English. *Intercultural Pragmatics*, 7/2, 221–255.

Hendriks, Berna, van Meurs, Frank & Kakisina, Bob. 2023. The effects of L1 and L2 writers' varying politeness modification in English emails on L1 and L2 readers. *Journal of Pragmatics*, 204/2, 33–49.

Herring, Susan. 2000. Gender differences in CMC: Findings and implications. *CPSR Newsletter*. 18/1, 1–9.

Kelly, Ryan & Watts, Leon. 2015. *Characterising the inventive appropriation of emoji as relationally meaningful in mediated close personal relationships*. Paper presented at Experiences of Technology Appropriation: Unanticipated Users, Usage, Circumstances, and Design. Oslo, Norway.

Lan, Li. 2000. Email: A challenge to Standard English? *English Today*, 86, 23–30. <https://doi.org/10.1017/S0266078400000511>.

Lewin-Jones, Jenny & Mason, Victoria. 2014. Understanding style, language and etiquette in email communication in higher education: A survey. *Research in Post-Compulsory Education*, 19/1, 75–90, <https://doi.org/10.1080/13596748.2014.872934>.

Marder, Ben, Houghton, David, Erz, Antonia, Harris, Lloyd & Javornik, Ana. 2019. Smile(y)—and your students will smile with you? the effects of emoticons on impressions, evaluations, and behaviour in staff-to-student communication. *Studies in Higher Education*, 45(11), 2274–2286. <https://doi.org/10.1080/03075079.2019.1602760>.

Níkleva, Dimitrinka. 2018. Markers of politeness and impoliteness in student-teacher interaction in the discourse genre of emails. *Revista Signos*, 51/97, 214–235.

Níkleva, Dimitrinka & Núñez, María Pilar. 2013. El correo electrónico como género discursivo: Percepciones y habilidades para su composición en estudiantes universitarios. *Revista Española de Lingüística Aplicada*, 26, 385–407.

Myrset, Anders. 2022. 'You could win Masterchef with this soup. Can I get some more?' Request production and the impact of instruction on young EFL learners. *Journal of Pragmatics*, 192, 56–76.

Pan, Ping Cathy. 2012. Interlanguage requests in institutional e-mail discourse. In Maria Economidou-Kogetsidis & Helen Woodfield (eds) *Interlanguage request modification*. Amsterdam: John Benjamins, 119–162.

Patrama, Hendi. 2019. *Linguistic politeness in online communication*. Semarang: LPPM Unnes.

Petrie, Helen. 1999. *Writing in cyberspace: A study of the uses, style and content of email*. Unpublished paper. University of Hertfordshire/Hatfield.

Pinilla, Raquel. 2020. El correo electrónico como género digital en estudiantes universitarios semipresenciales de Lengua Española. *Revista Estudios del Discurso Digital* (REDD), 3, 77–108. <https://doi.org/10.24197/redd.3.2020.77-108>.

Rahmani, Elahe & Rahmany, Ramin. 2014. Politeness strategies and politeness markers in email request sent by Iranian EFL learners to professors. *Journal of Teaching English Language Studies*, 2/4, 50–64.

Robles-Garrote, Pilar. 2020. La competencia pragmática en la comunicación digital: reflexión sobre la (in)adecuación en correos electrónicos del ámbito académico. In Eva Álvarez-Ramos & Javier Blasco-Pascual (eds) *Humanidades digitales. Retos, recursos y nuevas propuestas*. Valladolid: Agilice Digital, 235–246.

Rodríguez-Velasco, David. 2019. Análisis de los elementos pragmáticos en la interacción escrita académica: el caso de los correos electrónicos de universitarios norteamericanos. *Revista Nebrija de Lingüística Aplicada a la Enseñanza de Lenguas*, 13, 198–225.

Rodríguez-Velasco, David. 2023. 'Dear Dr John Smith. I refuse to obey this mark. That's mean. So, can you give me a higher mark?' *International Review of Pragmatics*, 15, 3–31.

Salazar-Campillo, Patricia. 2023. Address forms and politeness markers in Spanish students' emails to faculty. *Rael: Revista Electrónica de Lingüística Aplicada*, 21/1, 58–73.

Salazar-Campillo, Patricia & Codina-Espurz, Victòria. 2018. Politeness in first and follow-up emails to faculty: Openings and closings. In Ariadna Sánchez & Ana Herraiz (eds) *Learning second language pragmatics beyond traditional contexts*. Bern: Peter Lang, 87–108.

Savić, Milica. 2018. Lecturer perceptions of im/politeness and in/appropriateness in student e-mail requests: A Norwegian perspective. *Journal of Pragmatics*, 124, 52–72.

Savić, Milica. 2019. Relational practices in Norwegian students' email requests in English. *Journal of Intercultural Communication*, 19/1, 1–16.

Schauer, Gila A. 2021. Email communication in English and in German. In Economidou-Kogetsidis, Maria, Savić, Milica & Halenko, Nicola (eds) *Email pragmatics and second language learners*. Amsterdam: John Benjamins, 179–201.

Shah, Reena & Tewani, Ruchi. 2021. Mapping emoji usage among youth. *Journal of Creative Communications*, 16/1, 113–125. <https://doi.org/10.1177/0973258620982541>.

Shim, Young-Sook. 2013. Requests in students-to-professor emails of Korean EFL students. *English Language and Linguistics*, 19/3, 171–194.

Stephens, Keri K. & Houser, Marian L. & Cowan, Renee L. 2009. R U able to meat me: The impact of students' overly casual email messages to instructors. *Communication Education*, 58/3, 303–326.

Tang, Ying & Hew, Khe Foon. 2018. Emoticon, emoji, and sticker use in computer-mediated communications: Understanding its communicative function, impact, user behavior, and motive. In Liping

Deng, Will Ma & Fong Cheuk (eds) *New media for educational change*. Singapore: Springer, 191–201.

Tseng, Chia-Ti Heather. 2015. "You must let me pass, please!": An investigation of email request strategies by Taiwanese EFL learners. *Journal of ELT and Applied Linguistics (JELTAL)*, 3/1, 11–28.

Tseng, Chia-Ti Heather. 2016. E-politeness: An analysis of Taiwanese EFL learners' email discourse on request strategies. *International Journal for 21st Century Education*, 3, 35–62.

Vareberg, Kyle, Vogt, Olivia & Berndt, Maranda. 2023. Putting your best face forward: How instructor emoji use influences students' impressions of credibility, immediacy, and liking. *Education and Information Technologies*, 28, 6075–6092. <https://doi.org/10.1007/s10639-022-11421-w>.

Vela-Delfa, Cristina. 2018. La apelación en el género discursivo del correo electrónico: fórmulas nominales de tratamiento en las aperturas y los cierres de los mensajes de email. *Onomázein*, IV, 98–118. <https://doi.org/10.7764/onomazein.add.06>.

Waldvogel, Joan. 2007. Greetings and closings in workplace email. *Journal of Computer-Mediated Communication*, 12, 456–477.

Whitmell, Clare. 2014. *Business writing essentials, how to write letters, reports and emails*. Clare Whitmell.

Winans, Michael. 2020. Email requests: Politeness evaluations by instructors from diverse language backgrounds. *Language Learning & Technology,* 24/2, 104–118. <http://hdl.handle.net/10125/44728>.

Yule, George. 2002. *The Study of Language*. Cambridge: Cambridge University Press.

Zarei, Gholam & Mohammadi, Masoomeh. 2012. E-politeness in Iranian English electronic requests to the faculty. *Research in Applied Linguistics*, 3/1, 3–24.

Zhu, Wuhan. 2012. Polite requisites strategies in email: An investigation of pragmatic competence of Chinese EFL learners. *RELC Journal*, 43/2, 217–238. <https://doi.org/10.1177/0033688212449936>.

Section IV
Multilingual Pragmatics

PILAR SAFONT

From Interlanguage to Multilingual Pragmatics: The Case of the Valencian Instructional Context

Introduction

Despite the wide amount of studies describing multilingual language learning (Aronin, 2019; Cenoz et al., 2001) and the not so recent multilingual turn in Second Language Acquisition (May, 2013), pragmatics investigation has somehow been unenthusiastic about considering languages other than the target one, which in most cases is English. The Valencian context in Spain has been an exceptional case thanks to the work led and coordinated by Alcón-Soler (2008; 2013). In fact, members of this author's research group have been studying the pragmatics of multilingual Valencian learners for almost twenty years now (Safont, 2005; Portolés, 2015).

At present, some critical voices (Kesckes, 2022) have raised the need to account for the multilingual reality of instructional settings by adopting an intercultural viewpoint. Furthermore, recent state-of-the-art reviews (Taguchi, 2022) include multilingualism as one of the challenges and ideas for further research in pragmatics language learning. Bearing these ideas in mind, it is our purpose to describe how these challenges have been partially met in the Valencian context thanks to Alcón-Soler's work and the coordination of several research projects which aimed at acknowledging those factors that may play an important role in pragmatics teaching and learning. All this investigation has taken place within an instructional context which also fosters multilingualism. As we know, the world is multilingual (Cenoz, 2013) and the Valencian Community in Spain is not an exception. Spanish is the majority language which coexists with Catalan and English in instructional settings. Catalan is the minority language and, for decades, it has been included as a course subject or means of instruction in educational programs. English is the foreign language per excellence, as in many other countries and communities around the world, and its teaching starts in kindergarten in an attempt to guarantee its learning and for students to become effective communicators at the end of the compulsory education. However, high proficiency levels in English are not the general trend in the Valencian educational system. As we know, one of the aspects that could help improve the knowledge of a language refers to pragmatics because pragmatic competence is one of the main components of the construct of communicative competence. Hence, the Valencian instructional setting is perfect for conducting a number of investigations that relate to pragmatic teaching and learning. In addition to this, the fact that this speech community and educational centres include at least three languages present an ideal source for examining existing paradigms and theories about multilingual acquisition and development.

On that account, we have accomplished several investigations that focus on trilingual pragmatic awareness and production. This chapter includes an overview on some of these studies as they provide answers to some of the gaps that have been identified in previous research which adopted a monolingual perspective or a Second Language Acquisition (henceforth SLA) orientation.

In what follows, we shall first briefly refer to IL pragmatics investigation and to the multilingual turn that now seems to be taking place. After that, some of the main tenets describing multilingual language learning will be introduced and special attention will be paid to the call for disclosing multilingual pragmatic development. The last subsection shall be devoted to describe findings from our research on multilingual pragmatics which refer to pragmatic translanguaging in online discourse (Nightingale & Safont, 2019), requests and attitudes in classroom discourse (Safont, 2022), requests in emails (Safont, 2024a); and requests in Content and Language Integrated instructional interaction (Safont, 2024b). These four studies aimed at covering some of the gaps that have been pinpointed in Interlanguage Pragmatics research which are also described as follows.

Interlanguage Pragmatics Research and the Ideal Monolingual Norm

The notion of pragmatics adopted in most Interlanguage (henceforth IL) pragmatics research has been adapted from Leech's (1983) and Thomas' (1983) description of pragmatics which is regarded as one main component of the construct of communicative competence. In this sense, pragmatics includes pragmalinguistics which refers to the linguistic resources for conveying a given speech act, and sociopragmatics that relates to the social conditions underlying appropriate language use. As stated by authors like Thomas (1983) the interest for language learners' pragmatic competence is raised due to the fact that even advanced learners with perfect grammars and rich vocabulary fail to communicate, and this may be due to their lack of knowledge about the social rules of interaction. Since its origin IL (also termed Second Language) pragmatics research has paid more attention to pragmalinguistics, that is to the forms that learners employed, than to the contextual circumstances hidden in their use. In fact, native speakers' performance is regarded as the achievable goal in pragmatic learning. Learners' production is compared to that of ideal native speakers of the target language (i.e. English in most cases). Such dichotomy is made clear in the term IL Pragmatics itself, which is used by authors like Kasper and Dahl (1991) to refer and identify learners as non-native speakers.

In the early 2000s, the social conditions affecting the choice of pragmatic forms were more present in research dealing with learners' pragmatics in second languages. Alcón-Soler (2008) refers to the need to consider not only the pragmalinguistic but also the sociopragmatic component of pragmatic systems, and in this line, she revisits the taxonomy of requests by providing it with a sociopragmatic perspective (Alcón-Soler et al., 2005). This viewpoint is displayed in Alcón's work through several years (Alcón-Soler, 2008, 2013) creating a school of thought that has been followed by her former students (Martín-Laguna, 2020; Safont, 2005; Salazar-Campillo & Codina-Espurz, 2019; Sánchez-Hernández, 2018; Usó-Juan & Martínez-Flor, 2021) in their investigation on the pragmatic development of English language learners.

Parallel and related to Alcón's innovative approach, other authors like Kesckes also argue against the ideal native speakers' pragmatics as a learning target and they call for the need to adopt an intercultural perspective (Kesckes, 2022; McConachy, 2018) that reconsiders the native versus EFL (English as a Foreign Language) learner division.

More recently, studies on interlanguage pragmatics with a focus on instructional effects (Martínez-Flor et al., 2023) call for a deeper focus on "the teacher" and "the learner". Martínez-Flor et al. (2023) identify the need for empirical work on those individual differences influencing pragmatic development. Within the bulk of individual differences, several authors refer to acknowledging the influence of motivation, attitudes or multilingualism in learner's pragmatic performance and development.

Similarly, in a recent historical overview of IL pragmatics research, Taguchi (2022) refers to the newest contributions to IL pragmatics research by pointing to the Lingua franca framework in L2 pragmatic research. As quoted by this author, this new focus which originates in the 2020s involves how L2 speakers co-construct mutual understanding and establish common ground in intercultural communication (Taguchi, 2022: 19). This wider view goes beyond the traditional notion of politeness including pragmalinguistics and sociopragmatics. Additionally, and regarding the future directions for Second Language Pragmatics, Taguchi (2022) mentions multilingual pragmatic competence as an important topic to address under the influence of globalisation in L2 pragmatic research. This multilingual perspective in language learning, which relates to multilingualism and third language learners and users, is also described in the following section of this chapter.

Third Language Acquisition and Multiligual Language Learning

Interestingly, over twenty years ago several publications (Cenoz & Jessner, 2000; Herdina & Jesssner, 2002; Cenoz et al., 2001, 2003) referred to the need for a change regarding those paradigms employed in examining language learners' acquisitional processes and development. Such changes were in line with nowadays call for implementing multilingualism in pragmatics research. in order to obtain a more comprehensive picture of pragmatic development in a foreign language. Common existing publications on third language acquisition and multilingual education (Cenoz et al., 2017; Aronin & Singleton, 2012; Aronin et al., 2013; Singleton & Aronin, 2018) is the distinction between second and third language acquisition processes. As already argued by Cenoz and Jessner in 2000, second language acquisition paradigms see languages isolated from their wider contexts. Acquisition may be presented as linear, static and systematic. The learners' language background is often omitted and the native speaker is the goal or referent. On the contrary, third language acquisition frameworks see the language within the wider context of use in contact with the other linguistic systems that conform the learners' linguistic repertoire. Language acquisition is perceived as a dynamic and complex process. The learners' language background is fundamental. Additionally, the goal is to become competent multilingual and multicultural speakers. Therefore, as argued by some authors (Aronin, 2015; Cenoz, 2013) SLA research has traditionally focused on the individual psycholinguistic development of the learner (Pienemann & Johnstone, 1996) and the identification of internal and external factors. Moreover, the notion of L1 interference when analysing L2 acquisition and development in examining SLA processes is quite broadly extended.

Besides, third language acquisition researchers (Jessner, 2006) do not study the target language in isolation. Interdependence is the term employed rather than L1 interference, which bears negative connotations, as if the fact of being bi- or multilingual were an obstacle in itself. The linguistic competence of the multilingual learner includes all the linguistic systems that conform their verbal repertoire. As mentioned before, third language acquisition is viewed as a dynamic and complex process which is best described by Herdina and Jessner's (2002) dynamic model of multilingualism and whose main components are (i) the language systems (LSn), (ii) cross-linguistic interaction (CLIN), (iii) metalinguistic awareness (MLA), (iv) cross-linguistic awareness (XLA) and the (v) multilingualism factor (M-factor). As best described by Jessner (2006), the model explains the existing interdependence among all the languages of the multilingual speaker via the cross-linguistic interaction component. It also distinguishes between awareness of the forms and functions of each language involved, that is, metalinguistic awareness, and across all the languages of the learner which refers to cross-linguistic awareness. Finally, the M-factor component points out those linguistic and cognitive skills that multilingual users possess in comparison to monolingual speakers based on prior knowledge and experience.

The dynamic model of multilingualism has given rise to other paradigms and frameworks for the study of multilingualism. In our opinion, further work on specific components of the model illustrate the growing body of research on multilingual development. One example is the dominant language constellation approach (henceforth DLC) which stems from the existence of several language systems in the multilingual mind (LSn) and their constant interaction and interdependence (CLIN). According to Aronin (2019, 2020), DLC constitutes an active, working part of the pool of language repertoire and typically comprises three languages. Many publications to date have considered the pedagogical implications of adopting the DLC framework in language learning and teacher training courses (Krulatz & Dugan, 2021; Gabrýs-Barker & Vetter, 2024). Interestingly, authors like Gabrýs-Barker (2023) also wonder to what extent the language repertoires of multilingual learners based in officially monolingual territories turn their target languages into their DLCs, and thus, contribute to these speakers' identity. Another instance of the DMMs influence within multilingualism research may be attributed to the promotion of metalinguistic and cross-linguistic awareness through translanguaging which refers to the alternate use of the multilingual speaker's languages in a fluid and non-abrupt way. According to Cenoz and Gorter (2021), translanguaging develops metalinguistic awareness by softening the boundaries between languages. In the case of language learning settings, pedagogical translanguaging supports the development of all the learner languages for it activates the students' multilingual repertoires so that they can benefit from their own multilingualism (Cenoz & Gorter, 2022: 342).

The advantages of multilingual speakers in using additional languages have been identified in a number of studies (Cenoz, 2013) and some of them refer to multilingual pragmatic development (Safont,

2005; Alcón-Soler, 2013). Pragmatics refers to the appropriate use of languages. In the Dynamic Model of Multilingualism (DMM), language choice or use depends on the perceived communicative needs of the multilingual speaker. According to Jessner (2008), these needs are psychologically and sociologically determined and identified as the driving force of language learning and use. In doing so, the speaker decides which language to use with whom and in which situation, and also when and why another language should be added to the multilingual's repertoire (Jessner, 2008: 273). It is from this perspective that we have conducted research on multilingual pragmatic development, acquisition and use through several decades with a particular focus on requests. Furthermore, the definition of pragmatic competence adopted is the one provided by Taguchi and Sykes (2013) which refers to the knowledge of correct form-function-context mappings and the ability to retrieve and use this knowledge efficiently in actual performance. Additionally, we have considered those sociopragmatic conditions underlying the pragmatic behaviour of language learners which include the interactional and contextual factors affecting the use of requests (Culpeper et al., 2018).

The Pragmatics of Multilingual Learners

This section includes an overview of four studies on multilingual learners' pragmatic performance in which we followed Alcón's work (2008, 2013) on instructional pragmatics as well as the interpretation of the communicative needs of multilingual speakers on the basis of the dynamic model of multilingualism (Jessner, 2008). More specifically, we shall refer to pragmatic translanguaging in online discourse (Nightingale & Safont, 2019), requests and attitudes in classroom discourse (Safont, 2022), requests in emails (Safont, 2024a); and requests and CLIL classroom discourse (Safont, 2024b). In doing so, we aim at showing that some of the challenges and ideas for further research in IL pragmatics and recent state-of-the-art publications have partially been met in multilingual pragmatics. We also believe that from a multilingual perspective we may contribute to cover the gaps that are identified in SL pragmatics, like the presence of the L1 or L2 in the learners' discourse, or their motivation to use the target language.

A number of influential publications on SLA refer to L1 interference in L2 development and to the lack of pragmatic knowledge even when the learners' grammar or vocabulary proficiency is high (Corder, 1967; Krashen, 1992; Long, 1990; Thomas, 1983). However, a multilingual perspective may help us acknowledge a different idea/view/reality. For this reason, we conducted a study (Nightingale & Safont, 2019) which focused on what multilingual adolescents do with their languages online. The idea was to identify whether the teenagers' L1 or L2 would illustrate sources of negative interference or whether they'd rather be examples of pragmatic translanguaging. In our opinion, translanguaging itself creates a pragmatic effect because the illocutionary force does not stem from the discrete lexical items involved in language alternation but rather from their fluid meshing in the act of multilingual discourse (Nightingale & Safont, 2019). In this sense, pragmatic translanguaging may be referred to as consciously outcome-oriented language mixing motivations.

Participants in this study included 97 high-school students aged between 12 and 17 years. They were receptive and productive bilinguals with Catalan and Spanish, and in some cases, they also knew heritage languages (i.e. Arabic and Romanian). English was their L3 or L4. As mentioned above, the research question guiding the study wondered about which pragmatic functions would be covered by translanguaging online. Data were collected by means of semi-structured interviews which were transcribed and codified afterwards using thematic analysis (Creswell, 2014; Fereday & Muir-Cochrane, 2006). The results obtained point to the fact that teenagers' online translingual practices perform three main functions, namely those of (i) marking humour, (ii) marking identity and (iii) modifying requests.

(1) 01 S1: yo no suelo hacerlo, a veces, no sé, en plan broma o algo
02 así pero de normal no
03 Interviewer: *tú lo haces en plan broma? a veces cambias-*
04 S1: *sí, pero con alguien de mucha confianza.*
(Source: Nightingale & Safont, 2019: 11).

(2) 01 Interviewer: *por qué please y no por favor?*
02 S2: *suena mejor*
03 Interviewer: *suena mejor?*
04 S2: *sí suena no sé, es una sensación*
05 S3: *sientes anglosajón*
(Source: Nightingale & Safont, 2019: 14).

(3) 01 S5: please es como, más cariñoso, para que te lo deje antes (...)
02 S4: por favor suena muy- (serious tone of voice)
03 S5: [please] (sweeter tone of voice)
04 S4: muy serio, no?
05 Interviewer: y please suena menos serio?
06 S4: sí
(Source: Nightingale & Safont, 2019: 15).

As shown in Example 1 above, S1 confirms the idea that the purpose of changing language has to do with fun (E.1 l.03, *en plan broma*) and for this reason, he would only do that with somebody they know very well (E.1 l.04, *con alguien de mucha confianza*). Example 2 shows how identity is projected in using their target language, English, which helps them project their ideal L2-self (Dörnyei, 2005). Both S2 and S3 mention the fact that it's a feeling (*es una sensación*). It marks somehow their identity and willingness to become part of the target language community (*te sientes anglosajón*). Similarly, Example 3 above leads to another function of translanguaging practices which, in this case, affects requests. Participants S4 and S5 point to the idea that translanguaging with English when asking for a favour may ease the tension (*please suena menos serio*) (Baker, 2001) and it may also sound sweeter and as a consequence the request may be performed earlier than expected (*para que te lo deje antes*). Hence, this descriptive study presents instances of translingual practices and the function that they seem to perform as well as the actual intention of the multilingual speakers in using them. Given the nature of this piece of research (qualitative and descriptive), we cannot generalise its findings but they may still be interesting to the extent that they do not illustrate a deficient proficiency level or a need to overcome communicative difficulties in English but rather a way of multilingual communication.

Requests in online multilingual interaction are also the focus of the study discussed next (Safont, 2024a). The main purpose was to analyse email requests written by multilingual learners of English and identify the role of age and gender regarding the request form chosen in each email message produced. Previous research from an SLA perspective with a focus on age effects in email requests show that younger learners seem to be more direct than older ones (Barón & Ortega, 2018). Authors like Economidou-Kogetsidis (2021) attribute such directness and informality in email requesting to the overuse of smartphones for sending messages. Regarding gender, we believed that some influence could be identified since as argued by Kasper and Rose (2002), members of a specific gender develop their IL pragmatic knowledge based on social, cultural and situational L2 context including gender roles. Similarly, Tajeddin and Malmir (2014) stated that the identification as male or female relates to specific social positions and patterns of interaction in the L1 and L2. To this last statement, we could also add specific patterns in the L3 or L4.

Based on previous research, the hypotheses guiding the study referred to the idea that young learners would use direct unmodified requests (Barón & Ortega, 2018) and there would be a different pattern for female and male learners (Tajeddin & Malmir, 2014). In order to test this assumption, we examined 250 email requests written in Catalan, English and Spanish and addressing a Faculty professor. One hundred participants took part in the study and they were distributed in four groups according to their age (+18, n=66 and +32, n=24) and gender (that is, whether they identified themselves as male, n= 39 or female, n= 61). In our analysis, we took into account the request head act strategies and the peripheral modification items accompanying them which were identified in the email messages that were examined.

As shown in Figure 10.1 below, results regarding age effects show that older students used more direct request strategies than younger ones unlike predicted in Barón and Ortega's previous study (2018). However, participants in their thirties used more modification items that mitigated the impositive nature of their direct requests and the difference in terms of data distribution is statistically significant. Such finding coincides with Economidou-Kogetsidis' results (2021).

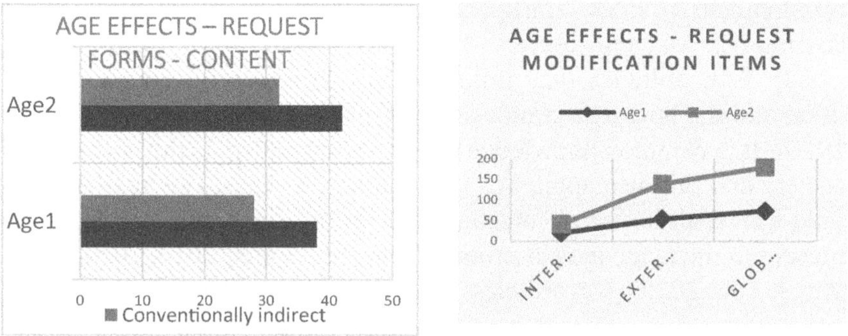

Figure 10.1: Request forms produced in email messages and age group (Source: Safont, 2024a: 1507).

Regarding the role of gender in email requesting, female learners mitigated their requests more often than their male counterparts in line with Pham and Yeh's study (2020). There are statistically significant differences regarding the use of attention getters, preparators, disarmers and the particle please. In fact, we may state that there were few instances of unmitigated requesting in our female subgroup unlike suggested by previous research (Alcón-Soler, 2013; Economidou-Kogetsidis, 2021; Felix-Brasdefer, 2012; Lorenzo-Dus & Bou-Franch, 2013; Schauher, 2021). Interestingly, male students were more direct to the extent that they made frequent use of intensifiers. In a nutshell, findings from this study both coincide and differ from former investigations. We found age effects as far as mitigation is concerned. Additionally, female and male requesting patterns were different from expected. We wonder whether such discrepancies might have to do with the inclusion of a multilingual viewpoint in our research. If so, these results would confirm the need for further studies on multilingual pragmatics.

In addition to age and gender effects, we have analysed language attitudes and how these may be displayed in the multilingual language classroom. More specifically, our study (Safont, 2022) dealt with teachers' requests as attitudinal reactions to learners' translanguaging discourse. We aimed at providing an answer to the ascertained need for more research on the relationship between attitudes and pragmatic development (Bardovi-Harlig, 2013) as these are an integral part of communicative competence.

In fact, attitudes may influence our reactions to other language users and the language choices we make as we communicate (Garrett, 2010). It is common knowledge that multilingualism is the norm in our society and this also applies to instructional settings. The alternate and fluid use of all learners' languages is a reality since translanguaging is present in the language classroom (Cenoz & Gorter, 2017, 2020, 2022; Wei & Lin, 2019). Nevertheless, there still seems to be a monolingual policy in most educational institutions. Qualitative CA (i.e. conversation analysis) studies signal out the monolingual bias (May, 2013) present in European teenage English classrooms (Dalton-Puffer, 2005; Dalton-Puffer & Nikula, 2006). Similarly, monolingualism is the norm in the University classroom too as shown by a recent study (Cots et al., 2022).

In an attempt to contribute to this line of research and meet the need for more studies on the relationship between pragmatics and language attitudes, our study (Safont, 2022) examined teachers' reactions to multilingual learners' translingual practices in the L3 English classroom. On the basis of previous research (Jakonen, 2016), we hypothesised that attitudes to normative language choice would be represented by teachers' directives to use the L2 (English). To test this hypothesis, we examined naturalistic classroom discourse which involved the participation of 268 Year 3 students and 12 English teachers. Participants belonged to 12 different schools in the Valencian Community which is an officially bilingual region in Eastern Spain with Catalan as minority and Spanish as majority languages as has already been mentioned earlier in this chapter. The schools adopted two different language programs. Six of them followed a Catalan-based program with Catalan, Spanish and English while the other six followed the Spanish based program, with Spanish and English as languages of instruction. We identified a total amount of 298 translingual instances and 295 teachers' reactions in discourse.

Results showed that teachers used five types of direct requests in these reactions, namely (i) modified direct request, (ii) direct request and intensifier, (iii) ignore and direct request, (iv) translate and Spanish direct request, and (v) Spanish direct request. Hence, the hypothesis guiding the study was confirmed as teachers' attitudes were represented by direct requests. Interestingly, we also found that the language program adopted in the schools had an effect on the way teachers reacted to learners' translingual practices.

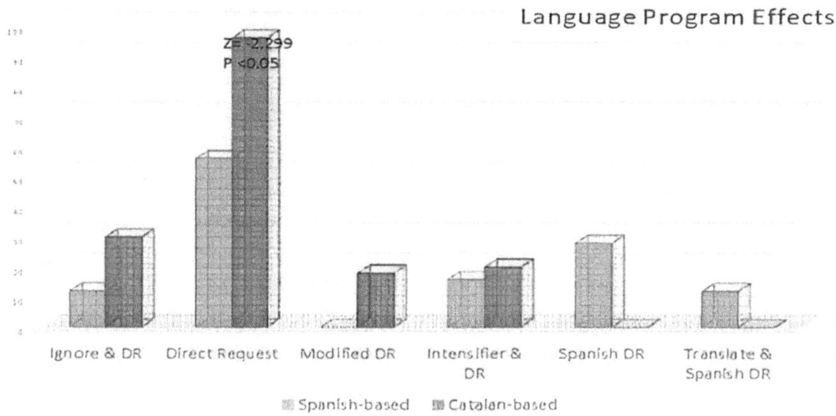

Figure 10.2: Teachers' attitudinal discourse and language program effects (Source: Safont, 2022: 330).

As shown in Figure 10.2 above, two different patterns emerged. Teachers in the Catalan-based program used modified direct requests more often than their counterparts in Spanish-based classrooms, and they also ignored the learners' translingual practices more often being such differences statistically significant (Z= -2.299; Z= -1.970; $p < 0.05$). Interestingly, attitudinal reactions in the Spanish-based group involved the use of Spanish direct requests and translation. In the light of our findings, we may say that teachers' attitudes towards translanguaging were displayed by means of their requestive behaviour and that the language program of the school seems to play a role in teachers' reactions. The Spanish-based program involved a frequent use of Spanish requests while the Catalan-program included requesting in the third language which was English in this case. All in all, we may state that in both cases an English-only policy motivated teachers' discourse choice.

Classroom discourse is also the focus of the study we shall describe next (Safont, 2024b) which deals with young learners' requestive behaviour in Content and Language Integrated Learning (henceforth CLIL) settings. According to findings from previous research on requests in CLIL contexts, it seems that CLIL may benefit pragmatic development (Nashaat-Sobhy, 2018; Tateyama, 2019), and it may also offer those sociopragmatic conditions that promote the use of a wider range of request forms including direct, indirect strategies and modifiers (Dalton-Puffer & Nikula, 2006). We should also consider those results that show how CLIL gains may be less obvious in teacher-fronted classrooms (Llinares & Pastrana, 2013). Interestingly, naturalistic discourse seems to include more direct request forms than elicited discourse behaviour (Economidou-Kogetsidis, 2013; Nashaat-Sobhy & Llinares, 2018). Nevertheless, no studies have accounted for the analysis of requestive behaviour in CLIL settings by adopting a multilingual perspective. In order to contribute to this line of research and meet the above-mentioned research gap, we examined and compared requesting patterns in CLIL and multilingual non-CLIL classrooms.

Authentic (non-elicited) classroom discourse from six non-CLIL and four CLIL lessons involving 125 learners and 5 teachers were analysed. Wc could identify 1,415 request instances in our data. The analysis included a pragmalinguistic and a sociopragmatic perspective. Therefore, we considered the request forms (i.e. direct, conventionally indirect forms and peripheral modification items), the request goals (i.e. request for action or request for information) and the classroom register (i.e. instructional, which relates to the provision of guidelines during tasks performance, vs regulative that has to do with teacher-students or students-students spontaneous interaction) in which these took place. Regarding the request goals, our findings show that CLIL settings included more requests for information in the instructional discourse and more requests for action within the regulative discourse. Furthermore, the non-CLIL multilingual classroom included more requests for information within the regulative discourse and there were no requests for action within the instructional discourse for any of the programs. These findings were in line with previous studies that relate the instructional discourse to requests for information and the regulative type to requests for action in CLIL settings.

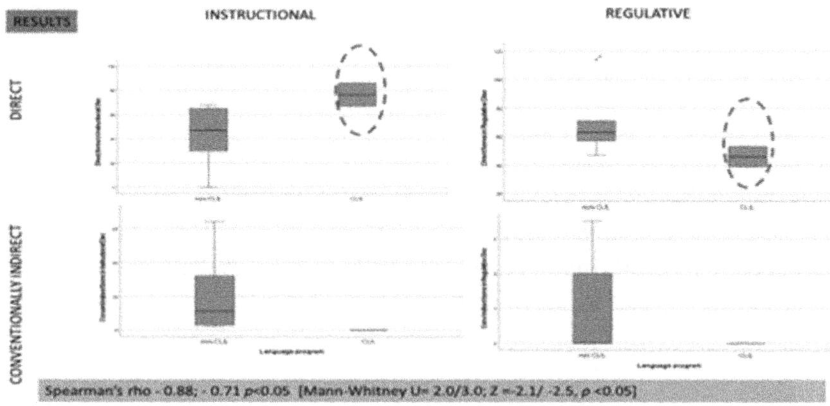

Figure 10.3: Requests forms in CLIL and multilingual non-CLIL classrooms (Source: Safont, 2024b).

As far as request forms are concerned, results showed that the instructional discourse of the CLIL classroom included more direct requests than the non-CLIL group. As shown in Figure 10.3 above, the CLIL classroom produced less instances of direct forms than the non-CLIL group within the regulative discourse. However, we should also point out that unlike predicted by some prior studies in CLIL settings (Dalton-Puffer, 2005), the multilingual non-CLIL group included more appropriate request forms, that is conventionally indirect request realization strategies, than the CLIL group both within the instructional and the regulative discourse type. In fact, conventionally indirect requests did not occur in CLIL classes at all. This contradictory result is partially in line with previous findings that relate CLIL naturalistic discourse to direct request forms (Economidou-Kogetsidis, 2013; Nashaat-Sobhy & Llinares, 2018). Furthermore, as has been previously mentioned, authors like Llinares and Nikula (2016) explain how CLIL gains may be less obvious in teacher-fronted classrooms and this could also be the case of our CLIL groups. Nevertheless, the reason why non-CLIL multilingual classroom discourse seems to offer better chances for appropriate pragmatic performance is not self-explanatory. We wonder whether a multilingual perspective might have induced the use of more varied request realisation strategies. Additionally, the fact that the three languages involved (i.e. Catalan, Spanish and English) do not share the same politeness orientation could have also generated a wider awareness regarding the need to employ conventionally indirect requests in the English classroom. In fact, former investigations on multilingual pragmatic development and learning point out the advantages of multilingual learners even from a very young age as far as request awareness and production are concerned (Portolés, 2015; Safont, 2013). Nonetheless, further research is needed that accounts for a multilingual perspective in CLIL discourse too in order to fully understand multilingual requestive behaviour in instructional settings.

Conclusion

The purpose of this chapter refers to meeting the ascertained need to rethink the existing monolingual bias in IL pragmatics research which sees the English native speaker as a feasible target for pragmatic learning. Drawing on Alcón's work on the pragmatics of trilingual (i.e. Catalan, Spanish and English) language learners (Alcón-Soler, 2013; Safont & Alcón-Soler, 2012), we have offered a portrayal of some recent findings in the Valencian multilingual context while pointing to some challenges and ideas for further research. More specifically, the studies described in this chapter have adopted a multilingual perspective in examining adolescents' online discourse, young adults' email requestive behaviour, the analysis of teachers' attitudinal discourse and CLIL interactional patterns in primary education.

We have tried to demonstrate that some of the gaps that have been identified by SLA research on pragmatic learning may also be met if a multilingual perspective is adopted. Additionally, our studies go beyond an exclusive focus on the target language to consider the learners' whole linguistic repertoire when describing interactional discourse. From a monolingual angle, using languages other than the target one may be considered as interference or as a sign of language deficiency. Nevertheless, results from Nightingale and Safont (2019) show that teenagers' online discourse includes translingual practices which perform a variety of functions, namely those of marking humour, identity or request mitigation.

Modifying requests online is also the focus of our study on multilingual email requests (Safont, 2024a). Findings on age and gender effects contradict previous results which adopted an exclusive focus on the target language (Barón & Ortega, 2018; Pham & Yeh, 2020); an aspect that calls for further research on classroom requestive behaviour. The speech act of requesting has received a lot of attention in IL Pragmatics as it is widely present in instructional discourse, yet a multilingual standpoint has not always been addressed. For this reason, we have also reported on findings from two more studies (Safont, 2024a, 2024b) dealing with requests that described teachers' attitudinal reactions to learners' translanguaging and CLIL interactional patterns involving the use of the target language (i.e. English) as well as the other languages that are part of the school program, namely those of Catalan and Spanish. Results from Safont (2024a) confirm the monolingual policy of the English as L3 classroom (Jakonen, 2016) and they also signal out the effect of the language program as different discourse patterns emerged when comparing the Spanish-based to the Catalan-based classrooms. Interestingly, comparing CLIL versus multilingual non-CLIL programs seemed to shed more light on the importance of the language policy adopted in the classroom. As raised before, results from such analogy (Safont, 2024b) show that the non-CLIL multilingual classroom provided more instances of appropriate requestive behaviour than the CLIL group. However, we dealt with naturalistic teacher-fronted discourse in the CLIL classroom which as ported by Llinares and Nikula (2016) may lead to more direct formulas. On that account, more research is needed in CLIL settings adopting a multilingual perspective in order to confirm or contradict current findings.

The studies described in the present chapter are subject to a number of limitations. All of them were conducted in the same sociolinguistic setting, namely that of the Valencian community in Spain. We would need to replicate them in other contexts to validate and generalise the results obtained. What is more, an almost exclusive focus has been drawn on requests and a wider range of pragmatic phenomena should be taken into account especially within multilingual and multicultural classrooms. For instance, research on implicatures, compliments, intonation patterns or pragmatic markers of emotion in multilingual language learning and teaching is very scant. Given the culture-bound nature of these pragmatic aspects, we believe that findings would be highly interesting both for the study on multilingualism from a educational perspective and for the analysis of the pragmatic development of language learners around the world.

References

Alcón-Soler, Eva. 2008 *Learning how to request in an instructed language learning context.* Bern: Peter Lang.

Alcón-Soler, Eva. 2013. Mitigating e.mail requests in teenagers' first and second language academic cyber-consultation. *Multilingua*, 32/6, 779–799.

Alcón-Soler, Eva, Safont, Pilar & Martínez-Flor, Alicia. 2005. Towards a typology of modifiers for the speech act of requesting: a socio-pragmatic approach. *RÆL: Revista Electrónica de Lingüística Aplicada*, 4, 1–35.

Aronin, Larissa. 2015. Current multilingualism and new developments in multilingual research. In Pilar Safont & Laura Portolés (eds), *Multilingual development in the classroom: Current findings from research.* Cambridge: Cambridge Scholars Publishing, 1–27.

Aronin, Larissa. 2019. What is multilingualism? In David Singleton & Larissa Aronin (eds) *Twelve lectures in multilingualism.* Clevedon: Multilingual Matters, 3–34.

Aronin, Larissa. 2020. Dominant language constellation as an approach for studying multilingual practices. In Joseph Lo Bianco & L. Aronin (eds) *Dominant language constellations: A new perspective on multilingualism.* Cham: Springer, 19–33.

Aronin, Larissa & Singleton, David. 2012. *Multilingualism.* Amsterdam: John Benjamins.

Aronin, Larissa, Fishman, Joshua, Singleton, David & Laoire, Muiris Ó. 2013. Current multilingualism: A new linguistic dispensation. In David Singleton, Joshua A. Fishman, Larissa Aronin & Muiris Ó Laoire (eds) *Current multilingualism: A new linguistic dispensation*. Berlin/Boston: De Gruyter Mouton Current multilingualism, 3–23.

Baker, Colin. 2001. *Foundations of bilingual education and bilingualism*. Clevedon: Multilingual Matters.

Bardovi-Harlig, Kathlin. 2013. Developing L2 Pragmatics. *Language Learning*, 1, 68–86.

Barón, Júlia & Ortega, Mireia. 2018. Investigating age differences in e-mail pragmatic performance. *System*, 78, 148–178.

Cenoz, Jasone. 2013. The influence of bilingualism on third language acquisition: Focus on multilingualism. *Language Teaching*, 46/1, 71–86.

Cenoz, Jasone & Jessner, Ulrike. 2000. *English in Europe: The acquisition of a third language*. Clevedon: Multilingual Matters.

Cenoz, Jasone & Gorter, Durk. 2017. Minority languages and sutainable translanguaging: Threat or opportunity? *Journal of Multilingual and Multicultural Development,* 38, 901–912.

Cenoz, Jasone & Gorter, Durk. 2020. Teaching English through pedagogical translanguaging. *World Englishes*, 39, 300–311.

Cenoz, Jasone & Gorter, Durk. 2021. *Pedagogical translanguaging*. Cambridge: Cambridge University Press.

Cenoz, Jasone & Gorter, Durk. 2022. Pedagogical translanguaging and its application to language classes. *RELC Journal*, 53, 342–354.

Cenoz, Jasone, Gorter, Durk & May, Stephen. 2017. *Language awareness and multilingualism*. Cham: Springer.

Cenoz, Jasone, Hufeisen, Britta & Jessner, Ulrike. 2001. *Cross-linguistic influence in third language acquisition. Psycholinguistic perspectives*. Bristol, Blue Ridge Summit: Multilingual Matters.

Cenoz, Jasone, Hufeisen, Britta & Jessner, Ulrike. 2003. Why investigate the multilingual lexicon? In Jasone Cenoz, Britta Hufeisen & Ulrike Jessner (eds) *The multilingual Lexicon*. New York, Boston, Dordrecht, London, Moscow: Kluwer, 1–10.

Corder, Pit. 1967. The significance of learner's errors. *International Review of Applied Linguistics*, 5, 161–170.

Cots, Josep M., Gallego-Balsà, Lidia & Llanes, Àngels. 2022. Promoting translanguaging (or not) in the ESP classroom: An analysis of monoglossic and heteroglossic practices and discourses. *System*, 107, 10279.

Creswell, John W. 2014. *Research design: Qualitative, quantitative and mixed methods approaches*. Thousand Oaks, CA: Sage.

Culpeper, Jonathan, Mackey, Alison & Taguchi, Naoko. 2018. *Second language pragmatics: From theory to research*. London: Routledge.

Dalton-Puffer, Christiane. 2005. Negotiating interpersonal meanings in naturalistic classroom discourse: Directives in content-and-language-integrated classrooms. *Journal of Pragmatics*, 37, 1275–1293.

Dalton-Puffer, Christiane & Nikula, Tarja. 2006. Pragmatics of content-based instruction: teacher and student directives in Finnish and Austrian classrooms. *Applied Linguistics,* 27, 241–267.

Dörnyei, Zoltán. 2005. *The psychology of the language learner: Individual differences in second language acquisition*. Mahwah, NJ: Erlbaum.

Economidou-Kogetsidis, Maria. 2013. Strategies, modification, and perspective in native speakers'requests: A comparison of WDCT and naturally occurring requests. *Journal of Pragmatics,* 53, 21–28.

Economidou-Kogetsidis, Maria. 2021. The effect of first language pragmatics on second language email performance. In Maria Economidou-Kogetsidis, Nicola Halenko & Milica Savi (eds) *Email pragmatics and second language learners*. Amsterdam: John Benjamins, 150–178.

Félix-Brasdefer, César. 2012. Email openings and closings. Pragmalinguistic and gender variation in learner-instructor cyber-consultation. In Eva Alcón-Soler & Pilar Safont (eds) *Discourse and language learning across L2 instructional contexts*. Leiden: Brill, 223–248.

Fereday, Jennifer & Muir-Cochrane, Eimear. 2006. Demonstrating rigor using thematic analysis: A hybrid approach of inductive and deductive coding and theme development. *International Journal of Qualitative Methods,* 5/1, 80–92.

Gabryś-Barker, Danuta. 2023. Language repertoires or individual dominant language constellations: The reality of instructed educational settings in a (mostly) monolingual context. In: Aronin Larissa & Melo-Pfeifer Sílvia (eds) *Language awareness and identity. Multilingual education*. Cham: Springer. 107–129.

Gabrýs-Barker, Danuta & Vetter, Eva. 2024. *Modern approaches to researching on multilingualism. Studies in honour of Larissa Aronin*. Cham: Springer.

Garrett, D. 2010. *Language attitudes*. Oxford: Oxford University Press.

Herdina, Philip & Jessner, Ulrike. 2002. *A dynamic model of multilingualism*. Bristol, Blue Ridge Summit: Multilingual Matters.

Jakonen, Teppo. 2016. Managing multiple normativities in classroom interaction: Student responses to teacher reproaches for inappropriate language choice in a bilingual classroom. *Linguistics and Education*, 33, 14–27.

Jessner, Ulrike. 2006. *Linguistic awareness in multilinguals: English as a third language*. Edinburgh: Edinburgh University Press.

Jessner, Ulrike. 2008. Teaching third languages: Findings, trends and challenges. *Language Teaching*, 41/1, 15–56.

Kasper, Gabriele & Dhal, Merete. 1991. Research methods in Interlanguage pragmatics. *Studies in Second Language Acquisition*, 13/2, 215–247.

Kasper, Gabriele & Rose, Kenneth. 2002. Pragmatic development in a second language. *Language Learning*, 52, 13–62.

Kesckes, Istvan. 2022. *The Cambridge handbook of intercultural pragmatics*. Cambridge: Cambridge University Press.

Krashen, Stephen D. 1992. The input hypothesis: An update. In James Alatis (ed.) *Georgetown university round table on languages and linguistics, 1991*. Washington, DC: Georgetown University Press, 409–431.

Krulatz, Anna & Dugan, Jennifer. 2021. Exploring identities and life stories of multilingual transnational couples through the lens of multilinguality and dominant language constellations. In Larissa Aronin & Eva Vetter (eds) *Dominant language constellations approach in education and language acquisition*. Cham: Springer, 173–201.

Leech, Geoffrey. 1983. *Principles of pragmatics*. London: Longman.

Llinares, Ana & Nikula, Tarja. 2016. Teacher and student evaluative language in CLIL across contexts: Integrating SFL and pragmatic approaches. In Tarja Nikula, Emma Dafouz, Pat Moore & Ute Smit (eds) *Conceptualising integration in CLIL and multilingual education*. Bristol, Blue Ridge Summit: Multilingual Matters, 189–210.

Llinares, Ana & Pastrana, Amanda. 2013. CLIL students' communicative functions across activities and educational levels. *Journal of Pragmatics*, 59, 81–92.

Long, Michael H. 1990. The least a second language acquisition theory needs to explain. *TESOL Quarterly*, 24/4, 649–666.

Lorenzo-Dus, Nuria & Bou-Franch, Patricia. 2013. A cross-cultural investigation of email communication in Peninsular Spanish and British English. The role of (in) formality and (in)directness. *Pragmatics and Society*, 4, 1–25.

Martín-Laguna, Sofía. 2020. *Tasks, pragmatics and multilingualism in the classroom. A portrait of adolescent writing in multiple languages*. Bristol, Blue Ridge Summit: Multilingual Matters.

Martínez-Flor, Alicia & Sánchez-Hernández, Ariadna & Barón, Júlia. 2023. *L2 Pragmatics in action. Teachers, learners and the teaching-learning interaction process*. Amsterdam: John Benjamins.

May, Stephen. 2013. *The multilingual turn. Implications for SLA, TESOL and bilingual education*. London: Routledge.

McConachy, Troy. 2018. *Developing intercultural perspectives on language use. Exploring pragmatics and culture in foreign language learning*. Bristol, Blue Ridge Summit: Multilingual Matters.

Nashaat-Sobhy, Nashwa. 2018. Pragmatics in CLIL. A comparison of CLIL and non-CLIL students' requests. *Revista Española de Lingüística Aplicada*, 31, 467–494.

Nashaat-Sobhy, Nashwa & Llinares, Ana. 2018. CLIL students' pragmatic competence: a comparison between naturally-occuring and elicited requests. In Ariadna Sanchez-Hernández & Ana Herráiz-Martínez (eds) *Learning second language pragmatics. Beyond traditional contexts*. Bern/Berlin/Bruxelles/Frankfurt am Main/New York/Oxford/Wien: Peter Lang, 173–199.

Nightingale, Richard & Safont, Pilar. 2019. Pragmatic translanguaging: Multilingual practice in adolescent online discourse. In Victòria Codina & Patricia Salazar (eds) *Investigating the learning of pragmatics across ages and contexts*. Leiden: Brill, 167–195.

Pham, Thi Minh Trang & Yeh, Aiden 2020. Politeness of Vietnamese students in writing request email in English: A course-based and socio-pragmatic study. *International Journal of Language and Literary Studies*, 2/2, 109–128.

Pienemann, Manfred & Johnston, Malcolm. 1996. A brief history of processing approaches to SLA: reply to Mellow. *Second Language Research*, 12/3, 319–334.

Portolés, Laura. 2015. *Multilingualism and very young learners*. Berlin, New York: De Gruyter.

Safont, Pilar. 2005. *Third language learners. Pragmatic production and awareness*. Bristol, Blue Ridge Summit: Multilingual Matters.

Safont, Pilar. 2013. Early stages of trilingual pragmatic development. A longitudinal study of requests in Catalan, Spanish and English. *Journal of Pragmatics*, 59, 68–80.

Safont, Pilar. 2022. 'In English!' teachers' requests as reactions to learners' translanguaging discourse. *Language, Culture and Curriculum*, 35/3, 317–333.

Safont, Pilar. 2024a. Multilingual cyberpragmatics in instructional settings. Exploring gender and age effects in Catalan, Spanish and English email requests. *International Journal of Multilingualism*, 3, 1494–1516.

Safont, Pilar. 2024b. Young multilingual pragmatics. A focus on requests in CLIL and non-CLIL settings. In Danuta Gabryś Barker & Eva Vetter (eds) *Modern approaches to researching on multilingualism. Studies in honour of Larissa Aronin.* Cham: Springer.

Safont, Pilar & Alcón-Soler, Eva. 2012. Teachability of request act peripheral modification devices in third language learning contexts. In Maria Economidou-Kogetsidis & Helen Woodfield (eds) *Interlanguage request modification*, John Benjamins Publishing, 275–314.

Salazar-Campillo, Patricia & Codina-Espurz, Victòria. 2019. *Investigating the Learning of Pragmatics across Ages and Contexts.* Leiden: Brill Rodopi.

Sánchez-Hernández, Ariadna. 2018. A mixed-methods study of the impact of sociocultural adaptation on the development of pragmatic production. *System*, 75, 93–105.

Schauer, Gila. 2021. Email communication in English and German. In Maria Economidou-Kogetsidis, Nicola Halenko & Milica Savic (eds) *Email pragmatics and second language learners*. Amsterdam: John Benjamins Publishing, 179–202.

Singleton, David & Aronin, Larissa (eds). 2018. *Twelve lectures on multilingualism.* Bristol, Blue Ridge Summit: Multilingual Matters.

Taguchi, Naoko & Sykes, Julie M. 2013. *Technology in interlanguage pragmatics research and teaching*. Amsterdam: John Benjamins Publishing.

Taguchi, Naoko. 2022. Second language pragmatics. A historical overview and future directions. In Nicola Halenko & Jiayi Wang (eds) *Pragmatics in English language learning*. Cambridge: Cambridge University Press, 7–28.

Tajeddin, Zia & Malmir, Ali. 2014. Knowledge of L2 speech acts: Impact of gender and language learning experience. *English Language Teaching*, 1, 1–21.

Tateyama, Yumiko. 2019. Pragmatics in a language classroom. In N. Taguchi (ed.) *The Routledge handbook of second language acquisition and pragmatics*. London: Routledge. 235–247.

Thomas (1983). Cross-cultural pragmatic failure. *Applied Linguistics*, 4, 91–111.

Usó-Juan, Esther & Martínez-Flor, Alicia. 2021. Teacher pragmatic awareness in English is an International language. In Zia Tajeddin & Minoo Alemi (eds) *Pragmatic pedagogy in English as an international language*. London: Routledge, 44–58.

Wei, Li & Lin, Angel M. Y. 2019. Translanguaging classroom discourse: Pushing limits, breaking boundaries. *Classroom Discourse*, 10/3–4, 209–215.

Richard Nightingale

Exploring Relationships Between Digital Media Contact, Language Attitudes, and Socio-Pragmatic Awareness in Multilingual Adolescents

Introduction

Both language attitudes and pragmatic competence are influenced by social factors. One such factor, which is particularly relevant for adolescent language learners, is contact with digital media. Existing research shows a relationship between positive attitudes to the Target Language (TL), and TL culture, and pragmatic competence, as well as a relationship between aspects of pragmatic competence and digital media use. However, much of this work takes a pragmalinguistic and/or Second Language Acquisition (SLA) perspective, in which the TL is usually English. While research on attitudes towards digital media as a language learning tool has received attention, there is a scarcity of work that places the focus on the potential influence of digital media contact on language attitudes. Nevertheless, what little work does exist points to a positive relationship between these two variables, especially with regards to minority and foreign languages in multilingual contexts. In spite of these positive initial results, further research is necessary on the relationships between language attitudes and digital media use in younger language learners, and research on different aspects of sociopragmatic awareness in multilingual contexts is still in need of further development. For these reasons, the current chapter aims to contribute to the literature by exploring the nexus between digital media contact, language attitudes and sociopragmatic awareness in multilingual adolescents in the sociolinguistic context of the Valencian Community, focusing on the three most salient languages experienced by young learners; namely, Catalan, Spanish, and English.

Literature Review

The first part of this section will provide a brief overview of the three variables involved in the current study; that is, language attitudes, pragmatic competence, and digital media in language learning. Subsequently, the remainder of the section will focus on some of the research that makes connections between the three variables discussed.

Language Attitudes, Pragmatic Competence, and Digital Media in Language Learning

In reference to the first variable, language attitudes refer to the feelings, beliefs, and predispositions individuals have towards different languages, varieties, speakers, speech communities, language learning, and even themselves as users of a TL (Garrett, 2010; Dragojevic et al., 2021). They can be positive, negative, or neutral and are shaped by social, cultural, political, and personal factors. They are closely interconnected with language learning motivation, in the sense that positive attitudes towards a language or its speech community can enhance motivation to learn and use the language effectively (Gardner, 1985; Masgoret & Gardner, 2003). They can also play a role in language education, in that language attitudes can impact educational policies as well as the resources allocated for language learning (Baker, 1992). In terms of what language attitudes influence, the attitude object tends to be either what we think about different language varieties, focusing mainly on structure, value, and sound, or what we think about speakers of different language varieties, focusing mainly on status and solidarity (Dragojevic et al., 2021). Moreover, there are strong correlations between beliefs about language structure and beliefs about speaker status. Likewise, there is a similar relationship between beliefs about language sound and speaker solidarity.

What has received less attention, however, is what might influence language attitudes. For instance, influential variables include age, gender, family values, personal experiences, global personality traits, language background, social dynamics, cultural milieu, educational contexts, and media representations, as well as broader economic and political influences (Baker, 1991, 1992; Cenoz, 2009; Dewaele, 2005; Lasagabaster, 2001; Nightingale, 2012, 2016; Pavlenko & Blackledge, 2004). Likewise, language-specific factors, such as perceived status, use potential, perceptions and stereotypes of language users, personal investment in language learning, and typological difference/similarity to L1, also play a powerful role (see Lasagabaster & Huguet, 2007). Attitudes change over time, making age an important variable to consider. Baker (1992) found an attitudinal dip at around 11–14 years old, this was corroborated by Nightingale (2016) who observed a similar dip in relation to the minority language at around 15–16 years old. In both cases, this temporary decrease in positive attitudes may be attributable to sociopsychological factors such as peer-pressure and group socialisation (Walqui, 2000). Maintaining positive attitudes towards languages is fundamental in order to capitalise on language learning gains (Lasgabaster & Huguet, 2007). As such, a focus on young and adolescent learners is of great importance.

In multilingual contexts, attitudes to minority languages are complex and contradictory. They may be valued for their identity and solidarity functions (Woolard, 1985), but not necessarily as linguistic capital (Bourdieu, 1992). Attitudes influence language policy and also serve as a barometer for assessing the vitality and prospects of minority languages, shaping their trajectory towards growth or decline (Baker, 1992; Fishman, 1991; Ó Riagáin, 2008). In the context of the current study, the Valencian Community, research reveals positive attitudes towards the minority language, Catalan, although Spanish retains its dominance (Safont, 2007; Nightingale, 2016). Moreover, some minority language speakers show resistance to English as a foreign language, potentially due to a perceived threat to ethnolinguistic vitality (Lasagabaster, 2004). Nevertheless, there is generally a positive attitude towards multilingualism (Lasagabaster & Safont, 2008; Portolés,

2015), which may help to mitigate potential conflict between languages and language ideologies. Despite this, a general monolingual bias is still present in language education (Guzmán-Alcón & Portolés, 2021; Portolés & Martí, 2020; Safont, 2022), highlighting the need for additional research with a multilingual focus.

In reference to the second variable, pragmatic competence is considered an essential skill for language learners to understand the contextual nuances of a target language and to successfully achieve interactional goals while using that language. In essence, pragmatic competence is knowing how to use language appropriately, given the context, the topic, and the relationship among interlocutors; in other words, "the ability to convey and interpret meaning appropriately in a social situation" (Taguchi, 2012: 6). Pragmatic competence is broadly divided into pragmalinguistic comprehension/production and sociopragmatic knowledge/awareness (Leech, 1983); respectively, the *forms* that can be used, and the *norms* that dictate their use. More specifically, the pragmalinguistic element refers to the "linguistic resources that speakers can make use of to convey a particular communicative act" (Martínez-Flor et al., 2006: 149). While the sociopragmatic element refers to knowledge of the "rules and conventions underlying appropriate language use in particular communicative situations and on the part of members of specific speech communities" (Alcón-Soler & Safont, 2008: 193). Language learners need to master both of these elements of pragmatic competence, however the latter is often considered to be more complex, as learners need to be aware of abstract concepts such as the specific utterance-production context, interlocutor roles within that context, as well as factors such as social distance, power, and degree of imposition (politeness variables) and their significance in 'saving face' during interaction (Brown & Levinson, 1987; Ishihara & Cohen, 2010); all of which play a paramount role in successful communication (Celce-Murcia & Olshtain, 2000; Martínez-Flor et al., 2006).

Research has shown that explicit instruction can enhance pragmatic competence by shifting learners' attention from the linguistic to the pragmalinguistic aspects of the communicative task (Safont & Alcón-Soler, 2012). However, instructed contexts have been shown to be less effective for increasing gains in sociopragmatic awareness (Alcón-Soler, 2012) due to the sometimes rather ambiguous nature of the social norms that govern communication in different cultures. So far, there is more pragmatics research that takes an Interlanguage or a SLA approach (Alcón-Soler, 2008) than there is in multilingual contexts (Safont, 2012). Very recent L2 pragmatics research (Taguchi, 2022) has begun to widen the scope by focusing on lingua franca and intercultural communication, and has also mentioned multilingual pragmatic competence as an important topic to address. Nevertheless, taking its lead from the pioneering work of Eva Alcón (2008, 2012, 2013), multilingual pragmatics research has been gaining traction (Safont, 2005, 2012, 2013, 2022, 2024a, 2024b; Portolés, 2015; Nightingale & Safont, 2019), yielding results on online translan-guaging, very young learners, pragmatic awareness in monolinguals vs. bilinguals, as well as requests and attitudes in classroom discourse, emails, and CLIL interaction. Although this work has demonstrated that some desiderata identified in SLA pragmatics research may be tackled from a multilingual perspective, there is still a need to expand our state of knowledge by focusing on a wider range of (socio)pragmatic phenomena in a wider range of cultural contexts (see Safont, this volume).

In relation to the third variable, digitally assisted language learning has existed for around 60 years (see Butler-Pascoe, 2011) but has evolved considerably with the advent of Web 2.0 applications, which increasingly allow users to "create, remix, and share digital content much more easily than before", marking a change from simple tools into "spaces for the *sociointeractional* use of tools" (Reinhardt, 2020: 235—my emphasis). Improved mobile devices and broadband connections mean that access to digital media has lost any spatiotemporal dependence and has become a personal, everyday tool that can expose its users to a never-ending supply of authentic language. Moreover, precisely because digital media now obviates the contingency between geographic, temporal, and social proximity, its users also have access to a wider range of linguistic variation than ever before. In spite of the increased presence of digital tools in language teaching, contrary to earlier predictions (Bax, 2011), digital media has become neither normalised nor fully integrated into classrooms. Instead, these technologies have become a simple fact of life outside of school for many young people (Reinhardt, 2020).

Digital media provides dynamic, flexible, and immersive opportunities for language learning as it offers greater control over learning experiences and promotes interaction in real-world contexts. Social networking platforms promote autonomy and user control. They help learners build friendships and acclimate to new situations, experiment with new languages and improve cultural competency (Harrison & Thomas, 2009; Mitchell, 2012; Reinhardt, 2020). Digital media frequently engages users in multiple threads and modes of discourse simultaneously, which can engender the type of meta-awareness that fosters language play and creativity (Herring et al., 2013). Furthermore, language use in digital gaming is a social action that may awaken linguistic and intercultural curiosity (Thorne, 2008), as well as sociocultural, pragmatic, and communicative competences (Peterson, 2010). Moreover, gaming constitutes a self-affirming activity, providing intense experiences and a sense of ownership and control (Henry, 2013), which helps to motivate learners and engenders positive attitudes.

With this in mind, Reinhardt (2020) proposes four new metaphors (window, mirror, doorway, and playground) for the language learning possibilities of current digital media. As a *window*, it affords exposure to authentic language use and cultural practices without the need to directly participate. This offers the protection of anonymity until learners feel ready to make themselves known. As a *mirror*, it not only provides a space for reflection on personal language skills, but also allows for the presentation of carefully constructed identities, which can enable learners to participate in communities they may not otherwise have access to. As a *doorway*, it allows language learners to participate in TL cultural, as well as intercultural, practices; that is, they are able to engage in and contribute to shared practices rather than just consume the practices of "others". Lastly, as a *playground*, digital media provides spaces for informal, autonomous, and gameful language learning and language play. This may look like taking on different persona to try out new perspectives, roleplaying using technological props and realia, or observing and participating in gaming communities. These metaphors are more appropriate for the inclusive and interactive nature of modern digital media as they move beyond the "tutor" or "tool" concept to capture the actions, perceptions, and reflections of the user.

Some of What We Know about the Relationships Between Language Attitudes, Pragmatic Competence and Digital Media

Some interest has been shown regarding attitudes towards digital media as a language learning tool (Billore & Rosén, 2017; Rosén & Billore, 2020), but there is still surprisingly little work that focuses on the attitudinal influence of digital media itself, and research that explores this potential relationship in multilingual contexts is almost non-existent. Nevertheless, there appears to be a strong link between digital media use and positive attitudes towards the languages they are used in (Nightingale, 2016). This connection is particularly strong in the case of minority and foreign languages and is attributed to digital media being eye-catching, engaging, authentic, empowering, and representative of lifestyle choices. In addition, digital media allows user agency in creating, choosing, and maintaining personalised multilingual and multimodal media environments. Moreover, in relation to younger language learners, digital media speaks to them in *their* language (i.e. appeals to their "digital native" literacies). Ongoing research (Nightingale & Zaharcenco, forthcoming) corroborates this, also finding that the strongest relationships between language attitudes and digital media contact are in relation to the minority language. To account for this, the study makes reference to existing work on digital media in minority language contexts (Eisenlohr, 2004; Soria, 2016), which suggests that language presence in digital domains establishes positive associations with modernity and relevance to current lifestyles and that, as so much of our lives is mediated through the digital arena, representation of minority languages in this domain equalises digital dignity and opportunities for language survival. Given the pivotal role of attitudes in shaping language growth/decline (Fishman, 1991) and the importance of digital representation to secure survival for minority languages (Crystal, 2010), married with the fact that, nowadays, most young people consume digital media through mobile devices, it puts the fate of minority languages (quite literally!) in the hands of their future speakers.

As mentioned above, what we think about speakers of different language varieties is one of a number of identified "attitude objects", and the way in which speakers, speech communities, and the culture surrounding the TL are perceived can influence interactions and communication. Related to this link between perception and performance, Kasper and Schmidt (1996) suggested that positive, supportive peer interactions can lead to more favourable attitudes towards language learning, which may be influential in the extent to which learners are willing to adopt TL pragmatic conventions. Since then, a limited range of studies have uncovered more specific links. For example, positive attitudes towards native varieties of English play a role in learning pragmatic behaviours (LoCastro, 2001), learners' positive attitude toward the TL community is related to their awareness of TL discourse markers (Takahashi, 2005), study abroad students show resistance to adopt the pragmatic norms of a variety of English that they show less preference for (Davis, 2007), attitudes towards the adoption of the TL culture is strongly related to the ability to comprehend conversational implicatures (Rafieyan et al., 2015), cultural interest in and positive attitudes toward the L2 community is positively correlated with appropriacy judgements (Kiyançiçek, 2023), and learners with preexisting positive attitudes towards English as an International Language show a higher frequency and range of use of pragmatic markers in L2 English (Sánchez-Hernández, 2023). Lastly, among the very few studies to approach this connection from a multilingual perspective, Safont (2013) found a connection between multilingual requestive development, interaction between languages, attitudes, and sociocultural factors, while Portolés (2015) found correlations between language attitudes and pragmatic awareness in the majority (Spanish) and minority (Catalan) language, but not the foreign language (English) in the context of her study. As we can see, as the bulk of this research focuses on the acquisition of pragmalinguistic competence in English as a second/foreign language (Sánchez-Hernández, 2023), there is still a clear need to further develop work on the possible ways in which sociopragmatic awareness may manifest and develop in multilingual settings.

Online platforms can be harnessed for developing pragmatic competence because they enhance communication and human interaction. In fact, digital media can provide exactly the kind of "positive, supportive peer interactions" that Kasper and Schmidt (1996) posit lead to positive language attitudes and enhanced pragmatic performance. Specifically, research findings indicate that use of digital media can facilitate interpreting implied meanings (Mirzaei et al., 2016), create informal communicative spaces in which to engage in varied interactions (Lantz-Andersson, 2018), raise awareness of sociopragmatic norms (Hasan & Idrees, 2020), and significantly improve conscious awareness of appropriate TL request forms (Quadha et al., 2021). This may be because digital media exposes learners to a broader range of sociopragmatic situations and contexts, in which they can test and develop L2 pragmatic competence (González-Lloret, 2021). Moreover, informal social media use also affords the development of audience awareness, which may improve intercultural and sociopragmatic skills (Reinhardt, 2019). Moreover, digital media discourse constitutes sociopragmatically authentic "encoded texts" (Knobel & Lankshear, 2008) with their own unique conventions and 'cultures-of-use' (Thorne, 2003). Understanding these conventions and cultures and especially the capacity to successfully flout pragmatic norms and contextual constraints using the affordances of digital platforms has been cited as evidence of sociopragmatic awareness (Reinhardt & Ryu, 2013). In fact, in relation to language play and creativity, it was found that adolescent learners are sociopragmatically aware of their language mixing practices on digital platforms and, in fact, point to the perceived outcomes (perlocutionary effect) of such practices as the reason for doing them (Nightingale & Safont, 2019). In sum, research shows that language learners are capable of identifying sociopragmatic elements in digital platforms and translating this to awareness-raising activities may be beneficial for sociopragmatic development (Blattner & Fiori, 2011).

As can be seen from the selection of studies in the literature review above, the variables of digital media contact, language attitudes, and pragmatic awareness show considerable overlap and mutual influence. However, much of the existing research tends to focus on only two of the given variables in the acquisition of a L2 (usually English). As far as we understand, there is a research gap to cover in terms of the mutual influence of all three variables in multilingual contexts.

The Study

With all the above in mind, the main goal of this study is twofold. On the one hand, we aim to ascertain the existing language attitudes of our sample of multilingual secondary school students in the Valencian Community, as well as their state of pragmatic awareness and the extent to which they use digital media in the languages most present in their daily lives. On the other hand, we will explore potential relationships between these variables. In doing so, we will also look for possible differences in the results by academic year to explore if the dip found in language attitudes is also present in digital media contact and sociopragmatic awareness. In order to meet these goals, we have formulated the following research questions:

- RQ1: What do the participants report regarding digital media use and language attitudes in three languages, and to what extent are they aware of request appropriateness in these languages?
- RQ2: What relationships exist between digital media contact, language attitudes, and sociopragmatic awareness in our sample?

Participants

The participants in this study are 81 students from two public secondary education schools in the Valencian Community, on the East coast of Spain. The sample was collected across three levels of *Educación Secundaria Obligatoria* (ESO), distributed in the following manner: 2nd ESO ($n = 21$); 3rd ESO ($n = 26$); 4th ESO ($n = 34$). As individual age and gender were not relevant variables for the current study, individual demographic data were not collected. Nevertheless, age differences are taken into consideration, but this is operationalised as the age range related to the three levels of ESO: 2nd (13–14 years old), 3rd (14–15 years old), and 4th (15–16 years old).

Sociolinguistic Context

It is relevant to mention that the participants are embedded within a specific sociolinguistic context which is manifest in their educational experiences. The Valencian Community has two co-official languages: Spanish and Catalan, of which the specific variety is often locally known as Valencian. Although these two languages share co-official status, Catalan is the autochthonous language of the region dating back to the 13th Century (Safont, 2007). It must also be noted the disparity of prestige between these two languages. While smaller towns and villages are usually Catalan-speaking, Spanish is generally considered to be the dominant or majority language, especially in larger urban centres. Catalan was supressed under Franco's rule and has gradually achieved more recognition, prestige and visibility over the years since the transition to democracy in Spain, but these advances cannot be taken for granted and require effort to maintain. All the above can lead to a complex relationship between Catalan and its speakers in the Valencian Community. Moreover, English as a third or foreign language is taught ubiquitously all over the country. Generally speaking, teaching English starts at the infant level and is included at all stages of education up to the university level, in which an increasing number of programmes are taught through English Medium Instruction. Nevertheless, English does not usually extend beyond classroom settings and there is little opportunity to use it in real-life extramural communication.

Instrument

This study triangulates data between two distinct, on-paper questionnaires that form part of a more extensive project. On the one hand, the first questionnaire collects data on digital media use (frequency of use, and in which languages), including 14 different popular platform types: Facebook, Instagram, Twitter, Tik Tok, Snapchat, Whatsapp, Telegram, Viber, Discord, FB Messenger, Forums (such as Reddit, Quora, etc.), Video games, YouTube, and streaming platforms (Netflix, Prime, HBO, etc.). Additionally, the questionnaire collects data on language attitudes towards Spanish, Catalan, and English, as well as towards specific attitudinal themes: (1) Education, (2) Internet, (3) Intercultural, (4) Engagement, and (5) Instrumental. On the other hand, the second questionnaire collects data on sociopragmatic awareness regarding the speech act of requesting. This questionnaire presents a total of nine requestive situations, three for each of the languages mentioned above, for which the participants are required to respond to a short series of questions. For the purposes of the current study, the focus was on questions 1a, which asks participants to evaluate the appropriateness of the request using a 5-point scale, and 1b, which asks them to give a brief explanation for this evaluation.

Data Analysis

In this study, the main variables were measured in the following way. The score for digital media came from part 1 of the first questionnaire mentioned above and was measured in terms of intensity of contact, that is a summation of all media types, in all languages, and the reported frequency of use. Given that the instrument was designed in such a way that the participants only had to indicate a frequency token (from 0—"never"—to 6—"(almost) every day") in the table cell relating to the language for each media type, this resulted in a maximum possible score of 252 points. From this hypothetical maximum, an average score was calculated. Scores were subsequently calculated for media use in each language using the same technique but with a maximum score of 84 points each.

Likewise, the score for language attitudes came from part 2 of the same questionnaire and was measured in terms of overall positive attitudes in all 3 languages. Similar to the digital media variable, participants simply had to mark agreement with each statement, resulting in binary data. One of the attitude statements (item 1.3) had to be reverse coded due to the wording of the statement. The overall maximum score for this variable was 75 points, from which an average was calculated. Subsequently, scores for each attitude theme were also calculated, extracting the average from a maximum score of 15 per theme.

The scores for sociopragmatic awareness were taken from the second questionnaire mentioned above. This variable was measured in terms of the answers to item 1a (an evaluation of request appropriateness) from all situations and item 1b (an open text space asking participants to explain their response to the previous item). In the questionnaire, item 1a was presented as a type of Likert scale, albeit non-categorical, with the extremes marked as "very correct" or "very incorrect". Nevertheless, for data analysis this was reduced to a binary response; in that, the participants either chose the right response or not. To this was added item 1b, the sociopragmatic reasoning behind the participants' evaluation. For this item, to score a point, participants must make explicit reference to pragmatic *norms*; that is the 'why' rather than the 'how'—for example, interlocutor relationship, power, distance, imposition (Brown & Levinson, 1987; Ishihara & Cohen, 2010). An average for this variable was calculated from a hypothetical maximum score of 18 points; one point for each correct evaluation added to one point for each explicit mention of pragmatic norms in each of the nine situations.

Results and Discussion Related to Research Question 1

In order to understand our participant sample, before exploring possible correlations, we will respond to RQ1, *What do the participants report regarding digital media use and language attitudes in three languages, and to what extent are they aware of request appropriateness in these languages?* This means that we focus on the three base variables: language attitudes (henceforth referred to as "attitudes"), sociopragmatic awareness (henceforth, "awareness"), and intensity of digital media contact (henceforth, "contact") in isolation. For each variable, an overall analysis was conducted and, subsequently, the sample was stratified according to academic year and analysed again. This will provide the necessary foundational information regarding the variables involved in this study for us to better interpret the relationships between them.

Results indicate that our participants have relatively low overall levels of contact (M = 0.25, SD = 0.095) in terms of the 14 popular media options offered to them in our instrument. Instead, they tend to gravitate towards specific platforms, such as Instagram, Whatsapp, Tik Tok, YouTube, and other streaming platforms. In contrast, our sample has fairly positive attitudes towards the three main languages they are in regular contact with (M = 0.56, SD = 0.126) but they are somewhat less explicitly aware of the sociopragmatic norms that govern the formulation of requests in these languages (M = 0.36, SD = 0.070). Breaking these results down further, we explore the possible differences over the three academic years in question; 2nd, 3rd, and 4th of ESO. As we can see from the results (Figure 11.1), there is relative consistency over the academic years. Respectively, contact (2 ESO, M = 0.21; 3 ESO, M = 0.26; 4 ESO, M = 0.26), attitudes (2 ESO, M = 0.56; 3 ESO, M = 0.55; 4 ESO, M = 0.57), and awareness (2 ESO, M = 0.35; 3 ESO, M = 0.38; 4 ESO, M = 0.35). Nevertheless, we observe that there is a slight overall increase in contact, a slight decrease in attitudes around age 14–15 (in line with Baker, 1992; Nightingale, 2016), and a slight increase in awareness around the same age.

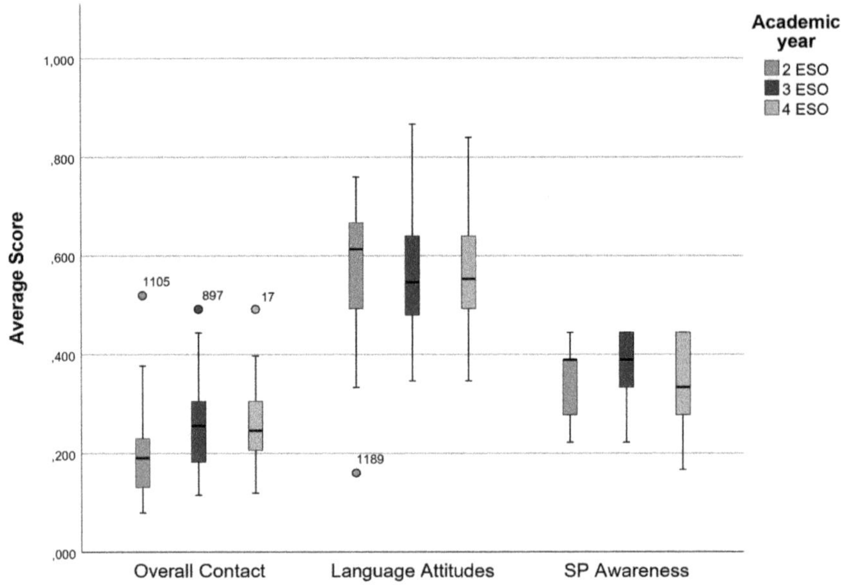

Figure 11.1: Base variables by academic year.

Moving on to explore the contact variable in more detail, results show that contact in Spanish (*M* = 0.43, *SD* = 0.134) is what accounts for most of the mean score reported above. In contrast, contact in English (*M* = 0.21, *SD* = 0.171) is lower, and contact in Catalan (*M* = 0.10, *SD* = 0.098) returned the lowest score. We do not find these results surprising given the dominance of Spanish over Catalan in the region in which the study took place, and the resulting, ongoing struggle for recognition and prestige faced by Catalan. The results are also in line with Safont (2007) who found a very low preference for the consumption of traditional media (TV, Radio, Press, and Music) in Catalan. The relatively low use of English, in spite of its global dominance online, was more surprising though, and can possibly be attributed to the participants' self-perceived, low competence in this language, as well as the general lack of contact with it in 'real life' situations outside the classroom. Again, on breaking these results down further to explore age differences, we can see (Figure 11.2) that there is relative growth over the academic years. Contact in Spanish appears to grow, slightly but consistently, over the years (2 ESO, $M = 0.40$; 3 ESO, $M = 0.41$; 4 ESO, $M = 0.45$). There is also slight growth in contact in Catalan (2 ESO, $M = 0.07$; 3 ESO, $M = 0.09$; 4 ESO, $M = 0.13$). Growth in contact in English shows a different tendency, which appears to spike in 3 ESO (2 ESO, $M = 0.15$; 3 ESO, $M = 0.27$; 4 ESO, $M = 0.20$). We consider these results encouraging as they show increased use of non-English language digital media, indicating that our participants become more amenable to using digital media in languages other than the 'dominant' language of the Internet (Crystal, 2010) as they get older.

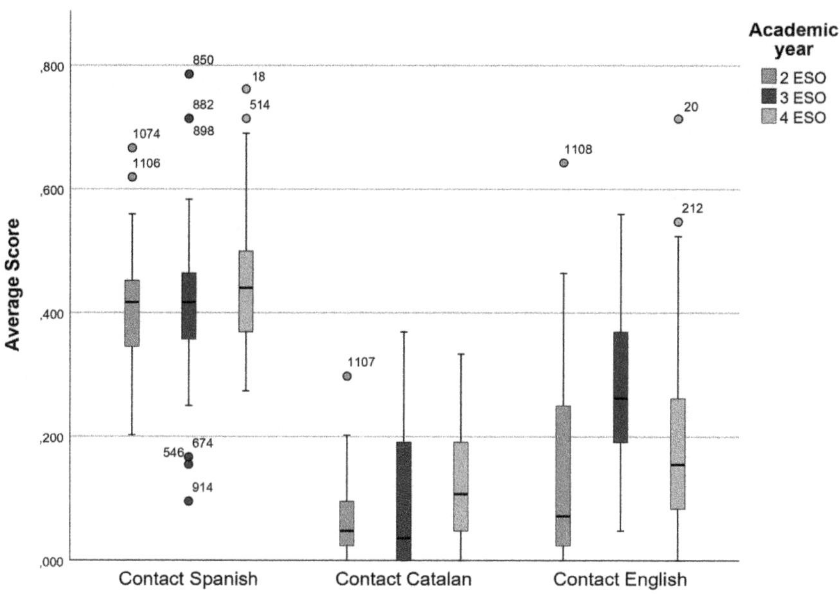

Figure 11.2: Contact intensity per language by academic year.

We now focus more attention on attitudes. Results relating to individual languages show the most positive attitudes from our participants are towards English ($M = 0.69$, $SD = 0.200$), followed closely by Spanish ($M = 0.62$, $SD = 0.172$), while attitudes towards Catalan are notably less positive ($M = 0.37$, $SD = 0.214$). This is similar to Safont (2007), in which Catalan returned the least favourable attitudinal results in university students. However, in contrast to Safont's results, the secondary school students in our sample slightly favour English over Spanish. The results are also contrary to Nightingale's (2012) study on adolescents, in which Catalan was the language that participants were most favourable towards. We propose that this points towards the instability of attitudes towards this minority language and the need to search for stabilising measures. Exploring possible age differences in these results, we find (Figure 11.3) that attitudes towards Spanish show a decline between 2 ESO and 4 ESO ($M = 0.69$ to $M = 0.61$, respectively), while attitudes stay stable for Catalan (no change at $M = 0.40$) and grow for English ($M = 0.60$ to $M = 0.69$, respectively). What stands out here is that 3 ESO shows a quite different pattern. This age range is the least positive towards both Spanish ($M = 0.57$) and especially Catalan ($M = 0.30$), but is the most positive of all towards English ($M = 0.77$). Here again we see parallels with the 'attitudinal dip' (Baker, 1992), which may be related to the intensity of peer pressure during the period of adolescence (Walqui, 2000), especially the desire to be seen to associate with a prestigious and fashionable language such as English (Nightingale, 2016; Nightingale & Safont, 2019).

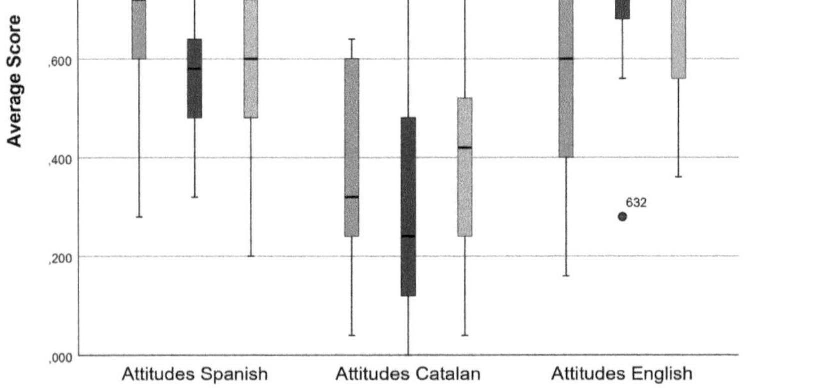

Figure 11.3: Language attitudes per language by academic year.

Now, we will explore attitudes by theme. The participants show the most favourable attitudes towards languages in education ($M = 0.61$, $SD = 0.173$), followed by their engagement with languages ($M = 0.59$, $SD = 0.201$), the instrumental value of their languages ($M = 0.57$, $SD = 0.161$), and the intercultural value of their languages ($M = 0.53$, $SD = 0.152$). The least favourable attitudes are towards languages on the Internet ($M = 0.49$, $SD = 0.137$). Exploring the age differences in these results (Figure 11.4), we can see a slight dip at 3 ESO for education ($M = 0.62$, $M = 0.57$, $M = 0.64$, respectively) and intercultural ($M = 0.59$, $M = 0.51$, $M = 0.52$, respectively), a slight increase and then plateau in Internet ($M = 0.48$, $M = 0.50$, $M = 0.50$, respectively), a slight increase in engagement ($M = 0.55$, $M = 0.59$, $M = 0.60$, respectively), and a decline in instrumental ($M = 0.58$, $M = 0.57$, $M = 0.56$, respectively).

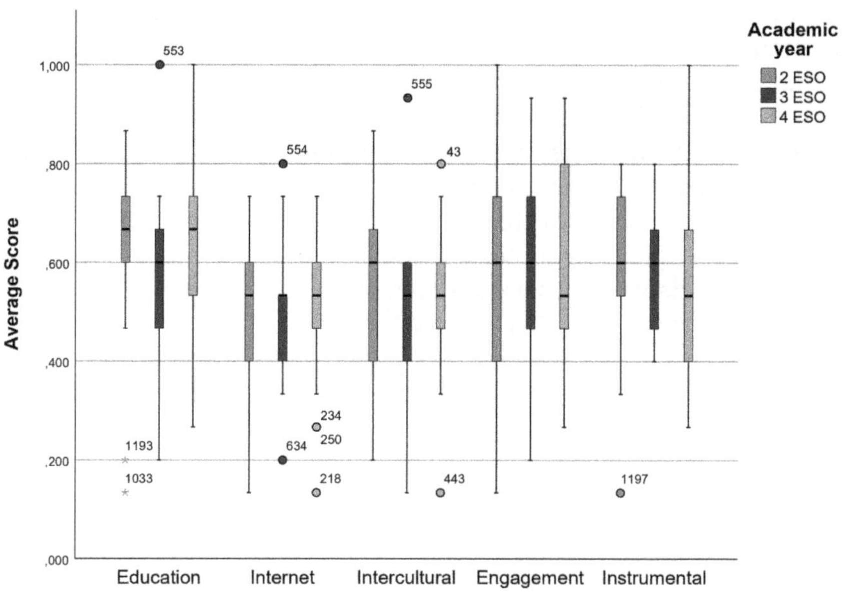

Figure 11.4: Language attitudes per theme by academic year.

To cover the last variable of the current study, we now look at awareness. This was measured via a rating of the appropriateness of the requests in each language, considering the contextual information that placed each request in a specific politeness context (Brown & Levinson, 1987; Ishihara & Cohen, 2010). As reported above, the global rating for awareness among our participants appeared to be quite low ($M = 0.36$, $SD = 0.070$). However, when we look at the differences between politeness orientations it is clear that they are more aware in the positive politeness orientation (Spanish and Catalan) ($M = 0.45$, $SD = 0.110$) than they are in the negative politeness orientation (English) ($M = 0.27$, $SD = 0.097$). It would appear that our participants are unable to transfer their innate understanding of sociopragmatic constraints to a language with the opposite politeness orientation. This is not a surprising result given the almost total lack of pragmatic instruction in secondary-school level language learning (Alcón-Soler, 2005; Alcón-Soler & Martínez-Flor, 2008), in which there is usually a focus on grammar, vocabulary and syntax rather than communicative competence or cross-cultural communication. This deficit of focus on pragmatic awareness means that the participants can only rely on intuition from their lived experiences as language users. Of course, in our context, they are unlikely to have had much lived experience in the foreign, and opposite politeness oriented, language. Regarding possible age differences (Figure 11.5), our results are not conclusive. We find very little difference across the age range for the positive politeness orientation (2 ESO, $M = 0.44$; 3 ESO, $M = 0.46$; 4 ESO, $M = 0.46$), while the negative politeness orientation increases somewhat for 3rd of ESO (2 ESO, $M = 0.25$; 3 ESO, $M = 0.31$; 4 ESO, $M = 0.25$) before returning to the same level.

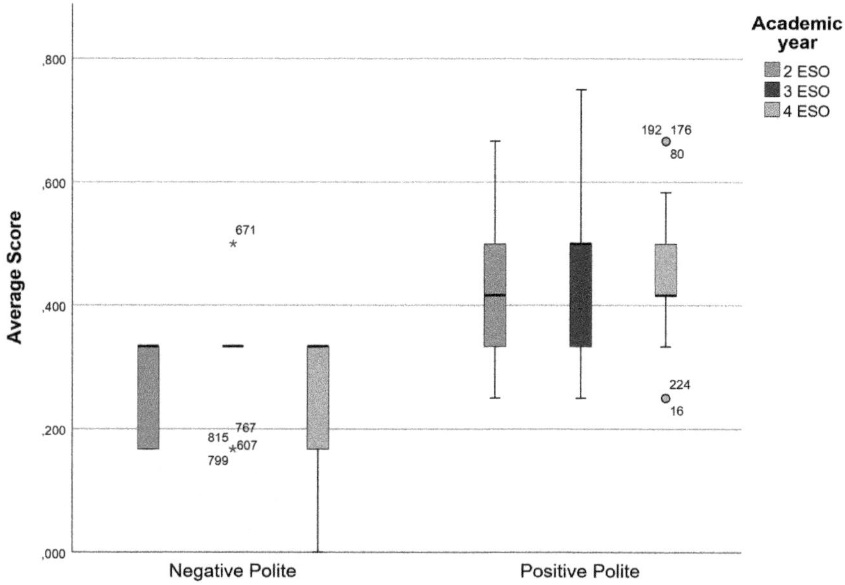

Figure 11.5: Sociopragmatic awareness per politeness orientation by academic year.

In sum, the data we have collected and explored in order to respond to Research Question 1 gives us an overall panorama of our sample in relation to the main variables of this study that shows parallels to existing research; specifically, that they are mainly drawn towards using digital media in the dominant language of their context, they show the least positive attitudes towards the minority language of their context, they are most positive towards languages in education, and they show little capacity to transfer knowledge of request appropriateness between opposing politeness orientations. We will now take this understanding of our participants as the foundation from which to explore possible relationships between these variables.

Results and Discussion Related to Research Question 2

In order to respond to RQ2, *What relationships exist between digital media contact, language attitudes, and sociopragmatic awareness in our sample?*, Spearman's tests were conducted (due to the non-normal distribution of some variables). As above, an overall analysis was conducted first, then the sample was stratified according to academic year and analysed again. In the results that follow, not all reported coefficients are statistically significant. Those that are will be indicated by asterisks, in the standard way: * $p =< 0.05$, ** $p =< 0.01$, *** $p =< 0.001$.

On exploring the resulting correlations between variables for the whole sample, we find a weak positive correlation between contact and attitudes ($\rho = 0.237$ *). However, if we break this result down into attitudes towards the languages individually, we find that overall contact most strongly correlates with attitudes towards English ($\rho = 0.369$ ***). Exploring this further by separating the contact variable into its component languages, we find what has already been established in other research (Nightingale, 2016; Nightingale & Zaharcenco, forthcoming), namely a strong and significant positive relationship between contact and attitudes towards minority and foreign languages; respectively, Catalan ($\rho = 0.621$ ***), and English ($\rho = 0.562$ ***). Analysing the attitudinal themes, we see a relationship between overall contact and the engagement attitudinal measure ($\rho = 0.369$ ***). We can attribute this result in large part to contact in Catalan and English, which both returned the exact same correlations. Moreover, contact in Catalan returned significant, albeit weaker, positive correlations for all the other attitude themes; Education ($\rho = 0.375$ ***), Internet ($\rho = 0.317$ **), Intercultural ($\rho = 0.268$ *), and Instrumental ($\rho = 0.226$ *). We find these results encouraging for the minority language as they indicate that participants who use Catalan-language digital media with greater intensity may be more positively engaged with this language; that is, they feel like they can use the language effectively, they can reflect on their language use, and they show volition in continuing to learn and improve their skills. This is a reassuring discovery for Catalan given the important roles of both attitudes and digital representation in the survival and growth of minority languages (Baker, 1992; Crystal, 2010; Fishman, 1991; Ó Riagáin, 2008).

With regards to awareness, contact in Catalan returns a weak, but positive, correlation with the positive politeness orientation (ρ = 0.235 *), and contact in English shows a stronger positive correlation with the negative politeness orientation (ρ = 0.359 ***). Again, this is very encouraging given the low levels of awareness in this orientation that were observed in the descriptive data (*M* = 0.27, *SD* = 0.097). We see this as an important result that potentially reflects earlier research on digital media as a sociointeractional space that affords a sense of audience awareness (Reinhardt, 2019, 2020), and thus builds awareness of sociopragmatically encoded texts (Knobel & Lankshear, 2008) and culturally-bound pragmatic conventions (Thorne, 2003). Regarding the attitudinal themes we see that the education measure positively correlates with both positive (ρ = 0.297 **) and negative (ρ = 0.328 **) politeness orientations. Moreover, the engagement measure also positively correlates with the negative (ρ = 0.232 *) politeness orientation, albeit to a lesser extent. Interestingly, in contrast to previous research (Kiyançiçek, 2023; LoCastro, 2001; Takahashi, 2005), it is not intercultural attitudes that best correlate with awareness, but rather how the participants feel about languages in education.

Now we will explore possible differences across the age range, stratifying the sample by academic year. The participants from 2nd of ESO show a strong positive correlation between contact and attitudes regarding English (ρ = 0.599 **), this is not the case for the other languages. Contact also correlates positively, albeit weakly, with all the attitudinal themes; the strongest being intercultural (ρ = 0.402) and engagement (ρ = 0.520 *). However, contact in English has only a negligible correlation with awareness in the negative politeness orientation. What does show a relationship in this regard is attitudes towards English (ρ = 0.332) and particularly attitudes towards languages in education (ρ = 0.560 **). We can see here that although there is a relationship between contact and attitudes, as well as a relationship between attitudes and awareness, there is no corresponding relationship between contact and awareness. As far as the other languages are concerned, there is no discernible relationship between contact in Spanish and attitudes towards that language, attitudes towards Spanish actually correlates negatively to positive politeness awareness (ρ = -.452 *), and the relationship between contact and awareness is weak (ρ = -.237). Regarding Catalan, we see a somewhat stronger relationship between contact and attitudes (ρ = 0.327) but, once again, a negative relationship between attitudes and awareness (ρ = -.351), and, for this language, also between awareness and contact (ρ = -.151), albeit quite weak. For these participants, the dominant/favoured position of English is clear. Of particular interest, given the very low scores for awareness in the descriptive results, is the apparent influence of contact on attitudes alongside the apparent influence of attitudes on awareness.

In general, the participants from 3rd of ESO seem to have weaker correlations for most measures. Nevertheless, these participants have the strongest correlation of all between contact and attitudes regarding Catalan (ρ = 0.757 ***). This appears to be mainly due to the education (ρ = 0.561 **) and engagement (ρ = 0.640 ***) attitudinal themes. Contact in Catalan also shows a strong positive correlation with awareness in the positive politeness orientation (ρ = 0.632 ***) for this section of our sample. This is also the case for attitudes towards Catalan (ρ = 0.543 **). In this sense, we observe a three-way reciprocal relationship for Catalan, in which contact, attitudes, and awareness in the positive politeness orientation all share strong significant correlations. With regards to English, we can see a similar pattern, albeit not as strongly correlated: contact with attitudes (ρ = 0.392 *), attitudes with awareness (ρ = 0.439 *), and awareness with contact (ρ = 0.287). For these participants, Catalan holds the dominant position, even though the descriptive results show low levels of contact and attitudes. In this sense, these results indicate that exposure to digital media may radically improve attitudes towards minority languages (Nightingale, 2016; Nightingale & Zaharcenco, forthcoming), and now we can suggest that pragmatic awareness may also be enhanced.

Lastly, the participants from 4th of ESO show a clearer pattern of positive relationships between contact and attitudes: Spanish (ρ = 0.287), Catalan (ρ = 0.699 ***), and English (ρ = 0.350 *), again here, Catalan holds the dominant position. Regarding attitude themes, contact in Catalan correlates with education (ρ = 0.341 *), Internet (ρ = 0.393 *), and instrumental (ρ = 0.421 *) themes, while contact in English correlates with the engagement (ρ = 0.338) theme. Attitudes towards Catalan correlates with awareness in the positive politeness orientation

(ρ = 0.377 *), and attitudes towards English correlates, albeit weakly, with awareness in the negative politeness orientation (ρ = 0.272). The contact variables return negligible correlations with awareness and, in fact, contact in Spanish returns a negative correlation (ρ = -.316) with the positive politeness orientation. Thus, similar to 2 ESO, we do not observe a three-way reciprocal relationship between the variables. Nevertheless, we can observe some reciprocity when we look at the attitudinal themes. On the one hand, engagement correlates with the negative politeness orientation (ρ = -.390 *), which itself correlates with contact in English. On the other hand, education and internet both correlate with the positive politeness orientation (ρ = -.350 * and ρ = -.382 *, respectively), which correlate with contact in Catalan. Although we do not see linear development over the three academic years, we see that Catalan is more represented as we move from 2 ESO to 3 ESO, and that this is maintained to a reasonable degree in 4 ESO.

Conclusion

The current study has explored, on the one hand, digital media contact, language attitudes, and sociopragmatic awareness in multilingual adolescents, and, on the other hand, the relationship between these variables. The descriptive results indicate that the young learners in our context mainly use digital media in the dominant language (Spanish), show the least positive attitudes towards the minority language (Catalan), and show little capacity to transfer their existing sociopragmatic knowledge to the foreign language (English). The results from the correlation analysis, in line with existing research, indicate strong relationships between digital media use and language attitudes for minority and foreign languages. Moreover, positive correlations between digital media contact and attitudes in these languages were found in relation to sociopragmatic awareness in the two politeness orientations. Additionally, the correlations by academic year show the strongest reciprocity between variables at 3 ESO for the minority language.

Of course, the current study is subject to a number of limitations and, as such, the conclusions drawn must be treated with caution. First, as the analysis for this study hinges on purely quantitative data, a follow up that includes in-depth interviews would be necessary to provide richer explanations that may help us to understand the mechanisms behind the relationships we have observed. Then, as we noticed that the participants tend to gravitate towards specific platforms, such as Instagram, Whatsapp, Tik Tok, YouTube, and other streaming platforms, a follow up study that targets these specific platforms would be beneficial. Lastly, we are aware that correlation is not the same as causality, and more robust analysis would be needed to certify if these variables can actually be considered mutual predictors or not. Notwithstanding, we believe that this exploratory study shines some light on the possible mutual influence between language attitudes, digital media contact and sociopragmatic awareness that we have been unable to find in the existing literature. We hope that our humble contribution to this research gap may inspire continuing work in this area.

Acknowledgements

As a member of the LAELA (Lingüística Aplicada a l'Ensenyament de la Llengua Anglesa) research group at Universitat Jaume I (Castellón, Spain), I would like to acknowledge that this study is part of the research project PID2020-117959GB-I00 funded by MCIN/AEI/10.13039/501100011033. Additional funding has been granted by Projectes d'Innovació Educativa de la Unitat de Formació i Innovació Educativa 51020/24.

References

Alcón-Soler, Eva. 2008. *Learning how to request in an instructed language learning context*. Bern: Peter Lang.

Alcón-Soler, Eva. 2012. Teachability and bilingualism effects on third language learners' pragmatic knowledge. *Intercultural Pragmàtics,* 9/4, 511–541.

Alcón-Soler, Eva. 2013. Mitigating email requests in teenagers' first and second language academic cyber-consultation. *Multilingua*, 32/6, 779–799.

Alcón-Soler, Eva, Safont, Pilar & Martínez-Flor, Alicia. 2005. Towards a typology of modifiers for the speech act of requesting: A socio-pragmatic approach. RÆL: *Revista Electrónica de Lingüística Aplicada*, 4, 1–35.

Alcón-Soler, Eva & Safont, Pilar. 2008. Pragmatic awareness in second language acquisition. In Jasone Cenoz & Nancy Hornberger (eds), *Encyclopedia of language and education.* 2nd Edition, Volume 6: Knowledge about Language. New York: Springer, 193–204.

Baker, Colin. 1991. *Foundations of bilingual education and bilingualism*. Bristol: Multilingual Matters.

Baker, Colin. 1992. *Attitudes and language*. Bristol: Multilingual matters.

Bax, Stephen. 2011. Normalisation revisited: The effective use of technology in language Education. *International Journal of Computer Assisted Language Learning and Teaching*, 1/2, 1–15.

Billore, Soniya & Rosén, Christina. 2017. A cross-cultural study of attitudes to digital tools among students and teachers in the European language classroom. *Extended Papers of the International Symposium on Digital Humanities*. Växjö, Sweden, November, 7–8, 2016: 10–28.

Blattner, Geraldine & Fiori, Melissa. 2011. Virtual social network communities: An investigation of language learners' development of sociopragmatic awareness and multiliteracy skills. *CALICO. The Journal*, 29/1, 24–43. <https://doi.org/10.11139/cj.29.1.24-43>.

Bourdieu, Pierre. 1992. *Language and symbolic power*. Oxford: Polity Press.

Brown, Penelope & Levinson, Stephen. 1987. *Politeness: Some universals in language usage*. Cambridge: Cambridge University Press.

Butler-Pascoe, Mary. 2011. The history of CALL: The intertwining paths of technology and second/foreign language teaching. *International Journal of Computer-Assisted Language Learning and Teaching*, 1/1, 16–32.

Celce-Murcia, Marianne & Olshtain, Elite. 2000. *Discourse and context in language teaching: A guide for language teachers*. Cambridge: Cambridge University Press.

Cenoz, Jasone. 2009. *Towards multilingual education: Basque educational research from an international perspective*. Bristol: Multilingual Matters.

Crystal, David. 2010. *Language death*. Cambridge: Cambridge University Press.

Davis, John. 2007. Resistance to L2 pragmatics in the Australian ESL context. *Language Learning*, 57, 611–649. <https://doi.org/10.1111/j.1467-9922.2007.00430.x>.

Dewaele, Jean-Marc. 2005. Sociodemographic, psychological and politicocultural correlates in Flemish students' attitudes towards French and English. *Journal of Multilingual and Multicultural Development*, 26/2, 118–137.

Dragojevic, Marco, Fasoli, Fabio, Cramer, Jennifer & Rakić, Tamara. 2021. Toward a century of language attitudes research: Looking back and moving forward. *Journal of Language and Social Psychology*, 40/1, 60–79.

Eisenlohr, Patrick. 2004. Language revitalization and new technologies: Cultures and electronic mediation and the refiguring of communities. *Annual Review of Anthropology*, 18/3, 339–361.

Fishman, Joshua. 1991. *Reversing language shift*. Clevendon: Multilingual Matters.

Gardner, Robert. 1985. *Social psychology and second language learning: The role of attitudes and motivation*. London: Edward Arnold.

Garrett, Peter. 2010. *Attitudes to language*. Cambridge: Cambridge University Press.

González-Lloret, Marta. 2021. L2 pragmatics and CALL. *Language Learning & Technology*. 25/3, 90–105. <http://hdl.handle.net/10125/73451>.

Guzmán-Alcón, Irene & Portolés, Laura. 2021. Les actituds lingüístiques del professorat en actiu del sistema educatiu valencià: l'efecte del model lingüístic i de la L1. *Caplletra. Revista Internacional De Filologia*, 71, 121–146. <https://doi.org/10.7203/caplletra.71.21034>.

Harrison, Richard & Thomas, Michael. 2009. Identity in online communities: Social networking sites and language learning. *International Journal of Emerging Technologies and Society*, 7/2, 109–124.

Hasan, Atyaf & Idrees, Fatima. 2020. A socio-pragmatic analysis of social media comments on online learning at the time of COVID-19. *ELS Journal on Interdisciplinary Studies in Humanities*, 3/4, 638–650. <https://doi.org/10.34050/elsjish.v3i4.11525>.

Henry, Alastair. 2013. Digital games and ELT: Bridging the authenticity gap. In Ema Ushioda (ed.) *International perspectives on English language teaching: Motivation*. London: Palgrave McMillan, 133–155.

Herring, Susan, Stein, Deiter & Virtanen, Tuija. 2013. *Pragmatics of computer-mediated communication*. Berlin, Boston: De Gruyter Mouton. <https://doi.org/10.1515/9783110214468>.

Ishihara, Noriko & Cohen, Andrew. 2010. *Teaching and learning pragmatics: Where language and culture meet*. New York/ London: Routledge. https://doi.org/10.4324/9781315833842

Kasper, Gabriele & Schmidt, Richard. 1996. Developmental issues in interlanguage pragmatics. *Studies in Second Language Acquisition*, 18, 149–169. <https://doi.org/10.1017/S0272263100014868>.

Kiyançiçek, Ezgi. 2023. *The relationship between motivation and pragmatic awareness: A case study of Turkish EFL learners*. Bursa: Bursa Uludağ University.

Knobel, Michele & Lankshear, Colin. 2008. Digital literacy and participation in online social networking spaces. In Colin Lankshear & Michele Knobel (eds), *Digital literacies: Concepts, policies and practices*. Bern: Peter Lang, 249–278.

Lantz-Andersson, Annika. 2018. Language plays in a second language: Social media as contexts for emerging Sociopragmatic competence. *Education and Information Technologies*, 23/2, 705–724. <https://doi.org/10.1007/s10639-017-9631-0>.

Lasagabaster, David. 2001. University students' attitudes towards English as an L3. In Cenoz Jasone, Britta Hufeisen & Ulrike Jessner (eds) *Looking beyond second language acquisition: Studies in tri- and multilingualism*. Tübingen: Stauffenburg Verlag, 43–50.

Lasagabaster, David. 2004. Erratum: Attitudes towards English in the basque autonomous community. *World Englishes*, 23/1, 211–224.

Lasagabaster, David & Huguet, Ángel. 2007. *Multilingualism in European bilingual contexts: Language use and attitudes*. Bristol, Blue Ridge Summit: Multilingual Matters.

Lasagabaster, David & Safont, Pilar. 2008. Un análisis de las actitudes lingüísticas en dos comunidades bilingües. In Carmen Bretones (ed.) *Applied linguistics now: Understanding language and mind. Proceedings of the XXVI AESLA Conference*, Almeria: Universidad de Almería.

Leech, Geoffrey. 1983. *Principles of pragmatics*. London/ New York: Longman.

LoCastro, Virginia. 2001. Individual differences in second language acquisition: Attitudes, learner subjectivity, and L2 pragmatic norms. *System*, 29/1, 69–89. <https://doi.org/10.1016/S0346-251X(00)00046-4>.

Martínez-Flor, Alicia & Usó-Juan, Ester & Alcón, Eva. 2006. Towards acquiring communicative competence through speaking. In Ester Usó-Juan & Alicia Martínez-Flor (eds) *Current trends in the development and teaching of the four language skills*. Berlin, Boston: De Gruyter, 139–158. <https://doi.org/10.1515/9783110197778.3.139>.

Masgoret, Anne-Marie & Gardner, Robert. 2003. Attitudes, motivation, and second language learning: A meta–analysis of studies conducted by gardner and associates. *Language Learning*, 53: 123–163. <https://doi.org/10.1111/1467-9922.00212>.

Mirzaei, Azizullah, Hashemian, Mahmood & Khoramshekouh, Amin. 2016. L2 learners' enhanced pragmatic comprehension of implicatures via computer-mediated communication and social media networks. *Iranian Journal of Applied Linguistics*, 19/1, 141–179.

Mitchell, Kathleen. 2012. A social tool: Why and how ESOL students use facebook. *CALICO Journal*, 29/3, 471–493. <https://doi.org/10.11139/cj.29.3.471-493>.

Nightingale, Richard. 2012. *Bridging the gap between the internal and the external: The effect of sociocultural factors in adolescent learners' attitudes towards English*. Lambert Academic Publishing.

Nightingale, Richard. 2016. *The effect of out-of-school media contact on language attitudes in multilingual adolescents: a complex psycho-sociolinguistic system*. Castelló de la Plana: Universitat Jaume I.

Nightingale, Richard & Safont, Pilar. 2019. Pragmatic translanguaging: Multilingual practice in adolescent online discourse. In Victòria Codina & Patricia Salazar (eds) *Investigating the learning of pragmatics across ages and contexts*. Leiden: Brill, 167–195.

Nightingale, Richard & Zaharcenco, Daniela. Forthcoming. A comparative study of language attitudes and digital media use in two diverse multilingual contexts: Implications for minority languages.

Ó Riagáin, Pádriag. 2008. Language attitudes and minority languages. In Hornberger Nancy (ed.) *Encyclopedia of language and education*. Amsterdam: Springer. https://doi.org/10.1007/978-0-387-30424-3_159

Pavlenko, Aneta & Blackledge, Adrian. 2004. *Negotiation of Identities in Multilingual Settings*. Multilingual Matters.

Peterson, Mark. 2010. Massively multiplayer online role-playing games as arenas for second Language learning. *Computer Assisted Language Learning*, 23/5, 429–439. <https://doi.org/10.1080/09588221.2010.520673>.

Portolés, Laura. 2015. *Multilingualism and very young learners*. Basel: De Gruyter. <https://doi.org/10.1515/9781501500022>.

Portolés, Laura & Martí, Otilia. 2020. Teachers' beliefs about multilingual pedagogies and the role of initial training. *International Journal of Multilingualism*, 17/2, 248–264.

Qadha, Adil, Al-Wasy, Baleigh & Mahdi, Hassan. 2021. Using social networking tools for teaching requests to undergraduate Arab EFL learners: A study of pragmatics. *Learning and Teaching in Higher Education: Gulf Perspectives*, 17/2, 95–106. <https://doi.org/10.1108/LTHE-09-2020-0041>.

Rafieyan, Vahid, Behnammohammadian, Nazanin & Orang, Maryam. 2015. Relationship between acculturation attitude and pragmatic comprehension. *Journal of Language Teaching and Research*, 6/3, 504–512. <http://dx.doi.org/10.17507/jltr.0603.05>.

Reinhardt, Jonathon. 2019. Social media in second and foreign language teaching and learning: Blogs, wikis, and social networking. *Language Teaching*, 52/1, 1–39.

Reinhardt, Jonathon. 2020. Metaphors for social media-enhanced foreign language teaching and learning. *Foreign Language Annals*, 53, 234–242.

Reinhardt, Jonathon & Ryu, Jieun. 2013. Using social network-mediated bridging activities to develop socio-pragmatic awareness in elementary Korean. *International Journal of Computer-Assisted Language Learning and Teaching*, 3/3, 18–33. <https://doi.org/10.4018/ijcallt.2013070102>.

Rosén, Christina & Billore, Soniya. 2020. Consumption of digital education—A cross-cultural study of students' attitudes towards digital tools for language learning. *Huma Netten*, 45, 256–290. <https://doi.org/10.15626/hn.20204511>.

Safont, Pilar & Alcón-Soler, Eva. 2012. Teachability of request act peripheral modification devices in third language learning contexts. In Maria Economidou-Kogetsidis & Helen Woodfield (eds) *Interlanguage request modification*. Amsterdam: John Benjamins Publishing, 275–314.

Safont, Pilar. 2005. *Third language learners. Pragmatic production and awareness*. Clevedon: Multilingual Matters.

Safont, Pilar. 2007. Language use and language attitudes in the Valencian community. In David Lasagabaster & Ángel Huguet (eds) *Multilingualism in European bilingual contexts: Language use and attitudes*. Bristol, Blue Ridge Summit: Multilingual Matters, 90–114.

Safont, Pilar. 2012. Pragmatic competence in multilingual contexts. In Carol Chapelle (ed.) *The Encyclopedia of Applied Linguistics*. Oxford: John Wiley and Sons. <https://doi.org/10.1002/9781405198431.wbeal0927>.

Safont, Pilar. 2013. Early stages of trilingual pragmatic development. A longitudinal study of requests in Catalan, Spanish and English. *Journal of Pragmatics*, 59, 68–80.

Safont, Pilar. 2022. 'In English!' teachers' requests as reactions to learners' translanguaging discourse. *Language, Culture and Curriculum*, 35/3, 317–333.

Safont, Pilar. 2024a. Multilingual cyberpragmatics in instructional settings. Exploring gender and age effects in Catalan, Spanish and English email requests. *International Journal of Multilingualism*, 3, 1494–1516.

Safont, Pilar. 2024b. Young multilingual pragmatics. A focus on requests in CLIL and non-CLIL settings. In Danuta Gabryś Barker & Eva Vetter (eds) *Modern approaches to researching on multilingualism. Studies in honour of Larissa Aronin*. Cham: Springer, 191–119.

Sánchez-Hernández, Ariadna. 2023. Language attitude effects on L2 pragmatics. In Alicia Martínez-Flor, Ariadna Sánchez-Hernández & Júlia Barón (eds) *L2 pragmatics in action: Teachers, learners and the teaching-learning interaction process*. Amsterdam: John Benjamins, 215–239. <https://doi.org/10.1075/lllt.58.09sen>.

Satomi, Takahashi. 2005. Pragmalinguistic awareness: Is it related to motivation and proficiency? *Applied Linguistics*, 26/1, 90–120. <https://doi.org/10.1093/applin/amh040>.

Soria, Claudia. 2016. What is digital language diversity and why should we care? *Linguapax Review*, 4, 13–28.

Taguchi, Naoko. 2012. *Context, individual differences and pragmatic competence*. Bristol: Multilingual Matters. <https://doi.org/10.21832/9781847696106-002>.

Taguchi, Naoko. 2022. Second language pragmatics. A historical overview and future directions. In Nicola Halenko & Jiayi Wang (eds) *Pragmatics in English language learning*. Cambridge: Cambridge University Press, 7–28.

Thorne, Steven. 2003. Artifacts and cultures-of-use in intercultural communication. *Language Learning & Technology*, 7/2, 38–67.

Thorne, Steven. 2008. Transcultural communication in open Internet environments and massively multiplayer online games. In Sally Magnan (ed.) *Mediating discourse online*. Amsterdam: John Benjamins, 305–327.

Walqui, Aida. 2000. Contextual factors in second language acquisition. *ERIC Clearinghouse on Languages and Linguistics, Document ED444381,* 1–6.

Woolard, Kathryn. 1985. Language variation and cultural hegemony. *American Ethnologist*, 12, 738–748.

Gema Gayete and Laura Portolés

Multilingual Pragmatic Instruction in a Primary School Context: The Synergies Among Languages

Introduction

Previous literature has confirmed that pragmatics is teachable and should be taught inside the classroom (Derakhshan & Shakki, 2020; Taguchi, 2015). Research on pragmatic instruction of requests has focused on instructional effectiveness, such as comparing explicit and implicit approaches (Alcón-Soler, 2015; Martínez-Flor & Usó-Juan, 2020; Usó-Juan, 2021, 2022; Usó-Juan & Martínez-Flor, 2021). On the whole, most of the studies appear to confirm the effectiveness of explicit pragmatic learning over implicit learning. However, these instructional treatments have been conducted in secondary and higher education and followed a monolingual bias. A limited number of studies have explored the effect of explicit pragmatic instruction on primary students' pragmatic awareness of requests (Myrset, 2021, 2022). These studies have shown that being taught about pragmatic aspects of the languages enhanced young learners' pragmatic awareness. Hence, pragmatic instruction resulted to be beneficial from the early beginning of education.

From a multilingual viewpoint, only a few studies have examined the pragmatic awareness of requests in young children (Portolés, 2015; Portolés & Safont, 2018; Safont, 2018, 2024; Safont & Portolés, 2015, 2016). These studies have shown that students' multilingual repertoire positively influenced their pragmatic awareness in multiple languages. In addition, the benefits of multilingual instruction through translanguaging pedagogies on language awareness have also been confirmed. Translanguaging pedagogies refer to "the planning, application and extension of multilingual pedagogical strategies and practices based on the student's whole linguistic repertoire" (Cenoz & Gorter, 2021: 19). According to the authors, pedagogical translanguaging can be implemented at the morphosyntactic, lexical, phonetic, discourse and pragmatic levels (Carbonara, 2023; Cenoz et al., 2022; Cenoz & Santos, 2020; Leonet et al., 2020; Leonet & Saragueta, 2023). However, pragmatic awareness has not been considered in any of these prior investigations. Considering this lack of research on multilingual pragmatics, the present study aims to contribute to the field of research by exploring the influence of multilingual pragmatic instruction based on pedagogical translanguaging on primary students' pragmatic awareness of Catalan, Spanish and English requests, as well as to investigate the pragmatic synergies among the three languages.

Theoretical Background

Pragmatic Awareness and Instruction

Pragmatics focuses on how speakers interpret and express meaning in social interactions and requires understanding of the social rules of language (Usó-Juan & Martínez-Flor, 2021). As stated by McConachy (2022), pragmatic awareness refers to learners' ability to notice and understand pragmatic norms of appropriateness.

According to Brown and Levinson (1987), the notion of pragmatic awareness involves two main dimensions: pragmalinguistics and sociopragmatics. Whereas pragmalinguistics concerns the strategies used for performing speech intention as well as the linguistic elements to express these intentions (Takimoto, 2014), sociopragmatics refers to the social conditions that dictate language use to be socially appropriate (Leech, 1983). The politeness theory suggested by Brown and Levinson (1987) claims that three sociopragmatic variables (social distance, relative power and degree of imposition) influence speakers' language choices. Social distance principles explain that a language user does not employ the same language forms with a friend or relative than with an unknown person. In relation to the relative power of the speakers, interlocutors do not normally talk to a doctor in the same way they talk to a friend. The degree of imposition also influences linguistic choices since a speaker does not address another speaker in the same way when asking for a sweet than when asking for a car.

This investigation sets requests as the principal pragmatic aspect examined. The most popular definition of request is provided by Trosborg, who defined requests as "an illocutionary act whereby a speaker (requester) conveys to a hearer (requestee) that he/she wants the requestee to perform an act which is for the benefit of the speaker" (1995: 187). In other words, a request is considered an attempt by the emissor to get the receptor to do something. Requests are normally employed in daily conversations, might include different desired things or services, can be performed between interlocutors who share the same status or not, are related to be a face-threatening act, and can be formulated in many different linguistic forms that can differ across cultures and languages (Schauer, 2009). For these reasons, requests are considered the most widely studied speech act, suggesting that request awareness and production should be taught in language classrooms.

As seen in previous research, explicit pragmatic teaching is necessary to develop students' pragmatic knowledge and awareness at all educational levels (Alcón-Soler & Martínez-Flor, 2008; Derakhshan & Shakki, 2020; Taguchi, 2015), especially in the context of primary education. Following this line of research, the study of Myrset (2021) explored the impact of explicit pragmatic teaching of requests on 51 primary students' pragmatic awareness of requests in English, considering both pragmalinguistic and sociopragmatic aspects of the language. Results of the study showed that pragmatic instruction had a positive effect on students' use of request strategies, their engagement with specific pragmatic concepts used for metapragmatic reflection, and their critical reflection upon their progress in pragmatic learning. These findings suggest that the social dimension of pragmatics should not be underestimated and left apart in pragmatic research. Furthermore, Myrset (2021) reported that pragmatic instruction should be encouraged in the language classroom since it was proved to be beneficial for the pragmatic awareness and production of young learners.

In a later study, Myrset (2022) analysed the effect of explicit pragmatic teaching of requests on 51 primary students' pragmatic awareness. The instructional treatment on pragmatics was based on both pragmalinguistic and sociopragmatic aspects of the language. Findings indicated that explicit pragmatic instruction improved young learners' use and variation of request strategies that included modal verbs and supportive moves. Indeed, after the pragmatic instruction, students acknowledged certain sociopragmatic aspects such as the familiarity and age of the speakers in their pragmalinguistic choices for the production of requests. This study showed that primary students' sociopragmatic and pragmalinguistic pragmatic awareness enhanced due to explicit pragmatic teaching. As in his prior study (Myrset, 2021), the author demonstrated that pragmatic instruction should be fostered in the language classroom since it was observed to be positive for the pragmatic awareness of the very young learners.

Bearing in mind the relevance and teachability of pragmatics, multilingual classrooms should encourage the teaching of pragmatic aspects of the languages of the school curriculum. This is essential to enhance students' knowledge and awareness of pragmatics in contexts where several languages coexist. Nevertheless, the adoption of a multilingual perspective in pragmatic instruction is practically non-existent, although previous research has demonstrated the synergies among students' pragmatic systems and the benefits of using cross-linguistic comparison in the classroom setting (Cenoz, 2007; Martín-Laguna, 2022; Nightingale & Safont, 2019). Thus, the study of pragmatics, and more specifically, pragmatic awareness, should adapt to a more multilingual paradigm by considering multilingual students' whole language repertoire (Portolés, 2015; Safont, 2023). Following this idea, the next section presents several studies that investigated students' pragmatic awareness of requests from a multilingual viewpoint.

Multilingual Pragmatic Awareness of Requests

Multilingual classrooms have gained prominence since 1990 with the promotion of minority languages and the early introduction of English. They represent rich contexts where multilingual students engage in social interactions that involve multiple languages and where learners' language repertoire could be used to enhance language learning. Nevertheless, the area of pragmatics has not received much attention when dealing with multilingual classrooms, especially at the primary education level, as claimed by Myrset and McConachy (2023). With that in mind, it is paramount to examine students' multilingual pragmatic awareness of how to use languages appropriately and effectively depending on the context.

From this multilingual perspective, some studies have analysed students' pragmatic awareness of requests in primary education (Portolés, 2015; Portolés & Safont, 2018; Safont, 2018, 2024; Safont & Portolés, 2015, 2016), in secondary education (Nightingale & Safont, 2019), and in higher education (Martinez-Buffa & Safont, 2022; Safont, 2005; Safont & Alcón-Soler, 2012). These studies have demonstrated that multilingual students' language repertoire and previous experience as language learners have positively affected their pragmatic awareness of requests.

Since the present study focuses on the context of primary education, we have paid particular attention to the studies on students' pragmatic awareness of requests conducted in this level of education. For instance, Portolés (2015) examined the pragmatic awareness of Catalan, Spanish and English requests of 402 primary students who shared English as their L3 in the primary school context of the Valencian Community, where the three languages are offered as language subjects and languages of instruction. The author employed an audio-visual pragmatic comprehension test that contained direct and conventionally indirect requests in the three languages. Results showed that students displayed a high degree of pragmatic awareness in the three languages, even in the L3 English, and signs of pragmatic differentiation. More specifically, students demonstrated a greater pragmatic awareness in Spanish than in Catalan and English. The author suggests that the sociolinguistic status of Spanish and the frequency of input may have contributed to the increased pragmatic awareness of the participants. Young learners also identified request modifiers in three languages, such as the particle please and several grounders. In addition, students considered requests including grounders as more appropriate than requests with the particle please for the three language systems.

Similarly, Safont and Portolés (2015) explored 45 school students' pragmatic awareness of Catalan, Spanish and English requests. Regardless of their low proficiency in L3 English, learners demonstrated a high degree of pragmatic awareness in the three languages. According to the authors, pragmatic awareness was not influenced by their individual proficiency in each language, but by their global multilingual proficiency. The use and interaction of the three languages promoted transfer phenomena, which benefited young students' pragmatic awareness.

In a further study, Safont and Portolés (2016) analysed the pragmatic formulas produced by 184 primary and infant students in both Catalan and Spanish-based programmes where English is the L3 of students. Data were gathered from natural classroom discourse. Findings demonstrated that students produced requests in the three languages (Catalan, Spanish and English) to accomplish several pragmatic functions including group identity, manipulation and separate identity functions. Differences among students' use of pragmatic functions varied depending on the language employed. In particular, the group identity function was exclusively conveyed in English, whereas the other two functions (manipulation and separate identity) were mainly performed in Catalan and Spanish, as well as in English but to a lower extent. The authors concluded that a more multilingual perspective was needed in the English classroom to obtain a complete view of young learners' pragmatic behaviour since not only English but also Catalan and Spanish were used in the English classroom.

Safont (2018) explored young learners' (n=268) and teachers' (n= 12) multilingual requestive behaviour in primary schools. The author examined requests forms and modification devices, classroom registers and requestive goals. Classroom observations were conducted in twelve English lessons, which were video-recorded and transcribed. The results showed that students and teachers employed more direct and unmodified request forms in English, Catalan and Spanish. However, in contrast to previous studies of requests in EFL classrooms, some requestive behaviours were modified and variability among pragmatic forms was observed. The author encouraged the need for a more multilingual approach in the study of pragmatics.

In a much recent study, Safont (2024) examined the amount of modified English, Catalan and Spanish requests produced in multilingual CLIL and non-CLIL classrooms. The scholar also aimed to analyse the pattern linking request forms, goals and registers in both settings. Data came from video and audio recordings of 10 school lessons in which 125 students and 5 teachers participated. Findings demonstrated that, considering the three languages in conjunction, the number of modification items in CLIL and non-CLIL settings was very similar. Nevertheless, English requests tended to be more frequently modified by means of downgrades in the CLIL classroom, in line with the politeness orientation of language. In terms of strategies, more direct strategies were used by CLIL students, whereas conventionally indirect requests were frequent among multilingual non-CLIL groups.

Also in the Valencian context of primary education, Portolés and Safont (2018) examined 127 multilingual school students' pragmatic awareness and production of requests through natural classroom discourse and pragmatic test completion. Results showed that young learners had a preference for direct request strategies in the three languages (Catalan, Spanish and English). Indirect requests were also produced in Catalan, Spanish and English, while a greater number of conventionally indirect requests with some modifiers were used in English. These findings suggest that the request forms produced were not always in line with the politeness orientation of each language. However, findings extracted from the pragmatic comprehension test reported that students displayed high levels of pragmatic awareness and were aware of the politeness orientation of each language. The scholars suggested that pragmatic skills may transfer among languages.

In sum, studies on multilingual young students' pragmatic awareness have demonstrated that learners' multilingual skills and abilities benefited their pragmatic awareness of requests. Pragmatic transfer phenomena was noticed among the languages of students' multilingual repertoire, as well as some specific particularities among the pragmatic awareness students conveyed towards each language system. The overall findings report that learners developed a unified pragmatic system for all their languages. Several variations in pragmatic awareness were also seen in the use of request strategies, modification devices and pragmatic functions in each language. From this multilingual standpoint, more research is required to investigate pragmatic synergies among the languages used by primary school students.

The Study

This investigation adopts a multilingual perspective towards the study of pragmatic awareness since it explores the influence of multilingual instruction, referring to pedagogical translanguaging, on young students' pragmatic awareness in Catalan, Spanish and English, as well as the pragmatic synergies among the three languages. However, previous literature in the field has shown that multilingual pragmatic awareness has not been paid much attention. As far as we are concerned, only some investigations carried out in elementary schools have followed a multilingual bias in the study of pragmatic awareness (Portolés, 2015; Portolés & Safont, 2018; Safont, 2018,2024; Safont & Portolés, 2015,2016).

Previous research has also demonstrated that multilingual instruction based on pedagogical translanguaging improved young learners' language awareness (Carbonara, 2023; Cenoz et al., 2022; Cenoz & Santos, 2020; Leonet et al., 2020; Leonet & Saragueta, 2023). Nevertheless, to our knowledge, there are no studies that have examined the influence of multilingual instruction on primary students' pragmatic awareness. Taking into account this lack of research, the current study aims at exploring the influence of translanguaging pedagogies in young students' pragmatic awareness of Catalan, Spanish and English requests, focusing on both sociopragmatic and pragmalinguistic aspects of the languages. By considering each of the languages independently and not as a whole language system, we pretend to investigate synergies and interactions among the three languages involved in the multilingual pragmatic instruction. This main purpose has set our guiding research question:

Does learning pragmatics multilingually influence primary school students' pragmatic awareness in Catalan, Spanish and English? Is there any difference in terms of pragmatic awareness among the three languages?

Considering this twofold research question, we have formulated the hypothesis that guides the present investigation which is based on prior literature in the field:
Hypothesis: Multilingual pragmatic instruction will enhance young students' pragmatic awareness in Catalan, Spanish and English. Differences in the improvement of pragmatic awareness will be noticed among the three languages (Portolés, 2015; Portolés & Safont, 2018; Safont & Portolés, 2015).

Method

This study is part of a larger project conducted by the Laela research group exploring pragmatic awareness from a multilingual perspective. The present investigation focuses on the study of students' pragmatic awareness in each of the three languages under research (Catalan, Spanish and English) to observe possible influences of multilingual instruction on each of the three languages, paying attention to both pragmalinguistics and sociopragmatics.

In the following sections, we will provide information on the participants, the instrument employed, the data collection procedure and the process of data analysis.

Participants

The sample was composed of 28 primary school students from the 6th year of primary education. Young learners' ages ranged from 11 to 12 years old and their gender distribution was balanced since 50 % (n= 14) of the participants were male and the remaining 50 % (n=14) were female. Regarding their L1(s), 50 % of the students (n=14) were native speakers of Spanish, 39.29 % (n=11) had Catalan as their L1, and the remaining 10.71 % (n=3) shared Arabic as their L1.

Data were collected from a public school located in La Vall d'Uixó, a small city from the province of Castelló, in the Valencian Community (Spain). The school followed a multilingual program (PEPLI) where three languages were used as language subjects and languages of instruction. More specifically, the program combined the use of Catalan, the minority language of the region, Spanish, the majority language, and English. With regard to young learners' weekly exposure to languages, 11.5 hours were devoted to subjects instructed in Catalan and 5.5 hours to subjects having Spanish as the vehicular language. In relation to English exposure, 2.25 hours were devoted to EFL classes and 1.5 hours were devoted to CLIL lessons (i.e. arts and crafts in English), being a total number of 3.75 hours of English exposure per week.

Instrument

To measure students' pragmatic awareness, we employed a multilingual pragmatic written test. The instrument was composed of two main sections. While the first part gathered background information about the participants, such as age, gender and L1(s); the second part was constituted of a written questionnaire displaying nine request situations framed into the school context that were complemented with pictures showing the requests and the individuals (e.g. students, teachers, classmates, etc.) who asked for particular materials, actions or information. Each of the three languages under research (Catalan, Spanish and English) included three different request scenarios.

This pragmatic test was focused on both the sociopragmatic and pragmalinguistic dimension of Catalan, Spanish and English requests. Regarding sociopragmatic aspects of the languages, students were asked to judge request (in)appropriateness by paying special attention to the social distance of the interlocutors, their power relation, and the degree of imposition. In relation to the pragmalinguistic dimension, students were required to produce appropriate requests, which involves the formulation of forms and strategies for requesting according to the social situation.

Data Collection Procedure

The process for data collection was divided into three core stages and had a duration of 5 different sessions of 1 hour each. As illustrated in Figure 12.1 below, the three stages included the (i) pre-test, (ii) multilingual instruction and (iii) post-test.

Figure 12.1: Stages of the pedagogical intervention.

During the first session, students completed the multilingual pretest on pragmatic awareness with the help of the researchers and the regular primary teacher, who agreed to collaborate during the three experimental stages. Once completed the pre-tests, young learners received 3 sessions of pedagogical translanguaging of 1 hour each, which accounted for a total of 3 hours of pedagogical treatment. After the 3 sessions on multilingual teaching, students were distributed the post-test on pragmatic awareness during the fifth and last session.

Regarding the multilingual pragmatic instruction, which followed pedagogical translanguaging as the core teaching approach, students were encouraged to take part in planned pragmatic activities in Catalan, Spanish and English that focused on the concept of request, request types, request (in)appropriateness, politeness, social distance, relative power and degree of imposition. Hence, students were allowed to make use of their language repertoire as a learning strategy to develop simultaneous pragmatic knowledge in the three languages. As proposed by Halenko (2018), we developed computer-animated scenarios with Nawmal software to encourage a better understanding of pragmatic aspects of the three languages and to promote a higher engagement of primary students in the multilingual pragmatic classroom.

The first session was devoted to the study of request types (i.e. direct, conventionally indirect and indirect requests) using computeranimated videos. Students also identified appropriate request strategies for specific communicative situations. During the second session, students learnt the sociopragmatic dimension of requests in a multilingual way, that means how context may affect the production and interpretation of requests in Catalan, Spanish and English. First, learners watched a multilingual video on the notions of appropriateness, politeness, social distance, relative power and degree of imposition. The video had the aim of allowing students to further detect pragmatically (in)appropriate use of requests from a sociopragmatic perspective. After the video, students identified the degree of appropriateness of several requests and reflected upon the social distance, relative power and degree of imposition of the interlocutors in the situations. Finally, in the third session, students were asked to produce requests after watching different request situations in each language.

Data Analysis

Students' pragmatic awareness of Catalan, Spanish and English requests was compared both before and after the multilingual treatment to answer our research question and verify the hypothesis. A coding scheme was suggested to designate the scores for each of the answers of the multilingual test on pragmatic awareness. Three different raters were involved in the data analysis, including the authors of the study and a qualified researcher in pragmatics.

Quantitative data were examined and codified using SPSS statistical software. To compare the data in the pre and post-test, several paired-samples t-tests were carried out. Statistical significance was considered at 0.05 level. Qualitative answers were also quantified to explore students' reasons for justifying their pragmatic choices.

The present study followed all ethical principles of academic research.

Results and Discussion

This section presents and interprets the results on the influence of multilingual instruction, referring to translanguaging pedagogies, on young students' pragmatic awareness of Catalan, Spanish and English requests. Similarly, it describes the pragmatic synergies found among the three languages. From a multilingual viewpoint, we believe that students' pragmatic awareness as a unified system can be better understood by considering their entire language repertoire. However, the analysis of the relationship between languages may report the synergies and interactions among them. Thus, we paid major attention to the influence of multilingual instruction on students' pragmatic awareness for each language system (English, Spanish and Catalan).

To begin with, we explored the global degree of pragmatic awareness for each of the three languages before and after the pedagogical intervention. As Table 12.1 below depicts, young learners' pragmatic awareness of Spanish and English requests was enhanced after receiving multilingual instruction through translanguaging pedagogies. Better scores were obtained for both English (M = 9.91, SD = 2.49) and Spanish (M = 10.02, SD = 1.95) in the post-test than in the pre-test (English: M = 9.46, SD = 2.49; Spanish: M = 9.04, SD = 2.15). However, the pragmatic gains were higher in Spanish (N = 0.98) than in English (N = 0.45), and only statistically significant changes were observed for Spanish ($t(27)$_ = 2.560, p = 0.008). These findings indicate that multilingual pragmatic instruction had a greater positive influence on students' pragmatic awareness in Spanish, which is the majority and dominant language of the region.

Table 12.1 below shows the means and standard deviations for the scores in the two tests, the pre-post difference, t value and the degree of signification.

Table 12.1: Pre and Post scores on pragmatic awareness of requests for English, Spanish and Catalan.

	Pre-test		**Post-test**		**Pre-post difference**	***t* value**	***p* value**
	M	***SD***	***M***	***SD***			
English	9.46	2.49	9.91	2.49	0.45	-1.822	0.119
Spanish	9.04	2.15	10.02	1.95	0.98	-2.560	0.008
Catalan	10.25	1.43	10.18	1.41	-0.07	0.193	0.424

In spite of these positive results for Spanish, students' pragmatic awareness in Catalan was unaffected (Pre-test: $M = 10.25$, $SD = 1.43$; Post-test: $M = 10.18$, $SD = 1.41$). While this is true, it is important to keep in mind that young learners exhibited the highest levels of pragmatic awareness in this language (Catalan) prior to receiving the multilingual treatment. Interestingly, even in the post-test, Catalan pragmatic awareness scores remained the highest among all languages. This better performance in Catalan from the very beginning of the experiment could justify why primary students did not enhance their pragmatic awareness in Catalan after using their whole multilingual repertoire as a learning strategy. Yet, this leaves ground for further research.

Scenarios 3 (English) and 9 (Catalan) deserve special attention. For both scenarios, which share the same sociopragmatic and pragmalinguistic characteristics, the post-test means were lower than the pre-test means. The scenarios present direct requests produced by the responsible of the class and addressed to the rest of the students. It is relevant to consider that these were the only two requests of the test in which the request formula was produced by one of the classmates having more authority in the classroom context (student responsible). Therefore, participants' responses in both the pre- and post-tests indicate that young learners may have perceived their classmates as equals, independently of the role they have inside the classroom. This may explain the use of less formal request strategies among classmates and the lack of significant pragmatic improvement in English and Catalan after the multilingual treatment. This was also noticed in Rose's (2009) investigation, in which primary students tended to use more polite structures while addressing speakers they considered to share a higher status and not to their classmates since they regarded them as peers.

Notwithstanding both scenarios, these results indicate that multilingual pedagogies such as translanguaging may be beneficial for developing young learners' pragmatic skills and abilities, specifically referring to their pragmatic awareness of requests. Thus, employing all students' languages in the primary classroom was observed to positively influence students' pragmatic awareness in the majority and dominant language of the Valencian region, Spanish. A greater pragmatic awareness in Spanish than in Catalan and English was also noticed in the study carried out by Portolés (2015). The author suggested that the socio linguistic status of Spanish and students' frequent exposure to the language out of the school context may have contributed to the enhanced pragmatic awareness of the language.

We were also interested in exploring request production. In particular, students were asked to produce appropriate requests in the three languages (Catalan, Spanish and English) if they considered the requests to be inappropriate for each specific social situation presented in the pragmatic test. We examined the type of requests provided by students in each language focusing on two request strategies (direct strategies and conventionally indirect strategies). Students were supposed to produce appropriate request strategies. According to politeness orientations, while the English language requires more conventionally indirect strategies, Spanish and Catalan tend to use more direct request strategies.

Figure 12.2 below depicts the use of direct strategies for request production in both the pre and post-test. As seen in the figure, the amount of Spanish (Pre-test: 31.25 %, Post-test: 8.77 %) and Catalan direct requests (Pre-test: 33.33 %, Post-test: 11.11 %) diminished in the post-test. This indicates that young learners produced more polite pragmatic responses in Spanish and Catalan after the pragmatic instruction across languages. Thus, in our study, multilingual pragmatic instruction seems to increase young students' use of polite request strategies in Spanish and Catalan. Similar findings were found in previous studies in which explicit pragmatic instruction was proved to increase and improve primary students' use and variation of request strategies (Myrset, 2021, 2022).

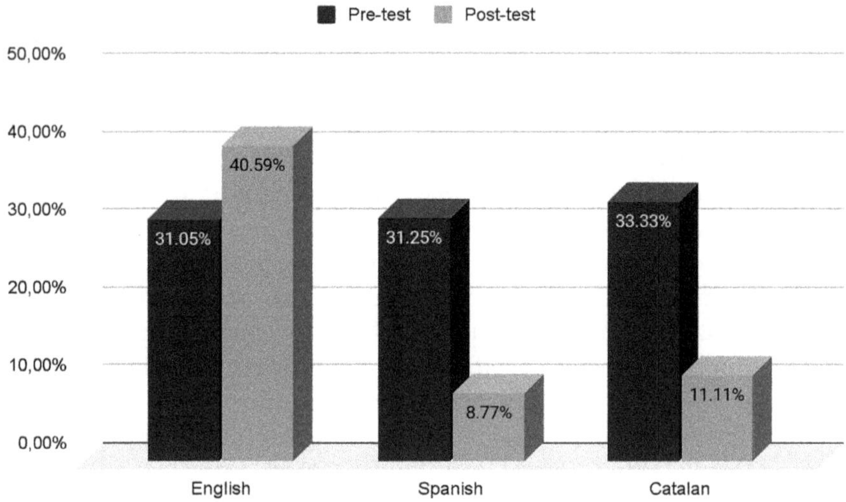

Figure 12.2: Students' use of direct request strategies.

In contrast, not as positive pragmalinguistic results were noticed for the English language since the employment of English direct strategies increased in the post-test (Pre-test: 31.05 %, Post-test: 40.59 %). Even though, according to its politeness orientation, this language demands to a higher extent the use of conventionally indirect request strategies. Instead of employing more conventionally indirect strategies in English after the multilingual treatment, students introduced the politeness formula "please" in direct request strategies, which is commonly used for softening the face-threatening nature of requests and sounding more polite. Some examples of English direct requests conveyed by students in the post-test include:

(1) give me the glue, please.
(2) please, now it's time to put the materials away.

This pattern was also seen in Safont's (2024) study, who found that CLIL students tended to modify English direct requests by means of downgrades, such as "please".

Regarding the use of conventionally indirect request strategies, primary students only produced more conventionally indirect requests in Catalan in the post-test (Pre-test: 33.33 %, Post-test: 55.56 %), whereas English (Pre-test: 68.95 %, Post-test: 59.41 %) and Spanish (Pre-test: 89.58 %, Post-test: 87.72 %) use of conventionally indirect strategies decreased in the post-test. Nonetheless, it is relevant to add that the number of conventionally indirect requests produced in English and Spanish was higher than the one in Catalan, even in the post-test. Consequently, despite the Catalan pragmalinguistic improvement, the majority (Spanish) and international language (English) of the classroom still obtained higher scores in the use of more polite request strategies. Some examples of conventionally indirect strategies provided by students in the post-test were:

(3) teacher, can you help me with my homework?

(4) *no he hecho los deberes, ¿te los podría entregar mañana?* (I haven't done the homework. Could I do it for tomorrow?).

(5) *t'importaria deixar-me el llibre, per favor?* (Would you mind lending me the book, please?).

For a better understanding, Figure 12.3 below illustrates the percentage of conventionally indirect requests in the three languages before and after the multilingual treatment.

It should be highlighted that general percentages obtained for the use of conventionally indirect strategies in each language were higher (English: 59.41 %, Spanish: 87.72 %, Catalan: 55.56 %) than the ones for direct strategies (English: 40.59 %, Spanish: 8.77 %, Catalan: 11.11 %), contrary to previous research that reported a more frequent use of direct strategies (Portolés & Safont, 2018; Safont, 2018). These greater percentages suggest that pragmatic instruction through translanguaging pedagogies may benefit students' pragmalinguistic awareness of requests, in relation to the appropriate use of request strategies under specific social conditions.

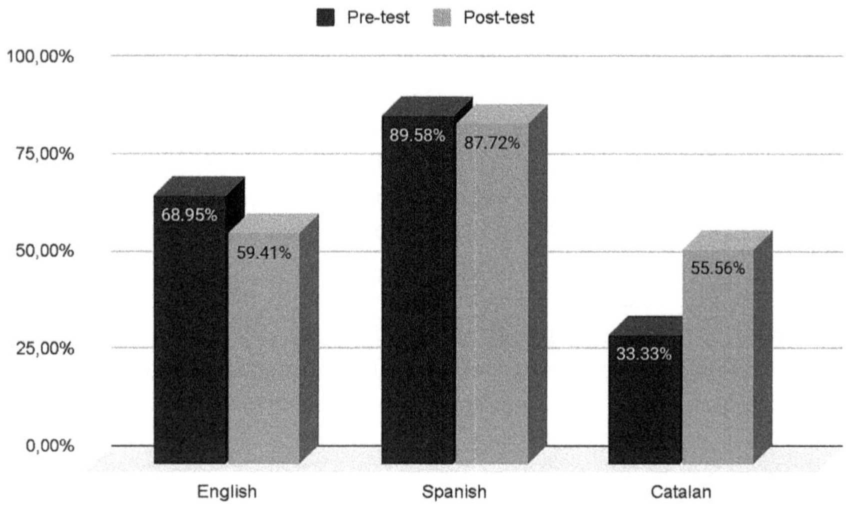

Figure 12.3: Students' use of conventionally indirect request strategies.

The results obtained for request production may be explained due to the language transfer phenomena produced in multilingual contexts of education where several languages are present and interact. In our study, the synergies among the three language systems (Catalan, Spanish and English) allowed for pragmatic transfer phenomena, as also observed in previous studies on young learners' pragmatic awareness (Portolés, 2015; Portolés & Safont, 2018; Safont, 2018). Through this phenomena, pragmatic features, such as language politeness orientations, are transferred from one language to another. This may explain why students employ direct request strategies in English and conventionally indirect request strategies in Catalan and Spanish. As observed, students did not distinguish between three different pragmatic systems and politeness orientations, but activated a single dynamic pragmatic system for their whole language repertoire, which was reinforced by explicit multilingual pragmatic instruction. Similar results were noticed by McConachy (2019), who stated that the study of pragmatic awareness should not be approached by considering politeness orientations of individual languages. In contrast, a more enlarged multilingual and intercultural bias should be followed for looking at pragmatic awareness.

We also paid special attention to students' identification of interlocutors' social distance, as a relevant sociopragmatic variable that can affect pragmatic choices, as mentioned by Brown and Levinson (1987). Table 12.2 below shows that young learners' recognition of the social distance of the interlocutors improved in the three languages since higher scores were observed in the post-test for English (Pre-test: $M = 1.93$, $SD = 0.98$; Post-test: $M = 2.32$, $SD = 0.77$), Spanish (Pre-test: $M = 2.43$, $SD = 0.57$; Post-test: $M = 2.64$, $SD = 0.73$) and Catalan situations (Pretest: $M = 1.79$, $SD = 0.74$; Post-test: $M = 2.04$, $SD = 0.58$). Regardless of the pragmatic improvement in the three languages, only statistically significant differences were observed for the English language ($t(27)$_ = -2.174, $p = 0.019$), which proved to be the language most favourably affected by multilingual instruction in this part of the test.

Table 12.2: Pre and Post scores on identification of interlocutors' social distance.

	Pre-test		**Post-test**		**Pre-post difference**	***t* value**	***p* value**
	M	***SD***	***M***	***SD***			
English	1.93	0.98	2.32	0.77	0.39	−2.174	0.019
Spanish	2.43	0.57	2.64	0.73	0.21	−1.652	0.055
Catalan	1.79	0.74	2.04	0.58	0.25	−1.426	0.083

These findings suggest that explicit pragmatic instruction across languages benefited students' awareness of sociopragmatic aspects in several languages, particularly referring to the social distance of the interlocutors. Therefore, employing students' language repertoire for pragmatic learning may be favourable to develop knowledge and awareness of sociopragmatic variables in multiple languages. These results are in line with the findings of the study conducted by Alcón and Pitarch (2010), which demonstrated the benefits of pragmatic teaching on students' awareness of sociopragmatic aspects, including social distance. Nevertheless, the scholars did not examine requests but refusals.

To sum up, findings of the present study show that our initial hypothesis (i.e. Multilingual pragmatic instruction will benefit young students' pragmatic awareness in Catalan, Spanish and English. Differences in the improvement of pragmatic awareness will be noticed among the three languages) is confirmed. Results demonstrate that learning multilingually through translanguaging pedagogies provides great opportunities for multilingual pragmatic learning in the primary classroom. Through the implementation of a multilingual approach, students' language repertoire could work as an efficient strategy for enhancing pragmatic awareness in multiple languages, focusing on both sociopragmatic and pragmalinguistic aspects of the languages. This study has explored possible differences and synergies in the pragmatic awareness of the three languages under research (Catalan, Spanish and English). Results have demonstrated that differences in the improvement of pragmatic awareness were observed among the three languages. Whereas students' pragmatic awareness in the majority language (Spanish) resulted to be the most favourably influenced by multilingual pragmatic instruction, several benefits were also noticed for English and Catalan. Regarding the English language, students developed a better ability to identify interlocutors' social distance in English situations. As for Catalan, young learners produced more polite request strategies in this language after receiving multilingual pragmatic instruction.

What is more, our results suggest that pragmatic transfer phenomena took place in the multilingual classroom due to the synergies among the three language systems. In particular, young learners transferred the language politeness orientations from one language to the others. This fact demonstrates that students did not activate independent pragmatic systems for each language, but a whole multilingual pragmatic system which was benefited by multilingual pragmatic teaching.

These positive pragmatic findings encourage more explicit pragmatic instruction in primary school contexts, as also claimed by Myrset and McConachy (2023), since as observed in the present study, pragmatic instruction across languages seemed to enhance young learners' pragmatic awareness in three languages (English, Spanish and Catalan).

Concluding Remarks

The results extracted from the present study may contribute to the research field of pragmatic awareness and multilingual education, and more specifically, multilingual pragmatics, which consists of an area of research that requires more and varied investigation, particularly at early levels of education. This study has shown that multilingual instruction based on translanguaging pedagogies has positively influenced young learners' pragmatic awareness of Spanish, English and Catalan requests, although differences in the improvement of pragmatic awareness were noticed among the three languages.

Dealing with individual languages, students' pragmatic awareness in the majority language (Spanish) resulted to be the most benefited by the multilingual approach. Some enhancements were also observed for pragmatic awareness in English and Catalan. Primary students were able to identify to a greater extent interlocutors' social distance in English situations after the multilingual treatment. Similarly, young learners were able to produce more polite request strategies in Catalan. However, it should be noted that pragmatic awareness in Catalan received the highest scores since the initial completion of the pre-test in most of the pragmatic aspects investigated (i.e. identification of request (in)appropriateness and decision of employing the same requests under specific social conditions in real situations), as well as in the general results on pragmatic awareness. These great scores made it difficult for our young learners to obtain even higher scores in Catalan after the multilingual instruction.

These results indicate that applying multilingual perspectives on pragmatic learning has a beneficial influence on primary students' pragmatic awareness in individual languages, that include Spanish, English and Catalan. Accordingly, these findings have confirmed our hypothesis (i.e. Multilingual pragmatic instruction will benefit young students' pragmatic awareness in Catalan, Spanish and English. Differences in the improvement of pragmatic awareness will be noticed among the three languages). This demonstrates that multilingual students' language repertoire should not be left apart in the study of pragmatics since multilingual instruction has proved to be a useful tool for developing a greater pragmatic awareness in multiple languages in primary contexts of education.

The present findings coincide with previous research that has demonstrated a positive influence of multilingual instruction based on the pedagogical translanguaging approach on several dimensions of primary students' language awareness (Carbonara, 2023; Cenoz et al., 2022; Cenoz & Santos, 2020; Leonet et al., 2020; Leonet & Saragueta, 2023). In addition, as claimed by some scholars such as Alcón and Martínez-Flor (2008) and Myrset (2021, 2022), explicit pragmatic instruction has proved to be beneficial for enhancing students' pragmatic awareness. This is even more relevant in multilingual classrooms, where multiple languages are present and used for pedagogical purposes. Therefore, students should develop pragmatic knowledge and awareness in all the languages of the classroom environment.

It is also relevant to mention that transfer phenomena was found in the primary classroom examined, as also observed in previous studies (Portolés, 2015; Portolés & Safont, 2018; Safont, 2018). The interaction among the three languages (Catalan, Spanish and English) has allowed our young students to develop a single multilingual pragmatic system. By acknowledging the three languages as a unified system, students transferred pragmatic features from one or several languages to the others, specifically referring to the use of request strategies according to the politeness orientation of each language. This multilingual pragmatic system developed by young learners has also seemed to be reinforced by instruction across languages. Accordingly, as also mentioned in previous research on multilingual pragmatics, a more multilingual approach towards the study and teaching of pragmatics is needed from the early stages of education (Safont, 2018, 2024; Safont & Portolés, 2016).

As findings suggest, educational policies and classroom practices should question the predominant monolingual paradigm found in education with the incorporation of multilingual strategies and pedagogies that encourage the use of students' language repertoire and previous linguistic knowledge. Our study has demonstrated that employing pedagogical translanguaging was beneficial for improving primary school students' multilingual pragmatic awareness, although multilingual instruction could also benefit other aspects of language learning. Yet, this leaves ground for further research.

Some limitations and further research ideas are proposed from this study. First, the number of participants is reduced and may not be depictive. Second, future investigations should include a control group to contrast the pragmatic awareness of students who learn through translanguaging pedagogies with those who follow monolingual pedagogies. Last, further research is needed that analyses the role of individual factors, such as gender and age, on students' pragmatic awareness. Thus, the conclusions extracted from this study claim the need for further research that contributes to the field of multilingual pragmatics.

Acknowledgements

As members of the LAELA (Lingüística Aplicada a l'Ensenyament de la Llengua Anglesa) research group at Universitat Jaume I (Castellón, Spain), we would like to acknowledge that this study is part of the research project PID2020-117959GB-I00 funded by MCIN/AEI/ 10.13039/501100011033. Additional funding has been granted by Projectes d'Innovació Educativa de la Unitat de Suport Educatiu 51020/ 24, and Ministerio de Educación y Formación Profesional under Grant FPU20/00220.

References

Alcón-Soler, Eva. 2015. Pragmatic learning and study abroad: Effects of instruction and length of stay. *System*, 48, 62–74.

Alcón-Soler, Eva & Martínez-Flor, Alicia. 2008. *Investigating pragmatics in foreign language learning, teaching and testing.* Bristol: Multilingual Matters.

Alcón-Soler, Eva & Guzmán Pitarch, Josep. 2010. The effect of instruction on learners' pragmatic awareness: A focus on refusals.

International Journal of English Studies, 10/1, 65–80. <https://doi.org/10.6018/ijes/2010/1/113981>.

Brown, Penelope & Levinson, Stephen. 1987. *Politeness: Some universals in language usage.* Cambridge: Cambridge University Press.

Carbonara, Valentina. 2023. The effects of multilingual pedagogies on language awareness: A longitudinal analysis of students' language portraits. *Linguistics and Education*, 78, 1–14. <https://doi.org/10.1016/j.linged.2023.101244>.

Cenoz, Jasone. 2007. The acquisition of pragmatic competence and multilingualism in foreign language contexts. In Eva Alcón & Pilar Safont (eds) *Intercultural language use and language learning*. Dordrecht: Springer Netherlands, 123–140.

Cenoz, Jasone & Gorter, Durk. 2021. *Pedagogical translanguaging*. Cambridge: Cambridge University Press. <https://doi.org/10.1017/9781009029384>.

Cenoz, Jasone, Leonet, Oihana & Gorter, Durk. 2022. Developing cognate awareness through pedagogical translanguaging. *International Journal of Bilingual Education and Bilingualism*, 25/8, 2759–2773. <https://doi.org/10.1080/13670050.2021.1961675>.

Cenoz, Jasone & Santos, Alaitz. 2020. Implementing pedagogical translanguaging in trilingual schools. *System*, 92, 1–9. <https://doi.org/10.1016/j.system.2020.102273>.

Derakhshan, Ali & Shakki, Farzaneh. 2020. The effect of implicit vs. explicit metapragmatic instruction on the Iranian intermediate EFL learners' pragmatic comprehension of apology and refusal. *Scientific Journal of Language Research*, 12/35, 151–175.

Halenko, Nicola. 2018. Using computer-assisted language learning (CALL) tools to enhance output practice. In Christian Jones (ed.). *Practice in Second Language Learning*. Cambridge: Cambridge University Press, 137–163.

IBM Corp. Released. 2021. *IBM spss statistics for windows, version 28.0.* Armonk, NY: IBM Corp

Martín-Laguna, Sofía. 2022. The multilingual turn in pragmatics: Is the use of hedges and attitude markers shared across languages in trilingual writing? *Applied Pragmatics.* 4/1, 63–91. <https://doi.org/10.1075/ap.20024.mar>.

Leech, Geoffrey N. 1983. *Principles of Pragmatics*. London: Longman.

Leonet, Oihana, Cenoz, Jasone & Gorter, Durk. 2020. Developing morphological awareness across languages: Translanguaging pedagogies in third language acquisition. *Language Awareness*, 29/1, 41–59. <https://doi.org/10.1080/09658416.2019.1688338>.

Leonet, Oihana & Saragueta, Eider. 2023. The case of a pedagogical translanguaging intervention in a trilingual primary school: the students' voice. *International Journal of Multilingualism*. 21/4, 1–19. <https://doi.org/10.1080/14790718.2023.2224009>.

Martinez-Buffa, Ignacio & Safont, Pilar. 2022. Multilingual pragmatic awareness in collaborative writing. *Language Awareness*, 1–22. <https://doi.org/10.1080/09658416.2022.2094389>.

Martínez-Flor, Alicia & Usó-Juan, Esther. 2020. Teaching speech acts in a second language. In Klaus P. Schneider & Eli Infantidou (eds) *Developmental and Clinical Pragmàtics*. Berlin: De Gruyter Mouton, 269–300.

McConachy, Troy. 2019. L2 pragmatics as 'intercultural pragmatics': Probing sociopragmatic aspects of pragmatic awareness. *Journal of Pragmatics*. 151, 167–176. <https://doi.org/10.1016/j.pragma.2019.02.014>.

McConachy, Troy. 2022. Pragmatic awareness in intercultural language learning. In Istvan Kecskes (ed.) *The Cambridge handbook of intercultural pragmatics*. Cambridge: Cambridge University Press, 766– 787. <https://doi.org/10.1017/9781108884303.030>.

Myrset, Anders. 2021. Scientific concepts as meaning-making resources for young EFL learners in the learning of pragmatics. *Intercultural Communication Education*, 4/2, 191–212. <https://doi.org/10.29140/ice.v4n2.485>.

Myrset, Anders. 2022. 'You could win Masterchef with this soup. Can I get some more?' Request production and the impact of instruction on young EFL learners. *Journal of Pragmatics*, 192, 56–76. <https://doi.org/10.1016/j.pragma.2022.02.010>.

Myrset, Anders & McConachy, Troy. 2023. Incorporating pragmatics into primary English language teacher education. In David Valente & Daniel Xerri (eds) *Innovative practices in early English language education*. Cham: Palgrave Macmillan, 305–327. <https://doi.org/10.1007/978-3-031-12922-3_15

Nightingale, Richard & Safont, Pilar. 2019. Pragmatic translanguaging: Multilingual practice in adolescent online discourse. In Patricia Salazar-Campillo & Victòria Codina-Espurz (eds) *Investigating the learning of pragmatics across ages and contexts*. Leiden, The Netherlands: Brill, 167–195. <https://doi.org/10.1163/9789004409699_009>.

Portolés, Laura. 2015. *Multilingualism and very young learners. An analysis of pragmatic awareness and language attitudes*. Berlin: De Gruyter. <https:// doi.org/ 10.1515/ 978150 1500 022>.

Portolés, Laura & Safont, Pilar. 2018. Examining authentic and elicited data from a multilingual perspective. The real picture of child requestive behaviour in the L3 classroom. *System*, 75, 81–92. <https://doi.org/10.1016/j.system.2018.03.012>.

Safont, Pilar. 2005. *Third language learners. Pragmatic production and awareness*. Clevedon: Multilingual Matters.

Safont, Pilar. 2018. Are classroom requests similar in all EFL settings? Focusing on a young multilingual learning environment. In Piotr Romanowski & Malgorzata Jedynak (eds) *Current research in bilingualism and bilingual education*. Cham: Springer, 123–141. <https://doi.org/10.1007/978-3-319-92396-3_7>.

Safont, Pilar. 2023. Multilingual cyberpragmatics in instructional settings. Exploring gender and age effects in Catalan, Spanish and English email requests. *International Journal of Multilingualism*, 1–23. <https://doi.org/10.1080/14790718.2023.2187811>.

Safont, Pilar. 2024. Young multilingual pragmatics. A focus on requests in CLIL and Non-CLIL settings. In Danuta Gabryś-Barker & Eva Vetter (eds) *Modern approaches to researching multilingualism: Studies in honour of Larissa Aronin*. Cham: Springer Nature Switzerland, 101–1019. <https://doi.org/10.1007/978-3-031-52371-7_7>.

Safont, Pilar & Alcón-Soler, Eva. 2012. Teachability of request act peripheral modification devices in third language learning contexts. In Maria Economidou-Kogetsidis & Helen Woodfield (eds) *Interlanguage request modification*. Amsterdam: John Benjamins, 275–314.

Safont, Pilar & Portolés, Laura. 2015. Pragmatic awareness in early consecutive third language learners. Current findings from research on multilingualism. In Pilar Safont & Laura Portolés (eds) *Learning and using multiple languages*. UK: Cambridge Scholars Publishing, 218–237.

Safont, Pilar & Portolés, Laura. 2016. Pragmatic functions of formulaic speech in three different languages: A focus on early L3 learners of English. *Journal of Immersion and Content-Based Language Education*, 4/2, 225–250. <https://doi.org/10.1075/jicb.4.2.04saf>.

Schauer, Gila. 2009. *Interlanguage pragmatic development: The study abroad context*. London: Bloomsbury Publishing.

Taguchi, Naoko. 2015. Instructed pragmatics at a glance: Where instructional studies were, are, and should be going. *Language Teaching*, 48/1, 1–50. <https://doi.org/10.1017/S0261444814000263>.

Takimoto, Masahiro. 2014. Evaluating the effects of input-based approaches to the teaching of pragmalinguistics and sociopragmatics in second language pragmatics: A case of English request hedges. *IAFOR Journal of Language Learning*, 1/1, 1–16.

Trosborg, Anna. 1995. Statutes and contracts: An analysis of legal speech acts in the English language of the law. *Journal of Pragmatics*, 23/1, 31–53.

Usó-Juan, Esther. 2021. Long-term instructional effects on learners' use of email request modifiers. *Email Pragmatics and Second Language Learners*, 328, 71–99.

Usó-Juan, Esther. 2022. Exploring the role of strategy instruction on learners' ability to write authentic email requests to faculty. *Language Teaching Research*, 26/2, 213–237. <https://doi.org/10.1177/13621688211066997>.

Usó-Juan, Esther & Martínez-Flor, Alicia. 2021. Fostering learners' (meta)pragmatic awareness through film analysis. *Language Value*, 14/1, 85–111. < https://doi.org/10.6035/languagev.5821>.

Notes on Contributors

Anne Barron is Professor of English Linguistics at the Leuphana University of Lüneburg in Germany. Her research interests in Second Language Pragmatics focus on pragmatic development, on pragmatic variation and on learner corpus pragmatics. Major publications in the area include *Acquisition in Interlanguage Pragmatics* (2003, Benjamins), Acquisitional Pragmatics in Foreign Language Learning (*Intercultural Pragmatics*, DeGruyter, 2007, co-editor: M. Warga) and Pragmatic Development and Stay Abroad (*Journal of Pragmatics*, Elsevier, 2019) and journal publications in *Intercultural Pragmatics, Journal of Pragmatics, Language Teaching and System*. She has co-edited *The Routledge Handbook of Pragmatics* (Routledge, 2017, with Y. Gu and G. Steen) and *Pragmatics of Discourse* (de Gruyter, 2014, with K.P. Schneider). She is also associate editor of *Applied Pragmatics* (Benjamins), series co-editor of *Studies in Pragmatics* (Brill) and a member of the advisory board of *Contrastive Pragmatics* (Brill), *Corpus Pragmatics* (Springer), *Journal of Pragmatics* (Elsevier), *Intercultural Pragmatics* (de Gruyter) and *Study Abroad Research* (Benjamins).

Victòria Codina Espurz is an Associate Professor in the Department of English Studies at the Universitat Jaume I in Castelló, Spain. Her research and teaching interests embrace the area of second language acquisition, mainly the role of affective factors and individual differences in L2 learning. She has conducted research on interlanguage pragmatics, in particular, the role of instruction of speech acts (i.e., requests) in fostering pragmatic development in English as a foreign language, and the effect of learner proficiency in refusals. Most recently, her research agenda has developed in the study of email communication between students and faculty in a university setting. In this context, her more recent publications include: "Students' perception of social contextual variables in mitigating email requests" (2022) in *The Grove—Working Papers on English Studies* and 'The influence of social distance and power in email politeness in an academic context' (2021) in *Estudios Interlingüísticos.*

Onur Çiçek, M.A in English Linguistics, is a research associate at the Leuphana University of Lüneburg in Germany. His research interests focus on Interlanguage Pragmatics, pragmatic instruction, pragmatic development. He is currently working on a follow-up study, which is on the effects of pragmatic intervention on the use of directives in ELF peer feedback. He presented this research at the International Association for Teaching Pragmatics conference in Barcelona in July 2024. This paper represents his first academic publication, reflecting his ongoing research into interlanguage pragmatics.

Ilka Flöck, PhD in English Linguistics, is a postdoctoral researcher at the Leuphana University of Lüneburg in Germany. Her research interests include Cross-cultural and Variational Pragmatics, Second Language Pragmatics, and Corpus Pragmatics. Most of her research focuses on requests and directive speech acts in naturally occurring interactions in different varieties of English and different languages. Her major publications include Requests in American and British English (2016, Benjamins), Preference Organization and Cross- Cultural Variation in Request Responses (2018, with Ronald Geluykens, *Corpus Pragmatics*), Requests in Informal Conversations: A Contrastive Study of English and German (2024), and Analyzing Pragmatic Variation in English (2024, co-edited with Ronald Geluykens, Lincom).

Gema Gayete Domínguez is currently a PhD student from the Applied Languages doctoral programme at Universitat Jaume I (Castelló, Spain), as part of a FPU grant from the Spanish Ministry of Education. She holds a MA in English Language Teaching and Acquisition in Multilingual Contexts (MELACOM) and a degree in English Studies. She has also conducted a three-month research stay at University of Rijeka (Croatia) in 2024 as part of her international doctoral programme. She is a member of the LAELA research group and her research interests include third language acquisition, multilingual education, language attitudes, CLIL and multilingual pragmatics. The findings of her studies have been published in international journals and editorials, such as *International*

Journal of Multilingualism and *Journal of Language and Culture in Education*, among others. She has presented her research in more than 15 national and international conferences, and she has been part of the organising committee of several international and national conferences and seminars. Moreover, she has participated in several research projects dealing with multilingual education, pragmatics and affective factors in education. Additionally, she has served as a reviewer for prestigious international research journals, such as *System and Applied Linguistics*, among others.

Marta González-Lloret is a Professor of Spanish Applied Linguistics at the University of Hawai'i Mānoa. She is among the world's 2 % most-cited researchers and among top 400 world linguists according to the 2023 Stanford University's ranking (Elsevier Data Repository). Her research focuses on technology-mediated language learning, Task-based Language Teaching, and L2 pragmatics. She has published extensively on these topics and given more than 80 invited talks/workshops and 17 plenary/keynote talks all over the world. She is currently co-editor of the *Task-based Language Teaching* book series (John Benjamins), editor of the *Pragmatics & Language Learning* book series (NFLRC) and serves in multiple academic journals and advisory committees.

Irene Guzmán-Alcón is an Assistant Professor in the Department of Language Didactics at the University of Valencia (UV). She has been collaborating with the LAELA research group since 2019. She holds an MA in English Language Teaching in Multilingual Contexts and an MA in English Language Teaching in Secondary Education. In 2023, she obtained her PhD in Applied Linguistics at University Jaume I, funded by a grant from the same university. Irene was also awarded a grant as a postdoctoral researcher. Her research interests include third language acquisition, young language learners, CLIL, and multilingual education. The results of her studies have been disseminated through various articles in internationally indexed journals, such as *English Language Teaching* and *Applied Pragmatics*, among others. She has presented her work at numerous international conferences, and has been involved in the organisation of several national and international conferences. Additionally, she has participated in several research projects focusing on multilingual pragmatics, CLIL, and individual differences in education.

Otilia Martí is a lecturer in the Department of Pedagogy and Didactics of Social Sciences, Language and Literature at Universitat Jaume I (Castelló, Spain). Her background is in Contemporary History (Universitat de València) and in Applied Linguistics (UJI) where she is member of the LAELA research group, coordinated by professor Pilar Safont. Committed to the initial training of Primary and Secondary teachers-to-be, she is currently responsible for courses on English Language Teaching in the degree of Primary Education and in the master degree for Secondary and Vocational teacher trainees at UJI. Her research interests include teachers' beliefs in multilingual education, pragmatics classroom discourse and service-learning projects around storytelling through picturebooks, with articles published in journals such as *Caplletra, Bellaterra Journal of Teaching and Learning Language & Literature, International Journal of Multilingualism, Language, Culture and Curriculum, System* or *Applied Pragmatics,* and chapters in *Tirant lo Blanch, Brill* or *Peter Lang*

Sofía Martín-Laguna is a lecturer at Universitat Jaume I. She graduated in English Philology from the Universitat Jaume I (Spain) with an Academic Achievement Award. She holds an MA in English Language Teaching in Secondary Education and another MA in English Language Teaching in Multilingual Contexts. She was awarded a grant from the FPU programme of the Spanish Ministerio de Educación, Cultura y Deporte to do her PhD, which Dr. Eva Alcón Soler supervised. Sofía's PhD thesis focused on transfer and development of pragmatic markers in multilingual learners, and was awarded Excellent Cum Laude with Extraordinary Prize. Sofía was a post-doctoral researcher at the University of Amsterdam. She is the author of *Tasks, Pragmatics and Multilingualism in the Classroom: A Portrait of Adolescent Writing in Multiple Languages* (Multilingual Matters, 2020). Her research interest includes discourse and pragmatic development, metadiscourse, Task-Based Language Teaching and multilingual education.

Ignacio Martinez Buffa (Universitat Jaume I) is a university professor and a secondary school teacher who holds a MA in English Language Teaching in Multilingual Contexts (MELACOM) and a MA in Teacher Training for Compulsory Secondary Education and Baccalaureate, Vocational Training and Language Teaching. In 2022, he obtained his PhD in Applied Linguistics in University Jaume I, as part of a grant from the Spanish Ministry for Science, Innovation and Universities. His research tackles the importance of engagement with the languages in student-student interaction as an opportunity to improve and develop learners' pragmatic knowledge and awareness. Ignacio's research interests include: third language acquisition, engagement, pragmatic awareness and pragmatic development. He has shared his research in international conferences like the International Pragmatics Conference (IPrA) and the International Conference on Third Language Acquisition and Multilingualism (IAML3) and published in well-known journals such as *Language Awareness*.

Alicia Martínez-Flor is a Senior Lecturer of English Linguistics at Universitat Jaume I (Castellón, Spain). She holds a PhD in Applied Linguistics. She is a member of LAELA (Lingüística Aplicada a l'Ensenyament de la Llengua Anglesa) research group at Universitat Jaume I (Castellón, Spain). Her main research interests include interlanguage pragmatics, instructional pragmatics and foreign language learning and teaching. Her publications include articles in international journals such as *Foreign Language Annals and Language Teaching Research.* She has co-edited the volumes *Pragmatics in Foreign Language Learning, Teaching and Testing* (Multilingual Matters, 2008), *Speech Act Performance: Theoretical, Empirical and Methodological Issues* (John Benjamins, 2010), *L2 Pragmatics in Action: Teachers, Learners and the Teaching-learning Interaction Process* (John Benjamins, 2023), as well as the special issue Pragmatics in Instructed Language Learning in *System* (2005).

Richard Nightingale holds a Ph.D in Applied Linguistics and is an Associate Professor in the Department of English Studies at Universitat Jaume I, where he teaches at undergraduate and postgraduate levels. He coordinates the MA program in English Language Teaching and

Acquisition in Multilingual Contexts. He is also a member of the LAELA (Applied Linguistics to the Teaching of the English Language) Research Group, and treasurer of the International Association of Multilingualism. His research mainly focuses on the nexus between language, society, and the self. Within this framework, his main areas of interest are multilingualism, sociolinguistics, pragmatics, affective factors, and the influence of digital media contact. His work has been published with Springer, Brill, Peter Lang, and John Benjamins, among others, and has been disseminated at numerous international conferences.

Laura Portolés Falomir is an Associate Professor at the English Studies Department and a member of the LAELA research group at Universitat Jaume I, Spain (http://gruplaela.uji.es/). She is also co-coordinator of the English Language Teaching and Acquisition in Multilingual Contexts (MELACOM) MA programme. Her research interests are third language acquisition, multilingual pragmatics, affective factors, and multilingual education. She currently works on research projects about pragmatics and translanguaging. She has published widely on those topics in international peer-reviewed journals, such as *International Journal of Multilingualism, Language, Culture and Curriculum* and *System*. Her most relevant and cited contribution is an international monograph entitled '*Multilingualism and Very Young Learners*' (De Gruyter, 2015), which received the 2016 outstanding book award (junior researchers category) from the AESLA association. A complete account of her publications is available in her ORCID profile (0000-0003-2916-7069).

Pilar Safont is Full Professor of applied linguistics and multilingualism at the Universitat Jaume I in Castelló (Spain). She is the coordinator of the LAELA research group and main researcher of several funded projects that focus on the analysis of young adults' and children's attitudes and pragmatic competence in multilingual instructional settings. Her work has been published in international journals, monographs, handbooks and encyclopaedias. She has supervised several theses on preschool and primary education pragmatic development. Her former positions and roles in academia include President of the International Association of Multilingualism and associate Editor of the *Journal Language, Culture and Curriculum* among others.

Patricia Salazar-Campillo is an associate professor at the Department of English Studies (Universitat Jaume I, Castelló, Spain). She is a member of the research group LAELA (Lingüística Aplicada a l'Ensenyament de la Llengua Anglesa) and her main interests include teaching and learning English as a foreign language, especially those areas involving corrective feedback. More recently, she has been conducting research on interlanguage pragmatics in online discourse, mainly on emails. Her research has been published in international and national publishing companies such as Springer, Peter Lang, International Journal of English Studies, English Language Teaching, Porta Linguarum, Sintagma and Ibérica. She co-edited the book *Refusals in instructional contexts and beyond* (Rodopi, 2013) and *Investigating the learning of pragmatics across ages and contexts* (Brill, 2019).

Naoko Taguchi is Professor in the English Department at Northern Arizona University where she teaches courses in applied linguistics and TESOL. Her primary research interests include second language pragmatics, intercultural competence, and technology-mediated language learning. Her recent book publications include *the Encyclopedia of Applied Linguistics Pragmatics Volume* (with Daniel Kadar; Wiley, 2024), t*he Routledge Handbook of SLA and Pragmatics* (Routledge, 2019) and *Teaching and Learning Pragmatics in the Globalized World* (special issue with Modern Language Journal, 2021). She is currently the co-editor of*Language Learning* (Wiley) and *Applied Pragmatics* (John Benjamins). She serves on the editorial board for 11 journals and book series. She also serves on the advisory board for the International Teachers' Association of Pragmatics (Barcelona, Spain) and the Center for Pragmatics Research (Dalian, China).

Esther Usó-Juan holds the position of Senior Lecturer in Applied Linguistics at Universitat Jaume I in Castellón, Spain. Her research focuses on interlanguage pragmatics, instructional pragmatics, and language learning and teaching. She has published in various international journals, including *The Modern Language Journal, Applied Language Learning, ELT Journal and Language Teaching Research.* Additionally, her other works, including edited books and book chapters have been published by renowned publishers such as Mouton de Gruyter, John Benjamins, Routledge, Springer and Rodopi, among others. Her recent publications have focused on analysing the pragmatic performance of Spanish learners of English, offering valuable insights into the complexities of cross-cultural communication. Moreover, she has explored innovative teaching approaches, particularly through the integration of audio-visual materials, to enhance the instruction of pragmatics in language learning settings.

Linguistic Insights

Studies in Language and Communication

This series aims to promote specialist language studies in the fields of linguistic theory and applied linguistics, by publishing volumes that focus on specific aspects of language use in one or several languages and provide valuable insights into language and communication research. A cross-disciplinary approach is favoured and most European languages are accepted.

The series includes two types of books:

- Monographs – featuring in-depth studies on special aspects of language theory, language analysis or language teaching.
- Collected papers – assembling papers from workshops, conferences or symposia.

Each volume of the series is subjected to a double peer-reviewing process.

Vol. 1 Maurizio Gotti & Marina Dossena (eds)
Modality in Specialized Texts. Selected Papers of the 1st CERLIS Conference.
421 pages. 2001. ISBN 3-906767-10-8 · US-ISBN 0-8204-5340-4

Vol. 2 Giuseppina Cortese & Philip Riley (eds)
Domain-specific English. Textual Practices across Communities and Classrooms.
420 pages. 2002. ISBN 3-906768-98-8 · US-ISBN 0-8204-5884-8

Vol. 3 Maurizio Gotti, Dorothee Heller & Marina Dossena (eds)
Conflict and Negotiation in Specialized Texts. Selected Papers of the 2nd CERLIS Conference.
470 pages. 2002. ISBN 3-906769-12-7 · US-ISBN 0-8204-5887-2

Vol. 4 Maurizio Gotti, Marina Dossena, Richard Dury, Roberta Facchinetti & Maria Lima Variation in Central Modals. A Repertoire of Forms and Types of Usage in Middle English and Early Modern English.
364 pages. 2002. ISBN 3-906769-84-4 · US-ISBN 0-8204-5898-8

Editorial address:

Prof. Maurizio Gotti Università di Bergamo, Dipartimento di Lingue, Letterature e Culture Straniere Piazza Rosate 2, 24129 Bergamo, Italy
Fax: +39 035 2052789, E-Mail: m.gotti@unibg.it

Vol. 5 Stefania Nuccorini (ed.)
Phrases and Phraseology. Data and Descriptions.
187 pages. 2002. ISBN 3-906770-08-7 · US-ISBN 0-8204-5933-X

Vol. 6 Vijay Bhatia, Christopher N. Candlin & Maurizio Gotti (eds)
Legal Discourse in Multilingual and Multicultural Contexts.
Arbitration Texts in Europe.
385 pages. 2003. ISBN 3-906770-85-0 · US-ISBN 0-8204-6254-3

Vol. 7 Marina Dossena & Charles Jones (eds)
Insights into Late Modern English. 2nd edition.
378 pages. 2003, 2007. ISBN 978-3-03911-257-9 ·
US-ISBN 978-0-8204-8927-8

Vol. 8 Maurizio Gotti
Specialized Discourse. Linguistic Features and Changing Conventions.
351 pages. 2003, 2005.
ISBN 3-03910-606-6 · US-ISBN 0-8204-7000-7

Vol. 9 Alan Partington, John Morley & Louann Haarman (eds)
Corpora and Discourse.
420 pages. 2004. ISBN 3-03910-026-2 · US-ISBN 0-8204-6262-4

Vol. 10 Martina Möllering
The Acquisition of German Modal Particles. A Corpus-Based Approach.
290 pages. 2004. ISBN 3-03910-043-2 · US-ISBN 0-8204-6273-X

Vol. 11 David Hart (ed.)
English Modality in Context. Diachronic Perspectives.
261 pages. 2003. ISBN 3-03910-046-7 · US-ISBN 0-8204-6852-5

Vol. 12 Wendy Swanson
Modes of Co-reference as an Indicator of Genre.
430 pages. 2003. ISBN 3-03910-052-1 · US-ISBN 0-8204-6855-X

Vol. 13 Gina Poncini
Discursive Strategies in Multicultural Business Meetings. 2nd edition.
338 pages. 2004, 2007. ISBN 978-3-03911-296-8 · US-ISBN 978-0-8204-8937-7

Vol. 14 Christopher N. Candlin & Maurizio Gotti (eds)
Intercultural Aspects of Specialized Communication. 2nd edition.
369 pages. 2004, 2007. ISBN 978-3-03911-258-6 · US-ISBN 978-0-8204-8926-1

Vol. 15 Gabriella Del Lungo Camiciotti & Elena Tognini Bonelli (eds)
Academic Discourse. New Insights into Evaluation.
234 pages. 2004. ISBN 3-03910-353-9 · US-ISBN 0-8204-7016-3

Vol. 16 Marina Dossena & Roger Lass (eds)
Methods and Data in English Historical Dialectology.
405 pages. 2004. ISBN 3-03910-362-8 · US-ISBN 0-8204-7018-X

Vol. 17 Judy Noguchi
The Science Review Article. An Opportune Genre in the Construction of Science.
274 pages. 2006. ISBN 3-03910-426-8 · US-ISBN 0-8204-7034-1

Vol. 18 Giuseppina Cortese & Anna Duszak (eds)
Identity, Community, Discourse. English in Intercultural Settings.
495 pages. 2005. ISBN 3-03910-632-5 · US-ISBN 0-8204-7163-1

Vol. 19 Anna Trosborg & Poul Erik Flyvholm Jørgensen (eds)
Business Discourse. Texts and Contexts.
250 pages. 2005. ISBN 3-03910-606-6 · US-ISBN 0-8204-7000-7

Vol. 20 Christopher Williams
Tradition and Change in Legal English. Verbal Constructions in Prescriptive Texts.
2nd revised edition.
216 pages. 2005, 2007. ISBN 978-3-03911-444-3.

Vol. 21 Katarzyna Dziubalska-Kolaczyk & Joanna Przedlacka (eds)
English Pronunciation Models: A Changing Scene. 2nd edition.
476 pages. 2005, 2008. ISBN 978-3-03911-682-9.

Vol. 22 Christián Abello-Contesse, Rubén Chacón-Beltrán,
M. Dolores López-Jiménez & M. Mar Torreblanca-López (eds)
Age in L2 Acquisition and Teaching.
214 pages. 2006. ISBN 3-03910-668-6 · US-ISBN 0-8204-7174-7

Vol. 23 Vijay K. Bhatia, Maurizio Gotti, Jan Engberg & Dorothee Heller (eds)
Vagueness in Normative Texts.
474 pages. 2005. ISBN 3-03910-653-8 · US-ISBN 0-8204-7169-0

Vol. 24 Paul Gillaerts & Maurizio Gotti (eds)
Genre Variation in Business Letters. 2nd printing.
407 pages. 2008. ISBN 978-3-03911-681-2.

Vol. 25 Ana María Hornero, María José Luzón & Silvia Murillo (eds)
Corpus Linguistics. Applications for the Study of English. 2nd printing.
526 pages. 2006, 2008. ISBN 978-3-03911-726-0

Vol. 26 J. Lachlan Mackenzie & María de los Ángeles Gómez-González (eds)
Studies in Functional Discourse Grammar.
259 pages. 2005. ISBN 3-03910-696-1 · US-ISBN 0-8204-7558-0

Vol. 27 Debbie G. E. Ho
Classroom Talk. Exploring the Sociocultural Structure of Formal ESL Learning. 2nd edition.
254 pages. 2006, 2007. ISBN 978-3-03911-434-4

Vol. 28 Javier Pérez-Guerra, Dolores González-Álvarez, Jorge L. Bueno-Alonso & Esperanza Rama-Martínez (eds)
'Of Varying Language and Opposing Creed'. New Insights into Late Modern English.
455 pages. 2007. ISBN 978-3-03910-788-9

Vol. 29 Francesca Bargiela-Chiappini & Maurizio Gotti (eds)
Asian Business Discourse(s).
350 pages. 2005. ISBN 3-03910-804-2 · US-ISBN 0-8204-7574-2

Vol. 30 Nicholas Brownlees (ed.)
News Discourse in Early Modern Britain. Selected Papers of CHINED 2004.
300 pages. 2006. ISBN 3-03910-805-0 · US-ISBN 0-8204-8025-8

Vol. 31 Roberta Facchinetti & Matti Rissanen (eds)
Corpus-based Studies of Diachronic English.
300 pages. 2006. ISBN 3-03910-851-4 · US-ISBN 0-8204-8040-1

Vol. 32 Marina Dossena & Susan M. Fitzmaurice (eds)
Business and Official Correspondence. Historical Investigations.
209 pages. 2006. ISBN 3-03910-880-8 · US-ISBN 0-8204-8352-4

Vol. 33 Giuliana Garzone & Srikant Sarangi (eds)
Discourse, Ideology and Specialized Communication.
494 pages. 2007. ISBN 978-3-03910-888-6

Vol. 34 Giuliana Garzone & Cornelia Ilie (eds)
The Use of English in Institutional and Business Settings. An Intercultural Perspective.
372 pages. 2007. ISBN 978-3-03910-889-3

Vol. 35 Vijay K. Bhatia & Maurizio Gotti (eds) Explorations in Specialized Genres.
316 pages. 2006. ISBN 3-03910-995-2 · US-ISBN 0-8204-8372-9

Vol. 36 Heribert Picht (ed.)
Modern Approaches to Terminological Theories and Applications.
432 pages. 2006. ISBN 3-03911-156-6 · US-ISBN 0-8204-8380-X

Vol. 37 Anne Wagner & Sophie Cacciaguidi-Fahy (eds)
Legal Language and the Search for Clarity / Le langage juridique et la quête de clarté. Practice and Tools / Pratiques et instruments.
487 pages. 2006. ISBN 3-03911-169-8 · US-ISBN 0-8204-8388-5

Vol. 38 Juan Carlos Palmer-Silveira, Miguel F. Ruiz-Garrido & Inmaculada Fortanet-Gómez (eds)
Intercultural and International Business Communication. Theory, Research and Teaching. 2nd edition.
343 pages. 2006, 2008. ISBN 978-3-03911-680-5

Vol. 39 Christiane Dalton-Puffer, Dieter Kastovsky, Nikolaus Ritt & Herbert Schendl (eds)
Syntax, Style and Grammatical Norms. English from 1500–2000.
250 pages. 2006. ISBN 3-03911-181-7 · US-ISBN 0-8204-8394-X

Vol. 40 Marina Dossena & Irma Taavitsainen (eds)
Diachronic Perspectives on Domain-Specific English.
280 pages. 2006. ISBN 3-03910-176-0 · US-ISBN 0-8204-8391-5

Vol. 41 John Flowerdew & Maurizio Gotti (eds)
Studies in Specialized Discourse.
293 pages. 2006. ISBN 3-03911-178-7

Vol. 42 Ken Hyland & Marina Bondi (eds)
Academic Discourse Across Disciplines.
320 pages. 2006. ISBN 3-03911-183-3 · US-ISBN 0-8204-8396-6

Vol. 43 Paul Gillaerts & Philip Shaw (eds)
The Map and the Landscape. Norms and Practices in Genre.
256 pages. 2006. ISBN 3-03911-182-5 · US-ISBN 0-8204-8395-4

Vol. 44 Maurizio Gotti & Davide Giannoni (eds)
New Trends in Specialized Discourse Analysis.
301 pages. 2006. ISBN 3-03911-184-1 · US-ISBN 0-8204-8381-8

Vol. 45 Maurizio Gotti & Françoise Salager-Meyer (eds)
Advances in Medical Discourse Analysis. Oral and Written Contexts.
492 pages. 2006. ISBN 3-03911-185-X · US-ISBN 0-8204-8382-6

Vol. 46 Maurizio Gotti & Susan Šarcevic´ (eds) Insights into Specialized Translation.
396 pages. 2006. ISBN 3-03911-186-8 · US-ISBN 0-8204-8383-4

Vol. 47 Khurshid Ahmad & Margaret Rogers (eds)
Evidence-based LSP. Translation, Text and Terminology.
584 pages. 2007. ISBN 978-3-03911-187-9

Vol. 48 Hao Sun & Dániel Z. Kádár (eds)
It's the Dragon's Turn. Chinese Institutional Discourses.
262 pages. 2008. ISBN 978-3-03911-175-6

Vol. 49 Cristina Suárez-Gómez
Relativization in Early English (950-1250). the Position of Relative Clauses.
149 pages. 2006. ISBN 3-03911-203-1 · US-ISBN 0-8204-8904-2

Vol. 50 Maria Vittoria Calvi & Luisa Chierichetti (eds)
Nuevas tendencias en el discurso de especialidad.
319 pages. 2006. ISBN 978-3-03911-261-6

Vol. 51 Mari Carmen Campoy & María José Luzón (eds)
Spoken Corpora in Applied Linguistics.
274 pages. 2008. ISBN 978-3-03911-275-3

Vol. 52 Konrad Ehlich & Dorothee Heller (Hrsg.)
Die Wissenschaft und ihre Sprachen.
323 pages. 2006. ISBN 978-3-03911-272-2

Vol. 53 Jingyu Zhang
The Semantic Salience Hierarchy Model. The L2 Acquisition of Psych Predicates
273 pages. 2007. ISBN 978-3-03911-300-2

Vol. 54 Norman Fairclough, Giuseppina Cortese & Patrizia Ardizzone (eds)
Discourse and Contemporary Social Change.
555 pages. 2007. ISBN 978-3-03911-276-0

Vol. 55 Jan Engberg, Marianne Grove Ditlevsen, Peter Kastberg & Martin Stegu (eds)
New Directions in LSP Teaching.
331 pages. 2007. ISBN 978-3-03911-433-7

Vol. 56 Dorothee Heller & Konrad Ehlich (Hrsg.)
Studien zur Rechtskommunikation.
322 pages. 2007. ISBN 978-3-03911-436-8

Vol. 57 Teruhiro Ishiguro & Kang-kwong Luke (eds)
Grammar in Cross-Linguistic Perspective.
The Syntax, Semantics, and Pragmatics of Japanese and Chinese.
304 pages. 2012. ISBN 978-3-03911-445-0

Vol. 58 Carmen Frehner Email – SMS – MMS
294 pages. 2008. ISBN 978-3-03911-451-1

Vol. 59 Isabel Balteiro
The Directionality of Conversion in English. A Dia-Synchronic Study.
276 pages. 2007. ISBN 978-3-03911-241-8

Vol. 60 Maria Milagros Del Saz Rubio
English Discourse Markers of Reformulation.
237 pages. 2007. ISBN 978-3-03911-196-1

Vol. 61 Sally Burgess & Pedro Martín-Martín (eds)
English as an Additional Language in Research Publication and Communication.
259 pages. 2008. ISBN 978-3-03911-462-7

Vol. 62 Sandrine Onillon
Pratiques et représentations de l'écrit.
458 pages. 2008. ISBN 978-3-03911-464-1

Vol. 63 Hugo Bowles & Paul Seedhouse (eds)
Conversation Analysis and Language for Specific Purposes. 2nd edition.
337 pages. 2007, 2009. ISBN 978-3-0343-0045-2

Vol. 64 Vijay K. Bhatia, Christopher N. Candlin & Paola Evangelisti Allori (eds)
Language, Culture and the Law.
The Formulation of Legal Concepts across Systems and Cultures.
342 pages. 2008. ISBN 978-3-03911-470-2

Vol. 65 Jonathan Culpeper & Dániel Z. Kádár (eds)
Historical (Im)politeness.
300 pages. 2010. ISBN 978-3-03911-496-2

Vol. 66 Linda Lombardo (ed.)
Using Corpora to Learn about Language and Discourse.
237 pages. 2009. ISBN 978-3-03911-522-8

Vol. 67 Natsumi Wakamoto
Extroversion/Introversion in Foreign Language Learning. Interactions with Learner Strategy Use.
159 pages. 2009. ISBN 978-3-03911-596-9

Vol. 68 Eva Alcón-Soler (ed.)
Learning How to Request in an Instructed Language Learning Context.
260 pages. 2008. ISBN 978-3-03911-601-0

Vol. 69 Domenico Pezzini
The Translation of Religious Texts in the Middle Ages.
428 pages. 2008. ISBN 978-3-03911-600-3

Vol. 70 Tomoko Tode
Effects of Frequency in Classroom Second Language Learning. Quasi-experiment and stimulated-recall analysis.
195 pages. 2008. ISBN 978-3-03911-602-7

Vol. 71 Egor Tsedryk
Fusion symétrique et alternances ditransitives.
211 pages. 2009. ISBN 978-3-03911-609-6

Vol. 72 Cynthia J. Kellett Bidoli & Elana Ochse (eds)
English in International Deaf Communication.
444 pages. 2008. ISBN 978-3-03911-610-2

Vol. 73 Joan C. Beal, Carmela Nocera & Massimo Sturiale (eds)
Perspectives on Prescriptivism.
269 pages. 2008. ISBN 978-3-03911-632-4

Vol. 74 Carol Taylor Torsello, Katherine Ackerley & Erik Castello (eds)
Corpora for University Language Teachers.
308 pages. 2008. ISBN 978-3-03911-639-3

Vol. 75 María Luisa Pérez Cañado (ed.)
English Language Teaching in the European Credit Transfer System. Facing the Challenge.
251 pages. 2009. ISBN 978-3-03911-654-6

Vol. 76 Marina Dossena & Ingrid Tieken-Boon van Ostade (eds)
Studies in Late Modern English Correspondence. Methodology and Data.
291 pages. 2008. ISBN 978-3-03911-658-4

Vol. 77 Ingrid Tieken-Boon van Ostade & Wim van der Wurff (eds)
Current Issues in Late Modern English.
436 pages. 2009. ISBN 978-3-03911-660-7

Vol. 78 Marta Navarro Coy (ed.)
Practical Approaches to Foreign Language Teaching and Learning.
297 pages. 2009. ISBN 978-3-03911-661-4

Vol. 79 Qing Ma
Second Language Vocabulary Acquisition.
333 pages. 2009. ISBN 978-3-03911-666-9

Vol. 80 Martin Solly, Michelangelo Conoscenti & Sandra Campagna (eds)
Verbal/Visual Narrative Texts in Higher Education.
384 pages. 2008. ISBN 978-3-03911-672-0

Vol. 81 Meiko Matsumoto
From Simple Verbs to Periphrastic Expressions:
The Historical Development of Composite Predicates, Phrasal Verbs, and Related Constructions in English.
235 pages. 2008. ISBN 978-3-03911-675-1

Vol. 82 Melinda Dooly
Doing Diversity. Teachers' Construction of Their Classroom Reality.
180 pages. 2009. ISBN 978-3-03911-687-4

Vol. 83 Victoria Guillén-Nieto, Carmen Marimón-Llorca & Chelo Vargas-Sierra (eds)
Intercultural Business Communication and Simulation and Gaming Methodology.
392 pages. 2009. ISBN 978-3-03911-688-1

Vol. 84 Maria Grazia Guido
English as a Lingua Franca in Cross-cultural Immigration Domains.
285 pages. 2008. ISBN 978-3-03911-689-8

Vol. 85 Erik Castello
Text Complexity and Reading Comprehension Tests.
352 pages. 2008. ISBN 978-3-03911-717-8

Vol. 86 Maria-Lluisa Gea-Valor, Isabel García-Izquierdo & Maria-José Esteve (eds)
Linguistic and Translation Studies in Scientific Communication.
317 pages. 2010. ISBN 978-3-0343-0069-8

Vol. 87 Carmen Navarro, Rosa Ma Rodríguez Abella, Francesca Dalle Pezze & Renzo Miotti (eds) La comunicación especializada.
355 pages. 2008. ISBN 978-3-03911-733-8

Vol. 88 Kiriko Sato
The Development from Case-Forms to Prepositional Constructions in Old English Prose.
231 pages. 2009. ISBN 978-3-03911-763-5

Vol. 89 Dorothee Heller (Hrsg.)
Formulierungsmuster in deutscher und italienischer Fachkommunikation. Intra- und interlinguale Perspektiven.
315 pages. 2008. ISBN 978-3-03911-778-9

Vol. 90 Henning Bergenholtz, Sandro Nielsen & Sven Tarp (eds)
Lexicography at a Crossroads. Dictionaries and Encyclopedias Today, Lexicographical Tools Tomorrow.
372 pages. 2009. ISBN 978-3-03911-799-4

Vol. 91 Manouchehr Moshtagh Khorasani
The Development of Controversies. From the Early Modern Period to Online Discussion Forums.
317 pages. 2009. ISBN 978-3-3911-711-6

Vol. 92 María Luisa Carrió-Pastor (ed.)
Content and Language Integrated Learning. Cultural Diversity.
178 pages. 2009. ISBN 978-3-3911-818-2

Vol. 93 Roger Berry
Terminology in English Language Teaching. Nature and Use.
262 pages. 2010. ISBN 978-3-0343-0013-1

Vol. 94 Roberto Cagliero & Jennifer Jenkins (eds)
Discourses, Communities, and Global Englishes
240 pages. 2010. ISBN 978-3-0343-0012-4

Vol. 95 Facchinetti Roberta, Crystal David, Seidlhofer Barbara (eds)
From International to Local English – And Back Again.
268 pages. 2010. ISBN 978-3-0343-0011-7

Vol. 96 Cesare Gagliardi & Alan Maley (eds)
EIL, ELF, Global English. Teaching and Learning Issues
376 pages. 2010. ISBN 978-3-0343-0010-0

Vol. 97 Sylvie Hancil (ed.)
The Role of Prosody in Affective Speech.
403 pages. 2009. ISBN 978-3-03911-696-6

Vol. 98 Marina Dossena & Roger Lass (eds)
Studies in English and European Historical Dialectology.
257 pages. 2009. ISBN 978-3-0343-0024-7

Vol. 99 Christine Béal
Les interactions quotidiennes en français et en anglais.
De l'approche comparative à l'analyse des situations interculturelles.
424 pages. 2010. ISBN 978-3-0343-0027-8

Vol. 100 Maurizio Gotti (ed.)
Commonality and Individuality in Academic Discourse.
398 pages. 2009. ISBN 978-3-0343-0023-0

Vol. 101 Javier E. Díaz Vera & Rosario Caballero (eds)
Textual Healing. Studies in Medieval English Medical, Scientific and Technical Texts.
213 pages. 2009. ISBN 978-3-03911-822-9

Vol. 102 Nuria Edo Marzá
The Specialised Lexicographical Approach. A Step further in Dictionary-making.
316 pages. 2009. ISBN 978-3-0343-0043-8

Vol. 103 Carlos Prado-Alonso, Lidia Gómez-García, Iria Pastor-Gómez & David Tizón-Couto (eds)
New Trends and Methodologies in Applied English Language Research. Diachronic, Diatopic and Contrastive Studies.
348 pages. 2009. ISBN 978-3-0343-0046-9

Vol. 104 Françoise Salager-Meyer & Beverly A. Lewin Crossed Words. Criticism in Scholarly Writing?
371 pages. 2011. ISBN 978-3-0343-0049-0.

Vol. 105 Javier Ruano-García
Early Modern Northern English Lexis. A Literary Corpus-Based Study.
611 pages. 2010. ISBN 978-3-0343-0058-2

Vol. 106 Rafael Monroy-Casas
Systems for the Phonetic Transcription of English. Theory and Texts.
280 pages. 2011. ISBN 978-3-0343-0059-9

Vol. 107 Nicola T. Owtram
The Pragmatics of Academic Writing.
A Relevance Approach to the Analysis of Research Article Introductions.
311 pages. 2009. ISBN 978-3-0343-0060-5

Vol. 108 Yolanda Ruiz de Zarobe, Juan Manuel Sierra & Francisco Gallardo del Puerto (eds)
Content and Foreign Language Integrated Learning. Contributions to Multilingualism in European Contexts
343 pages. 2011. ISBN 978-3-0343-0074-2

Vol. 109 Ángeles Linde López & Rosalía Crespo Jiménez (eds)
Professional English in the European context. The EHEA challenge.
374 pages. 2010. ISBN 978-3-0343-0088-9

Vol. 110 Rosalía Rodríguez-Vázquez
The Rhythm of Speech, Verse and Vocal Music. A New Theory.
394 pages. 2010. ISBN 978-3-0343-0309-5

Vol. 111 Anastasios Tsangalidis & Roberta Facchinetti (eds)
Studies on English Modality. In Honour of Frank Palmer.
392 pages. 2009. ISBN 978-3-0343-0310-1

Vol. 112 Jing Huang
Autonomy, Agency and Identity in Foreign Language Learning and Teaching.
400 pages. 2013. ISBN 978-3-0343-0370-5

Vol. 113 Mihhail Lotman & Maria-Kristiina Lotman (eds)
Frontiers in Comparative Prosody. In memoriam: Mikhail Gasparov.
426 pages. 2011. ISBN 978-3-0343-0373-6

Vol. 114 Merja Kytö, John Scahill & Harumi Tanabe (eds)
Language Change and Variation from Old English to Late Modern English. A Festschrift for Minoji Akimoto
422 pages. 2010. ISBN 978-3-0343-0372-9

Vol. 115 Giuliana Garzone & Paola Catenaccio (eds)
Identities across Media and Modes. Discursive Perspectives.
379 pages. 2009. ISBN 978-3-0343-0386-6

Vol. 116 Elena Landone
Los marcadores del discurso y cortesía verbal en español.
390 pages. 2010. ISBN 978-3-0343-0413-9

Vol. 117 Maurizio Gotti & Christopher Williams (eds)
Legal Discourse across Languages and Cultures.
339 pages. 2010. ISBN 978-3-0343-0425-2

Vol. 118 David Hirsh
Academic Vocabulary in Context.
217 pages. 2010. ISBN 978-3-0343-0426-9

Vol. 119 Yvonne Dröschel
Lingua Franca English. The Role of Simplification and Transfer.
358 pages. 2011. ISBN 978-3-0343-0432-0

Vol. 120 Tengku Sepora Tengku Mahadi, Helia Vaezian & Mahmoud Akbari Corpora in Translation. A Practical Guide.
135 pages. 2010. ISBN 978-3-0343-0434-4

Vol. 121 Davide Simone Giannoni & Celina Frade (eds)
Researching Language and the Law. Textual Features and Translation Issues.
278 pages. 2010. ISBN 978-3-0343-0443-6

Vol. 122 Daniel Madrid & Stephen Hughes (eds)
Studies in Bilingual Education.
472 pages. 2011. ISBN 978-3-0343-0474-0

Vol. 123 Vijay K. Bhatia, Christopher N. Candlin & Maurizio Gotti (eds)
The Discourses of Dispute Resolution.
290 pages. 2010. ISBN 978-3-0343-0476-4

Vol. 124 Davide Simone Giannoni
Mapping Academic Values in the Disciplines. A Corpus-Based Approach.
288 pages. 2010. ISBN 978-3-0343-0488-7

Vol. 125 Giuliana Garzone & James Archibald (eds)
Discourse, Identities and Roles in Specialized Communication.
419 pages. 2010. ISBN 978-3-0343-0494-8

Vol. 126 Iria Pastor-Gómez
The Status and Development of N+N Sequences in Contemporary English Noun Phrases.
216 pages. 2011. ISBN 978-3-0343-0534-1

Vol. 127 Carlos Prado-Alonso
Full-verb Inversion in Written and Spoken English.
261 pages. 2011. ISBN 978-3-0343-0535-8

Vol. 128 Tony Harris & María Moreno Jaén (eds) Corpus Linguistics in Language Teaching.
214 pages. 2010. ISBN 978-3-0343-0524-2

Vol. 129 Tetsuji Oda & Hiroyuki Eto (eds)
Multiple Perspectives on English Philology and History of Linguistics. A Festschrift for Shoichi Watanabe on his 80th Birthday.
378 pages. 2010. ISBN 978-3-0343-0480-1

Vol. 130 Luisa Chierichetti & Giovanni Garofalo (eds)
Lengua y Derecho. líneas de investigación interdisciplinaria.
283 pages. 2010. 978-3-0343-0463-4

Vol. 131 Paola Evangelisti Allori & Giuliana Garzone (eds)
Discourse, Identities and Genres in Corporate Communication. Sponsorship, Advertising and Organizational Communication.
324 pages. 2011. 978-3-0343-0591-4

Vol. 132 Leyre Ruiz de Zarobe & Yolanda Ruiz de Zarobe (eds)
Speech Acts and Politeness across Languages and Cultures.
402 pages. 2012. 978-3-0343-0611-9

Vol. 133 Thomas Christiansen
Cohesion. A Discourse Perspective.
387 pages. 2011. 978-3-0343-0619-5

Vol. 134 Giuliana Garzone & Maurizio Gotti
Discourse, Communication and the Enterprise. Genres and Trends.
451 pages. 2011. ISBN 978-3-0343-0620-1

Vol. 150 Maurizio Gotti (ed.)
Academic Identity Traits. A Corpus-Based Investigation.
363 pages. 2012. ISBN 978-3-0343-1141-0

Vol. 151 Priscilla Heynderickx, Sylvain Dieltjens, Geert Jacobs, Paul Gillaerts & Elizabeth de Groot (eds)
The Language Factor in International Business.
New Perspectives on Research, Teaching and Practice.
320 pages. 2012. ISBN 978-3-0343-1090-1

Vol. 152 Paul Gillaerts, Elizabeth de Groot, Sylvain Dieltjens, Priscilla Heynderickx & Geert Jacobs (eds)
Researching Discourse in Business Genres. Cases and Corpora.
215 pages. 2012. ISBN 978-3-0343-1092-5

Vol. 153 Yongyan Zheng
Dynamic Vocabulary Development in a Foreign Language.
262 pages. 2012. ISBN 978-3-0343-1106-9

Vol. 154 Carmen Argondizzo (ed.)
Creativity and Innovation in Language Education.
357 pages. 2012. ISBN 978-3-0343-1080-2

Vol. 155 David Hirsh (ed.)
Current Perspectives in Second Language Vocabulary Research.
180 pages. 2012. ISBN 978-3-0343-1108-3

Vol. 156 Seiji Shinkawa
Unhistorical Gender Assignment in Lahamon's Brut. A Case Study of a Late Stage in the Development of Grammatical Gender toward its Ultimate Loss.
186 pages. 2012. ISBN 978-3-0343-1124-3

Vol. 157 Yeonkwon Jung
Basics of Organizational Writing: A Critical Reading Approach.
151 pages. 2014. ISBN 978-3-0343-1137-3.

Vol. 158 Bárbara Eizaga Rebollar (ed.) Studies in Linguistics and Cognition.
301 pages. 2012. ISBN 978-3-0343-1138-0

Vol. 159 Giuliana Garzone, Paola Catenaccio, Chiara Degano (eds)
Genre Change in the Contemporary World. Short-term Diachronic Perspectives.
329 pages. 2012. ISBN 978-3-0343-1214-1

Vol. 160 Carol Berkenkotter, Vijay K. Bhatia & Maurizio Gotti (eds)
Insights into Academic Genres.
468 pages. 2012. ISBN 978-3-0343-1211-0

Vol. 161 Beatriz Tizón-Couto
Clausal Complements in Native and Learner Spoken English. A corpus-based study with Lindsei and Vicolse.
357 pages. 2013. ISBN 978-3-0343-1184-7

Vol. 162 Patrizia Anesa
Jury Trials and the Popularization of Legal Language. A Discourse Analytical Approach.
247 pages. 2012. ISBN 978-3-0343-1231-8

Vol. 163 David Hirsh
Endangered Languages, Knowledge Systems and Belief Systems.
153 pages. 2013. ISBN 978-3-0343-1232-5

Vol. 164 Eugenia Sainz (ed.)
De la estructura de la frase al tejido del discurso. Estudios contrastivos español/italiano.
305 pages. 2014. ISBN 978-3-0343-1253-0

Vol. 165 Julia Bamford, Franca Poppi & Davide Mazzi (eds) Space, Place and the Discursive Construction of Identity.
367 pages. 2014. ISBN 978-3-0343-1249-3

Vol. 166 Rita Salvi & Janet Bowker (eds)
Space, Time and the Construction of Identity.
Discursive Indexicality in Cultural, Institutional and Professional Fields.
324 pages. 2013. ISBN 978-3-0343-1254-7

Vol. 167 Shunji Yamazaki & Robert Sigley (eds)
Approaching Language Variation through Corpora. A Festschrift in Honour of Toshio Saito.
421 pages. 2013. ISBN 978-3-0343-1264-6

Vol. 168 Franca Poppi
Global Interactions in English as a Lingua Franca. How written communication is changing under the influence of electronic media and new contexts of use.
249 pages. 2012. ISBN 978-3-0343-1276-9

Vol. 169 Miguel A. Aijón Oliva & María José Serrano
Style in syntax. Investigating variation in Spanish pronoun subjects.
239 pages. 2013. ISBN 978-3-0343-1244-8

Vol. 170 Inés Olza, Óscar Loureda & Manuel Casado-Velarde (eds)
Language Use in the Public Sphere. Methodological Perspectives and Empirical Applications
564 pages. 2014. ISBN 978-3-0343-1286-8

Vol. 171 Aleksandra Matulewska
Legilinguistic Translatology. A Parametric Approach to Legal Translation.
279 pages. 2013. ISBN 978-3-0343-1287-5

Vol. 172 Maurizio Gotti & Carmen Sancho Guinda (eds) Narratives in Academic and Professional Genres. 513 pages. 2013. ISBN 978-3-0343-1371-1

Vol. 173 Madalina Chitez
Learner corpus profiles. The case of Romanian Learner English.
244 pages. 2014. ISBN 978-3-0343-1410-7

Vol. 174 Chihiro Inoue
Task Equivalence in Speaking Tests.
251 pages. 2013. ISBN 978-3-0343-1417-6

Vol. 175 Gabriel Quiroz & Pedro Patiño (eds.)
LSP in Colombia: advances and challenges.
339 pages. 2014. ISBN 978-3-0343-1434-3

Vol. 176 Catherine Resche
Economic Terms and Beyond: Capitalising on the Wealth of Notions.
How Researchers in Specialised Varieties of English Can Benefit from Focusing on Terms.
332 pages. 2013. ISBN 978-3-0343-1435-0

Vol. 177 Wei Wang
Media representation of migrant workers in China. Identities and stances
198 pages. 2018. 978-3-0343-1436-7

Vol. 178 Cécile Desoutter & Caroline Mellet (dir.)
Le discours rapporté: approches linguistiques et perspectives didactiques.
270 pages. 2013. ISBN 978-3-0343-1292-9

Vol. 179 Ana Díaz-Negrillo & Francisco Javier Díaz-Pérez (eds) Specialisation and Variation in Language Corpora.
341 pages. 2014. ISBN 978-3-0343-1316-2

Vol. 180 Pilar Alonso
A Multi-dimensional Approach to Discourse Coherence. From Standardness to Creativity.
247 pages. 2014. ISBN 978-3-0343-1325-4

Vol. 181 Alejandro Alcaraz-Sintes & Salvador Valera-Hernández (eds) Diachrony and Synchrony in English Corpus Linguistics.
393 pages. 2014. ISBN 978-3-0343-1326-1

Vol. 182 Runhan Zhang
Investigating Linguistic Knowledge of a Second Language.
207 pages. 2015. ISBN 978-3-0343-1330-8

Vol. 183 Hajar Abdul Rahim & Shakila Abdul Manan (eds.)
English in Malaysia. Postcolonial and Beyond.
267 pages. 2014. ISBN 978-3-0343-1341-4

Vol. 184 Virginie Fasel Lauzon
Comprendre et apprendre dans l'interaction. Les séquences d'explication en classe de français langue seconde.
292 pages. 2014. ISBN 978-3-0343-1451-0

Vol. 185 Forthcoming.

Vol. 186 Wei Ren
L2 Pragmatic Development in Study Abroad Contexts
256 pages. 2015. ISBN 978-3-0343-1358-2

Vol. 187 Marina Bondi & Rosa Lorés Sanz (eds)
Abstracts in Academic Discourse. Variation and Change.
361 pages. 2014. ISBN 978-3-0343-1483-1

Vol. 188 Giuditta Caliendo
Rethinking Community. Discourse, Identity and Citizenship in the European Union.
240 pages. 2017. ISBN 978-3-0343-1561-6

Vol. 189 Paola Evangelisti Allori (ed.)
Identities in and across Cultures.
315 pages. 2014. ISBN 978-3-0343-1458-9

Vol. 190 Erik Castello, Katherine Ackerley & Francesca Coccetta (eds).
Studies in Learner Corpus Linguistics. Research and Applications for Foreign Language Teaching and Assessment.
358 pages. 2015. ISBN 978-3-0343-1506-7

Vol. 191 Ruth Breeze, Maurizio Gotti & Carmen Sancho Guinda (eds)
Interpersonality in Legal Genres.
389 pages. 2014. ISBN 978-3-0343-1524-1

Vol. 192 Paola Evangelisti Allori, John Bateman & Vijay K. Bhatia (eds)
Evolution in Genre. Emergence, Variation, Multimodality.
364 pages. 2014. ISBN 978-3-0343-1533-3

Vol. 193 Jiyeon Kook
Agency in Arzt-Patient-Gesprächen. Zur interaktionistischen Konzeptualisierung von Agency
271 pages. 2015. ISBN 978-3-0343-1666-8

Vol. 194 Susana Nicolás Román & Juan José Torres Núñez (eds)
Drama and CLIL. A new challenge for the teaching approaches in bilingual education.
170 pages. 2015. ISBN 978-3-0343-1629-3

Vol. 195 Alessandra Molino & Serenella Zanotti (eds)
Observing Norm, Observing Usage. Lexis in Dictionaries and in the Media.
430 pages. 2015. ISBN 978-3-0343-1584-5

Vol. 196 Begoña Soneira
A Lexical Description of English for Architecture. A Corpus-based Approach.
267 pages. 2015. ISBN 978-3-0343-1602-6

Vol. 197 M Luisa Roca-Varela
False Friends in Learner Corpora. A corpus-based study of English false friends in the written and spoken production of Spanish learners.
348 pages. 2015. ISBN 978-3-0343-1620-0

Vol. 198 Rahma Al-Mahrooqi & Christopher Denman
Bridging the Gap between Education and Employment. English Language Instruction in EFL Contexts.
416 pages. 2015. ISBN 978-3-0343-1681-1

Vol. 199 Rita Salvi & Janet Bowker (eds)
The Dissemination of Contemporary Knowledge in English. Genres, discourse strategies and professional practices.
171 pages. 2015. ISBN 978-3-0343-1679-8

Vol. 200 Maurizio Gotti & Davide S. Giannoni (eds)
Corpus Analysis for Descriptive and Pedagogical Purposes. ESP Perspectives.
432 pages. 2014. ISBN 978-3-0343-1516-6

Vol. 201 Ida Ruffolo
The Perception of Nature in Travel Promotion Texts. A Corpus-based Discourse Analysis.
148 pages. 2015. ISBN 978-3-0343-1521-0

Vol. 202 Ives Trevian
English suffixes. Stress-assignment properties, productivity, selection and combinatorial processes.
471 pages. 2015. ISBN 978-3-0343-1576-0

Vol. 203 Maurizio Gotti, Stefania Maci & Michele Sala (eds)
Insights into Medical Communication.
422 pages. 2015. ISBN 978-3-0343-1694-1

Vol. 204 Carmen Argondizzo (ed.)
European Projects in University Language Centres. Creativity, Dynamics, Best Practice.
371 pages. 2015. ISBN 978-3-0343-1696-5

Vol. 205 Aura Luz Duffé Montalván (ed.)
Estudios sobre el léxico. Puntos y contrapuntos.
502 pages. 2016. ISBN 978-3-0343-2011-5

Vol. 206 Maria Pavesi, Maicol Formentelli & Elisa Ghia (eds)
The Languages of Dubbing. Mainstream Audiovisual Translation in Italy.
275 pages. 2014. ISBN 978-3-0343-1646-0

Vol. 207 Ruth Breeze & Inés Olza (eds)
Evaluation in media discourse. European perspectives.
268 pages. 2017. ISBN 978-3-0343-2014-6

Vol. 208 Vijay K. Bhatia & Maurizio Gotti (eds)
Arbitration Discourse in Asia.
331 pages. 2015. ISBN 978-3-0343-2032-0

Vol. 209 Sofía Bemposta-Rivas, Carla Bouzada-Jabois, Yolanda Fernández-Pena, Tamara Bouso, Yolanda J. Calvo-Benzies, Iván Tamaredo (eds)
New trends and methodologies in applied English language research III. Synchronic and diachronic studies on discourse, lexis and grammar processing.
280 pages. 2017. ISBN 978-3-0343-2039-9

Vol. 210 Francisco Alonso Almeida, Laura Cruz García & Víctor González Ruiz (eds)
Corpus-based studies on language varieties.
285 pages. 2016. ISBN 978-3-0343-2044-3

Vol. 211 Juan Pedro Rica Peromingo
Aspectos lingüísticos y técnicos de la traducción audiovisual (TAV).
177 pages. 2016. ISBN 978-3-0343-2055-9

Vol. 212 Maria Vender
Disentangling Dyslexia. VenderPhonological and Processing Deficit in Developmental Dyslexia.
338 pages. 2017. ISBN 978-3-0343-2064-1

Vol. 213 Zhilong Xie
Bilingual Advantages. Contributions of Different Bilingual Experiences to Cognitive Control Differences Among Young-adult Bilinguals.
221 pages. 2016. ISBN 978-3-0343-2081-8

Vol. 214 Larissa D'Angelo
Academic posters. A textual and visual metadiscourse analysis.
367 pages. 2016. ISBN 978-3-0343-2083-2

Vol. 215 Evelyne Berger
Prendre la parole en L2. Regard sur la compétence d'interaction en classe de langue.
246 pages. 2016. ISBN 978-3-0343-2084-9

Vol. 216 David Lasagabaster and Aintzane Doiz (eds)
CLIL experiences in secondary and tertiary education: In search of good practices.
262 pages. 2016. ISBN 978-3-0343-2104-4

Vol. 217 Elena Kkese
Identifying Plosives in L2 English: The Case of L1 Cypriot Greek Speakers.
317 pages. 2016. ISBN 978-3-0343-2060-3

Vol. 218 Sandra Campagna, Elana Ochse, Virginia Pulcini & Martin Solly (eds)
Languaging in and across Communities: New Voices, New Identities. Studies in Honour of Giuseppina Cortese.
507 pages. 2016. ISBN 978-3-0343-2073-3

Vol. 219 Adriana Orlandi & Laura Giacomini (ed.)
Defining collocation for lexicographic purposes. From linguistic theory to lexicographic practice.
328 pages. 2016. ISBN 978-3-0343-2054-2

Vol. 220 Pietro Luigi Iaia
Analysing English as a Lingua Franca in Video Games. Linguistic Features, Experiential and Functional Dimensions of Online and Scripted Interactions.
139 pages. 2016. ISBN 978-3-0343-2138-9

Vol. 221 Dimitrinka G. Níkleva (ed.)
La formación de los docentes de español para inmigrantes en distintos contextos educativos.
390 pages. 2017. ISBN 978-3-0343-2135-8

Vol. 222 Katherine Ackerley, Marta Guarda & Francesca Helm (eds)
Sharing Perspectives on English-Medium Instruction.
308 pages. 2017. ISBN 978-3-0343-2537-0

Vol. 223 Juana I. Marín-Arrese, Julia Lavid-López, Marta Carretero, Elena Domínguez Romero, Ma Victoria Martín de la Rosa & María Pérez Blanco (eds)
Evidentiality and Modality in European Languages. Discourse-pragmatic perspectives.
427 pages. 2017. ISBN 978-3-0343-2437-3

Vol. 224 Gilles Col
Construction du sens : un modèle instructionnel pour la sémantique.
292 pages. 2017. ISBN 978-3-0343-2572-1

Vol. 225 Ana Chiquito & Gabriel Quiroz (eds)
Pobreza, Lenguaje y Medios en América Latina.
362 pages. 2017. ISBN 978-3-0343-2142-6

Vol. 226 Xu Zhang
English Quasi-Numeral Classifiers. A Corpus-Based Cognitive-Typological Study.
360 pages. 2017. ISBN 978-3-0343-2818-0

Vol. 227 María Ángeles Orts, Ruth Breeze & Maurizio Gotti (eds)
Power, Persuasion and Manipulation in Specialised Genres. Providing Keys to the Rhetoric of Professional Communities.
368 pages. 2017. ISBN 978-3-0343-3010-7

Vol. 228 Maurizio Gotti, Stefania Maci & Michele Sala (eds)
Ways of Seeing, Ways of Being: Representing the Voices of Tourism.
453 pages. 2017. ISBN 978-3-0343-3031-2

Vol. 229 Dino Selvaggi
Plurilingual Code-Switching between Standard and Local Varieties. A Socio-Psycholinguistic Approach
371 pages. 2018. ISBN 978-3-0343-2663-6

Vol. 230 Anca-Cristina Sterie
Interprofessional interactions at the hospital. Nurses' requests and reports of problems in calls with physicians.
371 pages. 2017. ISBN 978-3-0343-2734-3

Vol. 231 Xiaodong Zhang
Understanding Chinese EFL Teachers' Beliefs and Practices in the Textbook-Based Classroom.
189 pages. 2017. ISBN 978-3-0343-3053-4

Vol. 232 Manuela Caterina Moroni & Federica Ricci Garotti (Hrsg.)
Brücken schlagen zwischen Sprachwissenschaft und DaF-Didaktik.
345 pages. 2017. ISBN 978-3-0343-2667-4

Vol. 233 Dimitrinka Georgieva Níkleva
Necesidades y tendencias en la formación del profesorado de español como lengua extranjera
401 pages. 2017. ISBN 978-3-0343-2946-0

Vol. 234 Juan Santana-Lario & Salvador Valera (Hrsg.)
Competing patterns in English affixation.
272 pages. 2017. ISBN 978-3-0343-2701-5

Vol. 235 Francisco Salgado-Robles
Desarrollo de la competencia sociolingüística por aprendices de español en un contexto de inmersión en el extranjero
241 pages. 2018. ISBN 978-3-0343-2323-9

Vol. 236 Maria Chiara Janner
Sguardi linguistici sulla marca. Analisi morfosintattica dei nomi commerciali in italiano
345 pages. 2017. ISBN 978-3-0343-2667-4

Vol. 237 Bárbara Herrero Muñoz-Cobo & Otman El Azami Zalachi La primavera del árabe marroquí.
192 pages. 2017. ISBN 978-3-0343-3104-3

Vol. 238 Consuelo Pascual Escagedo
El papel del oyente en la construcción de la conversación espontánea de estudiantes italianos en su interlengua y en su lengua materna
295 pages. 2017. ISBN 978-3-0343-3186-9

Vol. 239 Stefania M. Maci
The MS Digby 133 Mary Magdalene. Beyond scribal practices: language, discourse, values and attitudes.
336 pages. 2017. ISBN 978-3-0343-3256-9

Vol. 240 Eliecer Crespo-Fernández
Taboo in Discourse. Studies on Attenuation and Offence in Communication.
326 pages. 2018. ISBN 978-3-0343-3018-3

Vol. 241 Jana Altmanova, Maria Centrella, Katherine E. Russo (eds)
Terminology & Discourse / Terminologie et discours.
424 pages. 2018. ISBN 978-3-0343-2417-5

Vol. 242 Xavier Blanco et Inès Sfar (dir.)
Lexicologie(s) : approches croisées en sémantique lexicale.
442 pages. 2018. ISBN 978-3-0343-3056-5

Vol. 243 Yunfeng Ge
Resolution of Conflict of Interest in Chinese Civil Court Hearings. A Perspective of Discourse Information Theory.
302 pages. 2018. ISBN 978-3-0343-3313-9

Vol. 244 Carla Vergaro
Illocutionary Shell Nouns in English
322 pages. 2018. ISBN 978-3-0343-3069-5

Vol. 245 Paolo Frassi
L'adjectif en français et sa définition lexicographique.
270 pages. 2018. ISBN 978-3-0343-3394-8

Vol. 246 Suwilai Premsrirat and David Hirsh (eds)
Language Revitalization. Insights from Thailand
328 pages. 2018. ISBN 978-3-0343-3497-6

Vol. 247 Wei Wang
Researching Learning and Learners in Genre-based Academic Writing Instruction
282 pages. 2018. ISBN 978-3-0343-3297-2

Vol. 248 Isusi Alabarte, Alberto & Lahuerta Martínez, Ana Cristina (eds)
La comprensión lectora de lengua extranjera
Estudio de los factores de familiaridad, interés, género y métodos de evaluación
336 pages. 2018. ISBN 978-3-0343-3493-8

Vol. 249 Mercedes Eurrutia Cavero
Approche didactique du langage techno-scientifique Terminologie et discours
374 pages. 2018. ISBN 978-3-0343-3512-6

Vol. 250 Aurora Ruiz Mezcua (ed.)
Approaches to Telephone Interpretation Research, Innovation, Teaching and Transference
268 pages. 2018. ISBN 978-3-0343-3330-6

Vol. 251 Morini Massimiliano A Day in the News A Stylistic Analysis of Newsspeak
188 pages. 2018. ISBN 978-3-0343-3507-2

Vol. 252 Ignacio Guillén-Galve & Ignacio Vázquez-Orta (eds.)
English as a Lingua Franca and Intercultural Communication Implications and Applications in the Field of English Language Teaching
414 pages. 2018. ISBN 978-3-0343-2763-3

Vol. 253 Bianca Del Villano
Using the Devil with Courtesy
Shakespeare and the Language of (Im)Politeness
216 pages. 2018. ISBN 978-3-0343-2315-4

Vol. 254 David Hirsh (ed.)
Explorations in Second Language Vocabulary Research
252 pages. 2018. ISBN 978-3-0343-2940-8

Vol. 255 Tania Baumann (ed.)
Reiseführer - Sprach- und Kulturmittlung im Tourismus / Le guide turistiche - mediazione linguistica e culturale in ambito turistico
270 pages. 2018. ISBN 978-3-0343-3402-0

Vol. 256 Ariadna Sánchez-Hernández & Ana Herraiz-Martínez (eds)
Learning second language pragmatics beyond traditional contexts
376 pages. 2018. ISBN 978-3-0343-3437-2

Vol. 257 Albert Bastardas-Boada, Emili Boix-Fuster, Rosa Maria Torrens (eds)
Family Multilingualism in Medium-Sized Linguistic Communities
336 pages. 2019. ISBN 978-3-0343-2536-3

Vol. 258 Yuyang Cai
Examining the Interaction among Components of English for Specific Purposes Ability in Reading. The Triple-Decker Model
296 pages. 2020. 978-3-0343-2913-2

Vol. 259 Catia Nannoni
Participe présent et gérondif dans la presse française contemporaine
176 pages. 2019. ISBN 978-3-0343-3631-4

Vol. 260 Nieves Rodríguez Pérez & Bárbara Heinsch (eds.)
Contextos multilingües. Mediadores interculturales, formación del profesorado de lenguas extranjeras
289 pages. 2019. ISBN 978-3-0343-3768-7

Vol. 261 Giuliana Elena Garzone, Mara Logaldo, Francesca Santulli (eds.)
Investigating Conflict Discourses in the Periodical Press
244 pages. 2020. ISBN 978-3-0343-3668-0

Vol. 262 Laura Nadal
Lingüística experimental y contraargumentación
233 pages. 2019. ISBN 978-3-0343-3791-5

Vol. 263 Claudia Claridge & Merja Kytö (eds.)
Punctuation in Context – Past and Present Perspectives
288 pages. 2019. ISBN 978-3-0343-3790-8

Vol. 264 Maurizio Gotti, Stefania Maci, Michele Sala (eds.) Scholarly Pathways
530 pages. 2020. ISBN 978-3-0343-3860-8

Vol. 265 Ruth Breeze, Ana M. Fernández Vallejo (eds.)
Politics and populism across modes and media
350 pages. 2020. ISBN 978-3-0343-3707-6

Vol. 266 Jean Marguerite Jimenez
Understanding the Effects of Immediate Electronic Corrective Feedback on Second Language Development
252 pages. 2020. ISBN 978-3-0343-3815-8

Vol. 267 Sergio Rodríguez-Tapia, Adela González-Fernández (eds)
Lenguas y turismo: estudios en torno al discurso, la didáctica y la divulgación
380 pages. 2020. ISBN 978-3-0343-3881-3

Vol. 268 Ana Bocanegra-Valle (ed.)
Applied Linguistics and Knowledge Transfer. Employability, Internationalisation and Social Challenges
344 pages. 2020. ISBN 978-3-0343-3714-4

Vol. 269 Beatrice Garzelli
La traducción audiovisual español-italiano.Películas y cortos entre humor y habla soez
202 pages. 2020. ISBN 978-3-0343-4013-7

Vol. 270 Iván Tamaredo
Complexity, Efficiency, and Language Contact. Pronoun Omission in World Englishes
292 pages. 2020. ISBN 978-3-0343-3902-5

Vol. 271 Silvia Domenica Zollo,
Origine et histoire du vocabulaire des arts de la table. Analyse lexicale et exploitation de corpus textuels
239 pages. 2020. ISBN 978-3-0343-3890-5

Vol. 272 Paola Paissa, Michelangelo Conoscenti, Ruggero Druetta, Martin Solly (eds.)
Metaphor and Conflict / Métaphore et conflit
385 pages. 2021. 978-3-0343-4068-7

Vol. 273 María Martínez-Atienza de Dios,
Entre el léxico y la sintaxis: las fases de los eventos
178 pages. 2021. 978-3-0343-4173-8

Vol. 274 Noelia Castro-Chao,
Argument Structure in Flux. The Development of Impersonal Constructions in Middle and Early Modern English, with Special Reference to Verbs of Desire.
300 pages. 2021. 978-3-0343-4189-9

Vol. 275 Gabriella Carobbio, Cécile Desoutter, Aurora Fragonara (eds.)
Macht, Ratio und Emotion: Diskurse im digitalen Zeitalter / Pouvoir, raison et émotion: les discours à l'ère du numérique
246 pages. 2020. 978-3-0343-4184-4

Vol. 276 Miguel Fuster-Márquez, José Santaemilia, Carmen Gregori-Signes, Paula Rodríguez-Abruñeiras (eds.)
Exploring discourse and ideology through corpora
293 pages. 2021. 978-3-0343-3969-8

Vol. 277 Tamara Bouso
Changes in Argument Structure The Transitivizing Reaction Object Construction
392 pages. 2021. 978-3-0343-4095-3

Vol. 278 Maria Luisa Maggioni, Amanda Murphy (eds.)
Back to the Future. English from Past to Present
250 pages. 2021. 978-3-0343-4273-5

Vol. 279 Luisa Chierichetti
Diálogos de serie. Una aproximación a la construcción discursiva de personajes basada en corpus
246 pages. 2021. 978-3-0343-4274-2

Vol. 280 Cristina Lastres-López
From subordination to insubordination. A functional-pragmatic approach to if/si-cons- tructions in English, French and Spanish spoken discourse
258 pages. 2021. 978-3-0343-4220-9

Vol. 281 Eleonora Federici, Stefania Maci (eds.)
Gender issues. Translating and mediating languages, cultures and societies
500 pages. 2021. 978-3-0343-4022-9

Vol. 282 José Mateo, Francisco Yus (eds.)
Metaphor in Economics and specialised Discourse
354 pages. 2021. 978-3-0343-4048-9

Vol. 283 Nicholas Brownlees (ed.)
The Role of Context in the Production and Reception of Historical News Discourse
376 pages. 2021. 978-3-0343-4181-3

Vol. 284 Catalina Fuentes Rodriguez, María Ester Brenes Peña, Víctor Pérez Béjar (eds.)
Sintaxis discursiva: construcciones y operadores en español
396 pages. 2021. 978-3-0343-4306-0

Vol. 285 Dominic Stewart
Frequency in the dictionary. A corpus-assisted contrastive analysis of English and Italian
178 pages. 2021. 978-3-0343-4368-8

Vol. 286 Carla Bouzada-Jabois
Nonfinite supplements in the recent history of English
386 pages. 2021. 978-3-0343-4226-1

Vol. 287 Sofía Bemposta Rivas
Verb-governed infinitival complementation in the recent history of English
340 pages. 2021. 978-3-0343-4227-8

Vol. 288 Mirella Agorni
Translating Italy for the Nineteenth Century. Translators and an Imagined Nation in the Early Romantic Period 1816–1830s
182 pages. 2021. 978-3-0343-3612-3

Vol. 289 David Hirsh (ed.)
Research Perspectives in Language and Education
276 pages. 2021. 978-3-0343-4219-3

Vol. 290 Federica Vezzani
Terminologie numérique : conception, représentation et gestion
238 pages. 2022. 978-3-0343-4394-7

Vol. 291 Stefania M. Maci
Evidential verbs in the genre of medical posters. A corpus-based analysis
498 pages. 2022. 978-3-0343-4521-7

Vol. 292 Francisco J. Álvarez-Gil
Stance devices in tourism-related research articles: A corpus-based study
170 pages. 2022. 978-3-0343-4555-2

Vol. 293 Annalisa Baicchi / Stefania Biscetti (eds.)
The Language of Fashion. Linguistic, Cognitive, and Cultural Insights
192 pages. 2022. 978-3-0343-4428-9

Vol. 294 Ana Maria Piquer-Píriz
E-learning in EMI. Academic language for university students
228 pages. 2022. 978-3-0343-4589-7

Vol. 295 Geneviève Henrot Sostero (ed.)
Alle radici della fraseologia europea
638 pages. 2023. 978-3-0343-4645-0

Vol. 296 Klara Dankova
Les fibres textiles entre synchronie et diachronie: études terminologiques
288 pages. 2023. 978-3-0343-4587-3

Vol. 297 Marta Carretero, Juana I. Marín-Arrese, Elena Domínguez Romero, Ma Victoria Martín de la Rosa (eds.) Evidentiality and Epistemic Modality. Conceptual and Descriptive issues
414 pages. 2023. 978-3-0343-3993-3

Vol. 298 Kim Grego, Alessandra Vicentini, Virpi Ylänne (eds.)
Age-Specific Issues. Language, Spaces, Technologies
280 pages. 2023. 978-3-0343-4411-1

Vol. 299 Giovanni Garofalo (ed.)
Estudios de género asistidos por corpus. Enfoques multidisciplinarios
290 pages. 2022. 978-3-0343-4548-4

Vol. 300 Giuseppe Palumbo, Katia Peruzzo, Gianluca Pontrandolfo (eds.)
What's Special About Specialised Translation? Essays in Honour of Federica Scarpa
298 pages. 2023. 978-3-0343-4411-1

Vol. 301 Raquel P. Romasanta
Probabilistic variability in clausal verb complementation in World Englishes.
374 pages. 2023. 978-3-0343-4703-7

Vol. 302 Giulia Adriana Pennisi
A linguistic Insight into Legislative Drafting. Tradition and Change in the UK Legislation
296 pages. 2023. 978-3-0343-4700-6

Vol. 303 Javier Fernández-Cruz, Antonio Moreno-Ortiz
Economic terms in the news during the Great Recession. A diachronic sentiment and collocational analysis
192 pages. 2023. 978-3-0343-4778-5

Vol. 304 Stefania Maci, Mark McGlashan (eds.)
(Critical) Discourse Studies and the (new?) normal. Analysing discourse in times of crisis.
400 pages. 2024. 978-3-0343-4767-9

Vol. 305 Ana Elvira Ojanguren López
Predications in competition and the rise of serial verb constructions in English. The verbal and nominal complementation of Old English aspectual and manipulative verbs.
534 pages. 2024. 978-3-0343-4644-3

Vol. 306 Stefania Maci, Giovanni Garofalo (eds.)
Investigating Discourse and Text. Corpus-Assisted Analytical Perspectives.
372 pages. 2023. 978-3-0343-4753-2

Vol. 307 Víctor Pérez Béjar
Las construcciones suspendidas en español. Un paradigma en gramática del discurso
494 pages. 2024. 978-3-0343-4799-0

Vol. 308 Javier Calle Martín / Jeús Romero Barranco (eds.)
Corpora and Language Change in Late Modern English.
408 pages. 2024. 978-3-0343-4642-9

Vol. 309 Cristina Petras / Sonia Berbinski / Daciana Vlad / Raluca Balaţchi (eds.)
Marqueurs métalinguistiques : émergence, discours, variation /Metalinguistic Markers: Emergence, Discourse, Variation.
758 pages 2024. 978-3-0343-4908-6

Vol. 310 Micaela Rossi (éd.)
Néologie, terminologie et variation – Neología, terminología yvariación – Neologia, terminologia e variazione.
418 pages. 2024. 978-3-0343-4696-2

Vol. 311 Sergio Maruenda-Bataller / Laura Mercé / Elena Castellano-Ortolà (eds.)
Discourse, gender, and violence: Insights from news and social media texts.
268 pages. 2024. 978-3-0343-4701-3

Vol. 312 Dario Del Fante
Migrating across times and cultures: Metaphorical images of migration in the U.S. and Italian newspaper discourse between the 20th and 21st centuries.
338 pages. 2024. 978-3-0343-4659-7

Vol. 313 Begoña Bellés-Fortuño / Francisco Alonso-Almeida (eds.)
Corpus-based Studies in Specialized Discourses.
276 pages. 2025. 978-3-0343-4261-2

Vol. 314 Elaine Millar
Multi-word Verbs in English Language Teaching. Insights from research and practice.
248 pages. 2025. 978-3-0343-5441-7

Vol. 315 Irene Guzmán-Alcón / Richard Nightingale (eds.)
New directions in Instructional Pragmatics Research.
424 pages. 2025. 978-3-0343-5099-0

www.ingramcontent.com/pod-product-compliance
Ingram Content Group UK Ltd.
Pitfield, Milton Keynes, MK11 3LW, UK
UKHW021835100926
8556IPUK00004B/346

9 783034 350990